THE DARK JOURNEY

THE DARK JOURNEY
John Whiting as Dramatist
by
ERIC SALMON

'You see, my life-loving darling, the dark journey to the **dark** home is sometimes sweeter than the summer's day'
— Edward, in *A Penny for a Song*

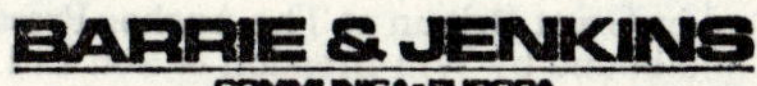

BARRIE & JENKINS
COMMUNICA-EUROPA

© Eric Salmon 1979
First published in 1979 by
Barrie & Jenkins Ltd
24 Highbury Crescent London N5 IRX

ISBN 0 214 20583 5

This book has been
written with the
financial assistance
of the Canada Council

Printed in Great Britain at The Anchor Press Ltd
and bound by Wm Brendon & Son Ltd
both of Tiptree, Essex

for

Janet and Jackie

with love and affection and thanks
in their proper proportions

Contents

(The dates given in the chapter headings above are the dates, as nearly as can be determined, of the writing of the plays and other works, not the dates either of production or publication. This is why a span of time is indicated in each case and why there is a great deal of overlapping between the separate periods shown. The question of the dates of individual plays is amplified in the text of the relevant chapter.)

John Whiting: a drawing by Feliks Topolski

Foreword

This book makes large claims for John Whiting; but if the British theatre since the war is viewed in perspective, I believe the claims are justified. His talent was undeniably that of a master, but his achievements were stopped short by a death which was as tragically mistimed as the appearance of most of his plays. I believe this book will help the plays to have a continuing life. It is comprehensive, accurate and enthusiastic.

I remember the physical shock of meeting *Saint's Day* at the Arts Theatre in the summer of 1951. It was romantic, but ferocious; it seemed as if a new Blake had stormed his way into the theatre. I was twenty and a stage-struck student, yet it was the first truly *modern* play I had seen in my life. For all the excitements of Eliot, of Ustinov and of Fry, the post-war theatre often appeared to be minimising great issues with self-conscious wit or self-conscious poetry. *Saint's Day* took them head on. It was contemporary, it was challenging and, as Eric Salmon fully illustrates, it was prophetic. Looking back now, Whiting seems a passionate and ironic evangelist, preparing the way for Beckett, for Pinter, for Arden, and for Bond.

Saint's Day had a terrible reception, and Whiting was bruised. I don't believe that bitterness ever limited his vision, but I know from a close friendship with him from 1952 until his death in 1963, that lack of recognition made it difficult for him to find creative energy. It was hard for him to write.

The theatre is the most public of the arts. Success or failure is instantaneous. A poet can, given sufficient courage and drive, go on writing, even if his verse is unread; an unregarded painter can continue to paint, even if only a handful of friends look at his paintings, but a playwright without a theatre is denied the main need of his art: communication with a living audience. I know that John Whiting, actor as well as playwright, would agree.

He was of course ambivalent in his attitude towards the theatre. So is everyone who works in it. We both love it and hate it, partly, I suppose, because it hands out public judgements without fear or favour.

It is as uncompromising as a battle or a bull-fight. For all his undoubted pride in his own work, Whiting wanted public approval. But whatever an artist's status, the theatre will never grant acceptance on a permanent basis. In Whiting's case, not until *The Devils* was acclaimed just before his death, did he feel the first full moment of acceptance. Although he had already written an impressive group of plays, I felt he was about to begin.

Eric Salmon believes that the theatre is frequently insensitive because 'public acts are, in a way, coarser, less subtle, less profound, than private acts'. This seems to me to ignore the theatre's ability to communicate complexities to an audience beyond the comprehension of its individual members. Whiting's best work lives through this ability. He is not easy to read, but he is triumphantly easy to act. It takes a scholar to unravel his tangled meanings from the page. But a good actor can bring a thousand people up to the same level of perception instantaneously. It is the proof that Whiting is a dramatist.

Initially, his audiences were not ready for him. They had to learn a new language – *his* language. It took them ten years. They were not helped by the response of the British critics who derided Whiting with a ferocity which is still bewildering. Perhaps the claims he made – intellectual and essentially European claims – seemed presumptuous.

He was in good company. Not only Whiting, but Beckett, Osborne, Pinter, Arden and Bond were dismissed by a majority of our drama critics when they first appeared. But they were more fortunate. They had time to work, time to be accepted.

An unfamiliar talent is as fragile as an egg placed in the hand. Drama critics will never appreciate their capacity to destroy until they themselves are regularly reviewed by equally ferocious critics. And that will only happen in an Artists' Utopia!

A great deal of the man also emerges from these pages. I directed *Saint's Day* in 1952 at Cambridge when I was still an undergraduate. This student production, presented only a little over a year after its first performance, attracted the London critics and there was some re-valuation of the play; it began to be accepted.

Whiting came to the production. He was from that time a ready friend and generous critic of my progress in the theatre. He seemed never far away from anything that I attempted. He encouraged me to present the first Ionesco play at the Arts Theatre, London, and was delighted when I followed it with Beckett's *Waiting for Godot*. Over the years, he translated Anouilh, Obey and Molière for the theatres I was directing. And when in 1959/60 the adventure began which led to the founding of the Royal Shakespeare Company with theatre in Stratford-on-Avon and London, he was there supporting our efforts and commenting on our productions and repertoire. He was the RSC's first 'House' dramatist.

I have often thought about his fate. Eric Salmon has traced, in his work and his life, Whiting's obsession with 'the innate tendency of the sensitive towards self-destruction'. I know this is accurate. But his work was not private. He was in fact growing more public as his talent matured; more equipped, like all great dramatists, to search out meanings from life and death.

His own death was just cruel bad luck. When the disease attacked him, he was looking forward to a strong creative future as a dramatist in a theatre which he could confidently call his own.

Sir Peter Hall

Preface

The case of John Whiting, the British dramatist who died in 1963, is a curious one. Virtually unknown to the layman, he is unanimously acknowledged, by all serious critics of twentieth-century drama in English, to be a major figure and a major force. This fact becomes all the more curious when one realises that he wrote only seven full-length stage plays and one one-act play in his short career; two of these were never performed in his life-time and one of them still has not been performed: and those that were produced, though they increasingly attracted the attention of discriminating critics, never won any sort of popular acclaim. The most 'successful' of them – in the sense in which theatre managements use that term – was the last, *The Devils*. At the time of their first performances, Whiting's plays tended to be taken more seriously on the European continent than in their native England: most of them were translated and played in France, Germany, Holland, Scandinavia, Czechoslovakia and Poland. *The Devils* even appeared in the southern Hungarian city of Pècs, but not until 1969. Yet in spite of this (quantitatively speaking) very slim record, it is no exaggeration to say that three or four of his plays are works of major importance and merit the closest of critical attention.

What this present study attempts to do is not only to look closely at individual works but also to trace Whiting's growth and development as a writer. For this latter purpose, the smaller works are also looked at in some detail, including some of the thirteen film scripts that he wrote. These, I think I am right in saying, have never been critically noticed before. This desire to demonstrate, as far as possible, the progress of the writer's craft as well as the growing depth of his art, has dictated the organisation and arrangement of this book and the system employed here for dating the plays. The dates given represent in each case, as far as is ascertainable, the period during which Whiting was working on each play. This, of course, is why in many instances the dates of one play overlap with those of another, since he often started work on one before he had completed the revising and rewriting of the previous one. These overlappings prove sometimes to be of considerable interest, demonstrating the movement of thought as well as the development of technique.

He wrote in many forms and tells us himself that he had, in effect, decided to become a writer before it even occurred to him to become a playwright – even though he had been trained as an actor and knew the theatre well. Though he published no verse, he quite obviously had an instinctive sympathy for and inclination towards the formal poet. He wrote one novel and started at least one other; he wrote several short stories; he published a good deal of dramatic criticism and theory. But, in spite of his not having thought of drama at first as his particular *métier*, what impresses one instantly about his work as a whole is its *dramatic* quality. This applies to his prose fiction as much as to his plays; it is even true, in a sense, of the critical writings. As an artist, his vision of the world was a dramatic vision, by which I intend to imply not simply a sense of exciting events but rather, and more precisely, that he possessed that particular quality of vision which sees the spirit of life as divided against itself, permanently and irrecoverably. To this vision, the poised opposition of dichotomous forces is part of the very structure: it is, indeed, to this view, the basis of the structure itself. It is not a problem capable of solution; in a sense there is no 'problem' at all, for the division is basic, existential. It can be reflected artistically but it cannot be 'solved'. John Whiting's intuitive view of life was of this kind. He was a dramatic writer and a major one. The demonstration of this fact, and the examination from play to play of the nature of the dichotomies, as Whiting saw them, will be part of the purpose of the present book.

The book owes a good deal to three people who have written on Whiting's work before me – Gabrielle Scott Robinson, Ronald Hayman and Simon Trussler. I have by no means always been able to agree with them and some of our differences of opinions are of a major sort, but their exploratory work has been most valuable to me in helping me in my own examination of Whiting and in the formulation of my own view of him. The reader will find a number of specific references to their opinions at various points and their own writings on Whiting are noted in the Bibliography. Another function of this present book is to correct some errors, both of fact and of omission, which occur in the works of these three previous critics of Whiting.

E.S.
University of Guelph
June, 1978

Acknowledgements

I wish to acknowledge my indebtedness to the following:

Mrs Asthorne Lloyd Whiting and Messrs A. D. Peters & Co. for their permission to quote from the unpublished novel *Not a Foot of Land* and the radio plays;

Heinemann Educational Books Ltd, for permission to quote from *The Collected Plays of John Whiting*, from *No More A-Roving* and from *A Penny for a Song* (Hereford Plays edition);

Thom Gunn and Faber & Faber Ltd, for permission to quote the poem 'Here Come the Saints';

Christopher Fry and Oxford University Press for permission to quote from *The Lady's Not for Burning*; also Christopher Fry for permission to reproduce a letter to John Whiting;

Alan Ross and *London Magazine*, for permission to quote from John Whiting's War Diaries;

M. B. Yeats and the Macmillan Companies of London and New York, for permission to quote the poem 'All things can tempt me', by W. B. Yeats, taken from *The Collected Poems of W. B. Yeats*;

Macmillan (Gill and Macmillan) Ltd, for permission to quote from *Sean* by Eileen O'Casey;

Rank Audio Visual Ltd and their managing director, T. E. Chilton, for generously placing their private theatre at my disposal and showing me a number of films from their library;

Miss Eugénie Babbage for typing the manuscript;

Mrs Laura Huxley, Chatto & Windus Ltd and Harper & Row, Inc., for permission to quote from Aldous Huxley's *The Devils of Loudun*;

The Canada Council and the University of Regina, for grants-in-aid to assist with research expenses and to make time available for the writing of the book;

Professor Bryn Davies, for valuable advice on Byron;

Dorothy Tutin, Christopher Fry, Peter Hall and Michael Powell, for most generously and kindly allowing me to question them about John Whiting and for giving me their recollections of him in valuable conversations;

Gabrielle Scott Robinson, for allowing me to read her unpublished Ph.D thesis, written for the University of London in 1968;

Ronald Hayman, for allowing me to see the printer's proofs of *The Collected Plays of John Whiting* before publication;

Elfrieda Lang, Curator of Manuscripts, Lilly Library, Indiana University, for allowing me to examine manuscripts of *The Gates of Summer*.

Quite apart from the formal acknowledgement for 'official help', mentioned in the foregoing list, I must record with gratitude my special debt to Jackie Whiting, John Whiting's widow. Not only did she place at my disposal all Whiting's letters and unpublished papers, allowing me the use of her library while I was engaged in the examination of these, but by her own conversations with me about her husband she suggested many lines of approach that I have found valuable and fruitful.

Chronology

1917	John Whiting born on 15 November, at Salisbury.
1922	His father is discharged from the army and moves with his family to Northampton, there to start in practice as a lawyer.
1930	Sent to public school in Taunton, Somerset.
1934	Leaves school to train as an actor at the Royal Academy of Dramatic Art, London.
1937	Completes course at RADA and begins acting small parts in various repertory companies; in the New Garden Theatre Company at Bideford, Devon, where he meets his future wife, who is an actress in the company.
1938	Member of the company of Croydon Repertory Theatre.
1939	Registers as conscientious objector on outbreak of war; recants and joins anti-aircraft section of the Royal Artillery.
1940	Marries.
1942	Commissioned as second-lieutenant.
1944	While still in the army, begins the novel, *Not a Foot of Land*.
1944	Discharged from army because of nervous debility and illness.
1944–5	Returns to acting, in repertory company at Peterborough.
1945	Joins White Rose Players, Harrogate; completes writing of *Not a Foot of Land*.
1946	Death of his father; birth of the first of his four children.
1946	Writes a comedy, *No More A-Roving*, which is rejected by Northampton Repertory Theatre.
1946	Writes a radio play, *Paul Southman: An Appreciation for Radio*, which is rejected by the BBC.
1946	Writes *The Conditions of Agreement* but does not offer it for production. Appears in O'Casey's *Oak Leaves and Lavender* in London.
1946	Begins the writing of *Saint's Day*.

1947   Moves to repertory theatre at York.

1947   Writes *Eye Witness*, a radio play (broadcast by the BBC in 1949).

1947   Begins the writing of *A Penny for a Song*.

1948   Completes *Saint's Day*; begins the writing of *Marching Song*.

1949   In addition to *Eye Witness*, the BBC broadcasts another short play of Whiting's called *The Stairway* and two short stories, *A Valediction* and *Child's Play*.

1950   Completes *A Penny for a Song*.

1950   Radio play, *Love's Old Sweet Song*, broadcast.

1950   Joins Scarborough Repertory Theatre.

1951   Joins Gielgud's company at the Phoenix Theatre, London, playing small parts in Shakespeare.

1951   In February, *A Penny for a Song* opens at the Haymarket Theatre, London; in September, *Saint's Day* is produced at the Arts Theatre Club and wins first prize in Festival of Britain play competition.

1952   Completes writing of *Marching Song*.

1952   Begins writing for films.

1953   Begins writing of *The Gates of Summer*.

1954   London production of *Marching Song*.

1956   Production of *The Gates of Summer* opens on tour and fails to reach London.

1956   Moves family residence from London to Nutley, Sussex.

1957   Writes the one-act play, *No Why*; begins *Nomad* but completes only one act.

1956–60   Writing of various film scripts, adaptations, etc.

1958   Begins work on new play, called *Noman* but writes only half of it.

1960   Peter Hall, of the Royal Shakespeare Company, commissions *The Devils*.

1961   London production of *The Devils*.

1961   Attempts to reorganise the theme and ideas of *Nomad* and *Noman* into a new form, beginning to rewrite it as *The Nomads*.

1961   Becomes dramatic critic for *London Magazine*.

1962   Royal Shakespeare Company presents revised version of *A Penny for a Song* in London and revives *The Devils* at the Edinburgh International Festival.

1962   Completes the film script *Young Cassidy*, based on the auto-
          biographies of Sean O'Casey.
1962   In November falls ill and is admitted to hospital.
1963   Is out of hospital in the early months of the year and working
          on a film treatment of Ibsen's *The Lady from the Sea*.
1963   Re-enters hospital 9 June.
1963   Dies of cancer 16 June.

It will be noted that there are some material differences, especially as to
the dates of the *beginning* of work on some of the plays, between the
above chronology and the dates given by both Ronald Hayman and
Simon Trussler. An exhaustive examination of all the various drafts of
the plays has revealed that Whiting began work, on some of the early
plays, a good deal earlier than was at first supposed and, more important, that he overlapped the writing of two and even three of them
in some cases.

I

BIOGRAPHY AND BACKGROUND

John Robert Whiting was born on 15 November 1917 at Salisbury, a fairly small country town in the south west of England. It is the 'county town' – that is to say, the administrative centre – of the county of Wiltshire and is dominated visually by a fine Gothic cathedral, the one that Constable painted framed in an arch of trees. Whiting's father was an officer in the regular army when Whiting was born but retired some five years later and moved back to his own part of England, which was Northampton, there to take up a new career as a lawyer. John Whiting's mother, Dorothy Herring, came of a west-country family that had moved from Devon to Wiltshire in the nineteenth century. There appears to have been no history of artistic activity on either side of the family except that Whiting's great-grandfather, J. F. Herring, had established a modest reputation as a painter of pictures of horses. Apart from this, neither side of the family had displayed any talent for the arts, or any special interest in them. There had been no previous writer in the family.

Whiting remembered his childhood as a happy one though once, almost as if his *feeling* about the nature of childhood was at odds with this happy memory of his own, he said 'I suppose I must have suffered the miseries and fears of childhood, but they have been lost in time.' Since children and the influence of childhood are such potent and significant symbols in his plays, it is worth remembering that in making them so he was drawing on his artistic and imaginative insight rather than on any direct, autobiographical memory.

He had one sister, six years his junior; no brothers. His education was unremarkable and undistinguished, the education of an upper-middle-class child: when he was very small he had a nanny who looked after him; from the age of five to the age of seven he went to kindergarten; then to a private preparatory school; then, when he was thirteen, to a minor public school in Taunton, Somerset. He did not like the school very much ('the particularly hellish life which is the English public

21

school', he said years later) but he remembered taking part in school plays and thought afterwards of these appearances as a possibly formative influence. The very first such appearance, he recalled, was as one of the gunmen in O'Casey's *The Shadow of a Gunman*. He remembered also writing some verse while he was still at school, but he did not regard it as remarkable or important. When the time came to choose a career, there was no question of his going on to a university since his academic standing (and interest) was too low: he said afterwards that he had never passed an examination in his life. Between him and his father and his headmaster it was decided, when he was seventeen, that he should train as an actor. It was a decision which Whiting himself welcomed, partly because it enabled him to escape from school and partly because the scheme seemed a sensible and reasonable one in itself. The idea of becoming an actor was one that he took seriously and was prepared to work hard for, though he did not at that time think of acting and the theatre as the career for which he was inevitably destined. He applied for admission to the Royal Academy of Dramatic Art, passed the entrance audition successfully and was accepted as a student. He began his studies there in the spring term of 1935. It was a very unhappy term for him. He was painfully shy and self-conscious, both in his contacts with other students (particularly the young women) and in the actual work and training. 'A very steady worker who will do much better when he has got over his paralysing nervousness', said Penelope Wheeler, his acting teacher, in his end-of-term report. The voice production instructor criticised his voice as being 'too nasal and too high – the words clear but superficial'. Another teacher said, in the report, 'His work at present is marred by nervousness. He needs much more vitality and attack' and the principal, Sir Kenneth Barnes, in his 'Remarks' offered this advice – 'You must summon a more confident spirit to help you in your acting. This means that you must set yourself to overcome self-consciousness, which you have in an acute form when appearing on the stage.'

Whiting, beginning to feel desperate about what alternative career was open to him if he failed as an actor, took Sir Kenneth's advice seriously. During the vacation between the first and second terms he contrived – and it must have been quite difficult to do – to get himself employed as a small-part actor in one of the smaller provincial repertory theatres where, because of the illness of one of the leading actors, he got his first chance to play a part of some size before a paying audience. The experience strengthened his self-confidence considerably and he went back to RADA with more determination. Sir Kenneth Barnes's report at the end of the second term reflects the result: 'He has made decided improvement. I did not regard him as promising in his first term; now I do. His performances were interesting and if he can go on making progress as he did last term, he may come out as an actor. He surprised me.' George Zucco, another of the academy's teachers, wrote in this same report a remark that was prophetic in its insight: 'Has what may grow into a very striking personality.' It did.

Whiting completed the RADA course early in 1937 with a final report that spoke optimistically of his abilities and chances as an actor. Work for young and inexperienced actors was even more scarce in England then than it is now: the provincial theatres were fewer and smaller; there was no television to absorb spare talent: he nevertheless managed to get some work. He was at the Croydon Repertory Theatre for a while. He got parts occasionally in radio plays for the BBC. He toured for three months in James Bridie's *The King of Nowhere*. The range of parts and of plays was quite wide.

He was now twenty years of age and there was no sign of his becoming or wanting to become a writer. His profession was acting, for which he was trained, and he thought of himself as an actor. Meeting him twenty years later, when his brief and modest acting career was all behind him and he was already an established dramatist, Michael Powell, the film producer and director, formed the impression that he had probably not been a very good actor. 'The personality was altogether too powerful', Powell said, 'to allow itself to be moulded by a character or put aside in favour of a character.' Certainly John Whiting never became a major actor: even if this was ever a possibility, various and different circumstances intervened to prevent it, the first of such circumstances being the outbreak of war in September 1939, when Whiting was almost twenty-two.

Idealistically, he registered as a conscientious objector. Like many young men, influenced by books like Dick Sheppard's *We Say 'No'* and A. A. Milne's *Peace with Honour* and by organisations such as the Peace Pledge Union and the Fellowship of Reconciliation, Whiting felt that the only sensible and honourable course for an intelligent and sensitive person to take was to register some kind of protest against another bout of the monstrous madness of modern warfare. However, he shortly afterwards changed his mind, cancelled his conscientious objector registration and became a reluctant soldier, hating it. The reason for his change of heart – or, at least, the thing that crystallised the change into actual action – was, according to his wife, his feeling of disgust and revulsion on attending a few pacifist meetings and finding them peopled by an insufferable collection of cranks, snobs, cowards and aggressive intellectuals. By the beginning of 1940 he was an anti-aircraft gunner at a camp on Merseyside and in a diary he kept at that time, he has left a vivid and moving account of his early impressions:

> I saw the guns firing for the first time today. First the
> 3-inch, then the 3.7-inch. Firing out over the sea at a
> target towed by a plane. First, the huge yellow flash from

the muzzle, then the report when all the sea seemed to
shake. You could hear the shell tearing upwards. Seven,
eight, nine, ten or eleven seconds later a tame black spot
of smoke after an initial flash. A long wait and a faint
explosion. The 3.7 brought down the 'sleeve' with two
perfectly placed rounds at either end of the target. It fell
limply into the mist on the sea.

A little later, he describes the use of the guns on a real target:

> The searchlight behind us hissed and the light climbed to
> the cloud bank over the river.
> 'Prepare to fire channel barrage,' said the telephonist in
> his queer Welsh accent.
> 'Barrage!'
> 'On Q.E. On bearing.'
> The slam of the shells into the loading trays.
> A pause.
> Startlingly the second telephonist with the earphones began
> to shout, '32. 31. 30. 29. 28. 27. 26. 25. 24. 23. 22. –'
> 'Fire!'
> A moment while the shells were rammed home and there
> was the metallic clink of the closing breeches – then the
> projectiles tore maliciously out over the sand banks far
> over the Mersey.
> Thousands of birds, white gulls, rose up from the beach
> and flew into the searchlight beams. They looked like paper,
> swaying, blinded.
> 'On Q.E. On bearing.'
> 'Fire.'
> Four more shells rushed away. Great blinding yellow flashes
> showed up the gun crews suddenly static in their places. The
> almost simultaneous crash of the four explosions and I
> smelled the burnt cordite and felt the rush of hot air and
> particles of dust in my face.
> Another four rounds and then quiet. Along the river in the
> beams of the lights were the black blobs of burst shells.
> Everyone looked to the sky. Nothing could be heard but the
> motor, and a screeching gull flew over us.
> We waited. No more reports came through. The G.L.
> station sent across to say the 'plane's either brought down
> or flown away.
> The telephonist smiled, replaced his receiver and said, 'Guns
> stand easy.'
> 'Replace covers. Stand down.'
> The ammunition was re-covered and in twos and threes the

gunners returned to their tents. A round cloud covered the moon.

I hung about for a few minutes tidying up. The searchlights were still fanning the sky. P. came out and looked up.

'I'm not satisfied with this. Blow that horn and let's have them out again, Whiting.'

I took up the toy tin trumpet and blew it with all my breath. Cursing in the tents and out came the little black figures running across the uneven ground, gathering like insects round their respective guns.

We waited. It was not an official 'stand to'. Had the G.P.O. made a mistake? G.O.R. was silent. The only indication was the searchlights over the city and up the mouth of the river.

I heard a 'plane flying low up the river. Then I was not sure: it was confused with the sound of the G.L. motor. The G.P.O. came out of the tent. I went over to him.

'Can you hear a 'plane, sir?'

'Where – ?'

As he spoke G.O.R. gave, 'Prepare to fire channel barrage.'

'30. 29. 28. 27. 26. 25. 24. 23. 22. – '

'Fire.'

The guns fired. Three rounds each. Then again the waiting silence.

Half an hour.

'Guns. Stand easy.'

I walked back to my tent and took off my tunic. I was hot and thirsty so taking my mug I went over to the ablution bench and drank a long mug of cold water. In my tent again I ate some chocolate and began to re-arrange my untidy bed. The other men were already lying down prepared for sleep.

The alarm sounded again. The short tinny sound coming nearer as the blower ran towards us. I grabbed my hat and respirator pulling on my greatcoat as I ran. I reached the command post and went into the telephonist's tent. The telephonist was repeating –

'190. 4000. 198. 4000. 195. Range constant. 193 – '

'How many 'planes?' I asked.

'They say six.'

'Is it our G.L. station?'

'Yes.'

I went out and looked to the bearing but I could see no 'planes. The sky was white with searchlights.

' 'PLANE!'

The G.P.O.A. indicated it with outstretched arm. It was

held, a great silver shape in two beams. Other searchlights
raced across the sky to meet it, until it was inescapably held.
'Hostile 'plane.'
The predictor and height-finder swung round to get it in
their telescopes. The guns clanked round following the dials
and the four muzzles went up to point accusingly at the target.
The 'plane was flying slowly up towards the mouth of the
river. It was not attempting to evade the lights but was
flying to a point directly before us.
'Height-finder on target.'
'Predictor on target.'
'Section on target.'
With half of my mind I was thinking, 'Hurry, hurry,' – with
the other half, 'Why don't you dive out of the light, you
bloody fool.'
The preparations went on.
'First. Two eight hundred.'
'Set three thousand.'
'Three thousand set.'
The 'plane came on, now almost directly over us. For a
moment our searchlight slipped behind it but again caught
up.
'Vertical steady.'
'Lateral steady.'
'Fire,' snapped the G.P.O. quietly to the predictor.
A moment then –
'Fuze 6.'
'Fuze 6,' to the guns.
'Fuze 6,' said the No 1 and then it was in the arms of an
ammunition number who ran to the tray. Into the tray:
over with the tray: back with the tray: back with the
rammer. The shells crashed into the breeches and the
breeches closed.
'Fire!'
'FIRE.'
'Fire' and away went the four shells. Four bursts in the
light beam beneath the 'plane. It swayed but flew on.
'Fuze 10.'
'FUZE 10!'
The eyes of the instrument numbers on their dials. The
guns slowly traversing across the sky.
'Fire.'
'FIRE.'
Ten seconds and then four bursts and the 'plane dropped out
of the light.

> Soon, 'Guns. Stand easy.'
> By 4 o'clock I was back in bed and asleep.[1]

His wife (he had married in 1940) says that even at the time Whiting often expressed the hope that the guns he helped to fire would never hit anything. The whole experience of the war obviously affected him deeply, but ambivalently. He himself said, in an interview some years after the war ended, that having abandoned his pacifist position he had wanted to get into an infantry regiment, for no other reason than that his father had been an infantry officer: the army authorities had ignored his expressed preference and put him in the artillery. The story is important in that it sets against his idealistic pacifism, which was unquestionably genuine and deeply felt, a sense of *noblesse oblige* and *esprit de corps* that, equally undoubtedly, he felt towards the country's military effort at that time. The clash of the forces of tradition, on the one hand, and conscious change on the other, is as clearly visible here in the parallel of his pacifism with his instinctive reverence for his father's old regiment as it was later to be in his plays.

In 1942 he was commissioned and moved to various other camps and duties in England: his military service never took him overseas. At about this time, too, an event occurred which was, indirectly, to have considerable effect on his technique as a writer in later years, in two different senses. He was sent by the army on a gunnery course, the materials of which he had both studied and practised before. He did not need the instruction, being thoroughly acquainted with the subject and he was faced, in consequence, with the prospect of the tedium of six months of lectures and note-taking on a subject he knew perfectly already. It happened that he had just then come across the handwriting of Frederick Rolfe ('Baron Corvo') and as a diversion he amused himself by submitting his military note-books in an imitation of this script. Rolfe, that extraordinary and paranoiac author of *Stories Toto Told Me*, *Hadrian VII* and *The Desire and Pursuit of the Whole*, had written in an elaborate pseudo-medieval script of a very distinctive kind[2] and it was this that Whiting now copied. His own handwriting, he said, was 'horrible and formless' and he welcomed the discipline. He adopted the script permanently and when he came to write his plays he made use of it by writing in this hand and in miniscule proportions – so small that it is practically impossible to read without a magnifying glass. The slowness which this practice forced on him helped him to concentrate and gave the ideas, so to speak, time to keep up with the hand. In some cases there are as many as five revisions of an entire play in this beautiful and infuriating italic hand, before the play was committed to a typescript. The original, handwritten drafts were apparently always written in Indian ink and one can readily imagine that this process must have demanded a fierce concentration of an almost hypnotic kind. The link between this and the actual creative process in the composition itself is a fascinating one.

As well as in the matter of calligraphy, it seems likely that Rolfe's work had a more important influence on John Whiting, namely as regards literary style. The exact extent of such influence cannot be guessed with any accuracy, but when one reads his first work – the novel called *Not a Foot of Land* – one is immediately struck in some of the formal, set-piece passages by a distinct similarity. The deliberately archaic style and the love of a recondite vocabulary recalls Rolfe quite strongly. Not that the total effect of the novel is even vaguely similar to any work of Rolfe's: Whiting's vision of the world is utterly different from Corvo's, but the stylistic echo is there and may well have been set off by his reading of Rolfe at the time of the gunnery note-books. The trait gradually disappears and is less discernible after that first novel, but his interest in Rolfe apparently remained: when Peter Hall commissioned Whiting to write a play for the Royal Shakespeare Company in 1960, the dramatisation of one of two books was considered. One was Aldous Huxley's *The Devils of Loudun*; the other was Frederick Rolfe's *Hadrian VII*, Whiting eventually chose the former: in view of the thin, impoverished, watered-down and cheaply melodramatic version of Rolfe's rich and strange book which eventually reached the stage in 1968 (dramatised by Peter Luke) one cannot help wishing, in a sense, that Whiting's choice had gone the other way.

He was discharged from the army late in 1944 and returned to his profession as an actor. Various minor pieces of work in and around London led to a two-year engagement with the White Rose Players in Harrogate, Yorkshire and it was here that he began to think seriously about writing, though not at first about writing for the theatre. He had already begun *Not a Foot of Land* during his last days in the army, and this he now completed. 'A casual remark in conversation with a friend led to the writing of the first play', he says in his Introduction to *The Plays of John Whiting* (1957):

> Exactly how casual this remark was intended to be I have
> never discovered. At the time I was engaged on other work
> and, although I had been actively concerned with the theatre
> as an actor, it had never entered my head to write plays
> since the age of twelve. To say the conversation was a
> challenge would be to put it too high. Rather, the attempt
> to write a play was a show-off. Every playwright must have
> something of the actor's desire for applause. During the
> war, when I was in my early twenties, I had written some
> poetry and stories. The circumstances of the time kept these
> from publication. It is just as well.

Five years after writing this he amplified slightly, in an interview,[3] the story of the 'casual conversation'. 'This was a girl among those that I knew,' he said. 'Young – she was twenty-one or something like that – who was interested in what I was doing and interested in my theories about the theatre and thought it was very strange that I didn't write for the theatre, being an actor. It's extremely difficult to say how you begin to write, or why you begin to write, or why you begin to write what you do.' The nature of his work in the next ten years was to prove that, no matter how accidental the choice appeared to be at the time, the instinct that drove him toward dramatic writing was a true instinct, leading him in the right direction for the proper expressing of his particular vision.

So he began to write plays as well as stories. Of the stage plays four were written (half his entire output) in the first three years and these four were completed before any one of them saw the stage, though in the meantime some of his radio plays had been performed by the BBC. Then suddenly his stage plays began to get productions. Two of them appeared in London within a single year – 1951; and immediately there became apparent the phenomenon which, perhaps more than any other, was to influence his artistic life from then on. On the face of it the matter was a simple one: neither the public nor the critics seemed to *like* his plays. In reality, however, it was a good deal more complex and sophisticated than that, involving in Whiting's mind large questions of artistic integrity and all the problems of an artist's making himself heard and understood. This question of the reception accorded his plays coloured the dramatic criticism he himself later wrote and even inhibited, to some extent at any rate, his style as a dramatist. Always something of an artist–aristocrat he had never expected or desired widespread popular acclaim of the *Charley's Aunt* or *My Fair Lady* sort. He knew he was writing 'serious' plays and he did not want to do anything else. But he *did* want to be understood and accepted by a serious-minded and intelligent audience and when he was not (or rarely, anyway) he tried more and more frantically through the form and frame of the play itself to solve the problem as if it were one of pure style. He would never compromise and put into the play the easy, predigested pabulum that he knew would satisfy the audiences and win him a glib success, yet – though at times he gave way to both cynicism and despair – he never entirely gave up the idea that one could somehow devise a dramatic form that would catch and hold even the most casual audience and yet not sacrifice anything of its artistic profundity, sensitivity or subtlety. It was a will-o'-the-wisp he was chasing and in a sense he gave the audience more credit in the matter than it deserved. Peter Hall, the director of the National Theatre of Great Britain, in discussing with me the difficulties he and Whiting had had in 1956 with the ending of *The Gates of Summer*, said that the problem was one of form and style occasioned, at least in part, by Whiting's intense desire to write a comedy, a play that was less austere and therefore more acceptable to an audience with which he desperately wanted to make contact. If the play were to be a comedy, then surely – the argument in Whiting's head went – the lovers, no matter how coolly rational and blasé they have been throughout the play, must finish up together: they do in *As You Like It*, for instance. But his instinct for the truth led him in a different direction: his genius knew that the sense of experience reflected in *The Gates of Summer* was of a radically different kind from that reflected in *As You Like It*. Both were true, but they came from different parts of Truth's spectrum and to compel either, by force, to seem like the other would be to falsify both. The constant revision of the ending of the play shows Whiting gradually abandoning both his desire to please and his erroneous theory of comedy in favour of a lonely and hard-won truth. He himself described the play afterwards as 'the harshest play I've ever written'. To his interviewer on that occasion he gave the sardonic advice 'Don't fall into the common error of believing that laughter is kind.' The over-statement betrays his own regret and longing: to be entirely rational and objective he should have said 'Don't fall into the common error of believing that laughter is *always* kind', but the buffeting the world gave him did not make for serenity of judgement. Except in his work. The sense of personal injustice, even of something close on paranoia, which shows sometimes in his dramatic criticism and in some of his personal utterances is never allowed to overbalance the fine poise of his work. The nature of the plots and characters he invents gives him chance after chance to indulge in self-pity and special pleading indirectly on his own behalf or on behalf of neglected artists in general. He dismisses the chances contemptuously, as he dismisses Harry Lancaster, the self-pitying mediocrity in *Marching Song*. It is the ability to make such dismissals that is one of the marks of his stature as a dramatist. His vision was absolutely clear but the sense of isolation it imposed made him sad. He was like a holy hermit whose life was given to God but who some-how regretted the loneliness. And to this frustration was added his acute realisation of the innate frustration of the theatre as an art-form. Compromise is of its essence and this was infuriating to a man who in matters of artistic truth could brook no compromise. He knew intuitively that there are certain senses of reality that can best be given artistic life and form in the theatre rather than in any other of the art-forms and that this is so *because* of the presence of the audience and because of the public nature of the theatre; yet he also came very quickly to realise that all public acts are, in a way, coarser, less subtle, less pro-found, than private acts, that where you have large gatherings of people you automatically lower standards, you work always to the lowest common denominator and that in the theatre this is complicated by the fact that you have large crowds, with massive conflicts of interest, on both sides of the legendary footlights. The dilemma is complete and exquisite and incapable of resolution except by the irrational, momentary magic that theatre at its best occasionally achieves. And at *his* best Whiting the dramatist, as distinct from Whiting the theorist, achieved it occasionally, too. But the horns of the dilemma dug deep into his side and from the first he was painfully aware of them. So were some others, for while his first plays got bad notices from the critics and a bland indifference from the public, they were from the first defended almost fanatically by members of the theatrical profession. In 1951, Tyrone Guthrie and Peter Brook wrote a joint letter to *The Times* in which they said:

> John Whiting's play *Saint's Day* has been described in the press as 'claptrap' and yet so admired by three distinguished judges that they have awarded it a prize of £700. May we express the independent opinion of two theatre workers who were both impressed and moved by what we saw – by a remarkable production and a remarkable play.
>
> *Saint's Day* may well be strange and obscure and entertainment is certainly a word that cannot be applied to it; but its passion and its unbroken tension are the products of a new and extraordinary theatrical mind. John Whiting is writing in his own idiom and describing his own world. For the moment this may be as strange to us as the private worlds of Kafka and Virginia Woolf must have appeared before familiarity added signposts to the scene. We offer no explanation of John Whiting's work; we only wish to record our own deep faith in his talent, integrity and promise and beg everyone truly interested in the theatre to go and see for themselves.
>
> Yours, etc.
> TYRONE GUTHRIE
> PETER BROOK

Tyrone Guthrie, who was at that time the director of the Old Vic Theatre, had before the appearance of the joint letter in *The Times* already written personally to Whiting about *Saint's Day*. His letter is worth quoting in full:

> Old Vic Theatre,
> Waterloo Road,
> London, S.E.1.
>
> Sept. 7, 1951
>
> Dear John Whiting,
> I saw your play last night and was very much moved and impressed.
> Douglas Campbell lent me a copy to read about 18

months ago. I thought then that it had great quality but
was a bit more baffled (specially by the last scene) than
seemed quite needful.

But last night it all seemed quite as understandable as
anyone has any right to expect of a serious work of art at
first contact.

Stephen Murray had, I thought, done a fine job; and the
actors all worked splendidly. I personally thought Valerie
White very terre à terre and lacking in 'overtone' but she
attacked her audience with a likeable grit and vim. My God,
it took some attacking. They didn't know *where* they were,
and didn't like what they were inclined to suspect.

This is reflected in the footling little notice in The Times
this morning (only one I've read). Don't let them depress
you *at all*. They can recognise nothing but 'success'. And
you can't in your wildest moments have thought this would
be a *George and Margaret*. Nor would you want it to be.
It's my view if a work of art succeeds right bang off it *must*
be mediocre. That, your work certainly isn't.

I still think what I remember thinking when I read it,
that the Soldiers don't quite do. I suppose they represent
Forces of Chaos or Destruction or Death-Wishes or quelque
choses comme ça (boring to try *exactly* to define symbols :
if they were exactly definable they'd be needless) but I
think they are too matter-of-factly explained (e.g.
'incorrigibles') and Christian Melrose rather sentimentally
treated (by you : very capably by Ralph Michael).

This letter's gone on *far* too long. It's intended merely
to offer you very sincere, hearty and respectful
congratulations. And bugger the critics.

Yours sincerely,
TYRONE GUTHRIE

The following month the same writer returned to the theme again.
Enclosing a clipping from the *Observer*, he addressed another long
and delicious letter to Whiting :

23, Old Buildings,
Lincoln's Inn,
London, W.C.2

Sunday, Oct. 23, 1951

Expect you've seen this. But thought I'd send it just in
case. Seems to me a very good, intelligent letter. And I
hope has been a nice poultice to your wounds. With it add
that one can't help *minding* what dull and often drunken

men write in the newspapers. When Aunts say 'but it's so
unlike anything one's ever really met; and anyway dear
there's enough sorrow and unpleasantness in Real Life
without having it in the theatre . . .' When Aunts go on
like that, one can 'understand' and Rise Above without too
big an effort, and without having to be madly 'superior'.

But of course Aunts haven't the power to destroy – in a
practical sense – one's chance to be Terry Rattigan or
Somerset Maugham. Or to push one to the sort of silliness
that says 'who wants to be Somerset Maugham anyway?'
Of course everyone wants to be wildly successful and
popular, with crystal chandeliers and Bentleys and holidays
in Tibet and the Harold Hobsons of this world casting
their nasty deformed little crowns into the glassy sea of
one's utter indifference. Everyone wants it. And one of the
subtly nasty things that can happen when one has been
pushed around, as you have been, is that one is forced into a
defensively superior attitude.

By the way, did you know (à propos of people *never*
'understanding' things at first) that after the first performance
of *Carmen* every critic in Paris (and they weren't all fools)
came out with patronising notices that said 'Clever but
impossible. Why can't this obviously promising boy write
a TUNE?' That was about *Carmen*.

And poor little Georges (?) Bizet who was silly enough
to be starving at the time, allowed it to 'get him down'; and
died soon after in great bitterness of spirit.

What a garrulous and rather didactic elderly person
I'm becoming!

Don't dream of replying.

Yours,

TYRONE GUTHRIE

The clipping he enclosed was from the newspaper's correspondence
column and read as follows:

Sir,

With what startling omniscience Mr Ivor Brown tells us
that 'there are no new answers to the problems of the world
or its emotional needs. They have all been made at some
time and in great diversity . . .' Then how silly of Mr John
Whiting not to have swotted up the answers to the riddle
of the universe and written them into 'Saint's Day' in
plain, simple terms.

The best that most of us can do, who find the mysteries of
life and death still awesome and unexplained, is to build

four walls out of the creeds and conventions we inherit and
shelter behind them, patching them up from time to time
with such scraps of knowledge and theory as science and the
arts can offer us. Occasionally an artist shows us a glimpse
of what he sees beyond his own four walls and what may
or may not lie beyond ours. Whether it excites or merely
frightens us depends not only on his powers of expression
but on our own experience – and, in the last analysis, the
experience of each of us is unique.

If the artist be a playwright and his experience is not
sufficiently shared his play may die. Or it may simply have
to wait until enough of us have plucked up courage to look
over our walls and get used to what we see. I doubt if the
content of 'Saint's Day' will be outside our vision for long.

Yours faithfully,
MARJORIE HAYWARD

All this related to the second Whiting play to appear in London that
year, but much the same sort of thing had happened over the first one,
A Penny for a Song, even though it was a very different kind of play
and, one would have thought, much less controversial. It nevertheless
divided its viewers in the same way – audience and professional critics
uneasy about what was going on and expressing their unease in utterances ranging from anger to bewilderment and from satirical scorn to
prim disapproval; a few enthusiasts, mainly from the theatrical profession
itself, almost beside themselves with delight and cheering Whiting on
to fresh efforts. The following two letters, from Dame Sybil Thorndike
and Christopher Fry, are typical of a whole group that Whiting received
at that time:

98 Swan Court,
Chelsea, S.W.3

17 April, 1951

Dear John Whiting,

I meant to have written to you before to tell you how
thrilled I was with 'Penny for a Song' as a play. I went to
see it just a bit swayed by some of the notices, but was
completely carried away by it. So was my husband. I had
read before and been extremely interested in your 'Saint's
Day' – I hope you aren't *too* discouraged by your short run –
I think in many ways it was beyond the critics! I think the
public would have liked it if they had been encouraged but
the public is fearful and won't risk if the critics have not
praised. I am completely mystified and disappointed at its
non-commercial success – I made several lots of people go
to it, among them Dame Edith Evans who was completely

34

carried away with the pleasure of it and the 'meaning'. The
meaning of the play was so exciting I really jumped in my
seat with joy.

Please go on writing and don't play down because of
stupid critics. 'Penny for a Song' will live, but of course
you have to live too, which is a worry! !

Sincerely yours
SYBIL THORNDIKE CASSON

27 Blomfield Road,
London, W.9
March 26, 1951

Dear John Whiting,

My wife and I would like you to know what very great
pleasure we got from your play when we saw it on Saturday
(it was my wife's second visit) – I don't remember when I
have laughed so much in a theatre, and I was touched too,
and made constantly aware of a most human and
understanding mind behind it all.

Whatever happens, don't be deflected one inch by the
critics: they'll come round in time. Cecil Day Lewis and
Jill Balcon were with us, also Jessie Evans: all equally
delighted.

With best wishes,
Ever sincerely,
CHRISTOPHER FRY

What is especially noteworthy about the tone of all these letters and also
about the critics' comments on Whiting's first plays, is the consciousness they both have of a newness and strangeness in his work. The critics,
by and large, disapproved of it; the theatre people welcomed it; but both
parties were acutely aware of it. To appreciate the full force of this
strangeness, one needs to remind oneself that the year in which *Saint's
Day* and *A Penny for a Song* were produced was five years before
Osborne's *Look Back in Anger*, seven years before Pinter's *The Birthday Party* and eight years before Arden's *Serjeant Musgrave's Dance*.
To a large extent the theatre at the beginning of the 1950s was dominated
by the mode of strict and literal naturalism, long after the vitality had
ebbed from that convention. Not that the dramatists of the time *set out*
to write dull, lifeless and timid plays: no one does that; but the limitations of their own vision combined with a stultifying technique produced
a dull, lifeless and timid effect in spite of intentions. There were a few
playwrights at the time who realised this and who tried consciously in
their plays to break the deadlock: these were the verse dramatists,
people like Norman Nicholson, Ronald Duncan, Patric Dickinson,

35

Gilbert Horobin and, most important of all, Christopher Fry. What they did was very welcome, very attractive and sometimes very lively; but it was not very big. It wore the air, in the cases of all but Fry, of a consciously esoteric 'movement' and it felt, therefore, like a piece of special pleading and, ultimately, a side-issue. This movement towards a modern verse drama had begun in the middle 1930s with Eliot, Auden, Spender and MacNeice and by the early 1950s the suspicion was more than a little developed that the insistence on formal verse, poetry so-to-say *imposed* on the theatre, was perhaps not, after all, the way to remedy the theatre's ingrown tendency towards a relative littleness and timidity. What the proper solution may be, however, defied augury. Meanwhile, for the most part the relentlessly neatly plotted plays in literal and self-explanatory settings (and depressingly literal and self-explanatory language) continued.

There are, of course, run-of-the-mill, made-to-order, built-to-a-formula plays in any age: the danger comes when these are mistaken for and become accepted as artistically serious and artistically lively work. One of the tests of the vitality, significance and importance of the theatre of a particular era is the extent to which its most distinguished theatre workers and its most perceptive critics can distinguish between the new play which really does have the echo of reality in its voice and the new play whose sole function is to 'while away the long age of three hours between our after-supper and bed-time'. (Nothing wrong in that in itself, of course, as long as one knows and recognises it: some people do suffer from intolerably long evenings.) Anyone can be mistaken about it occasionally and even the best critic will be wrong sometimes. One should always, as a sobering thought, recall that Felicia Hemans was buried in Westminster Abbey, in Poets' Corner, along with Keats and Wordsworth and Tennyson and the rest. The mischief comes when most of the critics are wrong nearly all the time, when a set of false and extrinsic criteria has so firmly been adopted that real life has been obliterated from the scene of art. The Victorians, for example, in the matter of the theatre got to the point of scarcely being able to make at all the distinction between the true and the false, the lively and the merely sententious. Something of the same danger, though not nearly to the same extent, existed in the British theatre in the early post-war years. It is not true that there were no good new plays being written in England at that time or that there was no interest in 'serious' theatre: it was in many ways a very lively time in the theatre. Barry Jackson had taken over the Stratford-on-Avon theatre in 1946 and had raised its standard immeasurably (as well as establishing Paul Scofield, whom he took to Stratford with him from the Birmingham Repertory Theatre, as a major actor); Lawrence Durrell had published *Sappho*, a distinguished and exciting play in verse, in 1950; all Christopher Fry's major plays had been written and produced between 1947 and 1951, the latter year seeing the opening of *A Sleep of Prisoners*; Eliot's *The Cocktail Party* had opened at the 1949 Edinburgh International Festival, and that festival itself was young and lively and promising – it had started, with Rudolf Bing as its director, in 1947; Peter Ustinov's *The Love of Four Colonels* was first produced in 1951. The British theatre of those years was devoid neither of intellectual excitement nor artistic aspiration, but there was a notable lack – realised at the time by the perspicacious and more obvious still in retrospect – of two things. These were, first, plays of major stature and, second, plays that reflected the tremendous unease of Europe after the brief post-war euphoria. Not that there were no plays that attempted to reflect this sense: Fry's *A Sleep of Prisoners* (among a good many others) was concerned with this theme, but neither it nor those others was large enough to compass the theme or resonant enough to set it throbbing in the heart. The theatre had retired, even if involuntarily, into a kind of faded elegance, a sincerity at one remove. The great distinction of Whiting's work is that, far more than the rather trite and (in my view) overvalued *Look Back in Anger* of 1956, it suddenly let into the theatre the frightening noise of the world outside, not in the obvious and outward manifestations of that world, but in the sickening lurch of its bared soul.

In the meantime, however, as Dame Sybil had remarked in her letter, Whiting had to live and in 1956 he turned his back, at least temporarily, on the ungrateful theatre and concentrated wholly on writing for films, a world in which he had gradually been establishing himself since 1952. There can be little doubt that this was a conscious decision on his part and that it was prompted both by economic necessity and disillusionment. He was by this time a married man with, in both senses, a growing family (there were now four children) and while there was certainly no question of scraping a living in a garret – he lived in a gracious country house on the edge of Ashdown Forest, in Sussex – the failure to find commercial acceptance in the theatre must, quite apart from any artistic considerations, have had its worrying moments financially. So he turned more fully to films. Not that he undertook them lightly or cynically or only with his mind on his bank balance. His wife was quick to point out to me – and rightly – that he spent a great deal of time and trouble on them and took great care over them. And they are, indeed, very workmanlike. One would like to think that what he was doing was exploring in a more popular medium the possibility of making contact in a serious-minded and meaningful way with a more broadly representative audience, but there are two difficulties about such a rationale. The first is that the writer has relatively little influence in the cinema – certainly nowhere near as much as he has in the theatre: the dominant figure in matters of artistic decision is the director. The second is that none of Whiting's film scripts are originals: all are dramatisations, at the behest of one or other of the film companies, of books (usually of novels that had for one reason or another acquired a momentary fame). There are one and a half exceptions to this statement, though still not in the direction of original film scripts: he prepared a film adaptation of Ibsen's *Hedda Gabler*, though it was never actually filmed; and at the time he died he was working on a film version of another Ibsen play, *The Lady from the Sea*. Apart from these two, in which – after all – the chief contribution is still Ibsen's, Whiting's film scripts are interesting now not for any intrinsic merit they possess but for the sidelights they here and there reveal on his working methods, his verbal and organisational techniques and his other works generally.

It was Peter Hall who persuaded John Whiting back into the theatre. Hall had just taken over as artistic director of the Shakespeare Memorial Theatre at Stratford-on-Avon and was in the process of turning it into the Royal Shakespeare Company. One of the elements of this change was to acquire the use, on a long-term basis, of a London theatre to which some of the Shakespeare productions from Stratford could be transferred and at which the new Royal Shakespeare Company could also produce plays by other authors, especially modern authors. Hall, who felt keenly that Whiting was being wasted and that he ought to be writing for the theatre, was determined that this was one of the first of modern dramatists to be included in the Royal Shakespeare Company's plans. The two men had been on very friendly terms ever since Hall, as an undergraduate, had directed a production of *Saint's Day* at Cambridge in 1952 and Hall was a great admirer of Whiting's work. Knowing of Whiting's especial interest in Aldous Huxley, and as a deliberate ploy to entice the dramatist back into the theatre, Peter Hall offered Whiting the job of dramatising *The Devils of Loudun*. When I asked Hall about it, he said 'You can't give a dramatist an *idea* and ask him to make a play out of it: you can give him a book. I knew of John's interest in Huxley and I therefore chose what I thought would be the book most likely to attract him.' They discussed, as has already been mentioned, another book by a favourite author of Whiting's – Rolfe's *Hadrian VII* – but the Huxley idea continued to seem attractive so Hall himself flew to Los Angeles to see Huxley and seek his permission for his book's being used. Huxley had never heard of Whiting but, on the evidence that Hall presented, his confidence was won and he gave his consent. Hall then returned to London and presented the matter to Whiting in terms of a challenge: 'I put it on the same basis as writing for a film: I gave him a deadline and told him to write to that. He did.'

The Devils opened in February 1961 at the Aldwych Theatre, presented by the Royal Shakespeare Company and directed by Peter Wood, the first modern play in the company's programme. It was kept in the repertory for the 1962 season, for which occasion Whiting slightly revised it. In the 1962 season also, the Royal Shakespeare Company included a revival of *A Penny for a Song* (also, unfortunately, revised by

Whiting, to its disadvantage) and in that same year he was working on a new play concerned with 'the Nazi period. Caught in as inexorable a passion as that of sex . . . Shifting society ("The Nomads") . . . The play is basically about the destruction of our ideal. Or at least, Western Europe's inability to come up to the ideal . . .' The theme was one with which he had attempted to deal in a play he had begun four years before, but had left unfinished. It is also a theme which had its roots, for him, in that first novel he wrote under the direct impact of the Nazi war nearly twenty years before. Now he was treating it again in dramatic form. John Whiting had returned to the theatre.

In January of 1963 he wrote on a sheet of paper:

THE NOMADS

a play in two acts

January 1963: definitive draft

Act One – Munich. Morning. Steps lead up from a river.

There is a bridge nearby . . .

And so on: but only six pages of it were ever written. On 17 April he wrote a letter of apology to the graduate student at the University of California for whom, in November of the previous year, he had made a tape recording of some autobiographical details: 'I very much regret my long silence . . . I must, of course, give you an explanation, which I would like you to treat as confidential. I mentioned to you that I had to go into hospital last November. Well, it turned out to be a longer and more tedious illness than expected and I am only really just recovering from convalescence . . .' He goes on to answer some questions that the student had put to him, questions about his handwriting, details about one or two of the plays. At the end of the letter he says 'I will try to make a short tape to cover any other points you make in your letters. I hope it will not come too late. I must say again how sorry I am that I have not been more helpful to you in these last months, but I am sure you will understand the circumstances.' Two months later, on 13 June, a letter to Whiting from the student said 'I am enclosing a final draft copy of the thesis . . . The first paragraph of the second letter[4] has been deleted from the final copy . . . Professor Shank informs me that he is corresponding with you about the possibility of your visiting our campus. Let me say from the other side of the fence [i.e. the students' side] that we would be honoured and excited to have you here as visiting lecturer.'

John Whiting never saw this letter. While it was still on its way across the Atlantic he was taken ill again; he returned to hospital in London and on 16 June he died of cancer of the brain. He was forty-five.

While writing this, I asked Michael Powell, the film producer and director, who knew Whiting and admired him greatly, for a comment on him. Powell wrote back to me at some length and very helpfully,

39

giving me some excerpts from his diary in which he had described two meetings with Whiting in 1958 when they were discussing the film script that, at Powell's invitation, Whiting was making from Cecil Woodham Smith's *The Reason Why*. The diary excerpts speak of Powell's admiration: 'I like J.W.'s mind (and manner) very much . . . I think he will be a success. No! Sure of it!' In addition to answering my questions and quoting from his diary, Powell also wrote on a post-card, which he enclosed with his letter to me:

> Whiting – an actress who met him once or twice (and who
> is acute) describes him as 'reticent'. When I think of him
> I think of velvet: quiet and strong: impersonal and
> inflexible: good-mannered: a cardinal of a man.

Others have expressed similar opinions of him: the impression one always gets is of a man who was compassionate but uncompromising, a man who readily and spontaneously inspired both admiration and devotion in those with whom he came into close personal contact. Though not arrogant, he was well aware of his own gifts. He himself once said that, in the ultimate analysis, the reason you went on writing was that you believed yourself to be better than the others. Peter Hall and Michael Powell, quite without any prompting from me along these lines, both remarked on this same trait. 'He knew he was good. He knew his time would come,' said Powell. 'But like Hardy's iceberg, the cancer knew, too.' And Edward Thompson, of Heinemann (who were Whiting's publishers), said that he seemed like a man almost consciously determined to kill himself. At a meal in a restaurant he would order something, eat a couple of mouthfuls and then light a cigarette, leaving the meal neglected. He would smoke furiously, savagely, throughout the meal, listening avidly, talking little – but trenchantly; and smoking, smoking, as if he had deliberately decided to ruin his health.

When he died, one of the actresses of the Royal Shakespeare Company, overwhelmed by a sense of personal loss and by a sense of grief at the thought of one with such great and unfulfilled gifts dying so young, herself committed suicide and bequeathed her estate to Whiting's children. Only a week before her own death she had attended Whiting's funeral at the little village church of Fairwarp in Sussex. There she had broken down completely and had been comforted and helped from the church by Whiting's wife, Jackie, who had taken her home with her and the children.

He was a man whom women very readily admired, his very reticence and austerity making him, no doubt, all the more attractive. During his marriage there were several quite serious love affairs with other women, though he always held his wife in high esteem, regarded her with great affection and had no thought of leaving her. She sent him, on one of his first nights, a little note that said 'All my love and best wishes for your success, darling.' The word 'All' was underlined, an emphasis that says a good deal about both of them. There is more than a passing echo in several of his plays of his awareness of the pain and the irony of divided loyalties and divided loves. The early *No More A-Roving* and the later *The Gates of Summer*, in particular, have scenes which strike one immediately as having been written from direct personal experience. The unexpected return of the wife at the end of *No More A-Roving*, for example, as well as being a very striking theatrical moment, has about it in its delicate ironies the curious feeling of being a piece of first-hand reporting as well as an artistic construct.

Though fond of his family and loyal to them, John Whiting was impatient of the constraints of family life: a man not made for domesticity. When one reads the plays, with their dark romanticism, this comes as no surprise. His life and his work were part of the same pattern, both informed by a kind of melancholy desperation. Yet there was another side to him – gay, gentle, a good companion – to which many of his friends bear witness and of which his wife still often speaks. John Whiting was a man of large ambivalences and ambiguities.

2

THE UNPUBLISHED NOVEL

Not a Foot of Land (1944–45)

After her husband's death in 1963, Mrs Whiting found the typed manuscript of a short novel stowed away in a packing case in the garage of their home in Sussex: it bore the title *Not a Foot of Land* and the date 1945. Whiting himself had, apparently, believed it lost and had said in November 1962:

> The first major attempt at writing that I made was when I
> was about twenty-four or twenty-five. It was while I was
> in the army. I wrote a short novel. Again, so far as I know,
> no copies exist of it, although a typescript was made. I
> didn't make any attempt to have it published. How shall I
> put it – I didn't write it for publication: I wrote it as an
> exercise, as a personal work. I think if I found a copy of it
> now and re-read it, I should think it quite unreadable and
> impossible.[1]

Though Whiting was discharged from the army in 1944 and the transcript of *Not a Foot of Land* is dated 1945, it is nevertheless fair to assume that this is the novel he is talking about, the one he wrote 'while I was in the army'. There is no trace of any other novel and his widow knows of no other. If the typescript was prepared in 1945, it is reasonable to suppose that the writing began a year or more before that date, during the latter part of Whiting's military service.

The novel is prefaced by two quotations, one from Cervantes and one from Dante, the former set down in an English translation, the latter in its original language:

> 'In Gods' name, let it live and let me die' quoth Master
> Peter at this juncture, with a fainting voice, 'since I am so
> unfortunate that I can say with King Roderigo "Yesterday

42

I was sovereign of Spain and today have not a foot of land
I can call my own".'

____

                       'Frate,
non far, ché tu se'ombra e ombra vedi.'
Ed ei surgendo: 'Or puoi la quantitate
comprender dell'amor ch'a te mi scalda,
quand'io dismento nostra vanitate,
trattando l'ombre come cosa salda.'

____

In view of the fact that the author had, before the war, trained as an actor and had practised briefly in that profession and in view of what we now know of the kind of writing which he would presently produce, the first words of the novel have a quirky and ironic significance. Whiting started thus: 'I shall give directions for the setting of the stage.'

And at once the scene which is set has the strange phantasmagoric quality with which the whole work is invested:

Here, in this village set on the southern slope of mountains, a day begins. The village, a group of wooden structures, can be called such only by the fact that it contains an actual community; a sisterhood of aged women, possessed of frail and useless wits; fled from former homes, from dead sons, husbands and lovers; driven by these memories to the mountains to form a simple centre of peace until their own not distant death. The foundations of the buildings were laid by the hands of forty women but this morning the woman in sight who is repairing her roof is one of only twenty-nine who remain. With the twenty-nine women there is one man, an interloper given refuge, a deserter. This man lies asleep on the open balcony of the centre dwelling house.

Old Tim Crashaw sleeps with his face to the sky and his mouth open. For an actor who may play this part[3] it should be stated that last night Crashaw sat up reading in a faulty light and drinking much sour wine. So this morning he sleeps, breathing heavily and with wine fumes in his head. Under the loosely drawn blankets he is dressed in a long smock, which has rolled up almost to his waist, and knee-high stockings; his rough shoes are upturned beneath the bed.

Within the house and adjoining the balcony is a small, square room. The furnishings are minimum. Beside the balcony door is a chair with a torn, once scarlet cushion. Beyond, against the wall, there is a table on which there is a book, an oil lamp, a jug of water, a few coins and, set before the table, a low stool. To the left of the inner door there is an old leather suitcase holding Tim Crashaw's

personal belongings. They are few: faded, stored away
but never forgotten. Some outdated clothes bearing the
label of a London tailor. A china terrier dog with the front
right leg broken away, wrapped in brown paper and bound
with string. A small handkerchief marked with blood, folded
to hold within it a dull, English penny. A box of matches
and a theatre programme. Finally, packed at the bottom
of the suitcase, there are some gramophone records and
many puppets, human figures with their controlling wires
wrapped about them and the wooden handles laid beside
them. Complementary to these are properties and scenic
materials for a puppet play set in this land where Tim
Crashaw now lives.

The day begins, for already the light has filled the long
and narrow Eastern sea and now, rising above the coastal
mountains, floods into the centre of the country which is a
plain lying within circling mountains. The daylight, now
falling on the tableland, shows the solitary city below. A
place of white buildings, untainted, compact, and isolated.

There is only a small penetration of light by the balcony
door into the windowless room behind Crashaw. Even at
full day this room remains shadowed and inhospitable,
merely a depository for Tim's belongings which, hidden in
the suitcase, are the necessaries to build in miniature all
this present scene.

Tim stares down at the plain and the city which now
appear to be closer, less remote, beneath the sun. It is
merely another day but Old Tim sees again all the familiar
forms, shapes, shadows, the houses and the towers of the
city, the hill surmounted by a single tree adjacent to the
village, each form being duplicated by the miniatures stored
within the suitcase; the models which are the only tangible
reminder of his last days in England, immediately
succeeded[4] by the Wednesday – November 16, 1938 –
when he had travelled to this foreign country to fulfil the
ending as he himself had portrayed it.

Even from these opening paragraphs it is obvious that Whiting's vision
automatically penetrates beyond both character and event to the senses
of an inner reality and sees, in the surface things, symbols of a more
complex truth and of larger issues than those which on the surface he
represents. The image of a man arriving in a foreign place with a model
of that place in his suitcase and a scenario of the action which is to
happen there, is a strange and powerful one. The puppets in Crashaw's
case immediately acquire something of the quality of a witch's wax

dummy into which pins are to be stuck: the whole question of life's tendency to copy art is raised: all the relationships of art and life are at once invoked and the Pirandellian enigma of illusion and reality, pretence and truth, acting and being, is raised by Tim's puppets and continued throughout the book by a series of similar devices (Tim at one point sits beneath a tree with three masks – Comedy, Tragedy and 'the final mask, a quaint composite of comedy and tragedy' – and speaks to the world through each of the first two in turn, changing them back and forth indiscriminately and speaking vacantly, unthinkingly, but reserving the final mask unused for some future occasion). And at the end of the novel in a flashback to the young Tim Crashaw, the chief characters are invited by Tim to a birthday party, there to watch by way of entertainment the re-enactment of a violent, revolutionary outrage which they themselves have already taken part in, but extended now into its ideal form and projected in a curious way into the future: it is played for them by Tim's puppets, who are, in fact, models of those chief characters themselves: so the real Sara watches the puppet Sara take part in a bloody revolution and Timothy-when-young watches and partly helps to operate the revolutionary fervour of Timothy-when-old. It is perhaps worth noting the similarity between this model world-within-a-world, this visual representation before an audience's eyes of a miniature of their own immediate environment, and the same kind of device (the model castle within a castle) used on the stage in Edward Albee's *Tiny Alice*, written some twenty years after Whiting's novel. The comparison is especially striking since Whiting's novel, as well as making constant use of the theatre and play-acting as one of its central images and basic metaphors, also reads almost as if it should have been a play itself.

The opening paragraphs of the novel are sufficient also to establish several other things which are typical of the whole work. Note, for example, the ferocious, fanatic attention to, and relation of, specific detail: '. . . immediately succeeded by the Wednesday – November 16, 1938 – when he had travelled to this foreign country . . .' 16 November 1938 did indeed fall on a Wednesday in very fact. And this is typical: throughout the book there are dozens of instances of this passion for minute detail, but also throughout the whole book, the terse, laconic and often sardonic reporting of minute detail of place and time and person is juxtaposed with passages of a wildly imaginative kind, so that the total effect is a surrealistic one – a hard, bright outline and a feverish vision. This does lead to the novel's most serious weakness – it is dangerously overwritten:

> As he sits, Sirs, delitescent, his voice begins the iterative
> phrases and he continues from time to time to clap against
> his face his playthings, the comic or the tragic mask. His

old eyes find difficulty in distinguishing the colours and
expressions of the different masks. Speaking hollow words
of misery his face contorts to laughter but, ignorant as
before, he holds the mask in his squamous hands and speaks
through the jeering orifice to a world which gives but small
attention to the past, present or future life of a Tim
Crashaw.

It was presumably, the memory of this sort of writing that made Whiting say, in some notes he prepared for himself while beginning in 1961 to write the play to be called *The Nomads*, 'Style: harsh, direct, idiomatic: cut the plush.' *Not a Foot of Land* is too lush and plushy, it has, in a word, the faults of a young writer's work, but in view of its merit and its promise these are faults one finds easy to forgive. One thinks of the early verses of Wilfred Owen and of his suddenly coming to maturity in another war. And the seriousness of purpose and the outstanding promise of *Not a Foot of Land* are everywhere apparent and undeniable.

It has two other qualities which make it an important document, so important that it surely should be published, in spite of Whiting's own statement that he did not intend it for publicaton. After all, Ibsen said *Peer Gynt* was not intended for the stage and was impossible to perform and Milton left a published note saying that *Samson Agonistes* must not be acted: both poets have been disobeyed, with happy results.[5] The two qualities to which I refer in *Not a Foot of Land* are these: first, it teems with images, situations, even whole characters, which recur later in almost all his plays and are obviously central to his view of the world; second, it shows again and again the way in which his own direct personal experience, transmuted into the figures and images of art, informed all his work. The central themes of *Not a Foot of Land* are the search for and the need for integrity of idea and ideal, the innate tendency of the sensitive towards self-destruction, the proper equipoise between individual and community, the defencelessness of innocence (especially as represented by childhood), the fear in the individual heart of rejection. In varying proportions and combinations, these themes and their attendant images recur in and form the backbone of all his plays. In this early novel, one sees them at their source, so to speak, in their most concentrated and purest forms (and although this also, therefore, implies that they are seen in their crudest forms, the crudity is really not disadvantageous so far as a study of the themes and their place in the scheme of Whiting's thought is concerned, even though that same crudity, and a certain confusion of thought and treatment, do make for a less than *totally* satisfactory work in the final analysis).

The close relationship of the senses (though not the incidents) of the novel to Whiting's immediate personal circumstances is not difficult to demonstrate. Take again, for example, that curiously-insisted-upon date: Wednesday, 16 November 1938, the date on which Timothy Crashaw leaves England. If, on his journey that morning, Timothy had bought a copy of *The Times*, he would have found that the chief news stories were concerned with the official pogrom, conducted by the Nazi government of Germany against the Jews, in reprisal (or so the official excuse went) for the assassination in Paris on 7 November by a young Polish-German Jew of the Nazi diplomat, von Rath. The anti-Jewish measures reported included a fine of £84,000,000 exacted on the entire Jewish community of Germany, the exclusion of Jews from all economic activity, the closing of all German universities to Jewish students, and thousands of arrests. Nazi-inspired mobs had looted, wrecked and burned hundreds of Jewish shops in Berlin and elsewhere. One headline in the paper said 'aryanisation of Munich bank'; a news item began 'All the Jews taken into custody are understood to be confined in the concentration camp at Dachau, near Munich. Three of them, it is learned from a trustworthy source, have died during imprisonment.' And one of the 'Letters to the Editor' contained this sentence: 'I cannot bring myself to believe that so great a leader as Hitler, who has achieved the amazing success of the complete resurrection of Germany, can have given his sanction to this deplorable action especially at this critical moment in the international situation.' The Munich Crisis was just over and though there was in both France and England a fairly general assumption (an assumption which by 1944, when Whiting started his novel, looked glib and pathetic) that the peace had been saved, there was still about the whole continent of Europe a pervading atmosphere of bizarre violence. On 16 November, *The Times* reported the end of one of the battles in the Spanish Civil War, with Franco's forces, liberally assisted by Italian and German aircraft, firmly holding the west bank of the Ebro. A few days before, the same paper had carried a report which said: 'In accordance with the wishes of Mr Neville Chamberlain the sum of 500,000 francs (£2,770) raised by public subscription under the auspices of the newspaper *Paris-Soir* to buy the Prime Minister a property in France as a thank-offering for his services to peace, will be paid over to French ex-service charities': on the same page appeared a report of the raiding by Swiss federal police of the offices of the Swiss-Nationalist-Socialist Party and the Bund Trevor Eidgenossen in the cities of Basle, Berne, Zurich, Saint-Gall, Lucerne and Schaffhausen. On 15 November the newspaper carried a map of Czechoslovakia, showing the pieces carved off by Britain, France, Germany and Italy at Munich. On 17 November a headline announced 'Japanese drive in Yangtze area' and, on the same page, was a report of the ratification of the Anglo-Italian agreement which recognised and legitimatised Italy's conquest of Abyssinia. On 18 November, among a number of items and photographs concerned with the state visit to England of King Carol of Rumania, was a short paragraph that said

'Vienna: Nov. 17 – It has been officially announced that all songs composed by Jews or with words written by Jews may no longer be sung and will in future be omitted from the school song-books.' And a headline on another page said: 'A.R.P.[6] Needs in the City – Poor Response by Volunteers.' To young men especially, 1938 seemed like the point of dissolution of all those ideals bred in the 1920s and 1930s; the world of the League of Nations, of the growth of idealistic socialism, of the pacifist determination to renounce war and to prevent all future wars, the world fit for heroes to live in which had been promised to those returning from the holocaust of 1914–18, just twenty years before. A young man might well feel that Chamberlain's Munich-England must somehow be left behind and that the course one steered must necessarily oscillate between a search for the impossible personal peace of some remote Shangri-La on the one hand (perhaps there is some significance in the fact that the trite name and facile image was taken from a popular novel of the later 1930s) and a plunging armpits deep in the honourable bloodshed of some final, apocalyptic revolution on the other (as many young Britons and Americans had done in the Spanish Civil War). Young Englishmen knew that their lives were about to be seized, disrupted, corrupted, uprooted. Whiting knew in 1938 that the onset of full-scale conscription (it should be remembered that there was no peace-time compulsory military service in England between the two world wars) would catch him in its earliest waves. Seen backward from 1944, the end of 1938 could well have seemed the cataclysmic, burning turning-point to one in Whiting's position. This sense of a world gone bad, a world to run from to somewhere purer, somewhere made more wholesome by one's own efforts, is strongly felt in *Not a Foot of Land*. As is also the nightmare quality of the whole experience of war, though the novel, except briefly at one point, is not about war as such. A story which Whiting himself told of an odd experience of his own in England during the war has particular relevance for the generally nightmare atmosphere of *Not a Foot of Land*. In reply to a magazine interviewer[7] who asked him about the source of *Saint's Day*, he said:

> 'It was a place, actually, and a mural in a house. A place
> where I was in the army – which is probably a reason for
> the soldiers in the play. It was in the early part of the war,
> in the Midlands somewhere. It was winter and it was
> miserable. We had nothing to burn, so we went out to see
> if we could find a house we could tear down. In quite large
> grounds we came across this obviously derelict house. We
> went in; there were no lights and we had to use flashlights.
> And *there* was this most extraordinary painting on the
> wall . . . Standing there in that house, I suddenly had the
> most extraordinary feeling, which stayed with me for six
> years.'

This eerie experience might well have been the origin of *Saint's Day* as Whiting, himself, suggested; the practical links of the presence of the soldiers, and of the picture, and of the decaying house itself – all of which appear in *Saint's Day* – indeed suggest a very close and direct connection. But the connection with *Not a Foot of Land*, though a connection of atmosphere rather than of actual object or incident, is equally observable and no less significant: the sense of an old life and an old world deserted, its artefacts left, defenceless, at the mercy of a present violence and destruction, is to be found everywhere in the novel. And the violence is, in the novel, all the more terrible for being incipient rather than actual, which again is the sense of the story of the deserted house. It is a violence of the spirit, rather than a mere physical violence; a feeling that that part of man which created the mural also created the war and the marauding soldiers that come to threaten it. Violence, in fact, is one of the basic parts of the nature of man and one that cannot be denied or permanetly sublimated or inhibited. There are relatively few scenes of overt physical violence in *Not a Foot of Land*, and most of those that are there seem curiously impersonal (and all the more horrible for that); there are no lovingly detailed brutalities; yet the overall sense of a world overturned, a dark, bitter, cold and dangerous world in which the individual soul is an isolated and irreconcilable alien, is very strong even in those parts of the book that seem confused and somewhat ill-defined.

Of course, many works by many writers – and especially first or early works by young writers – show a very direct impact of their authors' immediate personal experiences. There is nothing especially remarkable about this: indeed, it would be strange if this were not the case. Nevertheless, it is worth remarking it especially in the case of John Whiting and *Not a Foot of Land* because images which grew in this work from the direct and immediate impingement of his personal experiences spread outwards later and coloured a great deal of his future writing, acquiring in the process an obsessive quality for both him and his audiences. There is a sardonic little footnote to the particular example I have given – the story of the picture in the deserted house: Mrs Whiting told me that she very much doubted that it actually happened at all. She had always regarded it, she said, 'as one of John Robert's stories'. In other words, it was a part of art rather than life; not an instance of the raw material presently to be transmuted, but itself the first stage in the alchemy of transmutation. It does not matter: what stronger proof could there be of the closeness of his art at that time to his personal experiences than that eight years afterwards he could not tell the difference and had, in a sense, begun to think of himself, in this one regard at any rate, as a character in one of his own stories?

Not a Foot of Land has only one central incident: the destruction of a museum which has become a kind of shrine (a 'cenacle', Whiting calls it, with his love, at that time, for rare and overrich vocabulary).

The destroying of it is carefully planned by Timothy Crashaw and four others, three men and a girl. On the practical plane it is designed to be the start of a revolution or coup d'état (it is not clear which) for Crashaw links his plans with those of Everal, a military leader who has twice before made revolutionary attempts which have failed and now acts under Crashaw's commands. But the actual desecration of the shrine is carried out by Crashaw and his friends as an act of idealistic devotion, ceremonially. The museum is contained in a house once occupied by the leader ('the Master') who established the present regime. He was shot on the steps of the house and it is to him that the 'shrine' is dedicated. It consists of a museum display of memorabilia of the Master – his clothes, his gun, his diary and papers, photographs and paintings of him.

The actual act of desecration – the smashing of the glass cases, the ripping of the canvas of the portraits, the dashing to pieces of the plaster death mask, the sprinkling of gasoline and the final conflagration – is described minutely no less than five times in the course of the novel, sometimes with significant variation of detail. In one of the descriptions, for example, Sara, the young girl accomplice, is shot by the guard-cum-caretaker, caught in the rapid spread of the petroleum blaze and burned to death; in all the other accounts she escapes with the others, Crashaw being the last to leave, no caretaker or guard interrupting. Nor are these variations accountable for on the basis of any naturalistic rationalisation: one cannot, for example, say that they are the result of the accounts being given by different people, or from different points of view. The accounts differ, rather, because they attempt to incorporate at different times all the possible senses of so climactic and cataclysmic an act, all the responses, all the possible practical consequences. As if any great action subsists not only in the actual occurrences surrounding it and connected with it (which are in a sense only an accidental collection of incidents chosen by casual circumstance from all the things that could have happened and could have been thought about the central action) but also in all the complex possibilities of change and combination which it itself produces: its final 'meaning', its full gesture, can be realised only if all its possibilities, both practical and emotional, are known. Whiting has nowhere said, so far as I know, that this is what he was attempting. It nevertheless seems to be something of this sort which emerges and, one feels, valuably emerges. The style he uses to achieve this result is essentially an impressionistic one, with an intricate pattern of inter-relationships within it and between its elements. The burning of Sara, for instance, vividly recalls an earlier incident in the novel: Sara suffers a nightmare in which she sees herself punished for the crime of the desecration, her punishment being to be burned at the stake. The dream of the burning is described in detail, as if by someone inside the dream, so to speak. Similarly, in two of the five accounts of the attack on the shrine, Timothy is an old man and the rest are all young; in the other three accounts, all are young, including Timothy, and Timothy is Sara's lover. This change is not merely capricious or whimsical, however. It is built strongly into the pattern of the whole work, which begins with Timothy as an old man in the village built and inhabited only by women – he is the only man there. The women are voluntary exiles who have fled from the soulless and oppressive regime which had been started with such hopes and fervour by the Master, but has since degenerated into a totalitarian oppression. Old Tim has been there many years when the story begins, waiting for the chance to make his one stroke. The novel then flashes back to Timothy as a young man and the three accounts of his planning and executing of the revolutionary act occur within thirty pages. The first is a statement which Timothy himself imagines as made by a prosecutor at a trial. (After all five conspirators have successfully escaped and are back in England, Timothy, alone, suddenly comes upon a brief account of the crime in a newspaper. Momentarily, he projects his fear forward and in his imagination hears the voice of the prosecutor at the imaginary trial relating the details of the event in a mixture of drily factual official reportage and melodramatic official condemnation.) The second and third accounts are not naturalistically motivated in this way: that is to say, they neither of them represent a particular person's point of view. Both are given as part of the general narrative of the novel and they are subtly placed to serve as punctuation for the narrative as a whole. Many of the details are repeated in both of these accounts. Actual words spoken by characters are set down identically in the two accounts. On the other hand, some details appear in only one of the accounts and appear at some length. The general atmosphere of the second of the three 'young' renderings of the story is gay, factual, laconic; even with a little joke here and there, especially from Sara: 'What are you smoking, beloved? They'll smell you for miles', she says to Timothy about his cigar as they drive rapidly from the house after setting it ablaze. The atmosphere of the third telling is edgy, nervous, fraught with tension. Sara never once addresses Timothy as 'Beloved' in this version (she has used the epithet three or four times in the earlier telling). And there are two brief, elliptic references to the motive for the crime, or at least the origin of the plan, which are not there in the earlier versions.

Not that either of these references is explicit of motive or origin when one first runs across it, but together they become so, obliquely, when seen in the context of the fourth and fifth versions of the story. The first reference is to a priest, the second to a dancer. Timothy is thinking to himself of the escape after the crime: 'Slower, for they must turn right at the crossroads, a turning to take them on to a village, the birthplace of the priest.' There has been no mention at all, in any connection, of a priest before this, but in the fourth version, some hundred pages later, he re-appears as one of the conspirators, though in the background, not in the main assault. It is he who brings to Timothy (who is now 'Old Tim') the necessary information about 'the plans and the situation, of other men's schemes and ideas, of conditions in the city, the people's temper and the soldiers who, any day, might again occupy the city' and it is he who, after the attack on the museum–shrine has set the whole city in flames, comes back to Tim to tell him 'everything has gone thoroughly and well . . . the city was taken without force . . . there was no killing.' There is a description, at this point, of the priest: 'Tim recognised the priest, the face that was the beginning. The face with the dark, unlined skin, surmounted by a sloping forehead and fine clipped brown hair. The face that had led Tim over so many years.'

Just as the brief reference to the priest which occurs in the third version is then amplified in the fourth, so the reference to a dancer, occurring in the third version, is amplified in the fifth. The dancer's name is Frederick Sabine and Sara mentions him several times in tones of great admiration: she is especially impressed when Timothy also expresses his admiration and tells her that he is personally acquainted with Sabine. Then after the puppet-play at the birthday party ends (that is to say, *outside* all five versions of the story of the attack on the cenacle, the last two versions having been contained within the puppet play itself), Timothy introduces Sara to the man who has operated the puppets for the play. It is Sabine. 'All in the room looked at the long face with the fine, clipped brown hair' – the description of Sabine is identical with that of the priest. Sara speaks with him: 'So it was you who controlled us. Made us dress and behave like . . .' – she never finishes the sentence. Sara, in other words, identifies herself and the other conspirators with the puppets and attributes their inspiration to the dancer, just as Timothy, within the puppet play, has attributed his inspiration to the priest.

So Sabine, who is Sara's hero and an exquisite dancer, is identified with the priest who has in some mysterious way provided Timothy with the inspiration for his life's one significant action and has also operated the puppets in the play, controlled them, made them dream, fashioned their behaviour. The image, surely, is of the artist-as-priest: the purifier, the catalyst whereby the individual life realises coherence and nobility, the 'trumpets that sing to battle'. And it is significant that Sabine is one of the intrinsic connections between Sara and Timothy and that when the puppet play which he has devised is over, Sara disappears (as she does in the final pages of the novel).

Sara's awe and envy over Timothy's actually being acquainted personally with Sabine is referred to twice, both times in conversations which Timothy silently recalls to himself after the event. The first time is in the *third* version of the story of the despoliation, when the young Timothy recalls it. While the conspirators are crouched in hiding, waiting for the moment when their violent action is planned to begin, Timothy finds himself thinking over a conversation he has had that afternoon with Sara:

> 'Do you really know him?'
> 'Yes.'
> 'Do you really, really know him? To speak to him, I mean?'
> 'I say, yes.'
> 'Have you been to his dressing room?'
> 'Yes, and I have seen him dance from the wings of the
> theatre.'
> 'What?'
> 'Oh, *Le Chevalier d'Industrie* and others.'
> 'He's very wonderful, isn't he?'
> 'Very wonderful.'
> 'Some time you must tell me about him.'
> 'Some time; I will.'

This is how the conversation, as remembered by Timothy-when-young is reported in the third version. It is reported again, speech-for-speech and word-for-word, in the fifth version, in which Timothy-when-old, having told the young Sara in their hiding place that conversation would now be dangerous, thinks over an earlier conversation with her. In this version, there is an interesting comment on the conversation which did not appear in the earlier version, in which the identity of the dancer had been left unrevealed:

> 'Do you really know him?'
> 'Yes.'
> That question and answer had been applied to Sabine, the
> dancer, Sara's hero. The question had been asked and
> answered in the past; in the time preceding Tim's retirement.
> The transitional period had been spent in the village. The
> women had been kind to Tim even from the moment of his
> arrival, shy, as he had been, from failure. They had fed
> him as an invalid and in his long convalescence carefully
> re-taught him the meaning and sound of words as a symbol
> of expression. In return he had written and sung songs for
> them in a newly discovered language. In this way he had
> passed the major part of his life. The women had cared
> for him as tenderly when he was old as they had comforted
> him in his sick youth. They aided him in every way until
> he went from them an old man, never questioning his
> decision to depart. On leaving the women Tim came down
> to the city to explain the scheme.

'It is so simple. Come with me. All we need is a geometrical
plan.'
That again was the former episode.
'Do you really, really know him? To speak to him, I mean?'

And the remembered conversation then continues exactly as in the earlier
version. It is very significant indeed that Old Tim should recall simultaneously the image of the dancer and the moment of his decision to
leave the women's village and return to the city to 'explain the scheme',
for this return immediately brings to *our* minds – as the memory of it
obviously has brought to *his* mind – the figure of the priest. The description of the priest's visit to Old Tim, after he got to the city, occurs only
fifteen pages earlier; and it was the priest who gave him both the information and the courage to 'explain the scheme'; and because of this, he is
now crouching in hiding with Sara and awaiting the climactic event.
The thought of the dancer has led him spontaneously to the thought
of the priest and so in Old Tim's mind and in the reader's, the images
of the dancer and the priest are locked together.

The placing of this strange act of rebellion at the novel's centre, the
way the pattern of the book constantly returns to this point, the fact
that, in effect, a single act is made to occupy the whole of Timothy's
life and the way this act is linked over and over again with images of
sex and love and childhood (through Sara and through her childhood
and through Timothy's childhood) together make clear the central
posture and meaning of the work. It is not, I think, a nihilist one, as
might appear at first sight. Ronald Hayman, in his introductory note
to the unfinished play *Noman* in vol. 2 of *The Collected Plays of John
Whiting* (Heinemann, 1969) points out that there are marked similarities
between *Noman* and *Not a Foot of Land* and then goes on to suggest
that the novel (and therefore, presumably, the play) *is* nihilistic. He
says:

> And the play has a great deal in common with his
> unpublished novel *Not A Foot of Land*. In this, Timothy
> Crashaw and his accomplices, three men and a girl, plan
> to destroy the shrine of 'the holy Master',[8] who is venerated
> by the whole of society. Like so much else in the novel, the
> motives for the destruction are never explained, though
> Timothy seems to want to make a gesture against life. In
> one episode he recalls the fear he felt after a childhood fall.
> 'I looked up at the sky and was overcome with unreasoning
> terror. All acts of violence were inexplicable to me. Revenge,
> premeditated revenge of the bloodiest kind was the answer!'
> One character calls Timothy's attitude 'falling in love with
> death'.

It is true that the motives for the destruction are not 'explained' because this is not a discursive or didactic work but an imaginative and intuitive one. It is under no obligation to explain, so long as it reveals, illuminates and makes clear: which I think it does. If one considers the whole novel as a cohesive entity, the motive for the destruction of the shrine emerges clearly (and this is the very core of the work: I would concede that there are other, peripheral parts of the experience which *are* unclear and ambiguous). The destruction is not a 'gesture against life' but a gesture against a false life, a tawdry life, an empty life, especially against an emptiness which has claimed reverence by posing as fulness, completion, realisation. The 'Master' has turned out to be a false prophet; that is the point. In spite of his own heroic beginning and revolutionary ardour, the regime he has instituted is a dead and repressive one whose effect is to sap the vitality and individuality of the people and leave them dull, apathetic, resigned to a dusty existence in which the only targets are material ones, and they only modest and unexciting. Timothy's gesture – and be it noted it is the total gesture of a whole lifetime, the very meaning of his being, literally his *raison d'être*, for the fable makes his contemplation and execution of it cover the whole span of his life, makes him, in a sense, as Timothy when-young and Tim-when-old, perform the same simple act many times – is a plea for the awakening and revival of the spirit, a plea for the throwing off of the servitude of the soulless efficiency of the over-organised state, a plea for a return to a society where individual idiosyncrasy is valued. And the plea is not gentle, patient and reasoned, but exasperate and violent because it is an instinctive bursting forth of the imprisoned spirit. This is the significance of the child's cry of 'Revenge, premeditated revenge of the bloodiest kind was the answer!' John Arden, in his preface to *Serjeant Musgrave's Dance* written in 1957, expresses a similar sentiment when he says that *one* of one's responses to enormous injustice or brutality or violence, whether directed against oneself or against other people, is suddenly to wish to retaliate with some massive and outrageous stroke of violence oneself, an act which has some ceremonial, sacrificial quality in it, that somehow purifies, atones, redeems, like the striking-out of Oedipus' eyes or the crucifixion of Jesus.

The 'Master' against whose memory and legend Timothy is violently demonstrating started with great ideals and honest ones. His revolution was prompted by a love of the people and was designed to give them freedom. But it led to a police state and the establishment of a superstitious cult of leader-worship. The Master himself was assassinated (presumably by a counter-revolutionary) on the steps of the house where the 'shrine' now is and the assassination led directly both to the leader-worship legend and to the police state. The police chief, Podumus, is referred to at one point as having been the Master's friend and is presumably, therefore, carrying on the Master's policy; and the military leader in the Master's revolution, Kellinn, is now the commander-in-chief. One of the implicit questions, though one that is never explicitly explored, is the question of what might have happened had the Master remained alive to govern the society which his revolution had created. Another is the question of the antithesis between revolutionary aims and revolutionary achievements. The former of these questions was apparently one which especially interested Whiting, for in *Noman* he uses a central situation almost identical with that in *Not a Foot of Land* – a shrine to a dead leader, a plot to destroy and desecrate it – but his notes indicate that, had he finished the play, he intended to resurrect the dead leader: the assassination, though thought to be successful, was not; the leader, left for dead, was in reality wounded only; he now survives to be, under an assumed name, the caretaker of his own shrine, a situation rich in irony that, had it been carried out, would have given opportunity for the leader to comment both on the new society his 'death' had founded and on the disgust and disillusion of those who wish to break the shrine and destroy the legend.[9] In *Not a Foot of Land* no kind of character study of the Master is presented: indeed, it is fairly obviously in the interests of the central issues of the novel that he should remain shadowy and impersonal and this is what Whiting does with him. He is the subject of rumour, of veneration and of execration, a totem, not a person. It is the *idea* of a person in such a position, not the person himself, which interests Whiting. And the dilemma of the automatically self-defeating elements in the very act of revolution recalls very clearly the Communist dilemma and the totalitarianism of the Left. Old Tim seems particularly conscious of this dilemma and has toward it an attitude much more openly ambivalent than he had as Timothy-when-young. When they go to the house that is the museum, Old Tim tells his young collaborators, with admiration, the story of the Master's early struggles and of his triumph and of his death. Yet, he proceeds relentlessly with the plans for the despoliation of the shrine and, while waiting with Sara in hiding, waiting for the attack to begin, he writes out for her a song that he says used to be sung in that city:

> *Down from the hills the Master's come*
> *To make the city a boaster's home,*
> *Poor wee man with great big nose*
> *That it's useless to oppose,*
> *For it pokes and sniffs and pries,*
> *A hundred noses, two hundred eyes.*
> *Into my house, into yours,*
> *Up the stairs, behind the doors,*
> *Knowing what we have for dinner,*
> *Knowing that old Paul's a sinner.*
> *Look out!*
> *Run, run! Faster, faster!*
> *Or you'll be eaten by the Master!*

Tim explains to Sara: 'Old Paul was a local celebrity, a pamphleteer, who was hung for his lampoons. That song was sung less and less until it brought shots.'

Timothy's indictment of the Master's regime is not on grounds of physical repression of the populace (though armed patrols in city streets and the general apparatus of the police state do figure in the novel) but on grounds of causing a spiritual decay. When Old Tim returns to the city to begin his final assault on the cenacle, the following is the description of his arriving:

> So Tim Crashaw arrived in the city, an old man threading
> his way through barricades. No-one greeted him,
> acknowledged him or gave him any kindnesses for
> weak-headed old men were far too common in that place.
> Likewise no-one troubled him and for the first time he
> passed openly through the streets on this afternoon, without
> speed. The dry and dusty city was about him unwelcoming
> as he walked close against the walls of the houses, stepping
> his way through accumulated garbage, through the stench
> of filth and sewerage. There were few children and almost
> no wheeled traffic . . .

And at the house of the cenacle, when Old Tim and his small band of conspirators arrive:

> Through these historic rooms went Tim and his friends
> and the known story was told and heard again. Except for the
> caretaker, who was mending a hand-cart in the yard behind
> the kitchen, they were alone. For a moment, immediately
> after entering the house, they had seen a woman in a light
> raincoat come down the stairs. She had run off, slamming
> the door behind her. It was unusual for anyone to visit the
> house during the evening although it was accessible until
> 10 p.m. It was also unusual for more than six people to
> come in a day. Tim remembered in former times the
> tourists arriving in the mornings and in the afternoons the
> parties of school-children. There were no tourists and no
> children any more.

In other words, even the devotion to the secular saint has fallen off to a mere observance, a form only, pursued aimlessly, apathetically, yet still preserved with the status of an official religion. Tim leads his friends through the museum, telling its story as he goes. They come to the door of the room containing the 'shrine' itself:

> Together Tim and Sara put out hands to open the door;
> their hands touched and the door opened. Two lovers were

standing by the window but as Sara came into the room they
parted and began to look intently into the glass cases. The
action paused, confronted with the unexpected. Lovers?
There were, by right conduct, no more lovers. But two
stood before Tim, their hands and mouths parted by his
entrance into the room.

'There were, by right conduct, no more lovers . . .' At every point there
is evidence that all lively things, all productive things, all individual
things, were stifled in this city and it is to this stifling that Timothy –
and the novel – objects. The tyranny is a *foreign* one, not a native one:
the troops that parade the city are foreigners: the Master had apparently
sought the military help of some more powerful neighbour who, after
the Master's death, had kept its grip on the country. The parallels of
Russia in Hungary and Czechoslovakia are well-nigh irresistible, though
when Whiting's novel was written in 1944/5, Russia had invaded neither
of these countries, nor seemed, on the face of things, likely to do so.
Some of the descriptions of the once-gay city, however, now greyly
under the thumb of a proletarian dictatorship, could well fit Budapest or
Prague twenty years after Whiting was writing this novel.

There is one passage of description which not only captures very
vividly this atmosphere of general decay against which Timothy feels
that some final, awful gesture must be made, but which also illustrates
very aptly the surrealist quality of some of the writing and imagery. It
deals with an incident which occurs on the third day of Old Tim's stay
in the city (and is reminiscent, perhaps, of some German cities – Berlin
or Hamburg? – in 1945):

Beginning to cross the square Tim heard music.
Unbelievable: the sound of a large orchestra. Tim went
towards the music coming from the theatre on the east side
of the square. He walked towards the theatre, kicking his
way through a heap of filthy rags. Then standing beneath
the portico he saw the notice chalked on a blackboard which
leant against a column. He read that a symphony orchestra
would visit the city that day to perform three works, that
the soloist would be a violinist and that admission would
be free. Mounting the steps and passing through the
entrance, the doors of which had long ago been torn away,
he came to the foyer. The place was dark and dusty, the
gilded ornaments dulled and falling. On a wall still hung
a painting of some forgotten singer and beneath the picture
the fragments of a huge fallen chandelier were splintered
about. Tim looked down and his right foot was on an old
playbill. Before him was an entrance to the rear of the
auditorium and across the entrance, half-concealing, was

the remnant of a black curtain. Tim pulled this aside and
as he did so, whilst his hand was still on the curtain, the
music stopped. There was a patter of applause and,
following distantly, a clatter of instruments and a single
voice. The auditorium was not artificially lit but the large
doors at the back of the stage were open and the sunlight
entered from beyond the orchestra misting the individual
figures, silhouetting the raised conductor and shining
strongly upon the brass instruments. The light, flowing as
it was directly into Tim's eyes, softened the harsh lines of the
old theatre turning the dust to gold in the long shafts of
light and blinding the reflections from the cracked mirrors.
The conductor was turned towards Tim, his head bowed.
The audience was small, forty or so, mostly soldiers, seated
in the first few rows – the remaining seats had been removed
and replaced by wooden benches. The applause ended and
the conductor turned away to the orchestra and began to
arrange the scores before him. Tim walked to the centre
aisle and sat at the end of a wooden bench. Old political
pamphlets were about his feet, significant of dead, forgotten
fervour. Tim folded his hands on his lap and sat alone.
The conductor looked towards the wings of the theatre but
it was from a door in the auditorium that the violnist, who
was applauded, entered, brushing dust from his sleeve. He
stood almost at the centre of the stage beneath the rostrum,
staring confidently and with arrogance into the auditorium.
Together, the conductor raised his baton and the violinist
began to play. They broke Tim's silence of years with pure
music: the years through which he had relied upon half-
remembered melodies sung in his own harsh voice. The
sweetness of sound was so unbearable as it was unexpected
and Tim got up and ran from the building. His feet
cracked the glass of the fallen chandelier as he ran from
the theatre into the streets and back to the silence and
safety of his hired room.

This is two days before Timothy's final attack on the shrine of the
Master, the attack that will lead this time to the destruction of the
whole city by fire and to its capture by Everal, Timothy's military ally.

Ronald Hayman's suggestion of an entirely nihilistic explanation for
the gesture of despoliation seems inadequate when one examines all the
evidence. The gesture seems to me to be quite clearly a gesture *against*
the nihilist position, not in its favour. The violation of the shrine in
Noman is similarly motivated: Walter, who works in a public library,
and is one of the conspirators, says:

> 'People come to me and ask for books which will tell
> them how to paint the walls, make a table or a model
> railway train. I give out these books. A thousand and one
> ways to waste time, or How to Do for Yourself. That's all
> they want. Some guidance as to how to pass the time Lang[10]
> gave us. He set an end and a beginning to it all: he never
> fitted in the middle.'

And Meyer, the other principal among the revolutionary group, in *Noman,* agrees with him:

WALTER: Out into the streets.
MEYER: Sunday morning. People enjoying themselves. Happiness. Leisure. Desolation.
WALTER: The river steamers were pulling away from the banks. Shouts and music from across the water. Buses were setting off for the country-side. Comic hats and packed food.
MEYER: We sat at a safe table. Everything was laid on to impress us with the urgent need to accept ourselves as we are. Lovers went past. Nothing much can be given to the old and the ugly but at least they had dignity that day. Children's voices were silver, uncorrupted. It was a beautiful morning. And the horror and the emptiness of that beauty, the forsaken sorrow of that free human activity has brought us here tonight.

By 'here', he means to the museum–shrine, which they now mean to destroy.

The character in *Not a Foot of Land* quoted by Ronald Hayman as designating Timothy's attitude 'falling in love with death' is in fact the imaginary public prosecutor of Timothy's own fearful but momentary daydream. It represents, in other words, Timothy's saying to himself 'This is what those we oppose will say about us: this is the sort of accusation they will bring.' It does not mean that the description is one that Timothy himself accepts or that it can be taken by the reader as objectively accurate. The entire matter of the desecration of the cenacle should be taken as a poetic symbol, not as a factual account of a socio-political act. The politics are important only in so far as they illustrate the state of Timothy's soul, not the other way round. And his soul has been, according to the evidence of the novel, true to its objective, pure, successful at the heart of the matter. The self-exiled women in the mountain village 'had been kind to Tim even from the moment of his arrival, *shy, as he had been, from failure*'. In other words, he had tried before, many times perhaps: not specifically the destruction of the cenacle, but a general and constant assault upon false gods, tawdry ideals. The attack on the false shrine is a continuing thing, a life posture. There is, in this context, a possible significance in the fate of the death mask of the Master which is the most sacred relic kept in the shrine. In the first four accounts of the despoliation, the mask is lifted from the wall, laughed at, ridiculed and then Timothy asks

'Should we take it with us and set it up in the market-place?' Sara suddenly screams out 'Smash it; break it! Please destroy him!' and it is this scream which raises the alarm and causes the plotters to leave too hurriedly and so, in part at least, to bungle the job they came to do. As Sara screams, Timothy drops the mask to the floor in alarm and it is broken. But in the fifth account there is no scream and it is not broken:

> Reeves took the death-mask from the wall and holding it
> up in both hands said 'All of you look upon your Master'.
> He sneezed. They laughed. Tim crossed the room and took
> the mask. Holding it in the crook of his left arm he
> adorned the mask with his active painted fingers.[11] The
> false curving moustache gave the thinking face an expression
> of hilarity. A drop of paint ran from an eye of the mask
> like a tear. Taking the mask again in his hands Tim kissed it
> on the mouth, the paint leaving a mark on his face. He
> smiled at the mask, caressed the brow and asked: 'Should
> we take it with us and set it up in the market-place?' Again
> they laughed. Tim put the mask under his arm, the paint
> staining his coat and smearing over the plaster face. 'We
> must get on' he said. 'Let me have the petrol.'

And this time there is no alarm raised. The mask is taken with them when they leave and given as a souvenir to the one who has waited with the get-away car. And this time the whole city burns, the purifying fire sweeps away the garbage and the desolation and the materialism. This time, the gesture is triumphant and complete. And, half-ironically, the Master's mask is saved.

The novel's central sense of idealism on the one hand and of a fierce disgust with all compromise, chicanery and spiritual grubbiness on the other shows itself not only in the major incident of the destruction of the shrine but in the subsidiary and supplementary themes of the book. As was mentioned earlier, two of the most important of these are the instinct toward self-destruction and the sense of the fragility of childhood. The suggestion contained in the former of these is rather the same suggestion as Jean Anouilh attaches to the ermine which, he says (though I believe there is no biological authenticity in the legend), will kill itself if its white fur becomes soiled. All the way through *Not a Foot of Land* this pervading sense of desperation can be found, but the authority of the novel is given very firmly to the suggestion that this desperation should be viewed as an indication of a positive and idealistic response: romantic, but not nihilist. The world is a bleak and dangerous place; life is neither easy nor comfortable; but humanity nevertheless continues to breed an inveterate tendency to aspire. Everal, the revolutionary, describes his ambitions for himself and his country and links ambition with death:

'My ambitions were no less exalted: a complete restoration
of grace and by this my own entrance to power. I founded
my methods on those who had gone before me. That I
should have conformed, both in my methods and in my
ultimate failure is, perhaps, obvious. My mind is formed
for interpretation, not creation.[12]

So, my first two attempts had failed through treachery and
indecision.

On the penultimate day of the second campaign I had
seen the death of my lover.

I know now that she died.

Her body was raised from beneath the wreckage of a fallen
house – was finally exhausted by disease – was discovered
at dawn hanging from a tree, a solitary suicide – was
washed to the shore by the evening tide – she was destroyed
in the earnest endeavour of a great battle – burnt to death
by an accidental fire in a commercial hotel – she had died
under anaesthetic on an operating table – she was torn and
bloodied by an infuriated mob – crucified by strangers in a
foreign country and brought for me to see. She died in war.'

She died, in fact, all the deaths there are; she submitted to every form
of death for the sake of the revolution. She is the image and epitome of
all self-sacrifice. (The 'she' to whom Everal refers does not figure elsewhere in the novel: this is the only time she is mentioned.) Her loss is
also Everal's loss, the loss of his innocence and his essential self. They
have both given themselves to destruction rather than endure life's
sleazy compromise, a compromise which, the general tone of Whiting's
novel suggests (especially in passages such as the one just quoted), is
not the result only of social or political maladjustment but of the nature
of life itself, a malaise that is existential, not merely sociological.

In the same way Sara, with a curious will-less submission, gives herself over to destruction. There is an odd dreamlike quality in the way
she puts herself calmly and without resistance into those situations that
must lead to her immolation. Having 'died' twice by fire in the novel
and having been immured in a mental hospital, her mind partially
destroyed, she walks away from the party given on her sixteenth birthday (the gathering at which Timothy presents his puppet play of the
successful revolution) and quietly disappears. And no one goes to look
for her. When they notice that she has left the house – and they all
know that she has nowhere to go – Timothy tells the others that he will
wait for her: 'I shall go when Sara comes back', he tells Reeves, the last
to leave. And he does, indeed begin to look for her: on the stairway
outside the party room he calls her name. 'There was no answer, no
reply from any room, from the stairs or from any hiding place in the

house. His imaginative mind began the conception of a tragedy. He became aware of an atmosphere of ruin. Through his life violent imagery had provided him with the mental picture of a dead body, the face very white, the blood very red, the sacrifice conventional, banal. Perhaps, at last, he was at the verge of realisation.' He continues the search for a few minutes within the house. He calls her name again: ('Timothy went down to the first floor. There was no urgency in his manner. "Sara!" An uninformed observer would have gathered from his actions in the house that his position was a watchman; his searching a routine matter concerning locks, fire and burglary.' And a few moments later he gives up the search: ' "Sara! Sara. Ra." The name shouted, repeated, meant nothing. At last the word had lost significance: the name – Sara – had no connection with any living person of Timothy's acquaintance. There was realisation of this in his timid gesture towards the remaining door.')

Timothy does not go to look for Sara in the streets. He goes back to the room where the party was held and clears up the odds and ends of party debris. He packs the puppets from the play in a suitcase, which he takes with him when he leaves the house. This is on the night of 15 November, the night of Sara's birthday. On the next day, 16 November 1938, as we have been told at the very beginning of the novel, he 'travelled to this foreign country to fulfil the ending as he himself had portrayed it'. Sara has voluntarily, consciously, become the living and dying embodiment of Timothy's tragic sense of the world and, metaphorically, metaphysically, the self-immolation includes Timothy himself as well. The novel's cyclic structure is here perfectly suited to its theme.

The theme was to become basic to Whiting's plays and even to his personal life-style. Kenneth Tynan said of him, after hearing a lecture on the art of the dramatist by Whiting in 1957: ('I felt I was in the presence of a condemned man. There was resignation in the very set of his gentle, scolded face and the expression in his large dark eyes seemed to anticipate, even to embrace, defeat.' Tynan's view was borne out by John Whiting's response to his own position in the British theatre between 1951 and 1963. Always somewhat aloof, as an artist something of an instinctive aristocrat at a time when the theatre, like every other part of society, was beginning to bellow with a brash egalitarianism, his plays were never really accepted except by the minority. This rejection affected him deeply, but never by way of making him ingratiating. He rejected, in his turn, with a fine mixture of scorn and resignation, the views of the current theatre. His pieces of dramatic criticism, his published essays and lectures and, above all, his unpublished letters, make this very clear. And when I remarked to Christopher Fry, in a conversation in which we were discussing Whiting's work, that one was almost tempted to construe some eerily occult connection between his obsessive treatment in his plays of the resigned acceptance of a personal doom and his own early death (he was 45) from cancer, Fry replied by quoting Rilke – 'Every man makes his own death'.[13]

In *Saint's Day*, the central character, Paul Southman, withdrawn from a society which he hates and despises, is engaged in a policy of taking his revenge upon humanity by slowly destroying himself; Charles Heberden, the frustrated artist who is married to Paul's grand-daughter, fully supports the old man's position and is himself a self-immolator; and Procathren, the young poet who comes because he admires Paul but stays to murder him, destroys himself in the same gesture.

The same is true of Rupert Forster in *Marching Song*. A military commander imprisoned by his political enemies, he is offered the alternative of suicide or a rigged political trial deliberately designed to humiliate him and make him a scapegoat. His former love for Catherine de Troyes has faded and cannot affect his decision and though the flicker of a new passion for Dido Morgen, the young waif that chance thrusts at him in Catherine's house, momentarily deflects his will, the ultimate issue is never really in doubt. The only answer to the disgusting mess that life makes is to keep oneself clean and to leave the mess behind: some messes cannot be cleaned up.

In *The Devils*, Sister Jeanne unwittingly destroys herself (though not literally) through her pathological obsession with the physical imagery of sex and comes to realise the fact only after the destruction is complete; but Grandier goes open-eyed to the literal destruction which he has brought upon himself and taken no pains to avoid:

D'ARMAGNAC: Trincant has told me about his daughter. You have your whores. Why did you have to do this?

GRANDIER: It seemed a way.

D'ARMAGNAC: A way to what?

GRANDIER: All worldly things have a single purpose for a man of my kind. Politics, power, the senses, riches, pride and authority. I choose them with the same care that you, sir, select a weapon. But my intention is different. I need to turn them against myself.

D'ARMAGNAC: To bring about your end?

GRANDIER: Yes. I have a great need to be united with God. **Living has** drained the need of life from me. My exercise of the senses has flagged to total exhaustion. I am a dead man, compelled to live.

D'ARMAGNAC: You disgust me. This is a sickness.

GRANDIER: No, sir. It is the meaning and the purpose.

It is true that Grandier's death-wish is of a somewhat different quality from that of Southman, Procathren, Heberden or Forster, in that he himself consciously realises its presence and recognises its purpose, but there is a generic relationship between all of them nevertheless. They all represent a rejection of the ordinary, human life, for whatever reason. With Keats they repeat the Romantic litany:

> *. . . for many a time*
> *I have been half in love with easeful Death,*
> *Called him soft names in many a mused rhyme,*
> *To take into the air my quiet breath;*
> *Now more than ever seems it rich to die,*
> *To cease upon the midnight with no pain . . .*

Almost as a conscious counterpoint to the longing of the adult for a clean and decent death, Whiting employs in *Not a Foot of Land* the innocence, the instinct-to-believe, the yearning of children. The image of childhood is constantly before us in the book: sometimes in instances and incidents connected with the central characters; sometimes in memories and dreams; sometimes in incidents which seem quite separate from the general flow of the book; sometimes in glancing, passing references. But taken together, there are literally dozens of such references. and in nearly all of them the children are either alone, or threatened, or in some danger, or alienated from the adult world, or dead.

The second 'scene' in the novel, beginning on p. 6 and following immediately after the opening scene which has introduced us to Old Tim, now living in the Village of Women, begins with a vivid and gruesome description of a London street immediately after a street accident. The scene is written impressionistically. It has, on the face of it, absolutely nothing to do with what has gone before. It begins:

> Surrounded by the chattels of a street accident – a child's
> soft hat and cast-off upturned shoe, a discarded newspaper,
> some dispersed fragments of shattered glass and a group
> of six staring humans, four men and two women, including
> the woman driver of the car, her mouth open in a protracted
> silent scream – and sitting on the kerb of the pavement, lit
> by headlights from the car, was Andrew Colsin, awaiting
> the arrival of a doctor. The time was late in the fourteenth
> day of November 1938; the place a side street of London.
> The victim, a child, a girl, about twelve years old and a
> stranger to Colsin . . .

Colsin, as it turns out, does have a connection, a very firm one, with Timothy: two connections, in fact. He is the brother of the caretaker of the cenacle, who was killed (in four of the five versions, anyway) in Timothy's attack upon it; and he is suddenly and mysteriously accosted by Reeves, another of the conspirators, and taken, rather against his will, to the party where the puppet play is performed. But the twelve-year-old girl killed in the street has no plot connection with anything else in the book and is not mentioned again, once Colsin has left the scene of the accident. ('. . . the child opened her eyes and tears were seemingly released which ran down her face. She lay relaxed and looking up at Colsin. "Pain?" he asked. The child did not answer but stared up at his young face, his narrowed blue eyes, his short fair beard and pointed ears. As she was about to speak Colsin bent over her and the conical hat he wore threw shadow across her face and in that shadow she died.')

Only a few pages later, we are introduced for the first time to Sara, in the mental home, being befriended and waited on by another of the inmates, a circus clown. The clown has a vision:

> The faces of dead children laid in orderly rows for the
> purpose of identification. All sightless, all rigid, all dead
> with their heads to the centre of the room. Each covered in
> a uniform blanket blurring the contours of their bodies.
> The clown will walk along the line of children looking down
> at the inverted faces ... removing a blanket and smiling
> at the naked body; arranging an untidy pillow beneath a
> head and one at the feet; feeling a silver radiator to test
> the heat, then going on by a far door ... 'Save us' says the
> clown. 'A child alive in bed. God bless the child. Must
> speak to the child. Poor little Sara. Poor mad little Sara.
> What a sorry child Sara is, such a wretched child ...'

Neither the clown nor the dead children occur in the narrative again.

The next main reference to children is a description of the night Sara was born:

> Upon going into the house the father shut the door and
> closed himself into the darkness. Ascending the wide stairs
> he went into the bedroom. There he saw the child and the
> woman, his wife; kneeling by the bed he wept for he was
> an old man. His wife spoke to him, misunderstanding him:
> 'Don't cry. Don't cry. You are back to me from the war
> many years now. The fighting is finished. There is no need
> for sorrow, no cause for alarm.' As she spoke she touched
> the great scars on his shaven head.

This leads straight on, the peasant legend–folktale atmosphere increasing, into a long, detailed description of Sara's seventh birthday. She plays out-of-doors in a half-ruined courtyard full of ominous premonitions, with Everal, who is seven years older than she is. Then they go to her home for the birthday party. One of the guests is her old uncle, who does a strange, solo dance and sings while he dances.

> 'You are seven years old today, my sweet Sara. My darling
> is growing and she must never know misery. So I will dance
> again and again and let everybody know it is my Sara's
> birthday ...'

That night, Everal stays at Sara's house, his own home being distant.

The children are put to sleep in the same bed. One of the strangest pieces of description in the whole novel occurs. After they have undressed and Sara has scrambled into bed, Everal picks up Sara's clothes 'as if seeing them anew':

> Throwing them back to the chair he went to the bed to find the girl asleep. She was suddenly asleep. Everal saw her lying on her back holding a strange doll. Putting out his hands he caught the girl's hidden shoulders through the thick blankets and shook her into consciousness. Sara sat upright with her short black hair disordered. 'Marry me' whispered the boy. There was no response from the girl. 'Marry me' repeated the boy. Moving backwards from the girl he took up two lighted candles, setting them on the broad ledge at the foot of the bed. The boy beckoned to the girl but she remained unmoving. He took her hand and whispering encouragement drew her to the foot of the bed. There she clung for support while the boy made a cap for her by folding a linen table cover. This he placed on the girl's head and kneeling himself pulled her down beside him. Together they knelt silently, the girl's forehead resting against the bed.
>
> Before what god did these children kneel?
>
> Soon the boy impatiently muttered a benediction.
>
> Opening his eyes, raising his head, he took the girl's face between his hands and kissed her on the mouth in a manner strangely passionless for his mood.
>
> Together they stood up, the ceremony being done. The boy ungirded his waist and drew the robe over his head: he stood, displaying his nakedness.
>
> 'Take off your gown' was his order to the girl. By way of explanation he added 'That is the action of a bride'. 'I'm tired' said the girl, wearied of the game. At that the boy stepped forward and caught the folds of the girl's nightdress. He pulled upwards over her unwilling but lifted arms. The gown, being corded at the throat, caught beneath her chin. She gave a cry of pain from among the folds as the boy roughly stripped her. Together the children's nightclothes lay discarded on the floor and together the children stood naked.
>
> Sara snatched the ceremonial hat from her head and ran to the bed climbing in between the rough blankets. Everal laughed and pursued her. For a moment there was madness in the display of a mature woman's nude body, screaming mouth, disordered hair and, covering her, blood.

Then, as Everal looked down at Sara, they became children again.

Gently he lay down beside her. The bridegroom lay down with his bride in all righteousness. Then by his sudden movement the wooden doll fell and struck the floor like a rattle of bones; the movement which brought Everal down and upon Sara in which position he began an imitation, without penetration, of the sexual act as described to him by N[14] and witnessed by him enacted between his mother and his father. Sara was still, in pain beneath his weight. This was the first of the humiliations to be practised on her body.

This same Everal, when he is grown up and is exiled from his country because of his revolutionary activities, spends some months in London. Short of money, he gets a job as a teacher of his native language to a small English boy. 'This, employing me nine hours a week, continued for three weeks when the boy, Edward Gordon, aged twelve, was taken ill. Within three days he was dead. On the evening of his death I travelled to his home to enquire about him. His mother met me and, taking me into a large, seldom-used room, told me of her son's death.'

The mother gives Everal a small photograph of the dead boy as a memento; and shortly afterwards, when Everal is travelling back to his own country to take charge of the military operations in the new and final revolution, the photograph accidentally slips from his pocket to the floor when he is asked, on his journey, to produce his passport.

A clerk retrieved it and on looking at the face said 'A beautiful child' 'Dead' I said, 'He's dead' – and the words echoed in the brick-walled room causing me to look up as at the entrance of a new, but already known, voice. The preparations for the continuation of my journey went on between the three men. I sat on the wooden chair, Edward Gordon's photograph in my hand. Had the bringing together of two people been possible Sara and Edward Gordon should have been those two. Children together : the hiatus in my knowledge of Sara caused me to look upon her still as a child although I recalled her recent behaviour with Crashaw and the beginning of sexuality in a girl is the ending of childhood. The formalities for the remainder of my journey completed by the three clerks, I rose to leave when one of them, he who had commented on the beauty of Edward Gordon, came to me and asked to see the photograph again. I handed it to him and watched; I was again alert. The man stared at the picture without speaking and in silence returned it to me.

Edward Gordon disappears from the story at this point: he is not mentioned again.

Timothy Crashaw's childhood is referred to twice: once very briefly (though not casually) and once at some length. Both occasions are connected with Sara, who seems automatically to draw thoughts of childhood to her all the way through the book, whose birthdays provide the book with a structure and whose final birthday, linked in some mysterious way with the final act of revolution, has the climactic quality of orgasm.

As Timothy brings Sara back from the mental hospital, they pass in the train the house (a large aristocratic house similar to the one in Whiting's short story called 'A Valediction',[15] also about a child) where Timothy had been brought up. Timothy stares out of the window at the house: 'Within the train, Timothy leant forward, his hands upon his knees. He looked past Sara as the hill and the house approached . . . The train progressed. For an instant Timothy saw his former home. He stared as they, the woman and the child,[16] Sara and he all were swept inside the noisy tunnel. No cataclysm had occurred: all were safely within the tunnel.'

Seeing the house reminds Timothy of the only other occasion on which, in adult years, he had accidentally passed it, this time in a car. 'In the former journey the car had left the town and crossed the bridge. Sitting calmly on the parapet was a child, a usurper.'

These small, childish figures, vulnerable yet accusatory, obsessively haunt the substructure of this novel, appearing at significant moments and in strategic places, like Edgar Allan Poe's black cat.

Timothy's other childhood memory is provoked by a request from Sara. After she has suffered the nightmare of being burned at the stake, he tries to comfort her: when she is lying quietly once more she says 'Tell me a story. Don't ask me what kind of a story. Tell me the story you would tell to your child.'

> Timothy was silent.
> 'Go on, Tell me a story'
> She spoke and turned her head to him.
> 'Your enthusiastic anticipation puts everything out of my mind,' he said.
> 'Go on'. Sara closed her eyes and breathed firmly and deeply. Timothy again lay down in the bed, his body straight, his legs touching Sara's feet which were hot and dry and smooth. Sara again looked into the mirror and saw herself. Timothy, turning towards the girl and to the mirror, contemplated himself at eight years of age.

He begins to tell Sara a story. It is the story of a childish fantasy, of a child's sudden, overwhelming fear and instinctive rebellion, a rebellion

not only against the social structure of his life but also against the very
nature of life itself, a revolt against heaven.

> I was going beneath the trees and so along the road leading
> past the cathedral. There was no thought in my head but
> to return home and that idea was so strong in my mind that,
> hurrying forward, I did not notice a kerbstone and, tripping,
> I fell. On rising, natural tears came into my eyes at the
> sharp pain in my knees and from my right leg blood ran
> on to my stocking. The sight of my surroundings was misted
> with tears and, walking, I began to cry in earnest. Not from
> pain altogether but more from an idea that had occurred.
> Would all be well when I returned? My mother and my
> father safe? A little over a month before, burglars had
> broken into our house in the early evening of a Sunday
> when we were at church. They had rifled my father's desk
> and stolen a silk dress belonging to my mother. Also my
> grandmother had had two houses burnt down in the district
> within the last fifteen years. I looked up at the sky and was
> overcome with unreasoning terror. All acts of violence were
> inexplicable to me. Revenge, premeditated revenge of the
> bloodiest kind was the answer! I was no longer walking
> home. I had stopped and was standing at the beginning of
> the long narrow path which led to the northern entrance
> of the cathedral. Above me was the tolling of a single bell
> and I became suddenly determined it should also summon
> me. Turning so that the cathedral stood behind me, I called
> up my confederates. Immediately they stood before me,
> five of them, awaiting my instructions. I cannot remember
> now how I had named the members of that fantastic gang
> of mine, four men and one girl, but on that day I called out
> the names decisively enough and each one stood forward to
> receive orders from me, their leader. The orders were simple
> and I explained our motives: revenge for several acts of
> violence which I enumerated, inventing two of them. I
> described our action which was to enter the cathedral,
> creep forward in the distraction of worship and murder the
> small congregation as they knelt at prayer. I stressed the
> fact that under no circumstances was there to be any looting
> of the bodies; the crime was to be one of reckoning, not of
> gain.

Timothy's story goes on to describe how the small boy, who was once
Timothy himself, made his 'attack' on the cathedral congregation; how
the passers-by saw only one small boy, though *he* saw his accomplices
alongside him; how, when the attack was discovered, he dismissed the

accomplices who made a successful get-away so that the startled congregation saw again only one small boy, interrupting the service and being chased out of the cathedral by a verger.

The nightmarish quality of this incident links closely with other nightmare moments in the novel (and, it will be noted, has its origin in Sara's nightmare of being burned at the stake). It also has an obvious relationship to the desecration of the shrine, the cenacle, which Timothy plans and executes when he becomes a man. The whole idea that the clandestine revolt, the sudden attack on a smug and unsuspecting society, the revolutionary zeal and the religious purity of intent all had their roots in a child's disgust with the screaming injustice of man, god and the whole world, coupled with the adult–infant, woman–child image of Sara thoughout the book, is extremely significant and helps to give form and shape to the novel.

In passing, it is useful here to remind oneself that John Whiting was born in Salisbury, which is a cathedral town, and that his childhood was spent there. That magnificent and imposing Gothic building dominated his childhood's landscape.

The constant references to children and especially to the hurts of childhood in this first novel find equally constant echoes throughout Whiting's later work. The short story called 'A Valediction' has already been mentioned. The same collection of pieces[17] contains another also, called 'Child's Play', in which a small boy gropes his way toward a working relationship with the man his mother has just married. In the one-act play, *No Why*, produced by the Royal Shakespeare Company at the Aldwych Theatre in 1964, the child Jacob is locked in an unfurnished attic (Whiting often makes use of disused, unfurnished or derelict rooms) by his parents for some unspecified offence. A party is going on downstairs. His mother and father come and try to persuade him to confess his offence and say he is sorry: if only he will admit it and apologise he will be allowed to go downstairs and join the party again. The whole family come and try to persuade him. They talk of prisons and justice and the need for laws. They talk of sin and the need for repentance. They talk of expediency, the advisability of pretending to be sorry for the sake of future gains. The Grandfather, acting as a kind of judge sums up:

GRANDFATHER: Amy, you're used to everything. The whole bag of tricks. Lunacy, sickness, the lot. What's your opinion? How bad was this?
AUNT AMY: It was unforgivable. In my experience. A crime. An atrocity.
GRANDFATHER (*To* JACOB): You hear that? What do you expect us to do? Take you back as our little boy? Our hope and our future. You can't expect that.
JACOB'S FATHER: I've tried to explain to him how we live, father.
GRANDFATHER: Does he understand?
FATHER: I think he understands that the road back is long and hard.

GRANDFATHER: I'm too old to go back, Henry.
FATHER: We're talking about Jacob, father.
GRANDFATHER: Little Jacob? What's he done?
AMY (*Shortly*):   He exists, father. Look at him, there in front of your face.
He *is*, father.

In this last comment of Amy's, the sin and the crime move to the existential plane.

Except occasionally to look at his accusers, the boy Jacob never moves throughout the play. Nor does he speak: he never makes the demanded confession or apology. The family goes away, humiliated and defeated by his silence, which they interpret as pride. The father goes away, switching off the one electric light and leaving the child alone, in the dark, in a locked and empty room. Left, thus, alone, Jacob hangs himself from one of the roof beams by the cord from his pyjamas. Whiting's final stage direction reads: *He swings on the cord of his pyjamas, and the trousers have fallen around his ankles. He looks a useless object: a bag of bones. Cheap meat on a butcher's hook. The piano and laughter downstairs continue as the curtain falls.*

Almost always, children and death are associated and one is reminded again of Rilke: 'children had a little death within them . . .' In *Saint's Day*, a little girl with the same name as the young pregnant woman who has been shot by accident, at the end of the play 'performs a grave dance', alone and unnoticed. In *Marching Song*, an armoured division, advancing to take an enemy town, is suddenly impeded by an army of small boys. Rupert Forster, the efficient and fiercely ambitious general who was leading the attack tells the story afterwards:

> 'A little boy had come from the church and was standing
> on the steps . . . He blew the whistle and at once the
> children were upon us. Hundreds of them . . . They rolled
> like a wave towards us, some armed with sticks, some
> carrying flags. Reaching us, they beat themselves against
> the sides of our tanks. I saw my commanders and their
> crews laughing at them, cheering them on, encouraging
> them in their attempts to scramble over the armour. We
> might have been liberators and not an attacking force. Was
> I the only man to see the danger? We were virtually
> immobilized . . . Our concentration was broken. The
> attack – timed by seconds to co-ordination – was flinging
> itself to pieces. My central armoured force was the
> governing factor of movement. Delay it and the two
> infantry groups became as ineffective as naked men. The
> boy who had come first from the church had clambered
> on to my tank. He was black-haired and black-eyed and he
> carried a wooden sword which he swung above his head.

> He shouted something which I didn't understand and then
> spat at me. That was no provocation for what I did: I had
> already decided. I stretched out and drew his head to my
> shoulder like a lover and shot him in the mouth. I took him
> by the hair of his shattered head and held him up for my
> men to see. They understood. The shooting began.'[18]

The advance continues, leaving four hundred dead children behind; the town is successfully captured and all is ready for the attack across the river, as Forster had planned. Then, for no apparent reason, Forster halts and fails to give the order to press the attack. As a result, the battle is lost; he himself is captured, imprisoned, accused of cowardice and threatened with trial for treason. Bruno Hurst, one of the soldiers set to guard him, asks him why he hesitated when everything was going according to plan and victory seemed certain:

BRUNO: Then why didn't you act?
FORSTER: I was trapped. Trapped by the memory of the child. I couldn't free myself from that moment. The moment when I stood alone, sad, lost, childless, with the child in my arms. And looking down saw that it was a human being. Warm, as the bitter smell of its body struck up at me: dirty, fearful, brave and living. It was then the secret was forced on me. I'd shut it out until that morning by making my own prison, Hurst, years before they sent me to the camp in the mountains. A prison of pride and ambition. Then, when I caught the child to me, the secret was revealed. I suddenly understood what a man is. For I held it close.
BRUNO: If you felt this why did you shoot?
FORSTER: I had no choice. The way I'd chosen to live led to that encounter, which was in itself a challenge. Are you so great? Then fire! I fired, and the secret flew up leaving only blood on my sleeve. I became human. So I waited.
BRUNO: For twelve hours.
FORSTER: For twelve hours. It was my second-in-command who took the pencil from my hand and wrote the order for the attack across the river. It was too late.

The similarity between the symbolic use made of childhood in the pattern of *Marching Song* and in the fabric of *Not a Foot of Land* is quite remarkable: not only does the child, in both works, represent innocence and the innocent victim; in both, also, childhood is a symbol of the possibility of grace and of decency in human life; and very strongly in both the novel and the play there is the sense of the whole future of the individual enfolded, like petals in the bud of a flower, in the world and vision of the child. Some of the actual incidents have a distinct relationship to each other, too: the 'attack' on the cathedral in *Not a Foot of Land* relates in some ways to the halting of the armoured column (note that the Child–Leader in *Marching Song* comes out of a church to lead the attack); the double vision, deliberately imparted by the novel, of Everal both as a child and as a military commander obviously springs from the same source as the image of the encounter between Forster and the small boy; and the constant linking of Sara with childhood on the one hand and violence on the other looks forward also to the haunting of *Marching Song* by the ghosts of children who met with the violence of the adult world. It is worth noting that Timothy Crashaw, when he leaves England after the birthday party at which the puppet play was shown and from which Sara had disappeared, had in his pocket the manuscript of a children's story which he had intended to send to the editor of a boys' magazine and, earlier, Sara had asked him whether he had yet been able to sell any of his writings: he says 'No', and she then says: 'Not even that story about the little boy? You remember, the one you showed me.'

As a storehouse of future themes, *Not a Foot of Land* is invaluable, and as an early indication of Whiting's instinctive interest in big social questions and the movements of history not as didactic or sociological material but as symptoms of the unease of the human soul, it is important. (Whiting himself once said that the starting point for his work was always a *theme*, not a character or a plot or a conversation.) Apart, however, from its scholarly and academic importance as a source book and as a demonstration, *Not a Foot of Land* has *intrinsic* merit and value. One must be careful not to overstate one's case: the novel is not a major work, much less a masterpiece. But it is *real*, if minor: its sense of reality and of the undertow of human experience is a genuine and compelling one.

It suffers, as has already been remarked, from a lush sort of overwriting, and also from symbolism which is sometimes both brash and confused. Both the sexual and the religious symbolism (especially the latter) must fall under this interdict, at least at some points. Why, for example, is the pub where Everal and Sara go to meet Timothy and his accomplices, called the Crown of Thorns? (In an unfinished radio play, written slightly later and called *The Quarry and The Prey*, there is a pub called the Crown; once, the landlord explains, called the Crown of Blackthorn.) It seems gratuitously baffling and a bit pretentious. The same applies to the hill 'with a single tree' just outside the Village of Women: such a point is made of it, so often, that the image of Calvary, outside the walls of the city, is irresistibly invoked, especially since at one point the women decorate the lone tree 'like a Christmas tree'. Yet the image seems disconnected and leads nowhere.

There are more practical confusions, too. Themes begin but trail away without any kind of resolution; incidents are mentioned and then abandoned; characters who sound as if they should be important suddenly appear, but disappear as suddenly without a trace. One of these, and one of the most tantalising, is a girl called Mary Teresa. She is mentioned twice only. On the first occasion, Timothy is walking in the street near his London lodging after getting back to England from the attack on the 'shrine'. He is going to get a meal and is wondering, as he walks, whether he has anything with him to read while he is eating:

> It will have to be another evening paper. That and Sara's
> letter. Yes, I've that with me. I can read that. I'll go down
> and see her tomorrow – I've nothing else to do. I said I'd
> go on Monday but I'll go tomorrow. Look who goes driving
> past me in a large black car! Well, well! Up in the world,
> my darling, Mary Teresa! ('I love you, Timothy, *I* love
> *you*! Do you understand?') As blonde as ever and as
> beautiful but now being driven in a large black car and
> sitting waiting for the control lights to change. You don't
> know who is looking at you, do you?

That is on p. 36. And that is all, until p. 110 when she (presumably it *is* the same girl) is mentioned in Everal's narrative of the meeting at the Crown of Thorns:

> The waiter directed us into a small room. Six tables, four
> occupied, were laid for dinner. Standing within the room
> I noticed the decoration was similar to the main bars in
> ornate pretence. I felt ill at ease and suddenly tired in the
> artificial heat, with no appetite for the forthcoming meal.
>   A tall girl had risen from one of the tables and, passing
> me, spoke to Crashaw.
> 'Hello, Timothy'
> 'Hello, **Mary**'
> Reeves led Sara and I[19] to one of the two remaining
> vacant tables. We sat down.

That is all we ever hear of Mary Teresa or Mary. One cannot help wishing that it had been either a good deal more or a little less. If she is a part of Timothy's past, like Rosaline to Romeo before he meets Juliet, then her presence should be put to more significant use. If she is intended in some way as a contrast to Sara, then the point is not made sufficiently clear. If the memory of her is meant to disturb Timothy after he has moved away from her into another phase of his life, Whiting later forgets to mention this fact.

Just as there are momentary blemishes, there are also especially good moments. Here and there the laconic tone of the factual narrative of one of the many fragmented and non-chronological scenes is punctuated by the presence of what amounts to a long prose poem, whose effect is to extend the meanings from the particular incidents and individuals to wider and deeper planes of experience. As in the following, which comes after the quite practical and detailed description of Sara's leaving the mental hospital and returning to London with Timothy:

Think of it, think of it little by little until a final complete
realisation is achieved. Take T and S and they are together
and will not now be parted. So, over their world they are
meeting again, some in conscious, some in unconscious
preparation for the finality. Those others, human and by no
means symbols, who went together in infinite belief, who
went from each other in tears their minds unable to
encompass the idea of meeting in the furtive manner of the
future which is today, are together and will not now again
be parted. Those who faced the problems of Crashaw's
day and night, who walked solitary after friendship, which
was to them all and not based on love or kindness or
similarity of thought; not in environment, not in
graciousness of manner, not in political needs, not in love
of mankind and not in the love of any god but in endeavour
sprung from ambition were now sitting together or walking
up no longer lonely streets to sound the knockers and the
bells of doors and be admitted. Some were fetched to
others and in the meeting there was a dumb, remembering
silence and the facile noticing of new, unseen clothes; the
strangeness of a well-known, well-loved person in new
unknown surroundings. But the strangeness was dispelled
by understandings and in their scattered groups they
walked and chattered again before the second flight. With
some the strangeness gone the silence remained; with some
there were tears and with some there was excited laughter.
With all there was the knowledge that soon began the
second and final part. They knew that as they spoke together,
casually in the remaining hours, there would be no
reassembling, no second chance because the defeat has been
absolute. They knew that very soon the time would be
present and after that time when they went out again to
love again that action would be no part with this day or the
two hundred and fifty two preceding days.[20] They knew the
scars on their hands would remain and perhaps one night
a mouth pressed into the palm would ask how they came to
be there. The answer could be – while playing with a knife
as a child. There were other marks which could not be so
easily explained, but if not explained for the moment
forgotten in the fragment of reunion which ends by
the coming Tuesday morning.

There is still reference to the specific incidents of the story: the injured hands are Sara's; the 252 days make up the exact period between
the destruction of the shrine on 7 March and the reunion at the birth-

day in London on 15 November.[21] But the sense has broadened to include all friends and all lovers caught in the flux of terrible events and drawing strength and succour from a moment of peace with each other. And the poem becomes, because of its position in the text, the moment of stasis for Timothy and Sara, the pause in the battle, the quiet at the centre of the storm. It has in itself an incantatory quality, as also have some other moments in the book, as, for example, the reference to an ancient fable. 'It should be done in the moonlight for then the wound would never heal.' This is said twice about the act of desecrating the shrine. Timothy says it once; and once the author says it. It is an invocation of strange gods.

With all its faults and unevenness, *Not a Foot of Land* is much more than a piece of juvenilia. Some moments of it are very powerful indeed and none of it is either downright dull or downright silly. Its total gesture is impressive and has the feel of reality in it. It apprehends the intrinsic endemic moral dilemma of the human condition; its sense of the equipoise between violence and gentleness, innocence and compromise, is already mature and convincing. If it is a little confused, a little pretentious (sometimes) and a little self-conscious, that is not altogether to be wondered at: the task it attempts is a formidable one.

Not a Foot of Land is a document not only vividly reflective of the time of its composition – 1944/5 – but also of the era in which its author was growing up and becoming aware of the world – the 1930s. It is worth remembering that it was in those years that British poetry, in the hands of Auden, Spender and MacNeice, was more politically aware than at any other time in the twentieth century and it is, perhaps, no accident that John Whiting's 'Paul Southman', who makes his first, brief (though not unimportant) appearance in *Not a Foot of Land*, becoming in 1946 the subject of a radio play and finally in his full manifestation appearing as the central figure in *Saint's Day*, was both poet *and* political pamphleteer. But Whiting himself is no pamphleteer: neither his plays nor this early novel are didactic or doctrinaire. He saw the frame of society as a reflection of the corrosion of the individual soul and even in this early work, this vision is evident, powerful and persuasive.

3

BEGINNINGS OF DRAMATIC WRITING AND OTHER EARLY WORK (1946-1949)

I   No More A-Roving (1946)

In 1957 Heinemann published *The Plays of John Whiting*, a volume which contained *Saint's Day*, *A Penny for a Song* and *Marching Song*. Whiting himself wrote the Introduction to this book and in it he said: 'There was an earlier play, *The Conditions of Agreement*,[1] which has been destroyed. These, with one last play (*The Gates of Summer*) are my complete output for the theatre. No unproduced or unfinished plays exist.' Whether he really believed this to be true, or whether the statement was his way of officially disowning early work which he no longer regarded as speaking with his voice, it is now quite impossible to determine, but certainly the statement later proved to be inaccurate. Among his papers, after his death, Gabrielle Scott Robinson, assembling the bibliography for the Ph.D thesis she was writing, found two undated handwritten copies of *The Conditions of Agreement* and one bound typescript of that play, bearing the date 1946 very firmly and definitely on the front. She also found a similarly bound typescript, with the same date – 1946 – on the cover, of a play whose title is *No More A-Roving*. The typescript describes it as 'a comedy'. The typescripts of both plays bear, inside their front covers, labels which say 'John Whiting, 11, Beverley Road, Barnes. London. S.W.13'. Both labels have the slightly odd punctuation of full-stops, instead of commas, after the words 'Barnes' and 'London'. Both these typescripts are carbon copies (though both the aforementioned labels *are* originals, not carbon copies). *The Conditions of Agreement* was rescued after Whiting's death and was produced by the Bristol Old Vic in October 1965 in its Little Theatre programme, but *No More A-Roving* has had no such resurrec-

78

tion. It was not included in *The Collected Plays of John Whiting* (1969), though Heinemann have published it since (1975). (Incidentally, Ronald Hayman describes it, in his 'Biographical Outline' in *The Collected Plays* as a 'one-act comedy': it is, in fact, a full-length work, written in the then-conventional three acts.)

Though there can be no question but that *No More A-Roving* is a relatively immature work, far less impressive than *The Conditions of Agreement*, far more conventional and imitative, with little of the distinctive and individual quality of what was shortly to be recognised as Whiting's especial style and character, it would nevertheless be mistaken, I think, simply to forget its existence and allow it to slip into oblivion. Within its chosen *métier* it is very competent (the word is often used in a faintly pejorative sense, but is not so intended here) and has a distinctly good sense of the stage. And some of it is strangely moving, with a curious, compelling atmosphere sandwiched between the jokes and the rather obvious and antiquated theatrical devices. In any case, the very fact that *The Conditions of Agreement*, which is a strange, powerful play and, despite some unsatisfactory features, unmistakably mature and unmistakably Whitingesque, was written in the same year should in itself lend interest and importance to the other play and the force of this argument is increased when one also remembers that the first known copy of *Saint's Day*, a handwritten one, is also dated 1946. It must have been a quite remarkable year in Whiting's life, to see the completion of these three full-length plays, all written while still following a full-time career as an actor. There is an obvious kinship between *The Conditions of Agreement* and *Saint's Day* which is not shared by the humbler, slighter, less profound *No More A-Roving* and this fact in itself provokes one to look at the lesser play if only to see how it came to be written in the same year and by the same author as the other two and *after* the novel called *Not a Foot of Land*. And in looking at it one finds that even in this little comedy the dialogue and the characters have strange undertones, as if there stirred beneath this conventional surface an uneasy sense of a larger and more frightening world.

The three central characters of *No More A-Roving* are Angus Learoyd, Benedict Clare and Kirsty Winston. In the old days before the war they had been great friends, all three of them inseparable; but they had suddenly and rather mysteriously broken up and the unheavals of the time had then kept them apart, never seeing or hearing from each other, until now, eight years later, when Angus has invited both Kirsty and Benedict, without telling either that the other is coming, to stay with him for the weekend. Benedict is an actor and in the intervening eight years he has become quite famous as a film star. He is a little vain, a little shallow, very dependent and very likeable. His memory of their relationship of eight years ago is that he and Angus were very friendly with each other, as were he and Kirsty, but that Angus and

Kirsty did not seem to notice each other much. On his arrival, in their first conversation together, he confesses to Angus that he had been in love with Kirsty but had never summoned up the courage to tell her so: Angus says that he had been aware of Benedict's love for Kirsty and Benedict goes on to say that he thinks his feeling for her may still be the same, even though he has not seen her for eight years. However, before he tells Angus this we have already gathered from a conversation between Kirsty and Angus that *they* were in love with each other eight years ago and the reason the tripartite friendship had broken up was that Angus and Kirsty, without telling Benedict of their love or their intention, had suddenly left London, giving Benedict no explanation and not even saying 'Goodbye'. Benedict did not, in fact, know that they had gone together, only that both of his friends had suddenly disappeared. They had set up house together in a little village on the Thames 'about thirty miles west of London', very close to the place where Angus is now living; but after only six weeks they had quarrelled bitterly and had separated. Angus had gone to Falmouth and, shortly afterwards, the war had broken out. He had not joined the army: 'I seemed to spend years running away', he says in Act 1. 'First of all I ran from people and then I ran from the war. Oh, I couldn't have done anything had I stayed. They'd never have taken me on. I'm really a weak little fellow.' This is not elaborated upon or, indeed, mentioned again in the play, but it is perhaps worth recalling that Whiting himself, when war broke out in 1939, at first registered as a conscientious objector, though he changed his mind later. In the passage in which Angus describes to Kirsty how, after they had quarrelled, he went to Falmouth and then some time later returned to the house they had shared, there is a poignant example of a favourite image of Whiting's, one that constantly recurs – the deserted house, the empty room:

KIRSTY: Where did you go that afternoon? (*There is a pause*) Don't tell me if you don't want to.
ANGUS: I don't mind. I took the boat and went to Cornwall. I was there when the war started. I left the boat and came back by train.
KIRSTY: Came back?
ANGUS: To our house, yes. You had gone, of course; and you had left the place in an awful state. There was a detective novel you had been reading still lying in a chair. Wait – I can remember the title! – *Murder Must Advertise*. You had left your dog's lead behind . . .
KIRSTY: I couldn't find it.
ANGUS: It was hanging over one of the pipes in the kitchen. The radio was still tuned to Milan: we'd been listening to Mozart's 'Requiem' the evening before I left and you hadn't touched it after that. There was half a glass of water and a bottle of aspirin on the table by the bed and behind the bed some underclothes of yours. The clock had stopped at three minutes to five. There was one of your shoes standing upright on

the third stair. And my revolver had been taken out of the desk and left lying on the little round table. Very frightening.

KIRSTY: But there was no body.

ANGUS: No. That was something.

KIRSTY: Were you very angry?

ANGUS: Not then, no. I looked everywhere for a letter – a note. There was nothing.

KIRSTY: I didn't think you'd come back.

ANGUS: When did you leave?

KIRSTY: The day after you – and I remember nothing more than the clouds being very high and very white above the house. Nothing more.

This exchange is part of one of the two duologues that make up the bulk of Act 2 of the play: in one of these, which follows immediately upon a three-cornered conversation in which Kirsty, Angus and Benedict recall with warmth and affection their days in London together before the war, Angus and Kirsty warily edge around their former feelings for each other and wonder whether they are still in love. They show an affection, but also a good-humoured scorn, for Benedict, whom they have sent off to the local pub to buy some beer: they feel, however, that in their former relationship he was important to them, quite apart from mutual friendliness, as a kind of catalyst to their love. In the other duologue, between Benedict and Kirsty (Angus having been got out of the way by a piece of creaking dramaturgical machinery about as subtle as 'Tennis, anyone?'), Benedict says the same thing about Angus 'You must remember that it was Angus who provided us with the – well, background to the period when we knew each other. We owe him a lot.' He goes on to tell Kirsty how he fell in love with her eight years ago and he tries hard to get round to the point of saying he still loves her.

BENEDICT: Why did you go away like that? I thought it was because you knew I was in love with you and so you – well, ran away. But it wasn't that, was it?

KIRSTY: No.

BENEDICT: I was very lonely: quite naturally. For some time I'd had you and Angus as an audience and then suddenly there was no-one. At one moment there was all that we had together and the next moment you had gone with never another word from you until today. After you, Angus disappeared. No explanation, nothing until some weeks later when there was a letter from him: a letter I didn't understand at all – apparently begging forgiveness for something. I was left alone. I didn't understand it. You went and then Angus went and I . . .(*He stops*)

KIRSTY: What's the matter?

BENEDICT: Shut up a minute! I'm putting two and two together.

KIRSTY: I trust they'll eventually make four.

(*There is a long pause as* BENEDICT *stares at* KIRSTY)

BENEDICT: Was that it?

KIRSTY: Yes.

BENEDICT: Do you know when you are reading sometimes and you go over a sentence again and again and each time completely misread one word? That's what I've been doing, isn't it?

KIRSTY: Are you very angry?

BENEDICT: No, I'm not angry. Suddenly I said 'You went away and then Angus went away and I was left in London'. I've said that before, but this time, for the first time, I saw what it meant – you and Angus went together.

Then, a little further on, there is this:

BENEDICT: Then what happened?

KIRSTY: We quarrelled and parted after six weeks.

BENEDICT: I see.

KIRSTY: We didn't meet again until today.

BENEDICT: What am *I* doing here?

KIRSTY: You're here because we love you.

BENEDICT: (*He laughs*)   This makes all that I've said to you this evening seem rather ridiculous, doesn't it?

KIRSTY: We've bungled it horribly. We should have told you. But don't be angry.

BENEDICT: Stop saying that. I'm not angry.

KIRSTY: You have every right to be.

BENEDICT: Nonsense! I've no right at all.

When Angus returns, Benedict invents an excuse to absent himself and Kirsty and Angus are suddenly sure of their feelings for each other:

ANGUS: You're very lovely.

KIRSTY: I *am* very lovely?

ANGUS: You *are* very lovely.

KIRSTY: We have achieved the present.

ANGUS: May I say it now?

KIRSTY: Yes. Whenever you like. But another thing you said . . .

ANGUS: What?

KIRSTY: That I'm older and perhaps wiser.

ANGUS: Well?

KIRSTY: I'm not. Not a bit wiser.

ANGUS: I'm so glad.

KIRSTY: So am I. I should be a fool to be wiser. (*She suddenly laughs*) You have got a ridiculous face. As solemn as a pudding.

ANGUS: I was trying to disentangle the paradox of it being foolish to be wiser.

KIRSTY: Because then I couldn't be so happy.

ANGUS: And you are happy? At this very moment?

KIRSTY: Yes.

ANGUS: Then why these tears?

KIRSTY: They're not real tears.

ANGUS: You've never cried with me before.

KIRSTY: I know.   (*There is a pause*)

ANGUS: I can't say anything else.

KIRSTY: I don't think there is anything else to say. Except, having achieved the present, let us make some use of it.
ANGUS: We could go out.
KIRSTY: Yes. (ANGUS *has moved to the door*)
ANGUS: It hasn't rained. I said it wouldn't.
KIRSTY: The dancing has ended.
ANGUS: Listen!
(*Distantly, from the village hall across the fields can be heard* 'God Save the King'.[2] KIRSTY *and* ANGUS *embrace. The kiss and the National Anthem end simultaneously.*)
ANGUS: Now the dancers are saying goodnight . . .
KIRSTY: Foolish people!
ANGUS: . . . and whether happy or unhappy they are preparing to go home.
KIRSTY: Let us go home.
ANGUS: Where is that?
KIRSTY: (*She points through the door*) Somewhere out there. I don't quite know where – but somewhere. After all we don't ask for much.
ANGUS: It's no good. However hard we try we can't make a tragedy out of this.

        (*They laugh at themselves*)

KIRSTY: We should be ashamed!

        (*Their laughter suddenly stops: they kiss again*)

ANGUS: Come along. We can go by the lane.
KIRSTY: Yes, I remember. I remember the way.
ANGUS: Don't say that! (*There is a pause*) Don't say that. Please!

        (*They go out: there is a pause*)

CURTAIN

This is the end of Act 2 and it is significant that even in a slight, light comedy, imitative and derivative as it is, Whiting thus early in his work introduces a note of mysterious foreboding into the moment of ecstasy. Angus's last line somehow means more than 'I don't want to be reminded of the past. Let us live in the present' and it not only secures a strong curtain for the act – it also provides a faint hint of that mistrust of ecstasy and personal happiness that will show, later, in every one of Whiting's plays except *A Penny for a Song*. In *No More A-Roving* its symbol of expression, a broken love affair fleetingly renewed, is a cliché and a reach-me-down from the popular theatre of its day and its sense is no more than skin-deep. But it is a hint, nevertheless.

The action of Act 3 occurs on the following morning, the Sunday. Benedict invents an excuse and prepares to leave for London so that Angus and Kirsty can be alone. 'You are going to be happy together this time, aren't you?' he says to Kirsty. But they are not. Angus returns from making a mysterious telephone call and the conversation between him and Kirsty is as follows:

ANGUS: Good morning, Kirsty.
KIRSTY: Good morning, Angus.

ANGUS: Are you awake?

KIRSTY: Yes. Where have you been?

ANGUS: To speak to a man.

KIRSTY: What sort of a man do you speak to at half-past eight on a Sunday morning?

ANGUS: A man with a very long beard, very short legs and a great deal of money.

KIRSTY: Just the sort of man to speak to at half-past eight in the morning. Nice conversation?

ANGUS: Short but to the point.

KIRSTY: I heard you go, darling.

ANGUS: I thought you were asleep.

KIRSTY: No.

ANGUS: Why didn't you say something?

KIRSTY: I hadn't anything to say.

ANGUS: I might have known you weren't asleep. You were looking so very lovely.

KIRSTY: Meaning that I'm not when I'm really asleep?

ANGUS: Exactly. Yours is a very conscious beauty.

KIRSTY: How do I look at this moment?

ANGUS: Dreadful. Give me a cigarette.

KIRSTY: You don't want a cigarette.

ANGUS: Don't I?

KIRSTY: No. Come here. Kiss me.

ANGUS: Mind the coffee pot!

KIRSTY: Damn the coffee pot! (ANGUS *kisses her*) Now look at me. Well?

ANGUS: You haven't got any make-up on.

KIRSTY: No. I've washed my face.

ANGUS: It's a very good face. (*He pushes back her hair*) I can feel the pulse in your temple. One: two: three: four: five: six: seven: eight . . .

KIRSTY: That's very quick, isn't it? Apart from the lack of make-up can you see nothing else?

ANGUS: Stand up. (*She does so*) Not really, darling. Darling. My very sweet and unaware darling.

KIRSTY: And you. And you, my darling.

(*She puts her arms round him and they kiss. After the kiss they stand staring at each other in silence.*)

KIRSTY: Damn!

ANGUS: What's the matter?

KIRSTY: It's no good, is it?

ANGUS: No.

KIRSTY: I wonder why not?

ANGUS: We said we would never examine our reasons.

KIRSTY: The bloody old moralists would say it was just physical attraction between us.

ANGUS: You sound like an angry child. Yes, that's what they'd say.

KIRSTY: And they'd be quite right. You're very good in that sense. But there was something more – surely something more.

ANGUS: Friendliness, perhaps.

KIRSTY: A desire to please. (*They laugh*) It's quite useless trying to explain it.

[Twelve lines omitted here]

KIRSTY: We've both known the whole time.
ANGUS: Yes. Something you said.
KIRSTY: What?
ANGUS: Last night. You said 'And in the present I think I want you.' I *think* I want you. You were unsure.
KIRSTY: No! No, you're wrong. Last night I was certain I wanted you but I could see no further. You must know I wanted you. Darling, I've always found great delight in you. And it was that delight combined with a desire to please and friendliness that made us.
ANGUS: Made us what we are or what we were? (*He does not wait for her to answer*) You are standing there as I remember you one morning but you are saying things you have never said before.
KIRSTY: After all, we are told that love can never give us all we wish and therefore we must be grateful for the little it does give.
ANGUS: Which of your bloody old moralists is that?
KIRSTY: And it has given us each other. We should be grateful.
ANGUS: We have each other but we're just no good together.
KIRSTY: No good at all. Funny! We haven't quarrelled this time and yet we know more surely.
ANGUS: More surely than when we did quarrel.
KIRSTY: Angus . . .
ANGUS: Yes?
KIRSTY: Nothing. I must go and get dressed.
           (*She begins to move to the foot of the stairs*)
ANGUS: Kirsty! Just a minute! (*She turns*) Just a moment to look at you now that you're going away.
KIRSTY: Am I going away?
ANGUS: I think so. Soon.
KIRSTY: How soon?
ANGUS: Within an hour.
KIRSTY: In that case, I'd better go and dress now. (*But she remains standing there, facing* ANGUS) You're all right, aren't you?
ANGUS: What? Yes, I'm all right.
KIRSTY: Then I'm going to dress now.
ANGUS: Yes, run along.

Angus knows that she is leaving within the hour because the telephone call he went out to make was to her husband. When she arrived, the day before, neither Benedict nor Angus knew that she was married, nor had she told either of them during the brief time they had now been together. Although she does not yet know, Angus has discovered it by accident: looking in her handbag for a cigarette while she was sleeping, he came across a letter signed by her with her married name, Christiana Sotheran. The notepaper had a telephone number on it and he has called her husband, asking him to come and fetch her home, making out that this is a message and request from Kirsty herself. He is not angry with her for not telling him of her marriage; nor, indeed, is he in a position to be since he, too, is married and has not told her. Nor, for that matter does the audience yet know this. It is discovered at the very end of the play, after Kirsty has left with her husband. Elizabeth, Angus's wife, returns unexpectedly (but without either fuss or overtones of French farce) and the play finishes with them together, planning to go for a picnic and do some fishing and taking with them their baby son and the village girl who helps them about the house. So Kirsty never finds out that Angus is married: Benedict, just leaving for London by the late morning train, meets Elizabeth literally as he goes and just has time to realise who she is. The suggestion, however, in the scenes between Angus and Kirsty is not that they are deciding to separate for a second time because one of them has discovered that the other is married but that, as the passage quoted above indicates, they jointly discover that they are 'just no good together' – and this is not intended to refer to the sexual aspect of their relationship. When they meet for this second time, neither knows the other is married and when they fall in love all over again they still do not know. Somehow, during their one night of love-making, they discover that though they are sexually rewarding to each other there seems to be some kind of blank and arid barrenness at the heart of their relationship, now as in the past: it is when this realisation dawns on each of them separately that they each resolve, separately, not to pursue the matter beyond the weekend. Only after this are the ironic discoveries about other attachments made and the feeling the play gives is that these are purely practical problems which could have been easily dealt with in one way or another if the heart of the matter had been right and if the moment of bright ecstasy had been capable of being preserved in the ordinary daylight of a domestic day.

The general tone of the play is light, though it has certain strange, grave undertones. There is a certain stylishness of design and theatrical sophistication about some of it, as when, for example, in the opening stage description before the dialogue begins there occur the following: 'The room itself has great charm: it was obviously designed for no other reason than to contain the delightful happenings of the next twenty-four hours' and 'She is twenty-seven: a gracious, humorous and lovely creature, dressed as befits her part in this comedy.' The prevalent naturalistic mode of the day, which in most other respects is the one to which the play adheres, is here at the start tweaked gently by the tail. Early in Act 1, the play also acknowledges its own theatricality in another way:

KIRSTY: Do we need a starting-point, you and I?
ANGUS: Yes.
KIRSTY: Very well. Then we must start from this moment and we must

> do it properly. We must behave as though we haven't seen each other
> for eight years.
> ANGUS: Well, we haven't.
> KIRSTY: Then let us behave as if we hadn't.
> ANGUS: You'll have to begin. I don't know how to do it.
> KIRSTY: Something like this (*She pauses*) 'It was exciting to get a letter
> from you. But how on earth did you get my address?'

They then proceed to hold two conversations in parallel, simultaneously; in one they speak as their real selves, halting and embarrassed; in the other they speak in the *personae* of the lay figures Kirsty has just invented – purely theatrical figures, figures from a play. This kind of sophistication is a strength and a grace to the little play and is felt throughout, though here and there it is offset by a simple earnestness in some of the 'serious' speeches that is downright embarrassing.

It is a rather slight piece, of course, but as far as that goes, no slighter than, say, the comedies of Alan Ayckbourn and not as slight as *No Sex Please, We're British* or *Six of One* or *Shut Your Eyes and Think of England*. For the matter of that, *No More A-Roving* is no more slight than dozens of light comedies of its own time, either. Its chief weaknesses are its smallness of stature and its isolation from reality. It stems much more from the theatre than from life, such originality as it possesses consisting mostly – though not quite wholly – of interesting and piquant variations on themes, characters and psychological explanations drawn not so much from other specific plays as from that general atmosphere and ambience of theatrical performance in which recognisable figures behave in instantly recognisable ways. So familiar are we with them from knowing them on the stage that we tend to regard them as 'real' people, people with off-stage existences; but they are not, of course, except in those cases in which some particular type of character or imagined mode of society is so popularised by the stage that off-stage society begins to imitate it, producing a distorted parody of what was itself only an imagined shadow in the first place. Somewhere at the beginning of any particular one of these 'lines' of highly derivative groups or types there was a play that *did* freshly reflect a sense of real experience and the human dilemma from ordinary off-stage life; and the gradations through which this spirit passed in the gradual declension to the entirely formalised lay figures and stock situations of a set theatrical mode are often so small, from one play to another, as to be scarcely perceptible. This is why some plays acquire in their own day reputations for liveliness and significance and veracity which they afterwards lose and which, twenty years later (much less, in some cases), seems quite inexplicable. 'How could we have valued it so much', we wonder to ourselves, 'when it is so obviously pasteboard?' The early plays of Arthur Miller (though not those of Tennessee Williams) provide a good example of the phenomenon, as do once much-bruited plays such as *Johnson over Jordan* or

The Sacred Flame or the plays of Alfred Sutro or of Henry Arthur Jones. The style of these vast groups of characters who drift from play to play varies from one generation of theatre-goers to another but some are much longer-lived than others. The particular group on which *No More A-Roving* chiefly draws is the one that consisted of those charming, well-spoken, well-to-do, upper-middle-class people who seemed to live perpetually in mythical British drawing-rooms, were always down at somebody's place for the weekend and whose energies were concentrated wholly in the closed and overheated circle of their immediate personal relationships and concerns, especially the concerns of 'love'. 'Love' (and I put the word in quotation marks only because it became in the hands of those plays so much more a talisman, a conventionalised symbol, an ikon almost, rather than a description of an actual, living experience that it is now almost impossible to connect any objectified meaning with the word) is all-important, love in the pairing-off sense, the happy-ever-after sense, the someday-I'll-find-you sense. The *genre*, which is a direct derivative of eighteenth-century sentimental comedy, modified in technique but not in tone by the nineteenth-century mode of direct naturalistic representation, includes in its twentieth-century manifestations plays of four decades, stretching from such works as A. A. Milne's *Mr Pim Passes By* (1920) in which Dion Boucicault the younger played the name-part and *The Dover Road* (1922) which had Henry Ainley, Nicholas Hannen and Athene Seyler in the cast, through Coward, *French Without Tears* (Rattigan, 1936), Gerald Savory's *George and Margaret* (1937), Dodie Smith's *Dear Octopus* (1938) and Esther McCracken's *Quiet Wedding* (1939) to the plays of William Douglas Home and Warren Chetham Strode in the 1960s and even T. S. Eliot's unwise flirtation with the style in his last three plays, in the 1950s. But the heyday of the 'drawing-room comedy' in the British theatre was the decade of the 1930s, and as an actor in provincial repertory theatres just before and just after the war Whiting would have been called upon to appear in this kind of play more often than in any other. Quite apart from the very famous (in their time) examples which dominated the London theatre of the period, there were hundreds of others that appeared in London only briefly or not at all and whose titles have long since vanished from the records (who now recalls *Pink String and Sealing Wax* or *She Wanted a Cream Front Door*?). But in the 1930s the drawing-room comedy was the staple of ordinary, rather modest entertainment in the theatre and it was quite natural that Whiting, when he turned to writing for the theatre (especially if it was almost accidental, as he suggested), should approach the task by thinking, consciously or unconsciously, of what the theatre as he knew it as an actor usually did (he must have been required to play in dozens of trivial drawing-room comedies), and then by imitating that mode – though even in this early work he succeeded at certain points in bettering some of his models. The debt of *No More A-Roving* to the theatre of its day in style, subject and theatrical demeanour is obvious enough, yet it does bear some signs already of the hand of a different kind of playwright. In how many of those trite, well-made pieces would one expect to find the word 'miscreance'? Or the speech of Benedict's in which it occurs, for that matter:

> 'You know, Angus, long, long ago, when I was a little tiny
> child – I am told I was very beautiful – I had a trusting
> nature. I retained that trust until eight years ago but I
> regret to tell you it has now deserted me. It raises an
> interesting question that I think might form a basis for
> discussion between us this weekend. Must we consciously
> reconcile ourselves as we grow older to disbelief, miscreance,
> doubt and suspicion – and form our lives accordingly? Or
> must we fight against such things knowing that we shall
> fail?'

The second half of this speech, like the passage between Angus and Kirsty at the end of Act 2, which has already been quoted, is one of the occasional and subdued signs in the play that its author will shortly burst the bonds of this conventional form and begin to divert into his stage work that rich and sombre imaginative force whose first expression was that extraordinary unpublished novel. Meanwhile, he shows in this first play that he can already handle the conventional comedy conventionally well in its own terms, at least so far as the writing of lively dialogue is concerned. There are several sprightly exchanges, of which the following may be allowed to stand as a fair and fairly typical example:

BENEDICT: I am prepared to be noble, not to say self-sacrificing about you. I am only concerned with your future happiness. You and Angus made a mess of things before and I can see you doing it again. I don't want that to happen and I feel that I might be able to . . .

KIRSTY: Benedict . . .

BENEDICT: Yes?

KIRSTY: Is your pomposity inherited?

BENEDICT: Yes, from my father. You won't believe this, but his last words were 'Tell the world my final thoughts were of Shakespeare'. Then he died. Mother was furious. (*There is a pause*) You've changed the subject.

KIRSTY: I know. Don't go back to it, please.

The dialogue is a good deal better than the plotting and dramaturgy. In several places the machinery fairly creaks and groans in its efforts to keep the action flowing and to ensure that the right two people are, without too flagrant an illogicality, left on stage at the same time (and the right time) for the next duologue needed to move the plot forward. Once they are, the thing picks up momentum again, but getting them there and getting them alone is sometimes a bit of an effort, an effort that on occasion becomes all too visible. The worst example is the desperate device needed to isolate Kirsty and Angus for their final duo, in which not only is the relationship concluded, dramatically speaking, but also a number of pieces of practical information and explanation needed to bring the story to an understandable conclusion are revealed to the audience. To make this duologue possible, Benedict has to say to James (Kirsty's husband, who has now arrived, at Angus's invitation): 'Come along, Mr Sotheran. While your wife gets her bag and says her goodbyes, I'll come down with you and help you turn your car round. It's rather tricky.' Nothing could be more improbable. Benedict has been established all the way through the play as a rather vague and impractical sort of person, very dependent on others: he would be the last to think of the alleged difficulty of turning the car round (to which there has been no previous reference) and the last, even if he thought of it, to offer to help. Moreover, since he arrived at the house himself only the day before – and not by car – it is highly unlikely that he would be aware of any difficulty there may have been. And quite apart from the improbability of his involvement in the car-turning operation, in point of fact what would have been much more likely to have happened is that all four of them would have walked out to the car together.

Alongside these beginner's mistakes, however, is a very acute sense of what creating a part for an actor means. Kirsty is potentially a star role which would play on the stage extremely well. The servant girl, too, although of the general line of comic servants, is also something more: she is a genuine eccentric, the forerunner of the delicious comic eccentrics of *A Penny for a Song* and the sombre and compelling eccentrics of *The Conditions of Agreement* and *Saint's Day*. She would be very funny on stage if the play were performed but she could also, in the hands of a good actress, have something of a manic intensity about her that would move very close to the outer limits of humour and towards a darker life. She is fifteen years old and her name is Willy Yeats (the other characters comment – though rather feebly – on the comic name, but one feels that the play is not able to make as much use of it as Whiting had hoped when he invented it). She would make a very good 'part' for a young actress and she is an excellent example of the fact that, right from the start, Whiting had an extraordinarily well-developed instinct for the use of the stage. Notice his stage direction in the following and then picture what this small moment could be like on the stage:

ANGUS: Mind you, I don't think we can say there haven't been minor disasters. In fact, I think the incident of the coffee-machine might be classed as a major disaster. I still can't understand what you mean when you say the thing exploded: coffee is not an explosive...
WILLY: Well, I was holding it...
(She begins to demonstrate)

As he wrote his dialogue, even in this early play, Whiting was instinctively aware all the time of the visual elements that would be added in performance, without which any play is incomplete and the calculation of which is a proper part of the business of the dramatist.

The play has one or two interesting sidelights on Whiting's own views and personal position at the time. Benedict, talking about his war-time army service says 'Well, it was a peculiar branch of the service, as they say: rather difficult to describe. I believe some of the others in it actually had guns – but, of course, I was not allowed to touch anything like that.' Whiting, whose father had been a professional soldier, displayed in his attitude to the army a curious ambivalence. He wanted to join the infantry because his father had been an infantry officer: there was a kind of attachment, almost a love for it. But in the diary that he kept in the early days of the war, he wrote:

> I wonder if anyone in the ranks likes the Army? Some get
> satisfaction from it – I know I do – but only from the point
> of view of self-degradation. Not such a high-sounding reason
> really. I find an academic interest in the discomforts of my
> body. Not the masochistic, joyful acceptance of pain of
> Nietzsche, but a detached interest in this sometimes animal
> existence with its smell of sweat and urine and floor polish.
> I have always wished an experiment in personal denial
> but in my former life luxury came too easily. I no longer
> swear because there is so much swearing. I have given
> up drinking here and apart from discontinuing my
> usual relations with women, I find I do not need them. I
> even find myself slightly repulsed by physical contact.
> Perhaps, as I am driven to extremes because I witness an
> unrestrained animality among some of the men here – some
> indulge in queer little sexual games; harmless because they
> indicate sentimental longing rather than perversion – and
> although pleasant they are far from physical attractiveness.
> I have never been able to visualise any but the most
> attractive making physical love. Here I listen to them
> discussing the most intimate details of their life. There is
> a nostalgic longing left in me: last night I saw a soldier and
> a young girl kissing as they walked. It is not that I feel in
> any way superior to them. I have sunk my personality and
> my former existence these last weeks. As has been said,
> a man can rise to undreamt of heights but there must be a
> low level below which no man can sink. Not morally, but in
> his own estimation. It comes through an elimination of
> ambition. I do not mean a refusal of promotion. In the
> Army that is an automatic replacement of disciplined minds.

> Individual action I have forgotten. Everything for the
> present is automatic and strictly according to the textbook.
> I think it is mostly concerned with my *volte-face* with
> regard to pacifism. Now I find pleasure in the prospect of
> spasmodic promotion, if any. I shall be even more pleased
> if I remain where I am at present. An ignominious end
> probably awaits me. Death by tram-car. Sleep is my greatest
> luxury and pleasure here. To feel the coolness at my feet
> on first contact and to stretch my arms and grasp the rail
> above my head; turn to my side after the desultory
> conversation has died – and sleep.

This was in 1940, six years before he wrote *No More A-Roving*, but clearly Whiting had this sort of memory in mind when he invented the characters and situations of Benedict and Angus. In a way, they both represent himself (though he may not have known that), different sides of his own personality: Benedict the young actor, caught by the war, and both amused and horrified by it; Angus the sensitive young man who fled from the brutish stupidity of it. Obviously the whole question of the relationship between complex intellectual, cultural attitudes and simple, mindless, physical activity is one that exercises Whiting and the spectacle of a man of artistic, creative bent thrust into close and daily contact with repellent, gross, unproductive physical circumstance held a morbid and reluctant fascination for him. Though it does not become the theme of *No More A-Roving* (which would, in any case, have been too slight to bear it), there is in the situation of Benedict the actor a momentary glimpse of it and it is interesting to find it thus early in a frail and formal comedy. It will recur many times, in much more powerful and extended form, in later plays: the immaculate Procathren, for instance, suddenly surrendering himself to dirt and blood in *Saint's Day*, or the priest, Grandier, wallowing in a carnality which he knows will destroy him, discussing both the carnality and the destruction with a Sewerman and going half-gladly and wholly consciously to the pain of a terrible death.

Just as going into the army struck Whiting with its ironic contrasts, so did leaving it; and this irony, too, is reflected at one point in this little play. Benedict, talking about his release from the service, says: 'And so I went back to the theatre and found them making do with a few strange, androgynous creatures. I passed among them and on into films.' In the tape recording of biographical details made for Charles Slater, the Californian graduate student (see Notes on Chapter 1: note no. 3), John Whiting himself said:

> 'I came out of the army – I said in 1945: I should have
> said 1944 – I came out of the army before the end of the
> war, in 1944. I had married in 1940 and I had to get a

> job and there was nothing really that I was trained for. I
> was twenty-eight – I'm sorry, I have to work it out – yes,
> I was twenty-seven. So I decided to come back to acting.
> I went into – first of all I did a series of parts in and around
> London, and some broadcasting. The situation had changed
> very much from before the war because I was into the army
> early and I was out early and there was a great shortage of
> actors, so I got a certain amount of work. I went into a
> repertory company for about two years at Harrogate. I began
> to write for the theatre.'

Having made Benedict an actor, Whiting unconsciously reflects, also, something of his own ambivalence of attitude towards the theatre and the profession for which he himself was trained:

BENEDICT: I want to ask you something.
ANGUS: Yes.
BENEDICT: It was something you said to me years ago. You said 'Benedict, you're a very nice person but your sincerity is the sincerity of a clown – exaggerated to gain favour'.
ANGUS: Did I say that?
BENEDICT: Yes, and I found only little consolation in the fact that you were rather drunk at the time.

'The sincerity of a clown – exaggerated to gain favour': though he does not say so, here or elsewhere, this phrase applied to an actor seems aptly to sum up one of the uneasinesses that Whiting always felt about the theatre itself as well – its need, and its desire, always to please and be popular. 'Fallacy:' he once wrote in his note-book 'that any art is infinitely communicable to an unlimited number of people.' Neither popularity nor an easy accord were what he aimed at. 'I state what I believe to be true, but I don't try over-much to convince . . . I am only interested in taking a subject and extending it to its absolute limit, within my own experience. But that's all any of us are about', the same note-book said. And in another moment of despair and exasperation during rehearsals for one of his own plays he wrote in the note-book: 'I may have been meant for the Drama – God knows! – but I certainly wasn't meant for the Theatre.' He found the theatre distasteful because of its readiness to compromise and because of its constant efforts to ingratiate itself with its public. All its publicity aspects irritated him. He thought that artistic work should be judged on its artistic merit, not on its popularity potential, and he refused to equate the one with the other or to believe that there was any connection between them other than a purely accidental one. One recalls the phrase that he borrowed from James Joyce and used as the title of one of the published articles on the theatre – 'To the Playgue-house to see the Smirching of Venus'.

But this sudden glimpse, in *No More A-Roving*, of an early sign of what Whiting's attitude to the theatre would become is incidental to the play's main purpose: it is not even peripherally connected with the plot, nor does it help, really, to define either Benedict's character or Angus's. Both are, in any case, only very lightly sketched, as one would expect in a play of this kind. In plays of the drawing-room comedy *genre* all that there is in them is there on the surface, in explicit terms. They *tell* you what they mean and what they are 'about'. Except for some isolated moments when, as has already been noted, there is a faint sense of some deeper reverberation, this is as true of *No More A-Roving* as it is of any light, naturalistic comedy. It is much less striking as a first play than *Not a Foot of Land* is as a first novel and is technically less successful, too. Even though *The Conditions of Agreement* was apparently written in the same year, it can safely be assumed on the strength of the internal evidence alone (and so far as I know there is no other) that *No More A-Roving* was the earlier of the two and that what we are looking at as we read its typescript is Whiting's very first attempt at the form. Not only has it almost none of that dark intensity and complexity which is evident in all the other plays (even *The Conditions of Agreement*: the sudden deepening from the first to the second of these 1946 plays is astonishing) but, specifically, its actual dialogue is, compared with any of the other plays, thin, naive and over-explanatory, too literal and too slackly naturalistic.

I would nevertheless maintain that it was important to his development for Whiting to have written *No More A-Roving* and that it represents a particular and very interesting process in that development. After the imaginative outpouring – which in a sense was a piece of self-indulgence – of *Not a Foot of Land* and on deciding to turn to a new medium, he needed to explore, whether consciously or unconsciously, the relationship between the surface of events and their imaginative underpinnings, so far as expressing this relationship in the new medium of dramatic-theatrical terms was concerned. He already knew something of how it worked in a prose narrative: in *No More A-Roving* it is possible to see him experimenting for the first time with the new medium, for it is obvious from the start that he does not intend the conventional comedy to remain, in his hands, its usual vapid self. Predictably, what he writes in this first attempt is really only a description of the surface, but one can sense throughout and in some moments actually see his wary probing for the opportunity to get below the surface to the imaginative life underneath. He does not succeed as he will later succeed and the 'story' of this play remains a mere narrative: it never rises to the level of a fable; it never gains those mythic qualities that, at one level, are the mark of a great play and that Whiting himself will later be able to evoke.

In this first little play the characters remain as ordinary people, all too recognisable: they never come near to acquiring those mysterious, enlarged, archetypal dimensions that belong only to the characters of great plays. They are real enough, in the sense of being recognisably like people we know, but there is nothing more than that to them: and, of course, the truly vital and vivid dramatic character, like his counterpart in the novel, although he beguiles one with his 'naturalness' into supposing with half one's mind that he is an instantly recognisable person from the world of everyday, has yet that about him that increases his stature beyond the ordinary, endues him with a mystery and gives him, so to say, a huge shadow that stands tall behind him: he is not, when all comes to all, like an ordinary person in the least. On the other hand, the twentieth-century theatre has – partly through the historical accident of the cinema and television – become so thoroughly embroiled with documentary statement and the naturalistic mode that there is, in spite of some obvious rebellions and deviations, a very strong tendency to think of such literalism both as a theatrical norm and as a climax to 2,500 years of dramatic progress, so much so that it is probably necessary for almost all twentieth-century dramatists to begin by first writing plays of a mainly naturalistic-descriptive kind. It is a way of coming to terms not only with the dominant technical mode of the theatre of the time but also with the artistic dilemma itself – for naturalism dramatises, by its own limitations, the very function of art, which is to avoid the literal and to search for the hidden patterns and correspondences. While one can think of twentieth-century dramatists (Beckett and Fry, for example) who have not approached their craft in this way, one can also think of many who have, and who have moved away from literal representation later. There are two recent British examples who are especially interesting to compare with Whiting in this regard and whose work began fairly close to naturalistic representation but moved rapidly away from it (in two totally different directions, be it said). They are Harold Pinter and David Storey.

In 1946, when he wrote it, Whiting offered *No More A-Roving* to the Northampton Repertory Theatre. It was refused. In 1948 it was slightly revised and then offered, in its revised version, to one or two London managements. Again it was refused and at that point Whiting seems to have abandoned it. He offered it to no one else and never mentioned it again.

II   The radio plays

Between 1946 and 1950, in addition to the full-length stage plays *No More A-Roving, The Conditions of Agreement,* the early drafts of *Saint's Day* and the beginnings of *A Penny for a Song,* Whiting also wrote four plays for radio, began two others but never completed them, wrote three short stories for radio broadcasting and wrote the first (and, as it turned out, the only) chapter of a second novel. It is worth looking briefly at these minor writings – more particularly the radio plays – before going on to consider the major ones.

The radio plays are: *Paul Southman: An Appreciation for Broadcasting* (1946), *Eye Witness* (1947), *The Stairway* (1949) and *Love's Old Sweet Song* (1950). One of the unfinished pieces is a mere fragment, untitled and undated; the other, which is more striking than any of the finished ones, seems to be about half-finished and is called *The Quarry and the Prey*. It was written in 1950.

Paul Southman: An Appreciation for Broadcasting begins in this way:

ANNOUNCER: The impending death is reported of Dr Paul Southman, the celebrated pamphleteer and lampoonist, at his home in Essex. Here is Mr Edmund Lucock, the journalist, to speak of Dr Southman. Mr Lucock.

(EDWARD LUCOCK *speaks: a highly nervous young man*)

LUCOCK: Jonathan Swift wrote: 'The death of a private man is generally of so little importance to the world that it cannot be a thing of great importance in itself; and yet I do not observe from the practice of mankind that either philosophy or nature have sufficiently armed us against the fears which attend it. Neither do I find anything able to reconcile us to it but extreme pain, shame or despair; for poverty, imprisonment, ill fortune, grief, sickness and old age do generally fail.' Paul Southman wrote 'The loss by death of a man who has concerned himself with matters of social conscience – the death of a truly public as opposed to a private man – can be remedied by the building of a stone effigy, ornamental horse trough, bird-bath or garden of rest. Let this reconcile the public even though it does not reconcile the public man.' Dr Southman wrote that twenty-five years ago and tonight we are told he is dying at his house in Essex. By the way, the quotation from Swift with which I began was from his *Thoughts on Various Subjects* and the quotation from Southman from his famous pamphlet *The Abolition of Printing*. Well now, ladies and gentlemen, as we have some time to wait – how long, of course, is not for me to say, but for – well, yes. (*He coughs*) I think it will be best if I give you a short account of Paul Southman's life.

This he proceeds to do, but the play almost immediately deserts any kind of realistic or documentary style for a surrealist fantasy. The radio commentator is constantly interrupted by people who arrive from nowhere and suddenly announce themselves. They are all people who knew or claim to have known Southman at various stages of his life. Their evidence is in every case at variance with the comfortable official version of the story that poor Lucock, called on at the last minute and given time only to do the barest and briefest preparation by looking up a few facts in reference books, has to give. The play raises, in comic mode, three questions: first, the almost total disparity between the ordinary everyday messiness of everyone's life and the widespread public myths that tend to gather round 'famous' people; second, the possibility that both the mundane fact and the noble (falsely noble, perhaps) legend are irrelevant and unimportant if the man's work itself has any kind of permanence, importance or significance – with the attendant question of whether *any* work has any real permanence or significance in the long run; third – and ironically – that only to a small group of the initiated do any of these questions matter at all – the great mass of people pays no attention at all to the questions, let alone the answers. The 'great mass of people' is represented by a man and his wife (a little, perhaps, like Mr and Mrs A in *The Ascent of F6*, observing great events from the standpoint of everyday) who are listening to the radio programme about Southman. 'Never heard of him', the Woman says when her husband asks her to come and listen to the programme. The play allows these two, also, to talk directly with the broadcaster and at one point they interrupt to say they aren't enjoying it very much and to suggest that it would be improved by the addition of some music:

LUCOCK: Well, I don't really see how we can introduce music.
LISTENER: No need to introduce it. Put it on.
LUCOCK: Anything special?
LISTENER: Well, I realise it's a solemn occasion with Mr Southman dying so I should think something solemn. What about Handel's 'Largo'?
LUCOCK: Yes. Yes, that's solemn, isn't it? Just a minute: I'll see if I can arrange it.

He does arrange it and Handel's 'Largo' continues to play throughout his next long speech.

Finally, Lucock becomes so exasperated with the interruptions and opposition that he has the interrupters forcibly removed from the studio, *en bloc*, after a desperate bout of fisticuffs in which he himself gets involved, much against his will. He is just settling down to do his radio programme properly when he is interrupted yet again:

LUCOCK: Ladies and gentlemen, I cannot say how deeply, how very deeply, I regret this most . . . most regrettable . . . incident. I can only . . . you must forgive me, but my nose is bleeding rather badly . . . I can only say that I hope to be able to restore some reverence and tranquillity during these last few minutes of Dr Southman's life. That disturbance – dear me – that was the terrible Andrew Vince who was leading them. You know about him, of course: the man responsible for the burning of so many copies of *The Abolition of Printing* – among other things. I hope during these last few minutes of Dr Southman's life I can manage to restore some sense of reverence to the memory of a very great man. If I fail to do this completely, I at least hope that I succeed sufficiently to counteract the memories of those people who came here tonight with the purpose of calumniating Paul Southman. (*A pause*) At last we are alone – I may add, there's an armed guard on the door – and we may speak quietly and reasonably about Paul Southman.

AN OLD MAN: What are you going to say about him?
LUCOCK: How did you get in?
OLD MAN: I came in just this minute.
LUCOCK: You were allowed in?
OLD MAN: Yes.
LUCOCK: Really!
OLD MAN: Go on.
LUCOCK: Go on with what?
OLD MAN: With what you were talking about.
LUCOCK: I'm afraid I must ask you to leave.
OLD MAN: But I want to hear you.
LUCOCK: Will you promise to keep quiet and not interrupt?
OLD MAN: I promise. Your nose is bleeding.
LUCOCK: I know.
OLD MAN: I'll keep quiet.
LUCOCK: Very well. Ladies and gentlemen, I want you to put out of your
   minds all the things that have been said about Paul Southman this
   evening.
OLD MAN: They did go a bit far, didn't they?
LUCOCK: Everything, that is, other than the words spoken by myself. Paul
   Southman, as we must remember him . . .
OLD MAN: He wasn't a bad old dodger.
LUCOCK: Dr Southman was a genius, sir, not an 'old dodger'.
OLD MAN: All right.
LUCOCK: His genius extended . . .
OLD MAN: Look here, don't be angry . . .
LUCOCK: You promised not to interrupt.
OLD MAN: I know, but don't get upset. You see, I agree with you, Mr
   Lucock. I think all these people – poor stupid John Ussleigh, that
   horrible woman from Leeds, that smart young critic, the soldier and the
   awful man who grows begonias and the arch-enemy, Vince – I think they
   were all quite wrong.
LUCOCK: You do?
OLD MAN: Certainly I do.
LUCOCK: And you think I'm right?
OLD MAN: Well, you're nearer than any of the others.
LUCOCK: Thank you.
OLD MAN: Much nearer.
LUCOCK: Have you any memories of Paul Southman?
OLD MAN: Many.
LUCOCK: Would you care to tell the listeners?
OLD MAN: I'd like to – yes.
LUCOCK: Very well. May I introduce you?
OLD MAN: Certainly.
LUCOCK: Well, come along, then. What's your name?
OLD MAN: Paul Southman.
LUCOCK: Ladies and gentlemen, Mr Paul – What did you say?
OLD MAN: Paul Southman.
   (*There is a pause.* LUCOCK *gives a short scream. There is another pause*)

OLD MAN: He's run away! Ah, well, hats off everyone! Here goes! I suppose
all you people can hear me . . .
(*But they cannot, for a gramophone record of a funeral march is hurriedly
put on and played fortissimo.*)

The play is quite competent and some of its ironic points are nicely
made, but its chief interest and importance now is in the presence of
Paul Southman and in the many connections with other of Whiting's
plays. As has been noted in Chapter 2, there is a single mention of Paul
Southman in *Not a Foot of Land*, written a year or so earlier. There,
he is described by Old Tim as 'a local celebrity, a pamphleteer who
was hung for his lampoons'. In *Saint's Day*, which was begun in the same
year as the radio play, he is the central figure, is described as a 'poet
and pamphleteer' and is hanged (though not directly for his 'lampoons')
at the end of the play. *Saint's Day*, with none of the skittishness and
lightness of touch of the radio play, is nevertheless consciously dealing
with the same character, though in a more profound and penetrating
way altogether. There are some similarities of personality, however between these two Paul Southmans: the freakish sense of humour is still
there in *Saint's Day*, as are the blistering scorn for established society
and the quarrels with the neighbours. Several physical circumstances are
taken over, too, by the later play: Southman lives in the country, tended
by a younger man and woman; in the radio play they are his son and
daughter but have become his grand-daughter and her husband in *Saint's
Day*. In both plays there is a fastidious young critic, though in the radio
play he is a mere sketch and is opposed to Southman from the start:
Procathren, in *Saint's Day* is revealed in great depth and complexity and
is a fascinating and a highly ambivalent character. The whole incident
of the printing of the offending pamphlets by a printer called John
Ussleigh is taken over from the radio play – including the actual name
of the printer – and used satirically in *Saint's Day*, when Southman
describes the way in which he was, he says, arraigned for assaulting
'the well-known and much-loved whore, Society'; two of the witnesses
called against him in this fantasy trial are Andrew Vince and John
Ussleigh – both drawn from the radio play. Even the title of the offending pamphlet, for the writing of which Southman is ostracised, is the
same in both plays: *The Abolition of Printing*.

The surrealistic style – vivid naturalistic detail in bizarre surroundings – which characterises the radio play has connections with both
Saint's Day and *Not a Foot of Land*, as it also has in a general way with
the short stories. There is also one very specific connection with the story
written two years later, in 1948, and called 'The Honour of the Fire
Brigade'. Lucock says, while trying to put together a connected account
of Southman's career: 'The only fact that I have been able to gather
about Paul Southman's personal life at that period is this – he had a

passion for driving the local fire-engine which was, of course, at that time horse-drawn.' This is the situation of the central character in the short story ('The fire engine was not, of course, my grandfather's personal property,' that story begins) and it is also the entire preoccupation of Lamprett Bellboys in *A Penny for a Song*, written – in the main – in 1949. One other of these curious details in *Paul Southman* is significant: Ussleigh, the printer, describes how Southman, when he came to the printing works to bring the manuscripts of the fire-brand pamphlets, was always preceded by a small boy who arrived five minutes ahead of him and insisted on inspecting the room and its contents and cupboards and drawers in minute detail. The inspection completed to the child's satisfaction, he would then leave and summon Southman, who presently appeared. 'I assumed', says Ussleigh, 'after knowing Southman for some time that it was not to forestall assassination or attack but was for the purpose of deliberate mystification.' The incident is significant in that it illustrates once again that preoccupation of Whiting's with the figure of the innocent child, which is so noteworthy in the unpublished novel, *Not a Foot of Land*, and which occurs later in so many of the plays. In the case of the radio play, it also demonstrates that Whiting himself was not sure of *its* implications – hence the explanation that the child's presence was for the purpose of 'deliberate mystification'. The image came intuitively to Whiting's imagination: it was not an intellectually invented symbol of some specific point or idea. Its unconscious and instinctive origin usually makes it, of course, much more powerful and ultimately much more true, even if it also sometimes makes its presence bewildering to the author as well as to us. This child in *Paul Southman* is referred to once more and, again, significantly. Lucock says:

> 'Ladies and gentlemen, we have just been telephoned by
> Mr Henry Southman, the well-known medical practitioner.
> He wishes us to state that it was not *he* who preceded his
> father, Paul Southman, into Mr Ussleigh's office to conduct
> an investigation. He suggests that it may have been the elder
> brother, Oscar Southman, who died the following year at
> the age of nine, by falling from a fourth-floor window of
> the building occupied by a firm of engravers.'

The child, the innocent harbinger, is once more – as so frequently in Whiting – doomed to die.

Mention is made in *Paul Southman*, the radio play, but not in *Saint's Day* of an unpublished essay by Paul Southman. The supercilious young critic says of it: 'Southman's one work of merit is unknown. The essay "The Contemplation of an Empty Room". Fine stuff. No politics.' The title which Whiting has given to the lost essay is full of resonances. One thinks again of the way in which – in an interview for *Encore* – Whiting tried to explain something of the origin of *Saint's Day*: the story of suddenly coming upon a deserted, empty house, in war-time 'in the Midlands somewhere', with a strange, compelling mural painted on the wall of one of its rooms; and of Stella's use, in *Saint's Day*, of the image of 'a call from another room' and of the child Jacob in *No Why*, left alone to die in a disused and empty room. The same image appears again in the radio play called *The Stairway*, where one room only is used in an otherwise empty house and this, in turn, is very similar to the mysterious house in which Sara's strange birthday party, with the puppet play, is given in *Not a Foot of Land* (very like Aston's room in *The Caretaker*, too) and like the empty house to which Angus comes back, half-hoping to find Kirsty in *No More A-Roving*. Most significant of all, in its connection with the title of the earlier Paul Southman's lost essay, is the lament spoken by the later Paul Southman, in *Saint's Day*, over the body of the dead Stella: 'Dead. Dead. The doors are shutting in the empty house.' Like other powerful and recurring symbols to which reference has already been made, this one of the strangeness and the sinister quality of an empty room or an empty house is with Whiting an obsessive one. The way he anticipates the use of this particular image by Pinter some years later is quite uncanny (though I am in no way suggesting that Pinter *copied* it from Whiting: the spiritual ambience of the image as Pinter uses it, in *The Room, The Caretaker* and other plays, is too authentic, too truthful, too honestly felt and too much an integral part of the whole vision of the plays for that to be so) as is its affinities with the use of space and of common household objects in both Beckett and Ionesco, who were writing their first plays at almost exactly the same time as Whiting (*Waiting for Godot*, 1947–9; *The Bald Soprano*, 1950). At a more consciously literary level, the twin senses of aridity and half-hidden terror that the image of the dark house and the empty room is made to carry, are reminiscent of a similar and widely used set of images in Eliot's plays. 'Up and down, through the stone passages / Of an immense and empty hospital / Pervaded by the smell of disinfectant, / Looking straight ahead, passing barred windows, / Up and down. Until the chain breaks', says Agatha in one of the incantatory passages of *The Family Reunion*. And the Chorus in the same play, expressing its unease and unidentifiable fear, says: 'We do not like to climb a stair and find it takes us down./We do not like to walk out of a door and find ourselves back in the same room.'

Our physical environment plays us false. There is that about it which is unaccountable. It is not what it seems. It harbours an indescribable and irrational terror. *Murder in the Cathedral* ('. . . sometimes hesitating at the angles of stairs . . .') is full of imagery of rather the same character. It is, in fact, one of the basic images (perhaps one might even say *the* basic image) of all twentieth-century art, reaching its most obvious manifestation in the isolation, emptiness and desolation of the theatre-of-the-absurd plays. The astonishing thing is that Whiting should have caught and mirrored it so vividly and powerfully, and have translated it into such effective dramatic terms, before any of the absurdist plays had been written or the term 'absurdist' itself invented. Of course, in the little radio play here under discussion, the spirit of this awful emptiness is not present in itself, but there is at least a documentation of it, an indication of the author's emerging responses, in the title he chose to give to that 'unpublished essay' of his protagonist – 'The Contemplation of an Empty Room'. All his major characters in his later plays will feel that hollowness within and will reflect a nameless dread.

The same is true of the matter of public men and private men: though *Paul Southman: An Appreciation* does little more than hint at the dichotomy, later plays of Whiting's will show men riven by it. So even in this scrap of dramatic material for radio there can be seen the reflection of many of his dominant images and obsessions, seething and interacting in 1946 as they would continue to do through all his serious work for the next seventeen years. They represent a fairly narrow segment of observation and experience but one that, though narrow, was deeply felt, profound, vividly observed and resoundingly recorded.

Of the three more standard and conventional radio plays – *Eye Witness, The Stairway* and *Love's Old Sweet Song*, little need be said. They are efficiently plotted but flatly written. Their stories and characters are, for the most part, conventional stock ones, not exhibiting either the strange resonances of much of his other work or the fascinating connections with that other work that *Paul Southman* has. There is probably more than a slight tendency now, in the 1970s, to assume that no radio play could possibly be important, that all of them are time-serving pieces of conventional triviality; but it must be remembered that this was very far from true in Great Britain in the 1930s and 1940s. England, of course, has always tended to take radio drama a good deal more seriously than have Canada or the United States, and still does; moreover at the time Whiting was beginning to write, British radio drama was at its zenith. Louis MacNeice, for example, and D. G. Bridson both wrote some extremely important plays especially and solely for radio. The year in which *Paul Southman* was written was also the year in which MacNeice's *The Dark Tower* was broadcast. My point is that this was not, to Whiting, some minor pot-boiling activity designed to fill in an awkward gap until he could get down to his serious writing. The medium was one which he and others took perfectly seriously and the things he wrote for it were just as carefully prepared and are just as likely to be representative as the things he wrote for the stage (his work for films is another story). It is, therefore, worthwhile to distinguish between his radio plays which do show some marked originality and those which do not.

Eye Witness is about a wife who, with her lover's help, murders her husband, intending to leave the body with planted clues to suggest suicide. At the crucial moment, the murderers are interrupted by a blind friend and, thinking themselves to be safe since he *is* blind, the wife entertains him to tea in the room where the dead body lies and with the lover, who keeps silent, also present. The blind man has come to thank the dead husband for a loan of money that he has had from him for some very special purpose. The wife tells him that the husband is away from home and, apparently perfectly satisfied, he leaves. The murderers rejoice in their prowess at having deceived the blind man but realise that now, since the blind man will remember the *time* of his visit, they must abandon the suicide story and dispose of the body in some other way. They are planning how to do this when the telephone rings. It is the blind man, who tells them that the money he borrowed was for an operation on his eyes, which was at least partially successful. He is no longer totally blind: he can see a little. And he describes to the horrified wife, over the telephone, what he saw when he called on her that afternoon – the dead husband lying there and the lover, standing silent and pretending not to be there at all. It is an effective little tale, but nothing more.

The Stairway also concerns murder and suicide, but this time with the situation reversed. Max and Stephen come to murder Robert, who lives immured in one room at the top of an otherwise unoccupied house. They find that he, knowing the situation to be hopeless (there is the suggestion of vague political, revolutionary events in the background) has outwitted them by committing suicide after setting up a whole series of clues that will make the suicide look like murder and will point inescapably to *them* as the murderers. As they realise what has happened and set about the job of incriminating each other (and Max in the course of this murders Stephen), they are interrupted by the police who have eighteen minutes ago received a telephone call from Robert, reporting a murder at this address and even giving Max's name.

Love's Old Sweet Song is a little ghost story with a fairly ordinary, well-tried formula but with the emphasis much more on the general atmosphere of regret and decay than on the events. It is set in 1912, in a Victorian house overlooking a square in which a mysterious stranger stands and watches the windows. Though the season is late autumn, he is dressed in light summer clothes – a straw hat, a blazer, white flannels. In the house, two middle-aged sisters live. Grace is bedridden and has been for a long time, though Julia accuses her of malingering. Julia is deeply disturbed by the sight of the man in the square who, day after day, watches their house. Grace, who has not seen him because she is confined to her bed, talks endlessly and repetitiously of the days when they were both young and used in summer to meet the young men by the river. She remembers vividly how the young men were dressed: they wore blazers and white flannels and straw 'boaters'. She had eloped with one of them, who had later deserted her. Mr Henty, an old friend, comes to call. Julia tells him about the watcher in the square and of the feelings of unease and distress that, unaccountably to her, the sight of him produces in her. The old man only laughs and they do not tell Grace. The whole play has a touch of Gothic darkness about it that has the feeling of authenticity: a faint whiff of Edgar Allan Poe. It has some slight resemblance, too, to Pinter's *A Slight Ache* (which was written nine years later), though it is not brought to nearly as savage or thorough a resolution as the Pinter play is.

A good deal more interesting than any of these three, in many ways, is the unfinished *The Quarry and the Prey*, dated 1950. It was evidently intended to be more elaborate and ambitious than the other radio plays: the second draft bears a note saying that the running time was to be sixty minutes, where its four predecessors had all been thirty minutes; and in the scenes that were written there is more detail and more extended treatment of theme and climax than in the other radio plays. The first draft consists of $10\frac{1}{2}$ manuscript pages of the imitation medieval script in which Whiting wrote all his plays, seven pages of it written in red ink: the second draft, which has obviously been transcribed very closely from the first with relatively minor emendations only, does not get so far with the story as the first draft does; there are eight manuscript pages, written in the usual black Indian ink. The action of the play occurs on Christmas Eve. Henry Freeman and his wife Margaret (Mary, in the first draft: changed, perhaps to avoid any suggestion – in a play that is highly charged with symbols and is obviously intending to use them as part of both its structure and its meaning – that the name has a symbolic connection with the Christmas story) are at home, he having just got back from the little bookshop that he runs. He is gazing out of the window at the house opposite, where Alastair Napier lives. Napier's house is decorated with a Christmas tree and looks bright and gay; Freeman's house is drab and rather dark. Napier, we gather from Freeman's comments to his wife, hates the Freemans, though they are not sure why. He persecutes them in strange ways but, though they make some conjectures as to the reason, they are still not sure of it:

FREEMAN: Does he know? Does Napier know?
MARGARET: About us?
FREEMAN: About us. Does he know?
MARGARET: But even if he found out . . .
FREEMAN: Ever since we came here six months ago – from the moment of our arrival – he has made our lives a misery.
MARGARET: Even if he had discovered our – oh, no! – but what is his purpose? Why should he intimidate and persecute you with his questions, his jokes . . .
FREEMAN: His contempt, his ruthless inhumanity.
MARGARET: Why?

FREEMAN: I don't know.

MARGARET: You, an innocent man!

FREEMAN: An innocent man. Do people laugh at an innocent man? As he does – as he . . . (*He pauses*) That laughter! Yesterday – only yesterday – I came out of the shop and he was standing on the other side of the street. Squarely facing me, his hands in his pockets, waiting. The street was empty but for ourselves. He looked at me and then burst into laughter. He walked away, laughing, the sound echoing. The horror – listen to me, darling, whilst I tell you – the horror of his laughter is that it is not malicious – that I could understand, perhaps – no: it seems good, honest amusement, as if he saw a clown: as if I was his fool, his plaything. Indeed, he uses me with all the careless cruelty that children practise on their toys. His persecution is almost affectionate in its tenderness and love. (*He pauses*) Now, let us suppose that he knows about – (*The doorbell rings*) Leave it! There can be no-one of importance to us. They'll go away. Let us suppose that Napier knows about Dorothy. Let us suppose that he knows about her. And about Edwin George Price. Let us take it that he has found out, remembered the details and is aware of what has gone before in our lives. Is that reason to persecute us? And in such a way. If his attitude were stern, impartial – a second judge – that I could understand. But he seeks me out, follows me, waits for me. And then comes this boisterous, noisy derision. This laughter! (*The doorbell rings again*) And that I do not understand.

MARGARET: I have never understood cruelty.

FREEMAN: For in all of us is the misery that has gone before: every happy face contains a skull.

We never discover what was 'the misery that has gone before'. Whether we should have done so had the play been completed, it is impossible to say. One likes to think not, since to reveal the mystery at the end would make the use of it at the beginning a mere dramaturgic trick, a way of creating 'dramatic suspense', as in a thriller or whodunit, whereas to leave it unexplained is not only to increase its power (remember Coleridge's famous revision of 'Christabel'!) but also to make it actually a part of the inner sense of the play. And the play as it stands (fragmentary as it is) would seem to lean towards and lend its authority to some sense such as this.

After the conversation between Mr and Mrs Freeman, there is a conversation between Mr and Mrs Napier and a friend that shows up the persecution and hatred from the other side. The friend is an old school companion of Napier's, whose name is Gilbert Leppatt:

MRS NAPIER: Oh Gilly, it's dreadful (*But she, too, is laughing*) Alastair is so wicked. Mr Freeman lives over the way, with his wife, a funny faded little couple – and Alastair is cruel to him.

LEPPATT: In what way? (NAPIER *is laughing*)

MRS NAPIER: Oh, shut up, darling! They don't do anything. He keeps a rather smelly little bookshop – but I mean, they don't harm anyone.

Mild as rabbits. He wears thick specs and dark clothes and talks to him-self as he walks in the street. She's a dowdy thing, limps, wears strange hats and stinks of carbolic. Alastair hates them.

LEPPATT: Why?

MRS NAPIER: Yes, why do you, Alastair?

LEPPATT: Why do you hate them, Napier? (*Unanswered, he continues*) May I tell you something, Napier? Something to make you laugh. When I arrived this afternoon and you left me alone for a while in this room I began to admire the little house you have made for yourself. Charming, clean and colourful, but – if I may say so – very unlike the dream castles of your youth. However, having admired this room I went to the window and, looking out, I noticed something very odd. I noticed that the house opposite might have been a reflection – as in a looking-glass – of this house, your house. It appeared at first glance to be exactly the same until I saw it is rather shabby and dirty, whereas yours is bright and clean. But shabbiness is only a matter of time. A strange illusion. And mightn't you, Napier, be looking out of this window when you see a man come from that house. An ageing man, a lost man, a failure. And mightn't you amuse yourself with the notion that the man is a reflection – of yourself, perhaps – not now but, like the house, in some years to come. And then from the house you see a woman come, eccentric, a little crazy, ugly, deformed, diseased – and you would laugh, wouldn't you, because it might easily be – not now, but oh, so soon – it might easily be...

NAPIER: (*Shouting*) Shut up!

LEPPATT: Is that why you hate the Freemans?

NAPIER: Shut up!

MRS NAPIER: Alastair! Does he mean we might become like the Freemans?

NAPIER: I think he does.

It becomes apparent that Napier harbours, in relation to his old school-friend Leppatt, something of the same kind of paranoia and guilt complex that Freeman feels towards Napier. And as the scene just quoted demonstrates, he may well be trying to tyrannise over Freeman to compensate for senses of fear and guilt that he also feels in that direction. And Leppatt, too, is not outside this circle of hatred and inverse hatred. 'Gilly, you don't hate me, do you?' Napier asks him when they are alone. 'Not now,' Leppatt replies. 'You did once?' Napier asks. 'Oh, yes ...' says Leppatt. Napier interrupts him with 'Well, let's forget that' but Leppatt persists 'I hated you ...' 'Shall we? Let's forget it.' '... very much once,' Leppatt finishes. And a little earlier, the following exchange has taken place:

MRS NAPIER: Alastair, why send the carol-singers away all the time? I thought you were fond of music.

NAPIER: I am.

LEPPATT: Fond of music, Napier...

NAPIER: Oh, he's woken up!

LEPPATT: Do you still play the guitar?
NAPIER: You remember!
LEPPATT: I remember very well. You once tied a guitar string round my
    body and . . .

We never hear what happened because Mrs Napier interrupts with a
question addressed to Leppatt about what Napier was like when he
was a child at school. Not a very nice child, we infer.

It was presumably this pattern of mutual hatred, guilt and mistrust
in which it is impossible to see who is the hunter and who the hunted
that led to the choice of title for the play, though the title does not, in
fact, mean what it clearly seems intended to mean. Freeman himself
at one point, having decided to confront Napier, says: 'Which is the
hunter and which the hunted? There's a pretty problem.' And that
would seem to be the sense required of the title – the Hunter and the
Hunted. But this phrase, as a title, sounds a bit commonplace and crude,
so Whiting chose the much better-sounding the Quarry and the Prey,
not noticing, apparently, that 'quarry' and 'prey' are synonyms and
together represent only one side of his equation.

The decision to bring about a confrontation with Napier is taken by
Freeman after his house, hitherto thought by him to be sacrosanct, has
been 'invaded' by one of 'them', a strange and forbidding visitor, a Mrs
Malpas. (Though Whiting always said that his choice of characters'
names was a random one, it is hard to resist the temptation to believe
that there was a deliberate deviation from that rule in this case. The
idea of a Free-man being cornered by a character whose name means
False-Step has a ring about it that is positively Bunyanesque.) Mrs
Malpas comes to bring Christmas presents for Mr and Mrs Freeman:
she makes a yearly practice of giving presents to everyone in 'our little
community', she says. But there is nothing of friendship in the gesture,
which is carried out with a repulsive smugness and self-satisfaction. 'It's
very kind of you, but . . .' says Freeman; to which Mrs Malpas replies
'Kindness doesn't enter into it.' And when Freeman asks her if she
likes Napier, whom she has just mentioned in conversation, she says:
'A very extraordinary question, Mr Freeman, if I may say so – but I
will answer you. I like Mr Napier very much. You will find no discontent in our little community. If I may say it without being misunderstood, each member more than likes – they love each other. (*She
pauses*) You are strangers, of course. You came from far away, did
you not? – To this town. (*There is silence*) Some tragedy, perhaps.
(*She is unanswered*)' When she leaves, she goes to the outside door
alone and, as she opens it to go out, she says in a loud voice 'Peace
be on this house.' Whiting's stage direction says of this utterance
Baying as if it were a malediction. And after she has gone Freeman
says:

FREEMAN: I would not have believed they would come as Santa Claus.
MARGARET: What do you mean?
FREEMAN: They've never come inside our house before. Never dared . . .
MARGARET: A foolish old woman!
FREEMAN: One of *them* . . .
MARGARET: But Harry . . .
FREEMAN: Oh, make no mistake about it. Ruthless. Determined.
MARGARET: A foolish, mad, old woman. Nothing more.
FREEMAN: I'm not frightened – no, really – not fear: something – I don't know – but not fear. Not now. You must understand that I cannot comprehend what is happening but I am not afraid. Do you believe me?
MARGARET: Yes.
FREEMAN: It is important that you should believe me.
MARGARET: I believe you.
FREEMAN: Not afraid – no. Because I . . . (*He suddenly asks*) What's the time? I think we might go out for a drink – to somewhere near.
MARGARET: If you would like to go, yes.
FREEMAN: It being Christmas Eve. We can go to the Crown. We've never . . .
MARGARET: Harry . . .
FREEMAN: . . . been there. What?
MARGARET: Isn't that where Mr and Mrs Napier go?
FREEMAN: I believe it is. But don't be afraid.
MARGARET: Do you want to meet them?
FREEMAN: Yes. (*Then suddenly, forcibly*) Yes!

The 'Crown' had originally been called the Crown of Blackthorn. The landlord explains to the Freemans that the change was made in the early nineteenth century because 'doubtless they felt a drinking house so named might offend certain people's susceptibilities' (the crown of thorns worn by Christ on the cross was, according to legend, made of blackthorn). The scene in the pub is the last one that the unfinished manuscript contains and there is less than a page and a half of the scene written. The promised confrontation with Napier is never reached and the only participants of the scene are Harry and Margaret Freeman and the landlord of the pub, James Algar. Whiting says of him *His voice, charming and affected, is almost suffocated by the weight of flesh*. Margaret whispers to her husband that Algar is a nice man but that his clothes are odd and old-fashioned. Her husband adds, disapprovingly, that Algar 'uses scent'. They both notice a glass case of mementos about which they ask. Algar's reply is: 'The snuff-box belonged to Wainwright, the poisoner. The handkerchief is the very one that Palmer of Rugeley used to wipe away the sweat of fear. The shoe belonged to Seddon's child. The notebook fell from Madeleine Smith's hand and the rope – well, the rope is a part of that which hanged – (*Distantly a telephone begins to ring*) The telephone. Please excuse me. (*His voice recedes*) Behind you is an engraving of an execution at Tyburn. The series of engravings by Piranesi on that wall are of a famous prison . . .(*There is a pause.* MARGARET *whispers*)'

But what she was going to whisper we do not know; the manuscript, maddeningly, ends there, in the middle of a page.

One other feature of this unfinished play should be briefly mentioned: the presence of children in it. They are carol singers, going round from door to door, singing for pennies. In the first draft there are four of them but this is reduced to two in the second draft and the effectiveness of the image of childhood vulnerability is increased by this reduction. The older child says to the younger at one point: 'Can you remember "God rest ye merry gentlemen"? We'll sing that – we'll sing it over there – where the Christmas tree is in the window. Come along. What are they all about that they won't listen to us? What are they all doing, shut up in their houses? Come on, little one! Don't hang behind. You are funny – crying all the time without making a sound.' One is instantly reminded here of the child with its mother in the train in *Not a Foot of Land*, the child who wept silently throughout the journey. As in the earlier work, the children in *The Quarry and the Prey* are used structurally in the work only as ways of linking other passages together, but in the process they do two other things – they provide a norm of natural belief and spontaneous honesty against which the twisted enormity of the adult world is constantly measured; and they exist in their own right as children – frail, vulnerable, poignant and largely ignored. In the last glimpse we have of these two, the older says to the younger: 'Come on, little one – join in. Why are you holding yourself like that – do you want to wee-wee? Go on, there's no-one about. No-one but ourselves. Why are the streets so empty? Why aren't we frightened, I wonder? Frightened to be out alone on this dark night. You're not frightened, are you, little one? Come here and let me button your coat for you. Why, you're shaking! Are you frightened or cold? Stand close to me for a little and warm yourself.'

III Short stories and fragment of a novel

In the year 1947, with his radio plays beginning to be accepted by the BBC but with none of his stage plays yet performed, Whiting began to write a second novel. It was never given a title and only $8\frac{1}{2}$ printed pages were ever written,[3] but even so short a fragment is enough to show several things: that Whiting's vision is essentially dramatic[4] in quality, whether he is writing for the stage or not; that he still has not really decided to what medium of literature he really belongs; and that his whole concept of the novel and of fictional writing has altered in the eighteen months or so since he finished *Not a Foot of Land*. This brief fragment of the beginning of the second novel is much quieter in tone, much more sardonic and much less lyrical in style, than was the first novel. It sketches the situation of Margaret Anne Holden, a nineteen-year-old girl who was presumably intended as the central character of the novel. It is quite impossible to conjecture, on the basis of these few pages, what either the plot or the underlying sense of the novel was intended to be, but one immediately notices some familiar signs. Margaret is simultaneously the child-figure and the exile-figure. At nineteen, she is living a lonely, empty and frustrated life with a middle-aged woman who is briefly referred to at one point as her guardian. The death of her mother in a street accident, when Margaret was eight years old, is mentioned and the character of her father is lightly sketched. Where he is, now that Margaret is grown up, is not, in the brief section completed, explained. Margaret's childhood is described: the description is not introduced as a memory or reminiscence but baldly, thus: 'These were the circumstances leading to Margaret Holden being in that house at that time. Conceived rather casually one afternoon some seven months after the marriage of her parents, several attempts had been made on her life by her mother during the following three months.' Her mother had changed, however, after the birth: 'on seeing the child she was moved to a real and sincere affection – she was incapable of love.' An indiscriminate and unthinking attention had been lavished on the child by both her mother and her father, in the case of the latter not from any genuine love for the child but in order to give pleasure to his wife, whom he adored. Then at six years old Margaret had suffered a serious illness and while she was still convalescent, her mother was killed. Her father, represented as a weak and rather silly man, had abandoned himself to his grief and his daughter to the care of housekeepers and governesses. After some time, he just as suddenly recovers, throws out of the window the 'book on a religious subject' which he had been reading, goes off to the pub (he had given up drinking) and drinks half a bottle of whisky. The existing manuscript ends with these words: 'His grief was over, his sorrow ended and he was jolly little Tommy Holden again. The following day he met Kate Sessions. The circumstances in which they met are interesting, if farcical.' Kate Sessions is the forbidding guardian, disliked by Margaret, with whom, at the age of nineteen, the latter now lives.

Presented much more coolly and much more on the level of an everyday middle-class world than in *Not a Foot of Land*, here again is the sense of childhood's vulnerability and the way that this vulnerability extends forward into adult life and the constant association of children with death. Here again also is the sense that behind the smiling bourgeois afternoon, something chill and forbidding and slightly sinister lurks. If the few pages we have may be taken as typical of what the whole work would have been, the two novels together may be said to represent fairly accurately the two main strands of Whiting's sensibility – a darkly romantic, Gothic one and an ironic, laconic, objective one. As has been remarked already he could on occasion intertwine these two very effectively in the same work and it may be that this would have happened in the untitled second novel, though the opening pages seem to suggest otherwise, especially when compared with the opening pages of *Not a Foot of Land*.

A different kind of spirit entirely, and one which was to receive expression only once in his plays, is exemplified in the short story called 'The Honour of the Fire Brigade', written in 1948. It is a light, witty, humorous, delicious and altogether engaging piece. Everyone who knew John Whiting personally testifies to his gentleness, his friendliness and his love of people: these are the qualities that this pleasant little story reflects. It is set in 1911 (the coronation year of George V) in a Wiltshire town that is fairly obviously Whiting's native Salisbury and concerns a man who has a passion for fire engines. By becoming a patron of the local brigade, he acquires some influence over it and is elected by the town council to the position of honorary member of the fire brigade. He construes this in a much more active sense than did those who invested him with the honour, taking over the running of the brigade and constituting himself a kind of unofficial captain. (It should be remembered, of course, that this was in the days when British fire brigades were entirely voluntary organisations, operated on a part-time basis by men who, when not actually fighting fires, followed their own separate and varied occupations.) It was the pageantry and organisational excitement, not the actual efficiency, of the fire-fighting operation that appealed to the hero of Whiting's story, especially the driving of the horse-drawn fire engine, like a Roman chariot, pell-mell through the streets of the town to the fire. The culmination of this story is centred upon this gentleman's attempts to secure for the brigade a place of real glory in the coronation celebrations. He is contemptuous of the idea of merely taking part in the official procession and makes various counter-suggestions, from giving children rides on the engine in the main street at tuppence a time to having the engine stand in the cathedral close all day, attempting to direct a jet of water over the spire of the cathedral. When all these are rejected, he decides to take the matter into his own hands with a bold plan. On the day of the procession and celebrations, he provides a first-class fire for the fire-engine to deal with by himself setting fire to a house. He then seizes the engine from its place in the procession, drives it furiously to the fire and entertains the big crowds for the rest of the day with the spectacle of ladders and hoses and water-pumping and hair-breadth rescues in the imminent deadly breach. The story finishes thus: 'At dusk, still watched in awe by the silent crowd, the house was gutted. My grandfather, surrounded by his brigade, was heard to comment, "It makes a noble ruin." He regarded the devastation with satisfaction. Of course, we lost every-thing.' It was his own house he had deliberately fired.

The obvious comparison of the central situation of this story with one of the ingredients of *A Penny for a Song*, which was being written about the same time, had been alluded to already and has frequently been made elsewhere by other critics: it need not be laboured here. It is worth remarking, however, that not only the fire engine, so beloved of Lamprett Bellboys in the play, but also the balloon which is used by his brother, Timothy, has its origins in the same short story. The fire-fighting enthusiast invents a device whereby a dozen buckets of water and two firemen, on a wooden platform, are hoisted in a balloon so that the fire can be attacked from above. Needless to say, this never works out as it had been planned. 'This contraption proved its excellence at the first trial', the story says. 'While hovering directly above the fire, the balloon became ignited, precipitated the platform, the buckets and two men into the fire, which was immediately extinguished. The second experiment was less successful.' Although Whiting's wit and sense of humour show in his later plays, they are almost always used ironically and are of a darker quality. Only here at the beginning of his career as a writer do we see, in the instances of 'The Honour of the Fire Brigade' and *A Penny for a Song*, this warm and untroubled gaiety.

The best of Whiting's three short stories is the one called 'A Valediction'. It was written in 1949. The balance between robustness and an eerie strangeness which it achieves is remarkable, and both its sensitivity and its percipience are striking. Here again is a combination of two favourite Whiting themes – childhood and circuses, but the combination this time is not as casual and seemingly accidental as in some of the other instances. In fact, it is strongly wrought and purpose-ful and the whole story becomes a symbol of the eternal opposition of the life forces to the death forces and the equipoise that exists between the two. The story is about Edward, the child of an aristocratic family, who lives in the family mansion, a great house set in its own park-lands. There is no mother in the house and the father has just died. The boy is left to his own devices, tiptoeing about the silent house. 'On the way to his room he was stopped by a tall, fair woman. She was a frequent visitor to the house, in the past laughing with Edward's father. She now stared, unsmiling, at the boy. "Edward", she said "are you good?" "Yes", the boy answered directly. "We must pray tonight", the woman said, and then allowed him to pass.' Alone in his room, he sud-denly hears in the distance the sounds of a circus and is filled with an unaccountable excitement.

Two days later, Edward attends his father's funeral and watches the coffin being placed in the great family mausoleum on the hill in the park. We note in passing that the coffin is carried on a gun-carriage: in other words, Edward's father, like John Whiting's, was a soldier. On the evening of the day of the funeral Edward is again alone in his room staring out of the window at the hill behind which the circus is encamped. He hears again the distant sounds and is strangely attracted. Unobserved, he slips out of the house, runs across the park and joins the straggle of people going along the lane to the circus. As he goes he remembers the funeral and how the horses and carriages there had reminded him of the circus procession he had seen two days before. He falls in with three village children and, because the youngest, who is only a baby, keeps falling down, offers to carry him. They get separated from the other two and Edward is left to look after the baby and takes it to the circus by himself.

> He was very conscious of the child in his arms and held it,
> most gently, to himself. He felt beneath his hand the
> warmth and tenderness of the naked legs. He was also aware
> of the smell of the child; tart, animal, completely alien but
> in the very strangeness intimate, human and comforting.
> It was in this sensual knowledge, never before experienced
> by him, that Edward found an excitement, a sudden
> happiness he had never known.

As they go along, the baby points in excitement to the bronze cupola of the mausoleum in the park and Edward offers the explanation 'My father's house' to the child. The circus performance itself is for Edward a new world, a thing of magic wrenched from a drab existence. The galloping of the white horses reminds him again of the funeral, but without any sense of guilt. 'At the blast of the trumpets', says the story, 'Edward's head was not bowed.' There had been trumpets at the funeral, but then Edward *had* stood with bowed head. The parallels and comparisons and contrasts are everywhere. At the end of the performance, the grand procession of the performers reminds him of the funeral procession, since it moves at the same slow pace 'but the trumpets hooted and shrilled and the drums were possessed by a broken rhythm'. It is as if the boy is made to feel directly and simultaneously the forces of life and death themselves. When the older children come to collect the baby, Edward experiences a feeling of distress and a sense of loss which he cannot understand or define to himself. And left alone, he begins to walk home. He happens to come upon three of the circus clowns and stops to watch them. They are taking off their make-up and their comic faces. 'The third clown tore off his plaster ears and from all three the familiar, false hilarity of their faces was gone. Edward stared in horror at this dreadful decomposition and then, as the storm of grief and knowledge swept through him, stretched out his hands. "Dead men! Dead men!", he screamed.' He runs away and 'his flight carried him towards the domed building standing on the hill.'

The spareness and economy of means in the writing of the story are remarkable and the quality of its experience can be judged by that one phrase alone – 'as the storm of grief and knowledge swept through him': it brings powerfully together in the final paragraph the poised forces of the rest of the story and fixes them in a permanent balance through the expanding consciousness of a child.

The last of the short stories, written in the same year as 'A Valediction', is also about childhood, but is a slighter work. It is called 'Child's Play' and deals with the efforts of a man who is marrying a widow to make friends with her small boy. It is a charming story, told largely from the point of view of the child and it shows, as do all Whiting's studies of childhood, a remarkable insight into the child's mind and the child's world. It has not, however, the same disturbing mythic sense as 'A Valediction': its only virtues are the ones which are immediately obvious – charm, gentleness, compassion, accuracy of observation. These are not to be despised, either, but they lack in 'Child's Play' that penetration of vision that gives 'A Valediction', which is also charming, gentle and compassionate, a further dimension and makes it a paradigm of the eternal struggle between life and death. 'Child's Play' is more homely, more ordinary-real.

The three short stories, together with the fragmentary beginning of the second novel, constitute between them an absorbing comment on Whiting and his work. All of them – and especially when one considers them together – indicate the way in which his vision seeks automatically for dramatic expression: he sees the flux of life constantly caught at the very moment of turning; constantly he subconsciously translates his sense of the world into the metaphors of collision, confrontation, the striving for resolution. This being so, it is all the more surprising that he, who had himself been trained for the theatre, persisted so long with the narrative-prose form before giving all his attention to writing for the theatre. Not that the dramatic vision cannot be expressed in prose – it can; but the more obvious and the more immediate medium of its expression is the theatre, especially for one who already knew the theatre well.

But already, though he was still writing novels and stories, he had begun to write plays and the first of these to carry the indubitable stamp of his mature vision and to begin to show those qualities of coolness, strangeness, an incisively corrosive irony combined with a sort of passionate objectivity, a sense of life that is sombre yet headstrong, impulsive yet controlled, icily clear yet lit by a romantic fire, filled with a sense of underlying and inexplicable mystery yet analytical almost to a fault, was *The Conditions of Agreement*.

IV   *The Conditions of Agreement* (1946)

The play is a study in the individual's sense of inadequacy and of the network of fears that links together the unspoken and deep-seated misgivings of any group of people who are flung together by the accidents of circumstance. Not least among its discoveries is the fact that many frightened and frustrated people mask their fears and frustrations by deliberately and almost instinctively preying upon others (as Napier does on Freeman in *The Quarry and the Prey*). The plot which Whiting has devised and employed to reflect these senses is a strange one. Emily Doon, a widow of fifty-eight, is dozing in the afternoon, waiting for a visitor whom she expects for tea. She does not know, however, who the visitor is to be because the letter she received announcing his intention of calling had an illegible signature. It turns out to be Peter Bembo, an old friend (and possibly a lover – it is hinted at but never definitely affirmed), whom she has not seen for twenty-three years. Bembo has by profession been a circus clown (note the echo from both *Not a Foot of Land* and the short story 'A Valediction'), but is now retired. It is not clear why he has come but his reason for asking if he might stay, now that he is there, is made apparent, as is the excuse he uses to cover over that reason. This reason is a sudden determination to make a victim of and to subject to torture of sorts, a down-trodden little middle-aged man who lives next door and who appears to be in love with Emily. He is referred to throughout the play, by all the other characters, simply as A.G. Bembo's desire to wreak a vengeance on A.G. arises partly from the fact that the latter presents himself virtually as a sacrificial victim and partly – in a more immediately practical sense – from A.G.'s telling the story of his wife's death. She died, it seems, as a result of a fall from a grandstand, while watching a circus performance in Spain in which Bembo the Clown was the star performer. Bembo has confessed to Emily, before A.G. appears, that his one and only pride now left to him is in his remembrance that in the whole of his professional career no one at a performance of his ever wept: he had ever and always produced nothing but laughter. But on that day in Spain, A.G. had wept, wept for the death of his wife, wept at a performance given by Bembo. And for this, Bembo, who has only just met A.G. and heard the story, vows vengeance on him, though not openly yet; instead, he gives to Emily by way of excuse for wanting to stay, these reasons: 'I have travelled a long way – I am tired – it is natural at my age – I have no money but I expect a small sum to be made available to me in a matter of a week or so – there is you and – I want to interest myself in others – perhaps your son – I want – ' The mention of Emily's son is striking: Bembo has not met Nicholas yet, but he has heard a little about him (including the fact that his mother does not like him much), has seen his photograph, knows him to be lame and a moment before he asks Emily if he can stay has heard Nicholas call from offstage: 'I can manage. I'm very good on these stairs.' And he has instantly recognised, even on the strength of such slender evidence, a natural ally against A.G.

Nicholas is just returning from his honeymoon and is bringing his bride, Patience, back to his mother's home, where they are going to live. Nicholas is twenty-two; Patience is seventeen. She is socially and intellectually much his inferior and holds him in considerable awe, behaving toward him with deference and meekness, except in sexual matters. In these, she is the leader, sure of herself and of her power over Nicholas. 'There is no cause to be afraid of the night', she says to him. 'Why are you shy with me? You must have no shame with me. Together, we must be gay and impudent – and it must be you who comes to me to demand and be bold. I want that.' But Nicholas is afraid of sex and associates it with both shame and failure. 'The girl has degraded me beyond expectation', he tells Bembo. 'I was prepared as a necessity of marriage to give myself to a degree but she has made me debase myself until I . . . don't . . . sucking at . . . in the violence of . . .'

He is disturbed because these sexual encounters take place in the bedroom which he has occupied ever since he was a small child and he is horrified when Patience, entirely in innocence, clears from the shelves and cupboard all the toys that have been there, in the same place, for as long as Nicholas can remember. He is not only horrified by this, but extremely angry, so angry that he slaps Patience's face, very hard, and commands her to put the toys back immediately in their original places. Then he changes his mind and says that putting them back will not make the matter right because her moving of them has in effect destroyed them: 'You have destroyed them. Just as if you had burned them', he tells her.

Nicholas and Bembo, though they dislike each other when they first meet, do in fact become allies, realising suddenly that they have two things in common – their paranoic sense of inadequacy, symbolised by Nicholas's artificial leg and Bembo's lost eye (he wears a patch over the eyeless socket); and their hatred of A.G. Bembo explains his hatred to Nicholas by saying 'I shall give you only one reason. To tell you it is based (*He covers his face with his hand*) in some half-forgotten professional pride that he has destroyed. Unforgivable clumsiness.' Up to this point, Nicholas has not mentioned the fact that he also hates A.G., but he now replies to Bembo:

> 'In return for this confidence I shall give you my definite
> reason for hatred of A.G. I hate him because in his ignorance
> he cannot see our want. He avails himself of our company
> because he is a lonely man: we prove ourselves friends by
> giving him an audience for the continually reiterated story of

> the death of his wife: we allow him the impression that he
> is associated with gentle-folk (BEMBO *laughs*) – an intentional
> irony, Mr Bembo – we give A.G. all this and in return get
> nothing. He continually tells us he is fond of us but his
> stupidity does not allow him to see how he can practically
> express that affection – by hard cash.'

They enter into a kind of formal contract to act in some as yet unspecified way against A.G. In some odd way the precipitating of the sealing
of the final bargain between them is linked in Nicholas's mind with his
revulsion at his wife's sexual forwardness. 'I want you to listen to me',
he says to Bembo: 'Patience has . . . I have been gentle and considerate
but her violence to me – No. This is what I wish to say. When you
offered me your help you remember I said the only active thing within
me was my hatred of A.G.' He goes on to say that his love for Patience
is not active but passive and after only a slight hesitation decides to tell
Bembo of the incidents in the bedroom which have disgusted him. 'It is
relevant', he says. Bembo asks him 'What do you want to do, Saint
Nicholas?'

NICHOLAS: I don't know, Peter, I don't know (*He is terribly distressed*) I
    want some kind of revenge.
BEMBO: Now we're getting down to elementals. Revenge for what?
NICHOLAS: For my weakness.
BEMBO: Good. And on whom?
NICHOLAS: A.G.
BEMBO: I see. But why A.G.?
NICHOLAS: Because he is weaker than I am.

Nicholas specifies that there must be no actual violence and also that
the 'revenge' should have something to do with A.G.'s late wife. They
decide finally on the sending of an anonymous note, calculating that
though they know nothing to their victim's discredit, if there happens
to be anything hidden in his past, the note will catch him unawares and
cause him to confess, thus humiliating him. The note which they write
says 'You are discovered, therefore you are lost. She died in vain.
Actum est' and it has the desired effect on A.G. It distresses him terribly, makes him fearful and abject, throws him into their power. They
use that power to reduce him to a state of sycophantic dependence and,
in a ghastly pretence of bonhomie, they strike a 'friendly' bargain with
A.G., the bargain from which, presumably, the play derives its title.
The conditions of this agreement are that A.G. shall never mention his
wife's death again and, in return, Nicholas will befriend him, go for
country walks with him, take him riding in the car (which belongs to
A.G., not to Nicholas). Then, when all seems settled and A.G. has been
reduced to a pitiable yes-man, they inflict one further and devastating
punishment: they get A.G. to tell the story of his wife's death all over

again and, at the end, ask him why she committed suicide. A.G. hotly protests that she did not commit suicide, that the fall which killed her was accidental. Bembo then simulates great indignation and accuses A.G. of misleading them, of having implied all along that Helen's death was suicide. When A.G. protests that he has never suggested such a thing, Bembo says 'But you have implied, if not stated, so many reasons.' He goes on to enumerate various details that A.G. has included in his story of his wife's death: all of them are connected with Helen's feeling that she had failed as a wife, that the marriage was a sexual failure because of her. The parallel with Nicholas is underlined and we realise that Nicholas (who has also, earlier, threatened suicide) has quietly left the room. Bembo draws A.G.'s attention to this and, in effect, lays the blame for a second suicide at his door. A.G. is left alone, lying on the floor, after Bembo has pushed him with Nicholas's stick and addressed him as 'Vile: treacherous: insensate fellow. Evil: unkind: monstrous toad.' Slowly he collects himself and puts on his hat and coat. Without telling anyone he is leaving, he goes to the outer door, on his way home. As he opens the door, Nicholas's voice is heard off-stage saying 'Goodnight, A.G., my dear.' The tormenting of A.G. has been fairly savage, yet the play nowhere suggests that he is finally and totally destroyed by it. He becomes rather pathetically eager to be regarded by Bembo and Nicholas as a 'friend' and he abjectly agrees to their demand that he should ask Emily's forgiveness for having so often told the story of his wife's death, but he replies with a 'Goodnight' when Nicholas says 'Goodnight, A.G., my dear' and he walks home quite normally, Bembo and Nicholas watching him from the window. 'I knew it was a joke', says Patience: and the end of the play seems to agree. It treats the whole episode as a joke, or perhaps – more devastatingly – as a casual part of ordinary, everyday experience. Some critics have compared the triangle of Bembo–Nicholas–A.G. with Goldberg–McCann–Stanley in Pinter's *The Birthday Party* and there is one scene in Act 2 in which the resemblance is striking (*The Birthday Party* was written in 1958), but the plays are not really very similar. *The Birthday Party* is more purposefully and designedly savage: it is more single-minded and powerful but less subtle and complex. *The Birthday Party* in all its parts tends towards the same sleazy images and the same brute savagery, sometimes actual, sometimes incipient. *The Conditions of Agreement* matches its moments of savagery with disparate images, like the warmth and passion that underlies the relationship of Nicholas and Patience and the faint, sweet, nostalgic melancholy that Emily and Peter Bembo share. I am not arguing that one of these plays is better than the other but that they are different: such similarities as exist between them should not be overemphasised, nor should comparisons be pushed too far: the two plays reflect quite different views of the world. What is, perhaps, more interesting than the comparison of their content is a comparison between each of them and its author's later work. Both plays are early works: in Pinter's case, his first full-length play; in Whiting's case his second. Both are arresting and powerful but less than totally successful. Both (in spite of what I have said about the subtlety and complexity of the Whiting play) are simplistic versions of their authors' senses of life. And both are highly significant as prognostications of what the later works will be, both in its similarities to these early plays and in its differences and developments from them.

The Conditions of Agreement displays a number of those leitmotivs which we now recognise as basic to Whiting's vision. Notice once again, for example, the fascination with circuses and the use of the image of the circus both as a microcosmic world and as a delineation of the position of the artist in society: a serious clown who never makes children cry. Peter Bembo's concern about the exact nature of A.G.'s response at the performance in Spain epitomises and focuses all the complications of that image. What is important to Bembo when he hears the story of Helen's death is neither the sadness of the story nor how A.G. had actually felt at the time of the occurrence, but whether A.G. had actually wept or not: had there been actual tears? In one sense, he regards it as a sort of game or competition and he wants to know his score, so to speak, taking the precise technicalities of the rules into account. He had challenged his own professional integrity and even his existence with the rule that, since what he has set up to be is a circus clown, whose function, whose very *raison d'être*, is laughter, there must never be anything but laughter at his performances; not even the blemish of a single tear must mar his perfect record. Though craft is not art and though, therefore, the cleverness of a circus performance is not art, at least in the sense in which that word is used in relation to literature or the theatre (since its objectives do not include either the synthesising or the illuminating endeavours of the 'fine' arts), nevertheless Bembo's performances as a clown and Bembo's attitude to his professional standing are here used as a metaphor for the artist in relation both to his work and to society at large. This does not mean that Bembo-as-artist is not ultimately concerned with the feeling and the content of A.G.'s story of his wife's death, or that the artist is unfeeling and callous. But the concern is of a different quality and kind from that of immediate personal involvement. In the final analysis, its kind is a superior one, since it seeks to avoid the sentimental, that species of untruth and false feeling that, for the comfort of the individual, substitutes personal responses, personal concerns and personal emotions for the sense of the ultimate nature of human reality. Bembo, in fact, is concerned to know whether A.G.'s story reflects, by these absolute standards, any final truth. Its impingement upon his own position as an artist is one test of this, but there are two others which appear in the play, both put there by Bembo. One of them is concerned with the truth of artistic form, the other with the self-delusion and over-involvement of the teller of the story, which has led to a misinterpretation of the story itself, a failure of critical percipience. The former of these occurs early in Act 2 when Nicholas asks Bembo why his attitude to A.G. has changed, why he appears now to be laughing at the affair which the day before had made him so angry. In reply, Bembo says: 'Listen to me. I've explained to you the immediate impact on me of the story of the death of this man's wife. You know the tears he shed in that place at that time attacked my greatest conceit. You know that and understand.' Nicholas agrees, saying: 'Yes, I understand and sympathise. I'm no artist but I understand.' And with this assent, Bembo goes on: 'But consider: the woman's death was so fantastically comic in its elements. You admit? To hang by the heels, skirts about her head, distraught lover fluttering around in an agony of indecision and dismay while a clown in a circus ring below flew through a hoop and the immense audience howled with laughter. The woman fell, was killed. (*He laughs*) No, Nicholas, it's too much. I can't take it seriously. Perhaps, after all, A.G.'s tears were tears of laughter.'

Bembo's anxiety here is, so to say, an artistic one, the anxiety that the work of art – in this case the telling of the story of Helen's death – should have its true form, because the form of a work of art is an important part of its truth. To represent as quasi-tragic something that is *of its essence* comic, is to distort the reflection of reality and to obscure that reality itself. I have emphasised the phrase 'of its essence' because it is a tenet of artistic faith that aspects of that ultimate reality in which all the arts deal do have a natural 'essence', an actual recognisable posture in the world, a spontaneous gesture which can be identified and then reflected in the work itself. To make this identification correctly and to reflect it both truly and vividly is the central function of the artist. To fail to do so is the greatest of artistic failures. And wilfully to refuse to do so is artistic betrayal. Since the incident of Helen's death occurred at one of Bembo's performances, it became part of the 'work of art' which Bembo is considering (namely, that performance itself) and for A.G., either accidentally or deliberately, to tell the story in such a way as to alter its comic posture to a solemn one or a tragic one is to pervert the artistic perceptions themselves and to hide the truth that lies within the work. Bembo's apraisal of A.G.'s attitude to his wife's death is an elaborate and indirect defence of the importance of artistic form *per se*.

The other test of the validity of A.G.'s story is the more direct one that comes at the end of Act 3, when Bembo accuses A.G. of using the story not to reveal the truth but deliberately to conceal it. A.G. has always known, Bembo suggests, that Helen committed suicide in despair at her own failure; but to comfort himself, because the failure was his own as well as his wifes, A.G. had – according to Bembo – perverted the story to conceal the suicide in a supposed accident. Whether this really is the case or not is never finally settled: the play leaves the question open, though there is a feeling at the end that Bembo spoke the truth. The more important issue, however, is that the image of the artist and his work has been completed by the addition of audience and critic to the picture.

As well as serving as the symbol of artistic creativity, this circus image is again, as so many times elsewhere in Whiting, also associated with childhood. Emily recalls that she first met Bembo at a charity dance for crippled children which she had helped to organise and at which he had been engaged as a professional entertainer. She describes the moment when she was introduced to him:

EMILY: And you said 'How d'you do', and stood on your head. Your trousers slipped down to your knees and showed your yellow socks. I stood before you, your face at my feet, with my hand stretched out like a fool. All around us the children laughed and clattered their little wooden legs.
BEMBO: Such antics were expected of me.
EMILY: Yes, I remember. Dear Bembo, I was a little afraid of you and I couldn't understand then why the children were not afraid.
BEMBO: The children were never afraid.
EMILY: I only realised that from performances. There was your trick of leading a child from the audience whilst the band – what was that tune?
BEMBO: 'The Hill where Melchen Lives'. A child's song – forgotten now.
EMILY: You led the child out to hold your paper hoop. Never once in all the times I saw you do that was the child afraid.

There are connections between these early memories and Emily's later life. Nicholas, it will be remembered, is crippled, like the children who were there when Emily first met Peter Bembo; and Nicholas also tells Patience that when he was a little boy, his mother often bade him be nice to her admirers. 'I used to sing for them, the Harrys and the Andrews', he says, 'A little song called "The Hill where Melchen lives".' So Emily, who had loved and been a little afraid of Peter Bembo, had married a soldier called John Doon, who had died, and she had taught Nicholas to sing, to the succession of middle-aged admirers whom she rather wistfully entertained, the song that she had heard at Peter's clown performances long ago.

The image of the cripple,[5] both literal and metaphorical, permeates the play, which is fraught with references to impotence and weakness and ineffectuality – sexual, physical and spiritual. Bembo at one point says to Nicholas 'Not only your leg lets you down, eh? By the way, have you forgotten what you told me about your wife?' And A.G. explains that one of the most pathetic aspects of his wife's death was that he was not strong enough to lift her up as she hung there caught in the scaffolding of the grandstand, nor could he call for help, since his command of Spanish was insufficient. He says that he has 'grown stronger now to meet a similar eventuality which may never arise' and also that *now* his Spanish is fluent. His strength and capability have come too late: when Helen needed them they were not there. There is even a reflection of this general impotence in the behaviour of the weather: at the beginning of Act 2 a stage direction says: *The sun is shining into the room with an unnatural brightness*, yet a few minutes later Nicholas interrupts the flow of a conversation to ask Bembo: 'Do you find it cold in here? The sun should warm the room but . . .'

With one exception, this maimed and impotent spirit touches every character in the play: indeed, it more than touches them – it eats at their hearts. They are lives at a standstill. 'My hatred is the only active thing within me,' Nicholas says at one point, and then adds (*in sudden despair*, according to the stage direction) 'I must attempt a future as well as a present.' Emily, as far as one can tell (though one feels bound to agree with Simon Trussler that the character never develops as its first impact at the beginning of the play seems to suggest was intended), lives on regrets and past memories. A.G.'s life, so far as any strength or progress or development is concerned, stopped short with his wife's death, twenty years before, or perhaps even before that: 'Helen was ten years younger than me,' he says. 'We had wished during the three years of our marriage for children. In that third year Helen underwent an examination which proved she was unable to bear children.' And Bembo, as Ronald Hayman rightly points out, is the first of Whiting's long line of exiles. (The first in the published stage plays, that is. There are earlier ones in some of the other writings: Old Tim in *Not a Foot of Land* is an exile; so in a manner of speaking is Benedict in *No More A-Roving* and so are Harry and Margaret Freeman in *The Quarry and the Prey*.) Bembo tells Emily that he has been living for many years in Armenia which prompts Ronald Hayman to complain that this long absence is 'unexplained'. It hardly seems to need explanation – cut off by life from the roots of life, having been denied Emily's love, what did it matter where he was? All aims were now aimless. 'I remember exactly what you said the last time we met', he says to Emily. 'You said "Goodbye, you damned old clown!" Those were your last words to me before I went to – where on earth was I going that time?' Now that he is back at last and Emily asks him to stay at her home, Whiting's stage direction says: *The realisation that this is a definite invitation to stay at the Doons' house has a perceptible physical effect on* PETER. *He leans back in his chair and rests his head, his arms stretched and relaxed before him.* He begins a comment that is interrupted by the telephone and never finished: 'It is very pleasant to be . . .'

The contrast to these figures of sterility and fearfulness is Patience. She is laden with almost every possible disadvantage, except the limp death wish of the others. She is ignorant, socially inept, clumsy, gauche; she was born illegitimate and brought up in an institution – a pretty bleak one, it is implied; Nicholas has married her, so far as his overt, conscious intentions are concerned, out of friendliness and pity, not love. But she has roused him passionately in spite of himself and, in spite of her lack of intellectual grasp and understanding may yet, one feels at the end of the play, rescue him from emptiness and his fear of life by the sheer force of her own warm, wholehearted, unselfconscious sexuality. She is the play's one positive character – though it should here be emphasised that the play never reduces itself to the level of a programmatic struggle between 'good' and 'bad' or 'positive' and 'negative'. Although Patience has these positive qualities, they are not made brashly into the centre-focus of the play nor is *she* a central character or a resolving force; but her presence throughout, though not dominant (the part is the most lightly sketched of the five) nevertheless provides a robustness and a contrast against which the nihilism of the others shows up vividly. Simon Trussler, in his *The Plays of John Whiting: An Assessment*, postulates as a scheme – almost a convention – for the play the idea that all the characters are in a state of childishness: either they are retarded, like Nicholas, and held there, or they have wilfully regressed to childhood, like Bembo. There is something in this, though it is neither as thorough nor as schematic, I think, as Trussler makes it appear. To push the matter as hard and as far as he does is, it seems to me, to mistake the texture of a metaphor for its final and underlying meaning. Whiting, as has already been remarked elsewhere in this book, has the image and sense of childhood constantly before him and he uses it quite spontaneously and naturally to express many things as well as and other than the literal facts of childhood itself. *The Conditions of Agreement* is concerned at its heart not with childhood or childishness but with spiritual sterility.

The play has on occasion been criticised for its diffuseness, but the criticism seems unwarranted. The play is, in fact, extremely taut in construction, if one takes the marriage and death of Helen as the underlying, organising principle. The story of Helen dominates the whole play, recurring in a mesmeric, incantatory fashion at every new turn of events, its elements being echoed in those events and in the postures of the characters. And at the end, its spirit is exorcised by the Agreement: that A.G. shall tell the story for one last time and then never mention the matter again. And although the play makes no assertion and dramatises no conclusions, there is a distinct suggestion at the end that the exorcism has worked: A.G. has departed; the reading lamp which Nicholas had given to him and which had provided a kind of entrée for him into the Doon household, is left behind with the Doons. The story of infertility and death is done with and Nicholas and Patience are amicably preparing supper together. The flavour of the play is tart, but not altogether bitter; and not unwholesome. The play's one major fault is a slipping back here and there into a rather dull literalism, a failure to maintain throughout its own imaginative heat.

Stylistically, it is interesting in that it gives us another example of Whiting's grappling with that problem of theatrical diction with which he was preoccupied throughout his life and which, though he was always and very consciously working on it, he never entirely solved. He knew (and said many times) that so-called 'naturalistic speech' on the stage was a will-o'-the-wisp, an illusion. He knew it was quite impossible to obtain and that if it *were* possible to create absolutely 'natural' dialogue – indistinguishable from ordinary, everyday speech – then the play would have ceased to be a play at all. All stage speech is stylised, is written within a recognisable mode or convention and obeys the rules of that convention. It may be a unique convention, different from that of all other plays, devised by that one play for its own artistic purpose, as T. S. Eliot claimed, with some justice, he found after the event to be the case with *Murder in the Cathedral.* But even in such a case, the convention is still a recognisable one (I do not mean that it is similar to other modes or conventions but that its own inherent logic makes itself felt, announces itself) and the play recognisably worked within it. So far as language is concerned, the question is not whether it should be 'stylised' or 'realistic', but *how* stylised it should be and what convention of language is viable in a twentieth-century play. To some extent, of course, a dramatist's answers to these questions will be instinctive, uncalculated and spontaneous. To some extent, too, they will be dictated and conditioned by the nature of his vision, the particular segment of experience which he is impelled to reflect. But to *some* extent, especially in the twentieth century, these questions have to be approached by deliberate, reasoned intellectual process. Whiting tended always to a fairly formal language structure, a fairly 'literary' kind of speech (and the word 'literary' is not here intended derogatorily, though in regard to stage dialogue it is often so used). In other words, one of the assumptions of the convention within which he works is that all the language of the play will be articulate, even when used to represent characters who are in themselves inarticulate. This is not as paradoxical as might at first appear: it is, after all, no less illogical to suppose that consistently articulate language implies that all the characters are in their natural state articulate than to suppose that all characters in a Shakespeare play are intended to be poetically sensitive because they all speak poetry. Shakespeare is poetic *about* Shylock, but Shylock himself, as a character, is not poetic (indeed, the entire absence of that kind of sensibility is the most obvious weakness of the man). Similarly Whiting, through the things he makes them say, is articulate *about* his people: it does not follow that they themselves are all articulate or all equally so. It simply means that the style is a basically literary one. Not that this settles the matter, as if one chose styles by number from a catalogue. Whiting was still wrestling with the issue when he wrote that preparatory note for the *The Nomads*, 'Style: harsh, direct, idiomatic: cut the plush.'

In *The Conditions of Agreement*, the literary style – 'the plush' – can be seen beginning to take shape. The language, in spite of its effective colloquialism here and there, is splendidly formal, the speeches – especially the longer ones – shapely, well-formed, intrinsically conscious of their design. As well as the formality of structure, something of the luxuriant vocabulary of *Not a Foot of Land* also remains in the play, though not nearly to the same extent as in the novel, of course: stage dialogue does not give nearly as many opportunities for it as narrative prose. Nevertheless, the love of the exact word, the precise word, the highly coloured (but accurately coloured) word is still there. Interestingly, this is in fact more in evidence in *The Conditions of Agreement* than in *No More A-Roving*, even though the latter stands closer to *Not a Foot of Land* in point of time. The love of archaic diction, not in itself reprehensible (and, indeed, providing in some instances an actual convention within which the language of the play can operate), occasionally led Whiting into downright error or misuse. There are two interesting and rather amusing examples of this in *The Conditions of Agreement*.

On p. 43 of vol. 1 of the Heinemann *Collected Plays*, Bembo is made to say: 'I have arrogated myself to imagine his weaker moments and debased myself to observe . . . his stronger moments.' Obviously what is here intended by the word 'arrogated' is an antonym of 'debased' – some such word as 'elevated'. But to make the antithesis really work (and note, incidentally, that this antithetical structure is an excellent example of the formally structured, non-naturalistic style of speech and dialogue referred to earlier), the words needs a derogatory connotation also, as if to say 'falsely elevated' or 'uplifted myself'. The idea of self-assertion and *arrogance* is present, so the writer's mind has gone to an invented word, 'arroganted'. 'I arroganted myself . . .', meaning 'I made myself arrogant', 'I falsely set myself up . . .' Whiting knows, however, that there is no such word as 'arroganted' and so, by a simple declension, the slipping of a single letter 'n', he moves to 'arrogated' but leaves it to carry the sense of his invented word. In actual fact, the word 'arrogate' means 'falsely to assume' (powers, privileges, etc.). One cannot, within the meaning of the word, arrogate *oneself*; one arrogates *to* oneself the position or power in question. On p. 24 of the same volume, the other example occurs. And here Whiting appears not to know that the word he has used actually does not exist at all. He makes Nicholas say 'You people of the past sometimes come this way: all you wish to do is talk of the past. You revify Emily's memory and her faith in the better dead and forgotten.' It might be supposed that 'revify' was a simple misprint which had crept in when the volume of collected plays was set up in 1969 after Whiting's death, but a scrutiny of the 1946 typescript reveals that *it* also contains the non-existent word. There is no reference to 'revify' in any English or American dictionary except the earlier editions of the OED, which do, in fact, give 'revification' and say it is an erroneous form of, and probably a misprint for 'revivification'. Two or three examples of writers of the seventeenth and eighteenth centuries who used the erroneous form are given, including Steele, in no. 426 of the *Spectator*, so the error is committed in distinguished company. It is just possible – though not very likely – that Whiting knew of this entry and these uses and was deliberately seeking to promote a simpler form of the admittedly clumsy 'revivification'. What seems more probable, however, is that he simply missed out, by accident, one of the two 'vi' bits of the word in preparing the typescript and the mistake was perpetuated in the published play. It would be interesting to know – if anyone now remembers – what actual word was spoken from the stage when the play was produced at the Bristol Little Theatre in 1965.

4

THE CENTRAL PLAYS

I   *Saint's Day* (1946–1948)

Simon Trussler, in his *The Plays of John Whiting* (Gollancz, 1972) dates the writing of *The Conditions of Agreement* as 1948–9 and says that *Saint's Day* was begun before *The Conditions of Agreement*, in 1947. In point of fact, as has already been pointed out, there is in existence a typescript of *The Conditions of Agreement* dated 1946 and a manuscript of *Saint's Day* also dated 1946. So it is true that *Saint's Day* was written earlier than 1948–9 (though not acted until September 1951) but very doubtful indeed whether it was begun before *The Conditions of Agreement*. Whiting himself describes the latter as 'an earlier play' (see p. 78) and in the interview with Tom Milne and Clive Goodwin, published in *Encore* in 1961, he said 'So I sat down and wrote *Saint's Day*. I did write a play before that, but it didn't work out very well.' One could argue that the reference here was to *No More A-Roving*, except that he added 'Recently I rewrote it as a television play.' His only television play is *A Walk in the Desert*, which was shown by the BBC on 25 September 1960: while it may seem quite difficult for anyone but its author to regard it as a new version of *The Conditions of Agreement*, it manifestly *cannot* be regarded as having any connection at all with *No More A-Roving* (a play which in all Whiting's public utterances he never mentioned once). The television play does have a spiritual affinity with *The Conditions of Agreement* and, like the latter, does centre on a character whose physical lameness has produced a corresponding mental limp. One must conclude, therefore, that the play Whiting 'recently rewrote as a television play' was *The Conditions of Agreement* and that this was, therefore, the play written before *Saint's Day* that 'didn't work out very well'. In any case, the fact that in 1946 *The Conditions of Agreement* was already in typescript while *Saint's Day* was still in manuscript would in itself seem conclusive.

127

(There are two versions of *Saint's Day* in typescript one dated 1947 and the other 1948.)

The internal evidence of the plays themselves would certainly support the contention: to move from *The Conditions of Agreement* to *Saint's Day* is to move from the first signs of the mature Whiting to the full realisation of that maturity, though the quality and maturity of *Saint's Day* was not recognised by most observers at the time. It is possible to see now, however, that it is not only a very fine play and a major work of considerable stature, but is also probably its author's best. On the occasion of its first production it was greeted with derision by almost all the critics (J. C. Trewin was the one important and honourable exception and even he found himself defeated by the apocalyptic final act) and it became at once the object of fierce controversy, being defended chiefly by professional theatre people against the denigration of critics and the indifference of audiences.

Whiting had submitted *Saint's Day* in 1951 as an entry in the playwriting competition organised by the Arts Theatre, under its director, Alec Clunes, as its contribution to the Festival of Britain. Nine hundred and ninety-seven scripts had been received and the three judges – Peter Ustinov, Christopher Fry and Clunes himself – decided to pick out three of these for actual production, the prize to be awarded on the strength of the play's impact in the theatre rather than on the evidence of a mere reading of the script. The other two plays chosen were *Poor Judas* by Enid Bagnold and *Right Side Up* by C. E. Webber.[1] Each play was presented, with a distinguished cast, for three weeks at the Arts Theatre, *Saint's Day* being the last of the three to appear.

The critics' reviews of it were not only universally bad; they were more than usually savage and contemptuous. It received not a single good notice, or even a moderately good one. 'If these three plays are really the best of a big bunch, then it is a sorry look-out for the native theatre. As for the one judged best of the three, it quite defies description, far less analysis' said Iain Hamilton in *The Spectator*. Alan Dent in the *News Chronicle* declared it to be a 'strange, mad, baffling little play' and added 'At least it may be said that it is too startling to be tedious, too scatter-brained to be a bore. There is a queer kind of fascination in its stark and staring inconsequence.' The simple-minded critic of *The Stage* (not, in any case, a journal to which one would go for a reliable expression of opinion about plays) found *Saint's Day* 'meaningless' and demonstrated the naiveté of his own approach by justifying his view in these terms: 'Doubtless a profound symbolism lay behind the incomprehensible story but it is not much use being symbolic unless you can convey your ideas to others.' 'This extraordinary hotch-potch is going to carry off the prize, I suppose . . .' ventured Harold Conway in the *Evening Standard* before the result

John Whiting in 1954, one of the bright young men and great hopes of the theatre (Photograph Houston Rogers)

John Whiting in 1944 at the time of writing *Not a Foot of Land*

Scott Harrold, Michael Hordern, Valerie White and Robert Urquhart in the 1951 production of *Saint's Day* directed by Stephen Murray (Photograph John Vickers)

James Bree, Michael Hordern, Barry Justice, Sheila Allen and David William in the 1965 revival of *Saint's Day* directed by David Jones (Photograph Reg Wilson)

Rowland Emett's set for the original 1951 production of *A Penny for a Song* (Photograph Houston Rogers)

H. Gutschwager, Walter Bluhm and Clemens Hasse as Jonathan Watkins, Lamprett and Humpage in the first German production of *A Penny for a Song* in 1953 (Photograph Heinz Köster)

Diana Wynyard as Catherine de Troyes and Robert Flemyng as Forster in the first production of *Marching Song* (Photograph Angus McBean)

The first German production of *Marching Song*, at the Düsseldorf State Theatre in 1955: it was directed by Gristan Gründgens, who also played Forster (right foreground, nearest camera) (Photograph Dieter Heggemann)

of the competition was announced. *The Times* found *Saint's Day* 'of a badness that must be called indescribable . . . fantasy plunging portentously in a sea so dark and wide and stormy that the shores of reality are rarely glimpsed' . . . And the *Daily Telegraph* said 'John Whiting's *Saint's Day*, seen at the Arts last night, may have been more ambitious than the disappointing predecessors. It was certainly less rewarding.' T. C. Worsley, in the *New Statesman* made a comparison of the three competition plays thus:

> Miss Bagnold, though she launched far enough into
> symbolism as to be incomprehensible as a whole, couldn't
> quite discard a degree of realism which made stretches
> of her play all too plain sailing. Mr Webber's *Right Side
> Up*, though it escaped realism entirely, was founded on a
> fable so thin that we could see right through it. Mr
> Whiting's *Saint's Day* alone took the plunge into waters so
> deep that he never surfaced into comprehensibility for one
> single moment. I am quite prepared to accept the judges'
> decision, which must have been based on the view that the
> degree and kind of badness were such that only a promising
> writer could have achieved them. But I cannot go all the
> way with them; I hold back where they, joined now by
> Mr Tyrone Guthrie and Mr Peter Brook, recommend
> the play as an exciting and stimulating evening. I found it
> the opposite.

The critic of the *Daily Herald* was ready after its first two acts to concede the prize to *Saint's Day* but went on to say 'Alas, the third act proved a bewildering nightmare. If the last act, largely a debate on death while the artist paints with his dead wife as a model, has any meaning, it escaped me.' Philip Hope-Wallace in the *Manchester Guardian* resorted to the same adjective as several other critics: 'Maxwell Anderson and Strindberg in consort could not be more portentous. We sit stunned, anxious to catch on if possible (for the high-reaching earnest endeavour is not so common in our theatre that we can brush it aside because it is painfully boring). But Strindberg certainly would have started fewer hares running. In its present form the play makes just too many demands.' The *Daily Express* critic agreed: 'I did not understand a word of the plot . . . I did not understand the violent shootings, a village fire and the hanging of the principals by three lunatic soldiers . . . and finally, I did not understand why the audience – which included Tyrone Guthrie and Christopher Fry – were so patient with it all.' And another of the 'popular' dailies, the *Daily Graphic*, sounded much the same note – 'Despite its occasional dramatic power, *Saint's Day* is sententious and obscure', it said. J. C. Trewin, the dramatic critic and theatre historian, was in Edinburgh for the International Festival when *Saint's Day* opened in London. Reading his colleagues' reviews in the train on his way back to London he wondered what had gone wrong with so important a competition and why the judges had awarded the prize to a play which had been so thoroughly trounced by the critics. The next day he went to see for himself and found himself much moved though occasionally puzzled. 'I came out into the clanging street', he wrote afterwards, 'angry and baffled, yet haunted, oppressed, unable to throw off the weight of that dark house, that tortured world of query and symbol. And I wondered whether it could be right to dismiss simply as turgid nonsense a play that had so powerful an effect upon the mind: one that clung and would not release its hold . . . In my heart I could not reject it . . . It still flares smokily in the recollection . . .' (See Introduction, *Plays of the Year*, 1952.)

The fact that the critics were wrong, even that they were almost unanimously wrong, need not surprise us greatly. The history of the arts is littered with examples of purblind contemporary judgements. And in the case of some of the examples quoted above from the 'popular' press, the surprise is less still: no play of serious artistic intention is ever likely to receive their commendation and approval or, if it does, it will as like as not receive them for reasons quite unconnected with its actual merits. They are for a jig or a tale of bawdry or they sleep. But in the case of the more thoughtful critics the *reasons* given for their dislike are significant. All the talk of portentousness, obscurity, symbolism and sententiousness, coming from so many different critics, is a fairly sure indication that *Saint's Day* was operating in a mode to which they were unaccustomed, was breaking new ground. Just as it obviously owed nothing to the 'drawing-room comedy' or the realistic-naturalistic school, it had virtually no connections either with the only meaningful revolt, in England, against this school, namely the overtly poetic verse plays of Eliot, Fry, Ronald Duncan, Norman Nicholson, Patric Dickinson and others. It should be added also, as Ronald Hayman has pointed out in his Introduction to *The Collected Plays*, that though the style and manner of Whiting's plays was new, unique and highly idiosyncratic and though with the benefit of hindsight we can now recognise them in general spirit as the precursors of the 'absurdist' plays, yet there is no direct line of descent from them. They did not start a movement or a school of writing; they do not have obvious progeny; they have remained, like their author, slightly aloof and constitute a separate, distinct, isolated and highly original body of work.

Paul Southman, who has been mentioned several times already in connection with earlier works, is the central figure of *Saint's Day*. He is an octogenarian poet–pamphleteer, rejected long ago by society because of his savage and satirical sallies against the Establishment. He lives in a large, once-elegant house on the outskirts of a small village 'in

England'. The exact location is not specified (in the radio play about Southman the location was given as Essex). Some dates are very exactly specified, however: the house was built in the year 1775, say the stage directions; and the action of the play takes place on 25 January. It isn't mentioned in the play, but 25 January is the date assigned by tradition to the conversion of St Paul. It is also Paul Southman's birthday.

With Southman in his now-dilapidated house live his grand-daughter Stella, who is pregnant, her husband Charles and Paul's servant, John Winter (though the simple word 'servant' inadequately describes this strange character). Charles, who is twenty and twelve years younger than his wife, is an artist; on one wall of the room is a huge, half-finished mural on which he is working. The painting represents five human figures and a dog 'grouped about an, as yet, unspecified sixth person'. The household is a poverty-stricken one: Charles, though he was recognised as a prodigy at fifteen, now refuses to exhibit or try to sell his paintings; Paul Southman has refused, ever since he was hounded out of London twenty-five years before, to write anything at all or have anything to do with the outside world, which he regards with implacable hatred. The effects of their poverty are aggravated by the fact that Paul insists on treating the neighbouring villagers as active enemies, regarding them as representatives of the world that rejected him and as a sort of advance guard of an approaching army thrown against him. He speaks constantly in military metaphor and uses John Winter as an aide-de-camp, sending him out on skirmishes or to reconnoitre the current situation and balance of forces.

On this 25 January, they are expecting a visitor, an emissary from that literary world that drove Southman out twenty-five years before. He is Robert Procathren, a distinguished young poet and critic, who has been deputed by sixty other poets and writers to bring a presentation volume written by them in honour of Paul Southman's eighty-third birthday and to bring him to a dinner in his honour in London. It is designed as a gesture of goodwill and reconciliation. While Southman, Charles and Stella wait for Procathren to arrive they hear from John Winter, who has been down into the village to try to obtain food on credit, that three soldiers have escaped from a detention camp and are now marauding and looting in the village. Paul is exhilarated by the news and begins to talk excitedly of military strategy, alliance with the soldiers against the village, and so on, but Stella is suddenly terribly afraid, not so much of the soldiers as of the emptiness and barrenness and lovelessness of the life she has had to live, cooped up in this house since she was seven years old: 'As for myself', she says, 'if I die today my eternal happiness will depend on the tiny memory of you, Charles – you, on your first visit to this place, standing in the doorway, consciously picaresque and handing me the flowers from your hat. I thought then that we were to be lovers, but from our marriage you gave me no understanding, no explanation of the mysteries, only a child conceived in violence.'

When Procathren arrives, Stella takes him aside and asks for his help. She does not specify exactly what help she has in mind, except to urge that Procathren should keep in touch with her in the future and that Paul Southman should be 'restored to greatness in the world'. She asks this, she says, for the sake of her unborn child – 'In that way there can be a future for my child.' At one point she refers to the unborn child as 'the child Paul'. Procathren, though mystified, promises to help her in any way he can and promises to keep in touch with her in the future. A moment later, Procathren is asked to make an even stranger alliance: Paul Southman discovers that his dog is dead and immediately assumes that it has been poisoned by the villagers, though Charles and Stella assure him that it died of old age. He fetches his loaded pistol, swears revenge and asks Charles and Procathren if they will join him. Charles at once agrees but Procathren demurs:

PROCATHREN: I cannot – dare not – become engaged in something that is
    of no personal – no personal . . .
SOUTHMAN: Advantage, Mr Procathren?
PROCATHREN: No, sir! Not advantage, but . . .
SOUTHMAN: I have explained the circumstances to you. You are an intelli-
    gent man – you have undoubtedly understood. Will you or will you not
    help me?
PROCATHREN: My personal position . . .
SOUTHMAN: I don't understand your doubt and hesitation. With your
    admiration of myself surely you believe what I have told you to be true.
PROCATHREN: Of course.
SOUTHMAN: We need your help.
PROCATHREN: I will help you in any indirect way I can . . .
SOUTHMAN: No qualifications! Will you or will you not help me? I shall
    not ask again.
                    (*There is a pause*)
PROCATHREN: I will.
STELLA: You are being untrue to me!
PROCATHREN: What can I do? What else can I do?

Having contemptuously dismissed an appeal for help against the soldiers from the vicar of the village, the Reverend Giles Aldus, who comes to the house in great fear and distress, Charles and Paul give Procathren the pistol and ask him whether he knows how to use it and whether he will be willing to use it against the villagers. He says he will use it against the villagers but has never handled one before. While he is cautiously fingering it, it goes off. Apparently no harm is done; no one in the room is hurt. But when they try to open the door, they find it blocked by the body of Stella. She was just about to re-enter the room when the bullet, penetrating the door, struck her and killed her. The discovery works a sudden and desperate change in Procathren for whom, although the killing was accidental, the incident raises all the issues of ultimate personal responsibility. When the soldiers arrive, he asks their help. 'You're going to run away?' one of them asks. 'No, my friend', says Procathren 'I'm going to run towards the event. A thing I have never done before – but now I have the authority. Let us go.' He goes off towards the village with the three soldiers. As he leaves, he meets Paul Southman who is coming downstairs from the room where Stella has been laid.

SOUTHMAN: You killed her.
PROCATHREN: I did.
SOUTHMAN: Why, Robert?
(ROBERT is staring at PAUL)
PROCATHREN: Beast-face!
SOUTHMAN: Robert!
PROCATHREN: Beast-face!
SOUTHMAN: Robert!
PROCATHREN :   Satisfied? Satisfied by the shift of responsibility, eh?
SOUTHMAN: Robert!
PROCATHREN: Shan't step from under it this time. Surprised, eh?

From this point on, Robert Procathren becomes the mainspring of the plot (though not of the action). With the soldiers he goes to see Giles Aldus and talks to him to such good effect about the futility of a faith and belief that the parson, in tears, burns all his books and in doing so sets fire to the house. The fire spreads from the house to the church and to other houses and by the end of the day the entire village is destroyed. Some of the village women, one of them bringing a child with her, take refuge in Southman's house and he, instinctively recognising the broadening and deepening of the whole experience (though on the surface apparently taking refuge in madness), now withdraws his hostility and welcomes them. Meanwhile, Procathren – accompanied by the soldiers – has paraded through the burning village, talking to everyone in a terrifying way. Finally, they return to the house and the soldiers, on orders from Procathren, take out Charles and Paul and hang them. Charles has spent his last hours calmly working on the mural, using the dead Stella as a model and filling in on the painting the one missing figure.

More nearly, perhaps, than any other example that one could think of, *Saint's Day* approaches the status of that notoriously elusive phenomenon, the twentieth-century tragedy. Though its surface has great complexity, richness, even obscurity, its central design is essentially simple and it has something of that monolithic quality which was one of the characteristics of the classical tragedy. It is as if there were a great smooth steel shaft driven down the middle of it, giving form and firmness and providing a single-minded motive power. There is no need

– nor would it be helpful or appropriate – to take up here the general argument concerning the possibility of full tragic expression in the drama of a divisive and fragmented society: it does not matter whether *Saint's Day* be categorised as a tragedy or not, so long as its vision is perceived and its purpose recognised. Nevertheless, that perception and recognition may be sharpened if some note is taken of the close resemblance of the play to the classic tragic form and if the sense attaching to that form in the great standard examples of it is borne in mind. (Not that Whiting was engaged upon or interested in any academic exercise designed to demonstrate the feasibility of writing a modern tragedy – such a self-conscious exercise would, in any case, only produce a new *Gorboduc*; as, indeed, O'Neill did in *Mourning Becomes Electra*.) The greatest single advantage of taking cognisance of the fact that *Saint's Day* does in its form instinctively seek the true tragic mode is that an awareness of this will at least protect from the danger of judging the play by criteria that are false to it: it is not a character study in the naturalistic sense and its chain of causation is not a psychological one, any more than *Macbeth*'s is, or that of Racine's *Phèdre*. The psychology of the characters is acutely observed and accurately represented in the play, but the dramatic reasons for movement from one crux to another at the nodal points of the play are not psychological reasons; they are spiritual ones. It is, therefore, a false criticism – and one that some critics have been tempted to make – to say of the characters in *Saint's Day* that they would not have responded in the way they do 'in that situation', if by this phrase is meant a situation like that in the play but assessed in terms of ordinary, factual existence. They would not, of course: but we *know* what they would do in ordinary, everyday existence – we do not need to be told. What the play sets out to explore is the movement of the human spirit underneath those everyday events and occurrences. In short, we are dealing with a tragic poem, not a documentary sociological report. Perhaps the best example in the play of this difference of viewpoint is the effect on Procathren of the death of Stella. In 'real' life (which is, in fact, not real, having less contact with any ultimate sense of reality than has the poetic life), Procathren would have been very upset, Paul and Charles would have comforted him with the assurance that, though terrible, it was a complete accident for which he must try not to blame himself, someone would have called the police, an ambulance would have taken the body of Stella away, an inquest would have been held, the coroner would have repeated the assurance that Procathren was not to blame, a verdict of 'Death by Misadventure' would have been recorded, with a rider about the more careful use of firearms and Procathren would have spent the rest of his life, when he was alone and quiet in his room, half-wondering if he *were* to blame for Stella's death and mourning silently inside himself 'If only I . . .' Since this is not a play about the efficiency of coroners' inquests or the proper use of firearms, but about the progress of the soul, it misses out all the factual intermediaries and goes direct to that silent inward murmur 'Was it my fault?' and this it seizes upon, brings out into the light and dramatises: and it dramatises it not from the point of view of legalities or community ethics or the effect on the mind of the doer but from the point of view of how the deed and its antecedents and its results appear in – if the metaphor were still viable – the eyes of God. All this one deduces, if one is attentive and sympathetic, from the form of the play itself: it is tragic in the classic sense and declares itself to be so.

The element in it which first alerts us to the play's heightened and extended purpose is the language: as Christopher Fry noted, in a lecture on Whiting's plays read to the Royal Society of Literature on 17 October 1963, 'a natural speech which, without strain or pretension, sets up vibrations beyond itself'. Based on, though not a mere reproduction of, the quick interchange and muted, restrained expression of conversational prose, the language at the beginning of the play is spare and taut, capable of that sardonically abrasive humour so characteristic of Whiting, yet capable also of conveying indirectly, just under its surface, a sense of menace and tension and impending disaster. For most of the first act the subdued, almost naturalistic tone persists, sketching in and fixing the surface of life from which point the tragic statement, when it comes, will take its departure and thus establishing the frame of reference for the experience which is to be reflected. Now and again both the tone and the form of the dialogue rises – especially with Stella – to a more formal rhetoric which seems perfectly apt and which hints at the play's sense of direction. At the end of the act, it develops with a sharp upward lift that deserts the laconic exchanges of everyday conversation for a speech of Stella's that is three pages long and that owes nothing to the stammering incoherence and inconsequence of off-stage talk. It is constructed with a fine sweep and a progressively deepening intensity to a point towards its end at which is quite literally heard the trumpet of doom. It is the trumpet blown by the marauding soldiers as they approach: the sound is fairly distant on the first trumpet call; then nearer; and nearer still; finally, as the act ends, it is 'blatant, raucous, defiant'. The language and tension of Stella's speech are so framed as to lead quite naturally to the climax of the trumpet call and are entirely successful in doing so. Stella's statement of her fear is couched in non-conversational prose and this in itself should alert us to the fact that she speaks not only for herself but for the central purpose of the play at this moment. Naturalistic reporting has been transcended:

> But try to remember, Charles, that I am a woman – try to be
> conscious of that at other times than when I am naked. I
> am a woman and I have a child inside me. Does that explain

anything to you? Pregnant women have delusions, they say.
Do they? I only know that I am possessed by a loneliness
hard to bear – a loneliness which I should imagine attends
forsaken lovers. (*She stands silent – then*): Lovers. I am
innocent of such things. I have imagined what they do and
what they say – these lovers. It seems they find a great
delight in music and solicitude, in whispering and smiling,
in touching and nakedness, in night. And from these things
they make a fabric of memory which will serve them well
in their life after death when they will be together but
alone. They are wise, for that is the purpose of any memory
– of any experience – to give foundation to the state of
death. Understand that whatever we do today in this house
– this damned house – will provide some of the material
for our existence in death and you understand my fear. No
one who has lived as I have lived could be happy in death.
It is impossible.

One need hardly labour to prove that such a speech is far beyond the
range of naturalistic dialogue, both in form and content; and only those,
surely, who feel that all stage dialogue must be an uninflated copy of
ordinary conversation will want to quibble about its power and its
appropriateness, or to retort that 'people don't talk like that'.[2] The importance of this long speech lies far beyond the portrayal of the individual suffering of Stella, though the wider implications are allowed to
rise naturally from that suffering and to draw authority from it. The
speech as a whole proclaims the play's true-tragic objective (and I
now use the word 'tragic' in the full classic Aristotelian sense), summarising and epitomising that objective in a single sentence: 'The
purpose of any memory, of any experience, is to give foundation to the
state of death.' This, properly considered, removes both the terror and
the finality from death. The horror is not that life should be enclosed
by death but that, unless we exercise every nerve towards the maintaining of a sensitivity and a compassion, life will be enclosed in meaning-
lessness – death will be empty. Though the play throughout is drenched in death (Whiting himself once compared this particular play
with Webster), in the light of this speech of Stella's, those critics who
have seen the play as a nihilist document that regards death as a
ghoulish, Gothic horror have, I think, been incorrect. Stella's long
speech accepts the fact of death with calmness and dignity, regarding
it not only as inevitable but also as a natural and proper part of life,
not an unnatural and annihilating terror, though what fearful and
fearsome humanity can make of it is terrible. The consideration of
life as a preparation for a proper death is the true business and the proper field of tragedy and this speech finally affirms and makes explicit

what the whole of Act 1 has, in a rising curve, hinted at – that this is the frame of reference within which this play proposes to operate.

In the same way that the speech as a whole announces the general tragic intention, so one part of it vividly adumbrates the tragic method and structure itself: 'Whatever we do today in this house – this damned house – will provide some of the material for our existence in death.' One can prune the statement still further: 'today in this house – this damned house'. It is a description of the unities of time and place and a proclamation of the power that tragedy gains from them. The day, from the birth of dawn to the death of evening, from man's uprising to his lying down, is a paradigm for the life span; and the house, our dwelling, the place where we are for this brief span of a day, a life, is a paradigm both for the world and the body. The phrase 'this damned house', with its echo and reminder of the House of Atreus, reinforces this parallel: the house is cursed, as humanity itself is cursed. And the humanness of humanity and the very life of humanity grows from the same root as the curse grows from: they are of the same fabric: the life of the house and the doom on the house are inextricably intertwined and exist because of each other. It is well to remember that this chorus-like *aperçu* is spoken by a pregnant woman who has a sense of danger and a premonition of death. This single sentence reflects the exact intent of the tragic form's predilection for the unities of time and place, not applied arbitrarily as 'rules' in the eighteenth-century manner, but used when the tragic fable allows us both a structural device giving strength and clarity and a poetic device deepening insight and sensitivity. The play, in spite of its luxuriance of surface, is spare and austere and, as Whiting himself said, simple. The unity of structure just noted adds to these qualities and, in doing so, increases the play's power and, so to say, its poetic credibility. The play does, in fact, observe the tragic unities with almost startling consistency: the action begins at 9.30 a.m. with the family rising for breakfast; it ends at approximately 9 p.m. with the death of Paul and Charles, Stella being already dead; it stays within the one room of the house and preserves the purity and intensity of its artistic purpose astonishingly. It is fraught with a sense of menace and violence, but none of the violence takes place on stage – not even the death of Stella: we see the gun go off accidentally, but we do not see Stella die; her body is brought on later. In Act 3 the postman acts as The Messenger, bringing the news of the burning of the books and of the village and the destruction of Giles Aldus. The hanging of Paul and Charles takes place off-stage. What is portrayed on-stage is the progress of the spiritual motion, the outcome and result of the physical; and this is what provides the most important unity, the only truly Aristotelian one, the unity of 'action'. The action in *Saint's Day* is the movement towards final resolution of three great interconnected antitheses: Love and Violence; Contemplation and Action (within which is contained the more specialised and limited antithesis of Art and Life); Civilisation and Barbarism. These operate throughout the play obliquely, not by overt pronouncement and explication. The result of the action or movement, as in any tragedy, is the securing of an equilibrium between the opposing forces of each antithetical pair: not that one force 'wins', but that the matching tensions are recognised and the resultant poise and equilibrium is celebrated in a moment of calm, which is what happens at the end of *Saint's Day*. The deaths of Paul and Charles are proper, because both have deserted, turned their backs on life, become negative forces: though an unleashed and indiscriminate barbarism kills them, it would be artistically improper for them to be reprieved, because their deaths are *logical* and reprieve by any *deus ex machina* would be sentimental. But the countering force is there, nevertheless, in the figure of the child at the end of the play. She is one of the refugees from the burning village, brought to the house by her mother. Paul has talked to her while he was waiting to be taken away, talked gently and sympathetically, played a little game with her, danced for her and got her to wish him 'Many happy returns of the day'. So some of Paul's negative qualities have been redeemed by the child; he has regained his faith in life and love, has made partial expiation. After the soldiers have taken him away, the final moment of the play is given to the child:

The CHILD, *detaching herself from the group of* VILLAGERS, *moves across the room to where Stella's body lies. The* CHILD *stares from above at the dead face, and, extending a finger, touches for a moment the closed eyes. It is then the* MOTHER *calls to the* CHILD)
JUDITH: Stella! (*Startled by the call the* CHILD *stumbles among the bones[3] and so moves from the body. In doing so she accidentally knocks against the table and cries out in pain*) Stella, dear child! (*But the* CHILD *moves on and seeing the green scarf,* CHARLES'S *present to* PAUL, *lying on the floor, she picks it up and puts it around her neck*) Stella! We are strangers here, Stella.
The CHILD *takes up the copy of* Alice in Wonderland *from the table. The trumpet suddenly sounds from the garden: a raucous tune. The* CHILD, *with the book in her hand, performs a grave dance to the music.*

This dance is, in a sense, a continuation of Paul's dance performed for the child just before his death. He had asked her to dance for him then but she had been reticent and shy and had not done so. Now she dances for him as the play finishes. And her name is Stella, the same name as that borne by the pregnant woman who has died. The star of life still shines, even while the trumpet sounds for the death of Paul and Charles. (Notice, by the way, the grave formality, the non-naturalistic treatment of language, in the mother's last address to her child – 'Stella, dear child': it is intended to be more than a mere representation of realistic conversation.)

The co-existence at the core of humanity of the equal forces of love and violence, which is represented by the fine balance at the end of the play (not only in the antithetical structure of Paul *v* The Child, but also within the character of Paul himself), has been given expression both directly and obliquely throughout the play. In particular, one may note an overt and explicit statement of it by Stella (the grown-up Stella) early in Act 2, where she again functions as a chorus to the action. There is a clear indication in the stage directions that Whiting intended her to be seen in this way: he stylises the scene, thus:

STELLA (*She cries out*):   Then what is going to happen? (*There is a complete cessation of activity whilst* STELLA *speaks. She is swept by a sudden storm of fore-knowledge, awful in its clarity. The men, silent and unmoving, watch her*) Careful! We are approaching the point of deviation. At one moment there is laughter and conversation and a progression: people move and speak smoothly and casually, their breathing is controlled and they know what to do. Then there occurs a call from another room, the realisation that a member of the assembly is missing, the sudden shout into the dream and the waking to find the body with the failing heart lying in the corridor – with the twisted limbs at the foot of the stairs – the man hanging from the beam or the child floating, drowned, in the garden pool. Careful! Be careful! We are approaching that point. The moment of the call from another room.

Stella's image of the 'point of deviation' is an especially interesting one: it is the point at which life suddenly displays the other side of its nature: the ordinary comfort gives place to an extraordinary fear, the warmth of everyday contacts is exposed to the chill of disaster; the inherent ambivalences make themselves felt and known; love gives way to violence. The speech arises out of the struggle for Procathren's sympathy and help: Stella has begged it for the sake of the harmony and the preservation of the family group and for the sake of her child's future. Paul has asked it for the coming attack on the village. It is Paul who answers Stella's prophetic speech by saying: 'We are eagerly awaiting the shout from another room, for we know from whom it will come and to whom it will be directed. Also we are aware of the discovery – the destruction of the village – and so we have nothing to fear.' His sense of the 'point of deviation' is not only coarser and cruder than Stella's: it is also less profound. He translates her clairvoyant realisation of the nature of human reality into the gross terms of his own obsessive hatred and scorn. Trussler, incidentally, finds this speech of Stella's 'uneasy on the contemporary ear' and 'fraudulently ambiguous in its semantics' though he says later that the language of the play generally 'has an entirely successful formality and yet, syntactically, is casual and idiomatic'. Christopher Fry, too, felt some uneasiness about this one speech of Stella's. Whiting himself may have unconsciously set off this line of criticism when he said, about this particular speech, in the interview with *Encore* in 1961, 'That, of course, is a parody of Eliot . . . I used all sorts of literary devices and tests [in the writing of *Saint's Day*] such as parody and memories.' It is true that this speech does have an echo of Eliot about it but it is hard to see why this should be a disadvantage. Provided Stella's role at that moment is understood to be that of Chorus (in the same way that the characters in *The Family Reunion*, for example, sometimes function as Chorus) it would seem that both the formal abstractness of the language and the clairvoyant awareness of the content, used to fix and call attention to one of the themes and one of the nodal points of the play, are both entirely acceptable. The *deliberate* use of an Eliot echo, moreover, is no more than another example of that open and declared theatricality – the admission by a play that it knows it *is* a play – which one has noted in other Whiting's works. The speech is theatrically powerful in itself and the sense it conveys of the approach of a moment of irrevocable decision is neither untrue in itself nor out of keeping with the tone of the play as a whole. Both technically and poetically the speech would appear to strengthen rather than weaken the play.

The sense of life as being poised eternally between contemplation and action rests chiefly upon the figures of Paul and Charles. Socrates maintained that the unexamined life is not worth living and it is the artist's duty, along with the philosopher's, to examine. But to do so he must cultivate an objectivity, he must to a certain extent and in a certain sense withdraw from society, he must be in the world but not of it; and in such a withdrawal there are always the twin dangers of losing touch with reality on the one hand and of becoming spiritually self-centred and self-indulgent on the other. This is the irreducible dilemma of all artists and though neither Paul nor Charles spend time, as characters in the play, debating the issue, the issue is nevertheless constantly felt because of their presence, and the attempts by Stella and by Procathren (before his own disintegration) to persuade them to return to society and exercise their vision within society's bounds provide the other side of this equation. *Can* an artist live in an ivory tower? If he can, *should* he? In any case, both Paul and Charles have withdrawn from society not for the sake of objectivity and perspective but out of scorn, hatred and a desire for revenge. Now the despising by the artist of the corruptions and complacencies of society and his rejection of them are reactions which are both understandable and necessary: there is a nobility in the singleness of purpose, integrity of intention and refusal to compromise that prompts these responses. But to sit for twenty-five years nursing a grudge and fabricating an imaginary enemy out of a group of witless, but largely innocent villagers, is both childish and deadly. Paul and Charles are highly ambivalent figures: which of them is the more culpable – Paul for persisting in a blinkered hatred for so long, or Charles for giving in to despair so soon?

The dramatic and organic antithesis of civilisation and barbarism, which in a way contains all the other conflicts, just as it is also contained by them, is pointed up most vividly in the figures of Procathren and Melrose (the leader of the three soldiers). Melrose is all the unthinking, conscienceless violence and indifference of all humanity: he is that most evil of manifestations, the man who claims to be morally neutral. To Procathren, whom he has corrupted and debauched, he says, when the latter orders him to kill Paul and Charles:

> 'You're the boss now, you know. You can't get away from
> it now. If you want to order people like me around, you've
> got to take the responsibility – you've got to. It's always been
> like that. God knows, I wouldn't have it any other way. But
> it makes me laugh sometimes. "Melrose do such-and-such!"
> "Yes, sir!" – and then I look down and see their eyes and
> their eyes are asking me "Melrose, you think that decision
> is right, don't you? If you think I'm wrong for God's sake
> don't do it!" But I do it whatever I think – if I can be
> bothered to think.'

And to Charles, to whom he explains casually that they are going to hang both him and Paul, he says:

> 'Bobby doesn't think I'm capable. He's dared me to do it.
> That's a silly thing to do, isn't it? What does he think I
> am? What does he think I shall feel? You're nothing to
> me. Neither's the old man. Nobody's anything to me –
> because there is nobody – hasn't been for years. I care for
> nothing. They put it right when they said I was an
> "incorrigible". Look at me, what do you see?'

'A monster', says Charles, and Melrose replies:

> 'That's through your eyes – and quite natural. I don't take
> offence. But Bobby can't see me that way. And why?
> Because he's lived in the world where people – well, where
> they behave . . . You shouldn't have done it, you know.
> You've brought this on yourselves. People like us shouldn't
> do such things to people like that – people who live away out
> there with women and music. You've struck him very deep.'

Melrose is a terrifying figure. Though he reminds one sharply of Webster's Bosola and Flamineo, he is also instantly recognisable as a peculiarly mid-twentieth-century creature, one that was to become increasingly familiar in the plays of the sixties: it is with a shock that one recollects that Whiting caught him and fixed him so vividly as early as 1948, long before Joe Orton or Edward Bond. His type is the polar opposite from the civilised, decent and urbane Procathren's: and when Procathren suddenly disintegrates as a result of being brought into physical contact with an actual deed of violence (even though an accidental one), it is logical that his transformation should pitch him straight into the arms of Melrose. Procathren's liberal humanism could have faced the *idea* of evil and of brutal death, has, indeed, faced it and dealt with it before this, but the physical, animal fact of it and of his own complicity in it is too much for him. He suddenly sees dramatised before him the fact that the human race, which through centuries of breeding has produced a Leonardo da Vinci and a Goethe, is exactly and precisely the same human race that has produced a Himmler and a Stalin. And the line between the two strains suddenly looks frighteningly narrow. Procathren, as a civilised and cultured man, has always felt that in his minor and humble way he partook of something of the sense and quality of Leonardo, of Mozart, of Shakespeare. And he did, of course: it was true. But also and equally, he shared his humanity with Hitler and all other unspeakable monsters. The realisation is enough to throw him off his carefully devised and carefully guarded balance. The ease with which the civilised values can thus be overthrown by the growl of the ever-present beast is no indictment or condemnation of civilisation, but rather a warning of the need for constant vigilance and an assertion of the need for the preservation of civilisation's values, fragile though they may be, in the face of the ruthless political world. But the civilisation must be real, not a self-conscious affectation and it must be founded upon love, understanding and a real acceptance by individuals of their real and ultimate responsibility in all things: one must recognise and accept *and admit* the effect, on the interlocked and swaying forces within the human consciousness, of one's own stance, one's *persona*. One cannot contract out by some technical or legalistic definition; when the chicanery and double-talk of the law courts are applied to moral questions, morality and civilisation have already disappeared. Procathren, faced suddenly with the challenge, fails to stand firm. He fails, first, to recognise Stella's appeal for love and understanding, facing it with an unapprehending bewilderment. And then, trying to be diplomatic, he hesitates when the course of violence is proposed to him – violence in a good cause, be it noted. It is at that point that Stella cries to him 'You are being untrue to me!' From that moment he is locked in the dilemma of the twin existences of human barbarity and human compassion, both real, both as natural as is the life breath that sustains both. As with Oedipus, the riddles proposed by the Sphinx, though difficult, were capable of solution, the riddles proposed by human nature, not. In this fact the seat of tragedy subsists. And in the collapse of Procathren's humanism can be seen an image of the collapse of the religious and humanistic faith of Western civilisation after the Second World War. It is the genius of the play that, whilst faithfully and vividly mirroring the spirit of its own time in this way, it manages to transcend the disintegration of that time and synthesise a new, though sombre, faith, to reinstate a sense of human order and idealism, through the medium of tragedy. The play looks, in other words, beyond the immediate catastrophe to the possibility of reconciliation and recollection and contrives to do so (wonder of wonders for a twentieth-century play!) without being sentimental about it. '*Saint's Day* was written immediately after the dropping of the first atom bomb', said Christopher Fry in his lecture to the Royal Society of Literature. 'The whole play shudders with the fact.' He is right: it does (even including an extravagant – too extravagant – and complicated metaphor in which the infamous mushroom cloud is compared with a flower in the sky); but it seeks to subsume even this ultimate act of human barbarism in a broader vision of the human condition, one based on a longer view of mankind's civilised possibilities. The result is not a piece of slightly glib and slightly sentimental optimism, such as Fry's *A Sleep of Prisoners* (written about the same time as *Saint's Day* and first acted in the same year), but neither is it a piece of easy and modish cynicism or fashionable despair.

But Procathren, though he vividly illustrates one part of the inextricable human problem, is not the tragic protagonist. That is Paul Southman. He began as an idealist, a man with a fierce belief in human dignity and integrity, scornful of all compromise and courageous in his untiring and unremitting defence of standards and principles. He developed his skills to the utmost of their potential and he used them in the service of humanity. This is the kind of person the play invites us to imagine as the author of that pamphlet, *The Abolition of Printing*, which struck such a blow for the freedom of man's spirit. Since those days, however, the great figure has crumbled in two ways and for both, though the errors are understandable and though in the circumstances much might be said by way of mitigation and excuse, Southman must accept the ultimate responsibility. It is true that the load was hard to bear; but it is also true that he failed to bear it: this is the fate of all tragic heroes. The two particular ways in which he has failed are, first, to withdraw permanently from the fight; he has deserted the army of humanity: and second, he has allowed the righteous and generous anger which was once directed against the evils and follies of mankind to harden into an arrogant hatred of mankind itself. Both of these flaws, it will be noted, are the results of attitudes which are not evil in themselves but are extensions of admirable impulses to the point at which they become evil. To retire in order to survey the field, or to regain lost strength for a fresh attack, or to season a life of action with contemplation, is spiritually admirable; but to try to contract out of society and humanity is cowardice. Similarly, to detest compromise and shoddiness of spirit is laudable, but to treat all humanity with scorn and hatred and contempt because it is humanity that indulges in compromise is to fall from the hero's place and grace and to become abject and petty. Southman himself acknowledges his change from true to false values when, on two or three occasions, he quotes the Mock Turtle's plaint: 'Once I was *real* turtle.' He knows that he has surrendered to triviality and the world's slow stain. The dramatic sign in the play of Southman's fall and of his culpability is the fact that it is he who, in effect, initiates the destruction of Procathren, the agent of culture and civilisation. Procathren has come to the house because of his admiration for Southman, because he regards him as a leader and exemplar, because he reveres Southman's strength and greatness. It is Southman who bullies him into declaring his support for violence, on the excuse of its being a situation of emergency; it is Southman who mocks him into taking the gun into his hands; and it is Southman who seeks to evade his own responsibility in the matter by saying to Procathren 'You killed her.' Procathren himself, when he returns from the burning village at the end of the play, puts his own destruction and Southman's fall from grace in the wider perspective of mankind and the world when he says: 'Southman, I thought the power invested was for good. I believed we were here to do well by each other. It isn't so. We are here – all of us – to die. Nothing more than that. We live for that alone. You've known all along, haven't you? Why didn't you tell me – why did you have to teach me in such a dreadful way? For now – (*He cries out*) – I have wasted my inheritance!' And for the offence done to Procathren and all those he represents, Southman must die, yet the play refuses to lend its final authority to Procathren's nihilism, choosing rather, by its end, to endorse Stella's account of things – that life is a preparation for a a good death, in which the vital and compassionate part of every life is blended into and identified with the mythic memory and quality of the whole race, the whole world.

There must be some question as to whether the figure of Southman in the play is dramatically and theatrically big enough to serve the archetypal purpose that a tragic reading of the play would demand. Is the figure of sufficient stature? Is it sufficiently central to the action? And is it not, in the second half of the play, too passive? Certainly he is not the towering, complex tragic hero of the indisputably great tragedy: this is not a Lear or an Agamemnon. On the other hand, even when one only reads the play, Southman dominates it and sticks in the mind afterwards. He seems to us more than life-size. In the theatre, this is much more true; the reviews of the original production, even while mauling the play itself, almost all praised the fine, gripping and haunting performance of Michael Hordern as Southman. Hordern played the part again in 1965, in the only major professional revival there has yet been of the play (in English), and again the dominance and centrality of the character was immediately obvious. This was, on both occasions, partly due to Hordern's skill as an actor – which is of the highest order – but no actor can ultimately dominate a play, no matter how impressive he is momentarily, in a part that is empty. There is also the consideration that the other characters in the play regard him with awe and treat him as being a leader, a king, the typification of his people and clan. This, as has already been pointed out, is particularly true of Procathren. The size of the character and its central position seem sufficient, even though one acknowledges the legitimacy of the question. The other issue – of the relatively passive role of Southman in the last act of the play – is more serious. There is, indeed, some substance in this criticism: Southman does not grow in stature as a tragic hero should, nor is there that needed moment when, the fearsome struggle of decision over, we see the hero accept with clear eyes the inevitable state of things, the extent and limits of his own responsibility, and the inevitability of his own fate. Something of all this *is* there, in the scenes between Southman and Melrose; but it is not firm enough, big enough or unequivocal enough. Paul has by this stage realised the need to return to compassion – hence his welcoming of the village women, where he had before treated all those who lived in the village as being automatically his enemies. And his contact with the child, the new Stella, is a sign that he now recognises that life must be allowed to continue, cleansed of hatred; it must be revered, not reviled. (It is worth recalling that Stella, when she was pleading in Act 2 for Procathren's help for the sake of her unborn child, referred to that child as 'The child Paul. Innocent, you will admit . . .') But both of these instances of Southman's spiritual growth are so casually introduced as to appear uncertain and wavering: they could easily appear as inconsistencies or be passed over altogether, either in a performance or a reading of the play. There is, however, on the positive side, the sense that – though it is never stated – he knows he is going to his death and knows why: it is tenuous and somewhat muffled but it is there. He has not been told about the projected hangings and is still behaving, on the surface, as if he were still going to London to the celebration dinner. Charles and John Winter assume that his mind has simply given way under the strain. Charles actually says: 'Damn you, Paul! God damn you for the beastliness, the selfishness, of shutting yourself up in your tower of senility and lunacy at this moment – at this moment!' But there is a kind of clarity in the madness, as there is in Lear's. He has on his overcoat and he carries a little case and he sits down to wait and he says he will soon have to leave. But he never once mentions London or the celebration dinner and gradually the impression grows that he is thinking and talking of a different destination. To the child he says: 'There! I knew you could speak. Well done! "Many happy returns of the day" you said. And that is what they will say when I arrive – the great and famous people receiving me – they will say . . .' He does not mention London and, clearly, he is not thinking of London. He is thinking of his acceptance into the eternal company and this is emphasised by the little knot of village women who now wish him 'Many happy returns', one of them adding 'Good men are rewarded.' So the retreat into madness is not absolute and, indeed, becomes a liberating force rather than an imprisoning one. But the play's escape from a merely pathetic figure and a pathetic situation is a narrow one. Perhaps one could sum up by saying that this is an example of the one weakness which prevents *Saint's Day* from attaining completely the tragic stature at which (though not necessarily consciously on its author's part) it aims: its tone is at times too personal; it allows itself to become too engrossed in the fate of the individuals, but moving, thus, towards pathos, which is a dilution and diminution of the tragic spirit, it yet stops well short of sentimentality.

There has been some puzzlement, among various critics of the play, over the title and the connection they assume it to imply between Paul Southman and St Paul, because of the fixing of the date of the action of the play as 25 January, the anniversary of St Paul's conversion. 'Paul (Southman) is obviously the saint of the title though Robert also undergoes a conversion', says Ronald Hayman in his *John Whiting* (Heinemann, Contemporary Playwrights Series, 1969). Gabrielle Scott Robinson, in an article on the play in *Modern Drama* (February 1972) asks, about Southman: 'Is he not an evil man rather than a saint?' and in discussing the question says 'Also this "saint" blesses the soldiers who terrorize the village and are as savage as he himself would like to be. The Reverend Aldus believes him to be evil. It is difficult to pass judgement on Paul . . . The allusion to St Paul was meant to increase Paul's stature and the irony of the play, adding emotional depth to our response to him. But perhaps Whiting overreached himself here.' But surely the title of the play is not really intended to imply that Southman (or anybody else) is a saint. All that is being said, surely, is that 25 January is Southman's 'saint's day', in the sense in which the Russians in the nineteenth century celebrated the 'name days' of members of their families – the days designated in the church calendar for the saint after whom the particular person was named. There is no suggestion that the person *is* the saint or necessarily has the attributes of the saint: only that he has the same name as the saint. In the case of Southman, of course, it is no accident that the saint of whom we are by Southman's name reminded is St Paul, for Saul of Tarsus was a violent man and even after his conversion was a ruthless one, one who refused all compromise and held his views and his faith constantly at full stretch, a man who at every moment of his converted life, held his life and his belief *in extremis*, so to speak. In this respect, Southman does bear some similarity to his namesake. And yet one must recall that it was Saul of Tarsus who (given the glories of the Jacobean translation) said after his conversion: 'Though I speak with the tongues of men and of angels [which artists, such as Paul Southman, do] and have not charity [which, until the moment of conversion, Paul Southman had not] I am become as sounding brass or a tinkling cymbal.' The play's realisation of the need for charity comes through the tragic-cathartic experience of South-man's death. There is a significance for the play in the fact that St Paul's day in the calendar is fixed not by his birth or his death but by his conversion. And on this 25 January, Paul Southman, too, is con-verted from an opinionated exhibitionist, the empty shell of a one-time rebel, to an old man accepting the fact of and the necessity for death. The irony is twofold: on the one hand is the contrast between the palpably and obviously living Southman and the dead image of the sentimental conventional impression of what constitutes a saint (but this same irony could be evoked by setting any of the great Christian saints – St Paul, himself, for instance – alongside that sentimental, conventional, plaster-saint image); on the other hand there is the far deeper irony of comparison between the nature of the conversion of Saul of Tarsus and that of Paul Southman. Saul was 'yet breathing out threatenings and slaughter' when, on the road to Damascus, 'suddenly there shone round about him a light from heaven': Southman's way from his early breath-ings of threatening and slaughter is closed in with an ever-deepening dark. Under the stress of the twentieth century's violence and disillusion, the facile certainties of orthodox Christianity are seen as giving way before a sterner reality. The conversion is not to cynicism or nihilism, but it is not to the vision of a loving and saving personal God, either. Paul Southman's conversion is to the dark truth of a tragic reality and a tragic nobility. It is Stoic, pagan; not Christian. And therein lies the irony of the use of the word 'saint' and, for that matter, of the Western tradition of 'Christian' names, 'name days' and 'saint's days'. This is, in itself, an apt and telling comment on the confused state of moral beliefs in mid-twentieth-century Western society, where the forms of old faiths still partially remain but the life has deserted them and the truth of experience is elsewhere and must be expressed in other modes.

The tragic design of the play is reinforced, amplified and commented upon by the stage setting that Whiting had in mind. The mural that Whiting prescribes (and describes) as the dominant visual element of the staging of *Saint's Day* has some interesting implications for both the unity of the play's design and the tragic sense of the play. The figures in the mural, he says, are to be seen as greater than life-size. There are five of them at the start, with a central space for a sixth. There is also a dog. There are five principal characters in the play, not counting Charles, who is, in relation to the mural, the onlooker, the painter. So the un-finished mural prefigures the play, giving a sense of unity to it as well as a sense of progression. The action of the play exists within the bounds of the mural. The central, empty space is, in Act 3, filled by Charles painting in a portrait of Stella, using her dead body as a model. So the five male characters – Southman, Procathren, John Winter, Aldus and Melrose – are seen as being grouped round Stella and all looking at her. The play interprets the mural for us by showing the sense in which

Stella is central to the action. She is not central in terms of plot – that position is occupied by Procathren, who arrives from outside and causes everything to happen; nor is she central in terms of the tragic idea – Paul Southman is the tragic protagonist – but as a symbol of inveterate life she is central – that is why, in the picture Charles is painting, everyone gazes at her, for life and its meaning and the possibility of its continuance is what all of them are contemplating. It does not, of course, follow that because Stella is such a symbol that she is therefore merely, and only, a symbol, that she has no character and personality. It is the business of dramatic poetry to provide both and, indeed, a great play is great only by the measure to which it succeeds in blending these elements, the individual and immediate with the timeless and general. Whiting said that the idea of the whole play began from the idea of the mural, which was suggested to him by an actual mural that he saw. Obviously he intended this picture on stage to be a powerful and dominating factor in the play, one that is not only theatrically startling but is also bound to the deepest meanings of the play and in turn serves to bind the whole structure together.

John Whiting describes the theme of *Saint's Day* as being 'self-destruction', but the statement needs to be understood with certain qualification. What he was contemplating as he wrote it was the powerful urge toward self-destruction which paradoxically resides in human life and he draws portraits of several people in the play who do, in fact, bring about their own destruction. From the point of view of the immediate business of character portrayal, one can easily see that self-destruction might well be uppermost in his mind. But from the subtle chemistry of the play something far richer and more complex than a simple 'theme' or study of self-destruction emerges. To say that *Saint's Day* is 'about' (as they say) self-destruction is like saying that *Hamlet* is about revenge, a statement not so much incorrect as imaginatively stultifying in its state of half-truth. *Saint's Day*, as this present study seeks to demonstrate, has tragic scope and tragic depth. Simon Trussler even goes so far as to say that there is 'something Aeschylean' about its 'stripped-to-the-bone awareness' and he also points out, most acutely, that the main link between a simple study of self-destruction and the ultimate tragic shape of the play's experience is the question of responsibility. 'No single person's responsibility is absolute', says Trussler, 'but neither is any individual completely innocent. The process is indeed, as Whiting suggested, one of fulfilled self-destruction.' Self-destruction, then, was, in relation to the composition of the play, the artist's *donnée*, his point of departure, rather than the subject in a discursive sense (let alone the whole meaning) of the finished work.

It is, of course, one thing to construct a logical argument to show how a play's parts may fit an academic definition of a theory of tragedy, quite another thing for the play to work successfully in the theatre, even if the academic theory is valid. All that can be said, finally, is that the proof of the pudding is in the eating – no matter how refined and sophisticated the recipe – and in the case of *Saint's Day*, the proof is triumphant. Not only does the play work extremely well in performance, in the theatre it speaks direct to the senses with all the power and passion of the genuine tragic experience. It is said by some critics to be obscure but in performance I have not found it so, except in a few unimportant surface details. That is not to say, of course, that it offers simple explanations or makes explicit statements. No play of major stature does so, or should. It is composed not to explain but to celebrate a mystery, and that is what *Saint's Day* does; but in the process, a sense of the human condition is evoked which seems real; an impression is created of an inner reality which carries the stamp of authenticity. Gabrielle Scott Robinson, in an interesting and valuable article in which she compares the early drafts of the Whiting plays with their final published versions,[4] has pointed out that the early versions are almost always factually more explicit, the final versions being more resonant and being aimed at a statement of the more general, poetic truth rather than the particular fact. It is as if Whiting needed first to fix for himself the outward surface of the experience before proceeding to explore the inner nature of the experience itself. I would disagree, in the case of *Saint's Day*, with Mrs Scott Robinson's statement (in the same article) that 'in the final text too much is left to implication and guesswork'. It calls, in any case, not for guesswork, but for the exercise of a reasonable poetic sensibility, which, when allowed to operate on *Saint's Day*, yields the inner sense of the play quite clearly and quite readily.

Like a number of twentieth-century plays (Beckett and Pinter provide us with other good examples of this phenomenon), *Saint's Day* is informed by a deeply romantic spirit but is yet possessed of a structural yearning for the classic design. It is (unlike Beckett and Pinter, whose romanticism expresses itself in other ways) as given to a luxuriant proliferation of detail as a Gothic cathedral, complete with saints in niches, and is nevertheless austere at heart. It seems to me to be probably the best and most sizeable play written in English between *Heartbreak House* and *Serjeant Musgrave's Dance* and, though lesser than the former, not less than the latter. With these two and *Man and Superman*, *Major Barbara*, *The Playboy of the Western World*, *Juno and the Paycock* and *The Iceman Cometh*, this first major play of John Whiting's is among the best seven or eight of all twentieth-century plays in English. The dramatic critic of the *New Statesman*, when *The Devils* was first performed in 1961, said: 'Mr Whiting makes the best of our playwrights since the war seem mere by-ways in the drama. *The Devils* is our only highroad.' I would agree with his assessment of the playwright but would substitute *Saint's Day* for *The Devils*: the earlier play seems to me much the greater work.

Simon Trussler has grouped *The Conditions of Agreement* and *Saint's Day* together, saying that the former is about retarded childhoods and the latter about second childhoods, but the comparison does not seem very rewarding or illuminating. Both plays are, it is true, preternaturally *aware* of childhood, but this is true of all Whiting's work. Both plays use the images of children and childhood, but childhood is not at the centre of either play's ultimate meaning and the metaphor of childhood proves a hindrance rather than a help if insisted upon in too schematic a way. The best entrée to the world of *Saint's Day* remains the acceptance of the austere terms of tragic design which the play itself firmly postulates. Thom Gunn, the poet, realised this very clearly. He saw the play in 1952, when Peter Hall directed it at Cambridge. After seeing the play, Gunn wrote to Whiting:

Trinity College,
Cambridge
28 January, 1953

Dear John Whiting,
    I have been told I ought to send you the enclosed poem,
as it came out of the performance of *Saint's Day* (which
I so much enjoyed) in Cambridge last term. At the end of
the last act, 'The Saints Go Marching On' was played on
a trumpet. As the poem is only seven lines long it would
not waste much of your time to read it. Perhaps, if I ever get
it printed, I could dedicate it to you?
Yours faithfully,

THOM GUNN

The poem which was enclosed with the letter was later included by Gunn in a collection of his poems published by Faber & Faber under the title *Fighting Terms*. It reads as follows:

HERE COME THE SAINTS

Here come the saints: so near, so innocent
They gravely cross the field of moonlit snow;
We villagers gaze humbly at the show.
No act or gesture can suggest intent
They only wait until the first cock-crow
Batters our ears, and with abrupt and violent
Motions into the terrible dark wood they go.

II   *A Penny for a Song* (1947–1950)

The play was probably begun before the final revisions of *Saint's Day* were complete, but it was not finished until 1950 and it is safe to regard it, therefore, as the play which followed *Saint's Day*, so far as the writing of it is concerned. It was, however, staged a few months *before Saint's Day*, in March 1951, and was Whiting's first stage play to be produced. Eleven years later, after their success with *The Devils*, the Royal Shakespeare Company gave *A Penny for a Song* a London revival and for this occasion Whiting rewrote some scenes of the play, more particularly those between Dorcas and Edward Sterne. This rewriting was surely a mistake and tears the fabric of the original play. Whiting has nowhere said what motivated these revisions and while one can guess fairly shrewdly at the reasons, one cannot be sure. Ronald Hayman, in editing *The Collected Plays* in 1969, prints the earlier version of the play and appends to it some excellent notes in which he gives details of the changes and demonstrates very thoroughly (and, in my view, rightly) the ways in which the later version is less satisfactory than the earlier. Simon Trussler also follows the same line in his discussion of the play, pointing out that 1951, the year of the Festival of Britain, had about it an air of optimism and gaiety which by 1962, the year of the Cuban Missile Crisis and the peak of the Cold War, seemed downright irresponsible. Perhaps Whiting overreacted to the general mood of the time in 1962; or perhaps he responded to pressures from those who feel that a play is worthless unless it has a socio-political message; or perhaps some gradual but general darkening of his own horizon caused him to reject, at least in part, the sunshine of eleven years before. The second version of the play is published by Heinemann in their 'Hereford Plays' series (1964), edited by E. R. Wood.

In some handwritten notes dated July 1948 and headed 'Notes for a Comedy', Whiting quotes at length from Carola Oman's *Britain against Napoleon*, a light and 'popular' treatment of the history of the period, which had been published by Faber & Faber in 1942. *A Penny for a Song* owes something of its zany atmosphere to Carola Oman's descriptions of the panic-stricken and often comic preparations, especially among the civilian population, for the expected French invasion of England in 1804. Some of his practical details, such as the raising of local volunteer defence corps (the 'fencibles'), Whiting also drew from the same source. The title of the play he took from Yeats, and the Yeats poem, which it brings to our attention, is a reminder that even in the earlier, more logical version of the play, Whiting saw the happiness it reflected as a transient, not permanent, state. There, too, in the Yeats poem are Whiting's other perennial questions: of the relationship between the artist and the man of action, and, even more fundamentally, the possibility that the artist has no function at all to perform, that his is merely an exercise in self-indulgence better not undertaken at all. The poem, a single stanza, reads as follows:

> *All things can tempt me from this craft of verse:*
> *One time it was a woman's face, or worse –*
> *The seeming needs of my fool-driven land;*

Now nothing but comes readier to the hand
Than this accustomed toil. When I was young,
I had not given a penny for a song
Did not the poet sing it with such airs
That one believed he had a sword upstairs;
Yet would be now, could I but have my wish,
Colder and dumber and deafer than a fish.

The form of the play, too, is influenced by this same sense: it has a beautifully formal design, beginning as the household rouses to greet a new day and ending with a dying fall and the solemnity of evening: the final stage direction says *A single star stands in the sky*. The high spirits of the play's noon are subdued; the lovers are separated and a soft melancholy sighs in the air.

But that is the end of the play: the beginning is all gaiety. The year is 1804; the time, a summer morning; the place, Sir Timothy Bellboys' house on the Dorset coast. The house is inhabited by Sir Timothy himself, his brother Lamprett Bellboys with Hester, his wife, their daughter Dorcas and, at the moment, a visitor who arrived just the night before, an old friend of Timothy's, whose name is Hallam Matthews. One of the household servants, one Humpage by name, is posted permanently up a tree as a look-out. He has a telescope, a very large brass bell, a kind of portable weathervane and a complicated semaphore signalling device. Both Timothy and Lamprett claim his exclusive allegiance and he responds gamely to the commands of both. Timothy asks him to report immediately if he observes the arrival of Napoleon's troops on the British coast; Lamprett needs to know immediately if any fires break out. This seemingly fair division of authority and responsibility is not, as one might at first think, part of a carefully co-ordinated plan for dealing with the emergency but is, rather, evidence of a deadly rivalry. Lamprett is interested *only* in fires and his fire engine; he cares nothing for the invasion, which he regards as a nuisance and a distraction from the main business of life – fires. Timothy, on the other hand, sees the invasion as having been especially designed by Providence to enable *him* to fulfil himself. He has, he tells his friend Hallam, suffered one grave disappointment already, in that the little private army of fencibles he has raised has been declared illegal by the authorities and has been taken over as part of the regular military force. Not only that, but his application to the military for the command of the new unit has been turned down and the command given to George Selincourt, a stranger, brought in especially from Taunton. Timothy is not the one to take defeat lying down, however, and he now has a new plan whereby he will defeat Napoleon single-handed. He has asked Hallam to bring with him from London a box of theatrical costumes, borrowed from Drury Lane Theatre, and a French phrase-book. He has discovered that he looks rather like Napoleon and his plan is a simple one. He will dress up as the

Emperor in full military uniform: he will wait for the entire French army to land; and then, with the help of the phrase-book, he will address them in their own tongue and tell them that all is lost, that they are already defeated and that they must at once make the best of their way back to France. He has discovered that a disused and dried-up well in the garden has a tunnel leading into it, the other end of which comes out on the beach. He plans to descend the well at the crucial time, crawl along the tunnel and appear to the French army from its rear, as if having just landed behind it from the French ships.

Lamprett and Timothy each confides in Hallam that he is fearful for his brother's sanity. 'I think I should tell you', Lamprett says, 'that you will find him strange – very strange. God forbid that I should speak ill of my brother, but this threatened invasion by Bonaparte seems to have unhinged him completely. His behaviour has become eccentric in the extreme.' A little later, Timothy tells Hallam 'I am being made to understand with increasing force the impossibility of expecting Lamprett to take his life with the smallest degree of seriousness. He has, I'm afraid, an incontrovertibly frivolous nature. Father, had he lived, would have found an even deeper dissatisfaction with his younger son, I feel. During his lifetime he found Lamprett a sore trial.'

While Lamprett fidgets because no fires break out and Timothy busies himself with his disguise, Edward Sterne, a soldier blinded in the French wars and now being guided on his journey by a small boy called Jonathan (which was, incidentally, the name of John Whiting's first child, born in 1946), stops at the house to ask for a drink of water. He is on his way to London to seek an audience of the king, to ask him to stop the war. Jonathan, who has a journey of his own to make and is assisting Edward only incidentally, is going to Bethlehem because 'last Christmas he was told the story of the birth of a child in Bethlehem. From that story Jonathan recognised his brother. But the story ended and the story-teller forgot to say that the birth was over eighteen hundred years ago and that the boy has long since been dead.' There is an instinctive and immediate bond of sympathy between Edward and Dorcas and the sanity and seriousness of their relationship serves as counterpoint to the exuberant eccentricities of the rest. Jonathan is immediately taken over by Lamprett and spends the rest of the play, until the time comes in the evening for his departure, gravely helping to clean and operate the fire engine which Lamprett keeps permanently at the ready in the orchard. The boy never speaks throughout all this, but seems happy to be so engaged.

While Timothy is busy with *his* preparations for the invasion, George Selincourt, the new commander of the fencibles, has not been idle. He has planned a military exercise to give the local volunteers some experience of what it will be like. In the exercise, he explains to Hallam, two-thirds of his men will represent the French enemy and will 'attack' from the sea. For greater verisimilitude, he has borrowed a balloon from a local fair and will use it for purposes of reconnaissance. The spring of the farce is now wound tight and its swift and ebullient unwinding is no less amusing because perfectly predictable. Timothy, looking astonishingly like Napoleon, duly descends the well. Of course, he mistakes the fencibles for the French and of course they mistake him for Napoleon and there is a heroic chase and pursuit in the best farce tradition. In the process, Timothy accidentally comes upon the balloon, guarded by a single timid, rustic fencible who, taking one glance at the approaching French Emperor, deems discretion the better part of valour and flies for his life. So Timothy makes a triumphant entry in the gondola of the balloon but in an attempt to steer it accidentally deflates the gas-bag and precipitates himself for a second time into the well. Not to be thus thwarted of their quarry, the fencibles seal up the well with gunpowder which, when it explodes, propels Sir Timothy from the mouth of the tunnel over several acres of good Dorset land. He returns home tattered but undaunted, to be challenged by Selincourt himself. Timothy confesses his real identity but Selincourt is still dubious and insists on a number of tests by which to prove that Timothy is English and not French. The one that clinches the matter and makes firm friends of Selincourt and Sir Timothy is the miming of a game of cricket. Selincourt bowls an imaginary ball and Timothy at once faces him with an imaginary bat. The war and the invasion are forgotten and Selincourt and Timothy retire to the house to arrange a cricket match. Lamprett, who has spent the day enthusiastically extinguishing the signal fires lit by Selincourt's fencibles to warn the citizenry of the arrival (as they believe) of Bonaparte, joins them. Edward and Dorcas are left in the garden alone: they have spent the day simply, together, discovering each other and now she leads him to a seat in a little arbour:

DORCAS: I used to play here when I was a baby. Yes, it is a good place for us to be together for I have been happy here. It was my world within a world – peopled by folk who were all like me – and that is simple to understand for I was everyone.
EDWARD: I am a stranger.
DORCAS: No, No! We all greet you.
(Lightly, she kisses him)

She finds the place where as a child she carved her name on the seat and, taking a stone from the ground, she begins to carve again:

EDWARD: What are you doing?
DORCAS: I'm putting your name – Edward – here with mine. Isn't that a clever thing to do?
EDWARD: Indeed it is.
(As DORCAS works, she asks):
DORCAS: You're going away?

154

EDWARD: Yes.
DORCAS: Soon?
EDWARD: Yes.
DORCAS: Not before I've finished your name?
EDWARD: Not before then, perhaps, but soon – soon.
DORCAS: I shall be a long time. Perhaps, if I cut very slowly . . . I cannot
    come with you?
EDWARD: No.
DORCAS: There!
EDWARD: Finished?
                    (DORCAS *turns to him, her face distraught*)
DORCAS: Yes. Oh, yes. (*She cries out*) But we all love you – why can't you
    remain?
EDWARD: Poor Dorcas.
DORCAS: Forgive me. I don't understand.

Hallam sums it up for them. 'Circumstances', he says, 'deal with us in
a way we cannot approve. As you grow older you will understand that.'
Lamprett brings Jonathan back to Edward; the child is in his travelling
clothes again, after his day spent dressed as one of Lamprett's firemen.
The windows of the house show the rooms being lighted by candles and
the party goes indoors, except for Dorcas and Hallam. 'I shall sit here
for a while because I don't know where to go', says Dorcas, 'I've not
yet made up my mind, you understand? Can you see me?'

HALLAM: Yes.
DORCAS: It is getting dark. Day's end. Nightfall. I suppose there will be a
    tomorrow. I cannot believe that I shall wake to find the sun high. Do
    you know a song beginning 'All my past life is mine no more . . .'
HALLAM:

> *All my past life is mine no more;*
> *The flying hours are gone,*
> *Like transitory dreams given o'er,*
> *Whose images are kept in store*
> *By memory alone.*

    Yes, I know that.

It is the poem by John Wilmot, Earl of Rochester, and though Hallam
and Dorcas do not do so, one might quote the rest of it, since its
melancholy gravity sums up neatly the end of *A Penny for a Song* –
the sense of the bright sunshine of a single day, remembered with longing as the dusk of evening gathers:

> *The time that is to come is not;*
> *How can it then be mine?*
> *The present moment's all my lot,*
> *And that, as fast as it is got,*
> *Phyllis, is only thine.*

> *Then talk not of inconstancy;*
> *False hearts and broken vows;*
> *If I, by miracle, can be*
> *This live-long minute true to thee,*
> *'Tis all that heaven allows.*

The foregoing brief and rough outline of the play is based on the first version, the text of which appears in the 1957 *Plays of John Whiting* and in the 1969 *The Collected Plays of John Whiting*. There is no need to repeat here in any detail the points of comparison made by Ronald Hayman between this version and the second one: readers are again referred to his very perceptive notes on this subject. The general tone of the changes can be described by saying that a certain harsh abrasiveness replaces the gentle quality of the original; a worldly knowingness replaces wonder; and the eccentricities, though still comic, tend to be regarded – to some extent at least – as socially irresponsible instead of charmingly gay and innocent. In a word, the trust in the goodness of life which the play originally had has lost its self-confidence. The chief instrument of this change is the soldier, Edward Sterne: in the second version he is no longer blind, but is a returned, disgruntled soldier, carrying in his pocket a copy of Paine's *The Rights of Man* and journeying to London not – naively but attractively – to ask the king to stop the war but to preach revolution to the dispossessed. He sorts ill with the rest of the characters, not because he does not agree with them but because he really belongs to a different – and simpler – kind of play. The original Edward Sterne could hardly have been created by anyone but Whiting: the second Edward Sterne is not really a Whiting character at all. Not that Whiting characters cannot be serious: all the other Whiting plays give the lie to such a suggestion (and, ultimately considered, *A Penny for a Song* is serious, too). But the second Edward Sterne is not serious so much as solemn and pedestrian and his introduction into the play provides an interesting example of the declension from a general and spiritual, or artistic, sense of truth to the everyday specifics of social justice and injustice. The sentiments of what Sterne has to say are unexceptionable: any right-minded man would suscribe to them and act upon them. They need proclaiming loudly, especially at a time when the rights of man are, internationally, increasingly understood to refer exclusively to *material* rights. But to devote a work of art to such proclamation usually produces an embarrassingly poor work of art and to *superimpose* such proclamation on an already existing work, which is, in effect, what Whiting has done, is to run the risk of making the worst of both worlds. Interestingly enough, this move from the general to the naturalistically specific is the reverse of Whiting's usual practice in the revision of successive drafts of a play. Usually he seems to need the structure of surface description in the initial stages of his creative process in order to establish firmly the area of experience to be explored;

then, as he himself becomes more sure, he tends in his revising to dispense with more and more of the surface specifics in order to allow the underlying connections and juxtapositions poetically to assert themselves. If one bears in mind Dryden's dictum that 'delight is the chief, if not the only end of Poesie' then the second Edward Sterne neatly demonstrates for us the aesthetic implications of the difference between himself and his predecessor:

DORCAS: Are you going far?
EDWARD: To London.
DORCAS: Just for pleasure?
EDWARD: I don't do anything just for pleasure.

This second Edward has wit of a sort, but of such a lumpen and solemn sort as to make it sound always like special pleading. He notices Humpage perched in his look-out tree and observes: 'When I left England they used to keep the servants underfoot.' And on every available opportunity he is prosily explicit about his own alignment on the side of the angels, as witness the following exchange, on the subject of Dorcas, with the urbane, sophisticated and entirely delightful Hallam:

HALLAM: What I'm trying to say is this: she has been well brought up according to tried and tested ideas. You might say that she is a traditional child, and none the worse for that. I want you to think very carefully before you put these ideas into her head, ideas which are far below her station. The opportunities for revolution are few in this charming place. It would be sad, I think you'll agree, if you were to leave behind a convert with no material to work on.
EDWARD: Typical.
HALLAM: I'm sure I am.
EDWARD: You safeguard your own tottering position by chatter about tradition. This girl has a right to her own life. You make her look very small by taking it for granted that she wants to live in your way. She may have a conscience: have you thought of that? She may be ashamed to build her folly, as you do, on the labour of the poor.

He sounds like a student leader, espousing any virtuous cause in sight.

In the first version, both Edward and Dorcas declare their love for the other: they are separated at the end by what Hallam calls 'circumstance' – the details of which are unexplained, inexplicable and without any need of explanation within the ambience of the poem, which simply observes the fact that life parts lovers. In the second version, only Dorcas is in love; Edward specifically tells Hester, Dorcas's mother, that he is not. He leaves not because of the inevitable flux and tide of things but because he chooses to. One has the feeling that his choices would always be dour and pedestrian ones. He and Dorcas enter together at one point and we catch a fragment of conversation, broken off because something new obtrudes. In the first version, the fragment that represents the conversation is this (spoken by Edward): 'That's what laughter is, nothing more . . .' In the second version, this becomes 'That's what social reform is, nothing more . . .'

The play began as a gently ironic, comic fantasy: the revisions move it some way, though by no means all the way, towards factual earnestness. Yet paradoxically (as it might at any rate seem to a superficial view) the fantasy is truer than the fact and the first version of the play is more aware than the second of its true function as a work of art and fulfils that function more truly. In terms of Whiting's own particular vision of life there is a signal instance of this in the omission from the second version of a brief passage between Edward and Dorcas which appears in the first, a passage in which the authentic romantic vision asserts itself and immediately (and valuably) links the play with those moments in the other Whiting plays in which that quest for the Holy Grail of some absolute belief or attainment shows itself as one of the basic driving forces of Whiting's world. Dorcas has asked Hallam and Edward – the blind Edward, not the disgruntled revolutionary, 'Why do men fight each other?' Edward replies:

> 'Perhaps because there is a long-wished-for home they seek
> and they are too frail to take upon themselves the
> responsibility for the journey. Did you never, when you
> were a baby, know of something you desired but of which –
> oh, so humanly – you were ashamed? And did you not,
> perhaps – shall we say – engineer that thing to come about
> – oh, so sinfully – through the fault of another? (*He smiles*)
> You see, my life-loving darling, the dark journey to the
> dark home is sometimes sweeter than the summer's day.'

Dorcas says to him 'I think you must be a very serious and unhappy man to speak like that', but Edward denies this and in his reply returns to the image of the quest: 'Not unhappy, no. A journeying man, that's what I am.' Not only the quest for the Absolute is contained in this passage, but also the complementary theme of the unacceptability of compromise and the preference for death, the 'dark journey to the dark home'. This is not only a good deal more profound than anything of which the second Edward is capable, it is also, in its unargumentative and non-polemical style, a good deal more pleasant and persuasive. 'Don't, please, talk of such things,' Hallam says, 'I feel, somehow, as if the sun has gone in.' And Edward, instead of being solemn and pompous and heavily sarcastic as he would be in the revised version, says: 'I comprehend your distress. We will talk of other things.' It is the compassionate statement of the undogmatic poet, who sees the shadow that lies athwart the sunlight but does not feel the need to use his vision to frighten or destroy those less able than himself to understand or accept it.

The play contains several of Whiting's favourite elements and reminds us, therefore, of aspects of many of his other works – childhood, clowns, soldiers, fire engines. There are dozens of references to childhood throughout the play and there is also, of course, the silent, appealing and enigmatic figure of Jonathan. At one point, a stage direction reads: EDWARD *and* DORCAS *move across the garden.* JONATHAN, *standing beside them as they pass, for a moment, stretches out a hand towards them. But of course, he is unseen by* EDWARD *and even, in her blindness, by* DORCAS. *They go out by the gateway and the boy stares after them.* 'What is it?' Hallam asks him, 'Didn't they see you? Well, you're really very small, you know. Hasn't that got anything to do with it? You're right, it hasn't.' Hallam also likens adult life to childhood when he says: 'Rather than reveal our human imperfections we will turn ourselves, even for the beloved, into a fair-booth from which we offer for sale at extravagant cost the gayest and most useless toys. We cry our wares hoping the naked baby cowering at the back of the booth will not be noticed. We never give up our rattles: our thumbs will go to our mouths on our death-beds.'

Clowns and children are linked, as in Whiting they so often are:

DORCAS: What has been puzzling me is why you play the fool all the time.
HALLAM: Everyone does so.
DORCAS: Nonsense!
HALLAM: Everyone attempts to be other than they are.
DORCAS: I don't believe it. What about the saints?
HALLAM: Worse than any. It is clowning, you know. A most consequent factor of life.
EDWARD (*To* DORCAS):   He means, I think, that we find the reality unbearable. That factor within us – ah! the infrangible burden to carry: self-knowledge. And so we escape, childlike, into the illusion. We clown and posture but not to amuse others – no – to comfort ourselves. The laughter is incidental to the tragic spectacle of each man attempting to hide his intolerable self.

This figure of the tragic clown appears in several other places. Reference has briefly been made in Chapter 3 to his three-fold appearance at the end of 'A Valediction'; and in *Not a Foot of Land* is a brief statement about the Clown who comforts Sara: 'Weeping, the clown will walk on, the only sorrowing man in that happy city.' Again, Hallam says to Dorcas, when she gaily interrupts a conversation between him and Edward: 'You, in your youth, regard us as your clowns, do you not? The world, spinning about the centre of your untouched heart, somersaults for your amusement. Very well, but you must remember that there are some days when the clowns must sit together in the sun and talk of clownish things.'

The business of fire engines is less important, though a great delight. The way in which it connects *A Penny for a Song* with 'The Honour of the Fire Brigade' has already been pointed out, but this eccentric interest is not one of those powerful symbols that obsessively returns over and over again in all the plays and stories. Apart from the general situation of a man bewitched by fires and fire engines, though, the play does borrow one specific incident from the short story: Lamprett, talking to Hallam about a ruined cottage which was consumed by fire, says: 'It was burnt out two years ago – a magnificent conflagration! – the only occasion on which my brigade became sea-borne. An unfortunate legend credits me with firing the place – it was the first time my brigade was called out under my captaincy – but I can assure you it is nothing more than a legend.' It will be recalled that the hero of the short story set fire to his own house in order to provide himself and his fire brigade with a conflagration to quell. There is a very amusing account in *A Penny for a Song* of how Lamprett's eccentric passion for fire-fighting was first aroused. It is given by Timothy to Hallam:

> 'Instead of attending to his studies when he was at Oxford
> he became convinced that women should be admitted to
> the Colleges. To prove their worth he prevailed upon Hester
> – with whom he was friendly, both of them playing the
> bass fiddle – to dress in her uncle's second-best ceremonial
> breeches and coat. So dressed, she attended lectures for
> three weeks and might never have been discovered had not
> Lamprett then insisted that to complete the illusion she
> should begin to smoke. One evening, in his rooms, with
> Horace Walpole as his guest, Hester was standing before
> the fire, pipe in hand, when the breeches caught alight. She
> would have been burnt to the ground had not Lamprett
> extinguished the fire manually (*He demonstrates*). So,
> of course, he married her, and he's been fighting fires ever
> since.'

As well as being an amusing story in itself, this is also a very good example of a special Whiting technique: in several of the plays, he stops the overt stage action and carries on the dramatic action by narrative. Sometimes these narratives are sombre, as Rupert's story of the killing of these children in *Marching Song*; sometimes they are satirical, as Paul Southman's story of his assault upon 'the well-known and much-beloved whore, Society'; sometimes they are comic, like the story of Hester, saved only in the nick of time from being 'burnt to the ground' and, like the long story that Benedict tells in *No More A-Roving*, about a horse who so appreciated his sympathy and friendship that it followed him everywhere and finally got stuck in a revolving door while trying to follow him into a hotel.

Kenneth Haigh, Tracey Lloyd, Nigel Stock, Joyce Heron and Laurence Hardy in the 1960 BBC television production of *A Walk in the Desert* (BBC Copyright Photograph)

Eithne Dunn, Terence Hardiman, Frank Middlemass and David Burke in *The Conditions of Agreement* at the Bristol Little Theatre in 1965 (Photograph Derek Balmer)

V: Very well. Will you stand next to ~~Mr~~. Sergeant Thomson?
John: Who?
V: Next to the soldier — there. Is that everyone — oh, Miss Fairfax.
Jane: Yes, I'm here. Just been having a cup of tea.
V: Miss Fairfax. Was Paul Southman an ordinary man?
Jane: You bet he was. Why, he —
V: Will you stand there? Next to the gentleman with glasses.
Jane: Right-o.
V: Now then we'll take you in the order you stand, from right to left.
   (he calls)
   Mr. Ussleigh. Begin, please.
   (there is silence)
   Now, come along, Mr. Ussleigh. An appreciation of Paul Southman.
   (pause)
   Mr. Ussleigh. Because I didn't understand I lost all my money. Who did that to me?
John: ~~Who did I trust? Who used that trust to ruin me?~~
V: ~~Sergeant Thomson.~~ Next.
Soldier: Who is it writes songs that you can't march to?
V: ~~Mr Howell.~~ Next.
Howell: Who encourages his damned great dog to ruin my garden?
V: ~~The Critic.~~ Next. Who considers his jingles to be psalms?
Critic: ~~Whose work is distinguished by its meretriciousness?~~
V: ~~Miss Fairfax.~~ Good Next.
Jane: Who was born in the next street to me? Who is an ordinary man?

John Whiting's handwriting, reproduced here actual size. This is part of the script of the radio play written in 1946 (but never broadcast) called *Paul Southman: An Appreciation for Broadcasting*. All Whiting's plays – and critical works, too – were written in this tiny hand.

The theme of armies and soldiers is, of course, altogether more pervasive, so much so as scarcely to need emphasising. Obviously the fact of having a father in the regular army, coupled with his own direct, personal experience in the Second World War, has distinct bearing on Whiting's work in this regard, but even allowing for these factors the list of instances is a remarkable one:

Everal	in *Not a Foot of Land*
Benedict	in *No More A-Roving*
Melrose and the other two soldiers	in *Saint's Day*
Emily's husband	in *The Conditions of Agreement*
Sterne, Selincourt, Timothy and the Fencibles	in *A Penny for a Song*
Rupert and Hurst	in *Marching Song*

And, in *The Gates of Summer*, John Hogarth is on his way to be a soldier (even though he never gets there) and Selwyn Faramond is a retired soldier. Only *Marching Song* and *A Penny for a Song* are actually 'about' war, in the conventional military sense, and in neither play is warfare, in fact, the central experience of the play. It is, indeed, peripheral to the plays' main concerns, in both cases. At the centre of those concerns, *A Penny for a Song* can be regarded fairly accurately as the obverse of *Marching Song*, using its comic military plot as a structure to support the general sense of trust and love and well-being which the play, at least in the first version, distils. 'The historical references in the play are actual,' said Whiting in his Introduction, 'I have taken no liberties. It is rarely necessary to embroider the finer lunacies of the English at war.' But he makes it clear that this is the outward structure only: the inner heart of the play is a statement, he says, of 'Christian charity'. Ronald Bryden tends to miss the mark when he describes the play, in an article on Whiting in the *New Statesman* in May 1965 as 'a sardonic comedy, under Napoleonic disguise, of the gap between the real history of 1940 and the English view of it', though it is true that something of that extraordinary gaiety and bustle and ebullience of civilian life in the first years of the Second World War has got into the endearing antics of the Dorset citizens of *A Penny for a Song*.

Whiting's liking for a rarefied and recherché vocabulary is still in evidence here and there in this play, though its effects in the formal language of this work are advantageous rather than otherwise. We have 'infrangible' and 'catena' (both of which disappeared in the second version) and, in the description of Napoleon's preparations for invasion, 'praams'. I had to look it up. My OED told me it means 'flat-bottomed boats'. Where on earth had John Whiting, with all his breadth of reading, come across that? There is also, here and there among the glittering precision of language, the occasional syntactical gaffe, the worst one being: 'You must know, my dear Lamprett, that nothing is so necessary to a reading of Mr Wordsworth's book than a sense of security.' Presumably no one on stage ever actually *said* that and it is difficult to see how it slipped past editors in getting into print, but it managed the feat in the 1957 and 1969 editions: in 1964 it appeared correctly as 'nothing is so necessary to a reading of Mr Wordsworth's work *as* a sense of security'.

A Penny for a Song is a small play and it does not justify Whiting's own opinion, expressed in 1961: 'It's a better play than any of the others.' But though small, it is genuine. Its charm is not mere saccharin, nor is its optimism false or affected. Indeed, one of its chief values is that it shows for a moment, even if only on miniature scale, the other side of that dark romanticism which is the hallmark of Whiting's vision. In doing so, it lends an additional depth and perspective both to its own senses of reality and those of the other plays.

(There are some interesting examples of Whiting's own opinions of this play in a letter written to Peter Brook, the director of the original production, at the time that production was in preparation. The full text of that letter is given in Appendix 2 of the present work.)

III   *Marching Song* (1948–1952)

Writing about *Saint's Day* in the Introduction to the 1957 volume of plays, Whiting said 'The theme, which is self-destruction, is developed on other lines and with greater clarity in the later play, *Marching Song*.' As in the case of *Saint's Day*, the statement is true only in a certain limited sense and should not be taken as defining the whole experience or the ultimate gesture of *Marching Song*. The sense in which the statement *is* true is the immediate and surface sense of plot, event, happening. The central character, Rupert Forster, ends the play by committing suicide, having been given an ultimatum at the end of Act 1 offering him the choice of suicide or disgrace. The play, therefore, is 'about' his consideration of these alternatives and his final decision, but this should not be taken as implying that self-destruction, either literal or metaphorical, is the basic theme of the play. Forster himself, who is a soldier, treats death as incidental and his own death is, in fact, incidental to the play's main concern, which is with an exploration of the nature of, and possibility of, an ultimate, objective, identifiable reality in an individual life and individual experience. Rupert has believed in the possibility of achieving a permanent reality, an existence, through the doing of something, the making of something, *outside* oneself, so that there is an actual object, an artefact, left behind, quite independent of oneself and one's personal life. 'The night before that last battle', he says, 'I still believed that I could reach a point of achievement never before known to a man. The way I chose was conquest by war. Some men need an art to fulfil themselves. Saints need a religion. I had to pursue a triumph of arms. The greatest the world has ever known. By that I believed I could become myself, the man I was intended to be.' Rupert's interest, the play demonstrates, is not in self-realisation or self-fulfilment in any selfish or self-indulgent sense: his question is 'Can a human action have an objective existence?' and self-realisation is only a step towards proving or disproving the answer to that question. The word 'action' occurs over and over again in the play, especially in Rupert's mouth: the play explores the relevance of action, the possibility of action's permanent, non-subjective, recognisable reality. To Rupert, the test of life's validity, the test of whether it is really, objectively *there* at all, lies in the answer to this question. It is not so much a matter of whether one should or should not destroy oneself but whether one was ever there, in any real sense, in the first place.

The plot of the play is a simple one: in an imaginary central European country, Rupert Forster, the general commanding the army, has been imprisoned without trial for seven years following a military campaign in which, through a sudden and inexplicable hesitation and indecision, he and his army were badly beaten. Now, after seven years, he is released from his prison at the insistence of the political parties opposing the government, for the purpose of being brought to trial for 'treason arising from cowardice in the face of the enemy'. The real objective is, in fact, to create a scapegoat for the military disaster. John Cadmus, the head of the government, because of the pressure from the opposition, has been compelled to agree to Forster's being brought back from jail for trial, but, believing that such a trial would be politically disastrous both nationally and internationally, is determined to prevent its taking place, if possible. He dare not forbid it outright and so he comes to Forster secretly, points out the disgrace and shame that the trial would bring not only to Forster himself but also to the country as a whole and offers him the alternative of a quick, quiet suicide. Cadmus, indeed, provides the means for such an escape by giving Forster a capsule of poison and saying that it must be done within the next thirty-six hours. At his own request, Forster has been brought, on his release from prison, to the house of Catherine de Troyes, his mistress. Before the war and his defeat, they had been much in love with each other: Catherine, a foreigner with money of her own, had abandoned all her plans in order to be able to settle down here with Forster in the beautiful house she has had built. She is still very much in love with him, but he tells her shortly after his arrival that their relationship has no longer any meaning or reality in his life, which is now quite separate from hers. Catherine at first attributes this to the agony of the choice which has been offered to him, but comes gradually to realise that this is not the case and that she and Forster are now following quite separate paths. In the house also are three men to whom Catherine, partly for her own sake, partly for theirs, has given a temporary home. Catherine's motive for having them there is to provide company for herself sufficient to assuage the loneliness of her waiting for Forster's return but not sufficient to create real ties that might claim her loyalty and thus blur her vision of Forster. The three are Harry Lancaster, an American film director, Matthew Sangosse, a doctor and Father Anselm, a priest. All three, to a greater or lesser extent, have failed in their professions and are financially dependent upon Catherine and her hospitality.

As the play begins, Harry is just returning to the house with Dido Morgen, a nineteen-year-old girl that he has picked up in a bar: he thinks she may be useful in the film which he (on Catherine's money) is supposed to be making about the city. Twenty years ago he made another film about this same city, seeing it as gay, energetic and full of human warmth. His faith has now ebbed and the new film is intended to reflect the cynicism and disillusionment of the new era. Everyone knows, however – including Harry himself, at bottom – that he has no longer the will, imagination and energy to make any film at all. By order of John Cadmus, all those who are in the house at the time of Forster's arrival are detained there and no one else is allowed in, so the whole progress of the play is concerned with the progress of Forster's decision as it is influenced by the forces within the house – Catherine with her past love and her love of the past, Harry with his simplistic and flabby liberal humanism now grown childishly disgruntled and Dido with her fierce, young independence, her wariness and her instinct for life. At first, the decision seems an obvious one and Forster actually agrees with Cadmus immediately the idea of suicide is put to him. 'Cadmus knows I'll do what he asks because there is no future action for me', he tells Catherine. 'He knows there is nothing here, nothing anywhere, to detain me.' Catherine replies to this by saying 'I am here' and it is at that point that Forster says to her 'I am no longer in love with you, Catherine. Such things need to be said.' On the evening of the following day he is still saying to Catherine 'Why try to save me? I'm useless now. I've been tamed by long captivity' and yet when Cadmus revisits the house some few hours later in the early hours of the morning, Forster has changed his mind. He tells Cadmus that when he was in prison he had been sustained and persuaded to go on living by hearing, distantly, the sound of goatherds on the hills, singing. He could not understand the songs, which were in a foreign language, but he believed them to be simple love songs and they somehow signified a belief in and trust of life. During the one day he has known her, he has felt drawn to Dido, and she to him: she symbolises for him the same sense of hopefulness that he had attached to the goat songs and he has suddenly decided on the strength of this intuitive hope to reject the invited suicide and stand trial.

Cadmus is disgruntled and disappointed about this but admits that there is nothing he can do to force Forster's hand. He agrees to send an armed escort to conduct Forster to the city jail to await trial. When the escort arrives, Forster happens by chance to mention the goat songs to the captain in charge, who laughs and tells him the real meaning of the songs: they consist merely of a string of obscenities addressed to the goats; they *do* refer to love, but only in a mocking and belittling way and they have no connected sense at all. The captain then asks Forster about the crucial moment in the military campaign in which Forster was defeated. Having ruthlessly swept aside an 'army' of small boys with wooden swords in the town which was being invaded and having left four hundred of them dead, Forster had suddenly halted his army for no apparent reason and failed to press the attack though militarily the way was clear for him to do so. Forster explains that, at the moment his decision to cross the river should have been taken, he was immobilised by the thought of the leader of the little boys, whom he personally had shot. It was his second-in-command who gave the order for the attack, which, because of the delay, came too late. The captain asks Forster whether he has ever before made this admission to anyone and Forster says 'No'. 'You must consider yourself guilty', the captain says, and Forster admits that he does. 'Are you prepared to go on trial for this', the captain asks him 'to admit your error as you have to me, to be found guilty and to be sentenced? You'll serve the rest of time at the camp in the mountains. And your comfort will be the goat songs.'[5] Forster, though he gives no immediate sign, realises that he has wavered between two senses of life, diametrically opposed, and that now his life is meaningless, belonging to neither kind of life and having failed at the crucial moment in both. The lifeline which had been provided by the goat songs having now been broken by Captain Hurst, who has also compelled him to acknowledge the totality of his failure in the world of military action, Forster abandons the momentary hopefulness which Dido has inspired and, while the captain is for a moment called away by Cadmus, takes the poison. A moment later, loudspeakers in the city announce 'General Forster is dead' and when Dido and Catherine, who do not know of the suicide and who both thought Forster had decided to endure the trial, turn in consternation to Cadmus, he admits that he was so sure of Forster's character and the way he would decide that he had given the orders several hours before for the announcement to be made, without even waiting to hear from Forster as to what his decision was and without troubling to countermand the orders when Forster had said he preferred, after all, to go for trial. The play ends on a faint note of positiveness and hope: Catherine asks Dido, whom she views as her natural ally, to stay with her. The girl at first refuses but at the last moment changes her mind. The last line in the play is hers: 'Catherine. What I know. Can it be taught? I'll try.'

In considering the inner sense and total gesture of the play, it may be advisable at the start to dispose of an issue about which there could well be some confusion and misconception, namely the question of the morality or otherwise of modern warfare – or *any* warfare, for that matter. The story of the intervention of the army of small boys is so vividly and so movingly told that one may be tempted to regard the question of the necessity and justification for their deaths as being the main matter of the play. It is not, however. While death in war and violence generally are not treated by any means casually and are obviously intended to have a powerful emotional effect, the play seems consciously to brush aside the narrowly moral issue as if to indicate not that it is unaware of that issue's existence but that it considers such an issue, especially in its more overt and obvious sociological manifestations, to be a relatively minor one. Forster himself, in the speech already quoted earlier, compares his position with that of both the artist and the saint: what they have in common is that each has an aim outside himself, an objective to the achievement of which his whole being is entirely dedicated, an objective, moreover, which when achieved will be permanent, irrevocable, which will call into existence an actual en-tity – though not necessarily a physical one – that was not present before. The making of war must in this context be viewed as one would view a work of art. There is some indication of this in Whiting's original choice of title for the play: in the early drafts it is called *The Garland of the War*.[6] The setting-aside of conventional moral judge-ments in favour of a quite different view of the inner significance of the play is at one point explicitly stated in the dialogue:

RUPERT: You're young. You won't be free for long. You'll have to commit yourself and love because you're a woman.
DIDO: It's an easy excuse for weakness. You kept free for years. What's the secret? Being a man?
RUPERT: That and having an objective.
DIDO: Something you fought for in that war of yours?
RUPERT: Yes.
DIDO: They said it was for your country and for people like me.
RUPERT: It was for myself. Not for Cadmus or country or you, but myself. To impose myself.
DIDO: They say that's wrong. They say we should live, suffer and finally die for others.
RUPERT: Yes, that's what they say.

The central dramatic conflict of the play, then, is not between the rightness and the wrongness of Forster's murder of the children or even of his belief in war in general. It is between *his* concept of entity, reality on the one hand and Catherine's on the other. He believes that one must externalise one's sense of reality so that it issues in action and *making*, of one sort or another; she believes that reality exists only subjectively, in the creation of the perfect relationship, in loving. Dido stands somewhere between the two.

Like Forster, she is wary of over-commitment in personal relationships, fearful that something of her essential self will be engulfed and destroyed by the daily attrition of personal contact; like him, also, she is clear-eyed, objective and capable of staring truth in the face without flinching; yet she finds long-term, impersonal objectives arid and meaningless and her instinctive tendency is to identify that essential element of self in terms of personal relationship. Dramaturgically she is both catalyst to the action and the litmus by which, though faintly, the final outcome can be recognised. She says 'Everywhere I go there are the unhappy and the aimless waiting for me to put out my hand and walk into that trap made of human arms. Ach! this loving business.' And when Rupert asks her: 'A trap? Do you mean a conspiracy?' her reply is 'No, I mean a trap. The thing you catch wild animals in.' On the other hand, she says 'And you, Rupert. Catherine kept herself and this place for you in all kindness. You refused it. What's the matter with us? What are we afraid of losing? You know, we must think very highly of ourselves to keep ourselves so free.' She begins by being a neutral on the central issue, feeling that the existential reality of each moment and each experience should be tested as it comes along, on its own merits. 'People like me don't think about the future. We don't matter, you see. If we survive – that's good. If we go out – well, there's not much harm done. Mind, if somebody tries to put us out before we think it's time we fight. What for? Just to stay alive to see one more day end, have one more hot bath, be made love to once more, hear one more tune we've heard before and got fond of.' The start of a new day always takes her by surprise, she says: and her surname is Morgen, the German word for 'morning' (again Whiting's uncanny knack of unconsciously choosing for a character a name that subtly extends the meaning of that character from the particular to the general without seeming crude, naive or over-obvious and without sacrificing its credibility as a name – casual, seemingly accidental). In the pattern of the play, poised as it is between Being and Doing, between Love and Action, Dido Morgen is the renewal of energy, the dawning of a new day, the hint of resolution and reconciliation of the two poised forces. As she stands with Catherine at the end of the play, she shows herself ready to accept the implications and the commitments of the dawn that is just coming up, the same dawn that had been set by Cadmus as the signal for Forster's decision and his death.

The severely existentialist approach inherent in Forster's view of the world has its echoes in Whiting's own view of the theatre and, one supposes, of life. He several times in his comments on and criticism of the plays of others, and also in description of his own methods of work, emphasises the need for concreteness in the reflecting of experience and in the nature of the experience itself. In an article in *The Adelphi* magazine in 1952, called 'Writing for Actors',[7] he said 'The basic, the unalterable factor of drama is the moment "when"; the moment of happening which is contained in the action. The dramatist must concern himself with this moment of action and not leave it, as so often happens, to be imposed by the director or players. In other words, the dramatist must create what is done and *when*, and not only the words to be spoken.' Both Dido and Forster (like Stella in *Saint's Day*) have an acute awareness of the importance of 'the moment "when" '. At the moment in which Forster first changes his mind, from suicide to living and facing trial, Dido says to him: 'You and me – here. That's fine. My singing in the streets and you staring into the east[8] – that's the past. You going to prison and me going back to my room – well, that's the future. But you and me, here. That's now.' They are desperate to grasp and use the passing minute and turn it into something of permanent value. Similarly, in the notes Whiting made in preparation for writing *The Nomads* in 1961 he said 'total narrative. The necessity of "the happening" '. Forster several times in the course of the play expresses sentiments similar to this. To Harry Lancaster he says 'I have to act on my decisions, Lancaster. Unlike you, I don't make up my mind and regard it as an end in itself': and to Cadmus he makes a similar remark – 'Soldiers, you know, are forced to actions by their decisions. There's no getting out of it for men in my job. No going back and saying I didn't mean it, when in my hand I'm holding the casualty list for thousands. You'll forgive my contempt for men who think they've fulfilled their obligation by expressing an opinion.' He tells Catherine that when he was in prison he realised that, had he wanted to, he could have used the power of the imagination to make himself, in essence, a free man; but he did not desire this – he used his imaginative powers deliberately to reinforce the idea of imprisonment. 'That little space could have been my childhood nursery, my cadet's room at the military academy, my old battlefields, this room in the house with you – indeed, it could have been any of my particular heavens or hells. Imagination could have made it so. And I could have been any man I wished to be. A free man, if I liked. I chose that the room should be a brick and steel cell in a prison camp in the mountains and that I should be its occupant. A man called "Forster".' When Catherine says to him 'Some men would have tried to get out if only by imagination, by memory', he replies: 'Some men dream away their lives without having to be put behind bars. 'I'm not one of them.' Of Harry Lancaster's film-making he says: 'It's unwise and dangerous to distort the world around you to satisfy your longing.' Forster has the serious artist's longing for a bedrock reality and for the attainment of an Absolute that is compatible with that reality, and for which all sacrifices would be justified. 'What do you want to make of the present?' Dido asks him, and he answers laconically, 'A triumph'. One might put this reply alongside one given by Whiting himself in an interview. 'What do you hope to achieve?' was the question. Whiting's answer was 'What everyone in my job hopes for, I suppose. A masterpiece.' 'And how do you propose to set about it?' 'By becoming more sceptical, and less enthusiastic. By not marching anywhere. By reserving love for women and not spreading it thinly over the whole of humanity. By not going to the Royal Court Theatre. By detesting simplicity more than I do, if that is possible. By travel, by pleasure, by total rejection of knitted, woollen morality. By investigation. And, I suppose it will have to be so, by work.' There is a close kinship of spirit between Whiting's own ambition as an artist and that of several of the characters he created: Forster is one of this kind; so is Paul Southman; and so is Timothy in *Not a Foot of Land*. Like Whiting, they all hated compromise; like him, they yearned simultaneously for purity of soul and a concrete, definable, recognisable – and sizeable – achievement. Their dilemma is exquisite and irreducible. It is of the same kind as that described by Tanner in *Man and Superman*:

> 'But you, Tavy, are an artist: that is, you have a purpose
> as absorbing and as unscrupulous as a woman's purpose . . .
> Quite unscrupulous. The true artist will let his wife starve,
> his children go barefoot, his mother drudge for his living
> at seventy, sooner than work at anything but his art. To
> woman he is half vivisector, half vampire. He gets into
> intimate relations with them to study them, to strip the
> mask of convention from them, to surprise their inmost
> secrets, knowing that they have the power to rouse his
> deepest creative energies, to rescue him from his cold reason,
> to make him see visions and dream dreams, to inspire him,
> as he calls it. He persuades women that they may do this for
> their own purpose whilst he really means them to do it
> for his. He steals the mother's milk and blackens it to make
> printer's ink to scoff at her and glorify ideal women with . . .
> Perish the race and wither a thousand women if only the
> sacrifice of them enables him to act Hamlet better, to paint
> a finer picture, to write a deeper poem, a greater play, a
> profounder philosophy!'

The segment of experience which Shaw here explores and reflects (though it is not the central concern of *Man and Superman*) is the same as that reflected in *Marching Song* – the passionate belief in the possibility of achieving a permanence outside oneself, of leaving behind, embedded in the fabric of the world, the gem-like token of one's achievement, the sign of one's existence; and the paradox that this impulse, which springs from the creative roots of man, is always in inevitable conflict, both within the individual and (often) between the sexes, with that other and equally vital creative urge which is represented by woman. The area of experience is, at least in part, the same in *Marching Song* as in *Man and Superman*, but Shaw's essential vision is comedic where Whiting's is tragic.

For Catherine de Troyes, the personal relation itself *is* the reality; no material object or 'result' is needed to prove a real existence. 'It is the feeling for rightness which made me take you and will make me love you for ever', she says to Rupert. She explains to him that she brought the doctor into her house in the first place because she could not sleep and 'he had magic in his boxes and bottles'; and she brought the priest because she could no longer pray – 'the words that had been there since childhood weren't there any longer.'[9] As soon as Rupert returns, she tells them they must leave: 'You're back, Rupert. Why should I need anything more?' And a little later, when she is telling Rupert how she got to know Cadmus, there is the following passage:

RUPERT: Why didn't you ask him about me? He got a weekly report on my behaviour.
CATHERINE: I didn't want a weekly report on you – to hear of you growing older and sadder and more and more hopeless.
RUPERT: Why not? If it was true.
CATHERINE: I want to know you as you were! If they've changed you I don't know what I shall do. O God! I remember you, Rupert. But do you remember me – do you remember me?

Her love is not simply the selfish whim of a rich woman, nor a predatory or acquisitive impulse only. It is a real force and it represents for her the principle of life. Cadmus describes her as being made 'so intensely vulnerable by her love of life' and Harry, when he first brings Dido to Catherine's house says: 'Kate was in love. The house was built for Kate to get lost in with her man.' And Catherine herself says to Rupert, after she has realised that their lives are of different kinds, 'If I understand you, see you for what you are – I'll not be in love with you. Is that what you hope? There's your true weakness. Believing love can be recognised, evaluated, made to fit into the situation of the moment. It's not so. Not so at all. Even at the height of your power you could never control that.' For Catherine, the whole meaning of life somehow distils itself into that kind of personal relationship which commits one entirely to the other person. This is fullness: all else is emptiness. Her love is a real force, a living force, is indeed the sign of reality to her:

but it is, nevertheless, in her application of it, a conservative force. It harks back constantly to the past; it would forget the intervening years and recreate the past in the present. In this she is like Rupert, in that though she has realised a principle of life and has accepted it as hers, she has failed to integrate it with the whole business of living from day to day. Her absolute, her perfection, has an element of destruction in it, as Rupert's has. It is the avoidance of this destructive element that, she dimly realises at the end of the play, she can learn from Dido: she can learn to preserve and maintain the values of human warmth and human love without having to locate them sentimentally in the past and fix them exclusively and irrevocably on one person and isolate them from the world by imprisoning them in a beautiful house built especially for the purpose. (The description of the house at the beginning of the play acquires from Catherine a significance which is not obvious when one first reads it – or sees it – as the play starts: 'Built into the hillside which ranges high above the city, it transcends the mere purpose of a dwelling-place. The room is a shell caught within a web of glass and steel. It is dominated by the sky . . . Within the room there is an impression of air and space – an impression of delicacy, almost fragility, yet the place is a fortress in strength and position.') However, though there is the hint – it is little more – at the end of the play that Catherine's sense of the world is tentatively reaching out towards a new vision, that she can learn from Dido, the impression must not be given that this is either a clearly pointed 'victory' for Catherine's sense of reality as opposed to Rupert's or a didactic-argumentative conclusion designed to promote a particular point of view as being the 'meaning' of the play. This hint is a coda only: the structure of the main body of the work depends upon the equal validity and the poised forces of the two polar opposites represented by Rupert and Catherine. Indeed, the sense of the play is not only that they are of equal validity but that the structure of life, as of the play, depends upon the strength, authenticity and potency of both. It is not a question of choosing between them but of accepting both as part of the basic stuff of humanity. Individuals do not choose to ally themselves with one or other of these forces, though the forces themselves may, it seems, occasionally choose an individual and dominate him or her utterly: from such dominations come the great artists and the great (usually tragic) love affairs of the world. But such imbalance is the exception, rather than the rule. Ordinary mortals are, like the play, held in uneasy acquiescence, poised between the two.

Though the play is concerned at its deepest level with these two instinctive forces, both of which spring from the roots of life, and though they sufficiently emerge, obliquely, from the poetry of the play for the dramatic tension between them to hold the structure together adequately and to bring the main senses of the play to us, that emergence is not totally successful. The translation of inner sense into the outer forms and structures of the play is not as complete or as sure as it is in either *Saint's Day* or *A Penny for a Song*: Catherine, though an attractive and appealing character, is not central enough and is not drawn in sufficient detail; the compromise with realistic conversational speech is somewhat uneasy sometimes, being on some occasions so terse and muted as to be inexpressive and on others, when expansion and explication become essential, rather startlingly verbose and highly coloured, as if the maintaining of the stiffness of the upper lip for too long suddenly made a kind of desperation of explanation necessary; and elements peripheral to, but ultimately not really germane to the purposes of the central issue, are inadvertently allowed to acquire a dangerous degree of interest. In Aristotelian terms, the play, in the ultimate analysis, lacks that absolute unity of action which it really ought to have.

So far as the question of language is concerned, the reason for the uneasy compromise is not far to seek. It is part of Whiting's life-long struggle with that problem of style. Terrified always of falling into either a romantic lushness or a melodramatic overemphasis, he consciously sought a spare and austere style. 'My intention was to strip from the play everything unimportant to the theme, both in action and speech', he says of *Marching Song*[10] and in the notes for *The Nomads* 'Style, harsh: direct, idiomatic; cut the plush.'[11] Aware of and self-conscious about the natural luxuriance and extravagance of his own early style, as typified in *Not a Foot of Land*, he perhaps over-compensated in *Marching Song*, so that austerity, which is an artistic strength, tends at some moments to become bleakness, even thinness, which is not a strength but a weakness. Not that the failure is total, by any means: though some of the heightened passages do stand out rather awkwardly (Catherine, especially, has difficulty in expressing her deeper feelings without sounding just slightly stagey), there are many that do not. One of the best of these – and one that might have been particularly difficult and embarrassing – is the little lyrical duologue between Dido and Rupert at the end of Act 2. It contains a splendid description of the dawn in which each of them has a beautiful passage and it ends with the following, which is most surely and beautifully done:

DIDO: Would you like to roll up and sleep for a while? I'll watch. Oh, come on. I'm not such a fool. You've trusted people before me. Rest. I'll watch. Sleep.
RUPERT: Yes, you have to trust someone. That's the comradeship of soldiering. The knowledge that you're a man. And need to be watched over in the last hours of the night. Protected. From hurt. And death.
DIDO: Rest.
RUPERT: Watch.

The sudden lift at '. . . in the last hours of the night', when the flatness of everyday speech is suddenly transcended, is quite marvellous and the few words thereafter that take the scene to its conclusion have a sense and an importance out of all proportion to their literal meaning and the plot situation.

The intrusive elements which threaten to blur the central focus are almost all connected with John Cadmus and the political situation. We need either a good deal more of him or somewhat less: as it is, issues which he introduces cannot be pursued and yet are of such interest in relation to Forster's dilemma that they tempt us to move that dilemma into the socio-political arena and debate it there. This is a fascinating exercise but it debilitates the heart of the play. The play will work poetically, flawed as it is but, as Simon Trussler has demonstrated, it will not work politically. It does not, in fact, intend to; but Cadmus seems sometimes to be inviting us to consider it on that level and to do so is dangerous. So far as government and governing are concerned, the sense which the play, poetically considered, distils is that of the need for greatness and nobility in the governors and in the act of governing. As in *Not a Foot of Land* and *Noman*, the play is not so naive as to postulate that such greatness and nobility actually exist, but it does leave a residual sense that they *could*: they are not beyond the bounds of human capability. This general sense serves the play's purposes well: it is only the temptation to wander off into the details of dialectic that is dangerous. There is about the play, indeed, a pervading sense of nobility not only with regard to government but in reference to human nature generally and though the flawed structure has the final effect of making the experience of the play seem more limited than it really is and investing the whole with slight feelings of both unsureness and remoteness, yet this general ambience of an austere nobility does make itself felt. Ironically, it is Cadmus who, in the final moments of the play helps to ensure this. He makes two statements, after Forster's suicide, that invite us to regard Forster's life not in the context of political activity or of self-assertion, but much more as a spiritual quest. The statements, made to Catherine, are these: 'I knew him as a man to be very much like myself. But he'd something I've had to put away whilst I'm in office. Honour. So I knew what the end would be'; and secondly:

> 'We're all victims of injustice, Catherine, every moment of
> our lives. We can shut ourselves up in the day and lie
> awake at night dreaming of revenge. But revenge against
> whom? Against each other? Why? Forster had great cause
> to dream in that way. It was an injustice that we had to
> imprison him and he had reason to sit in that camp in the
> hills thinking up ways of reckoning. But he didn't do that.
> All he wanted was to be taken back into the service of the

world. The world wouldn't have him and so he turned away.
In acceptance. There was no hatred in him.'

The sense of honour which Cadmus attributes to Forster is not, surely, a politician's empty rhetoric; nor is it the conventional sense of patriotism, nor the kind of 'honour' that prefers death rather than face disgrace. What Cadmus is praising Forster for is the refusal to accept, just for the sake of staying alive physically, a life that, because it has irretrievably lost its contact with its own reality, has become meaningless. When this is so, the only logic is death; and honour, truth and the innate nobility of humanity demand that the individual recognise this fact.

There is a negative proof which goes to support this same conclusion and incidentally serves in the process to illuminate the one remaining principal character who has not so far been discussed. This is Harry Lancaster, the American film producer. He hates Forster and says so in various ways several times. At the very beginning of the play he says to Dido, about Forster, 'He was a terrible man. I mean that.' During his first real conversation with Forster himself, he says to Dido about Forster (and in Forster's presence): 'I'm talking to what looks like a man. They tell me he's something more, but he looks like a man. I guess the failure to see is in me.' To Cadmus he says, again about Forster, 'Is he breaking your heart, too? Don't let him do it. That kind break more than hearts. They're not often caught as you've caught this one and you don't often see the naked face out of its idiot covering. Don't let it go free.' And when Cadmus replies, 'But we're not, Mr Lancaster. Let me tell you: Forster is back here to be put on trial', Harry is overjoyed and tears into Forster: 'So they've finally caught up with you, Forster. What a chance for us all – all us little people – to take a smack at you. . . . I can't wait. I can't wait for the day when the whole world'll know what you are. How there was nothing back of those bloody murders but your lusting ambition . . .' This is in Act 2: he returns to the theme in Act 3 when he comes back, rather the worse for drink now, especially to tell Rupert: 'Forster, I want to say something t'you. Listen – now listen. It's this. You're wrong, see. The whole way you've gone is'n insult to what y'could be. Don't ask me why it's wrong. I d'know why. But I feel it here! Is that g'enough for you? . . . And the way I've lived has been right, Forster, and the way you've lived has been wrong. You know something? You're wicked. That's it! You're just wicked.' Harry's judgement and condemnation are on moral and ethical grounds and there can be no question but that he is sincere. He is also, by normal, everyday, conventional moral standards, correct in his judgement. But the play lends him no authority. Whiting himself called Lancaster 'a fool'[12] and the play, in fact, makes a fool of him. He is weak, self-pitying and sentimental, not a person whose judgement we could trust. The truth is that this judgement – which is explicitly given in the play as being on behalf of 'the common man' – is too glib, leaps to conclusions, oversimplifies the questions. Its effect is to discount the everyday mundane judgement, no matter how righteous and how worthy, and direct our attention to issues larger and deeper than those of fustian morality. The study is not of the rightness or wrongness of particular acts of Forster's, but of the nature of humanity that can make a Forster – and that nature is, the play suggests, innately noble.

Noble, but not happy – the play is marked with despair. Even Dido, who has of all the characters the best understanding of and the biggest capacity for happiness, is a wan little figure; brave and defiantly cheerful, but never far from the edge of sorrow. She deliberately hides or discounts this, however; in the mawkish and ugly colloquial slang of a period slightly later than hers, she 'keeps her cool'. As some other critics have pointed out, there is, in fact, an extraordinary prescience in the creation of the character of Dido. When one reads the play now she seems so vivid and so exact a typification of the young man or woman of the middle 1960s, those who were in early adulthood ten years after Jimmy Porter. But *she* was created three years before Jimmy Porter. She is in many ways one of Whiting's most successful portraits.

The inner and outer manifestations of the energy of the human spirit, with which the play is centrally concerned, are reflected at the play's perimeter in the implicit opposition between public and private life which to a greater or lesser extent affects all the characters. Harry sentimentalises it; Anselm and Sangosse (the doctor) are its victims; Dido rejects the whole structure out-of-hand, refusing even to acknowledge the existence of the 'public' life as anything more than a shadowy game, and a dirty game at that. But Cadmus, Rupert and Catherine all experience within their own souls the fury of the struggle between the private man and the public man. It is a favourite theme with Whiting, appearing in most of his plays in one form or another and he always sees it in terms not simply of reconciling the practical demands of public and private life but of trying to establish some permanent sense of reality and of values. Are those actions which we perform because society demands them (duty, social conscience, ambition, economic pressure) real? Or is only the inner heart of the individual real? And what is the link between the two? It is the dilemma which Rupert describes in himself when he says to Bruno Hurst, the captain, about the attack on the children: 'Then, when I caught the child to me, the secret was revealed. I suddenly understood what a man is. For I held it close.' Captain Hurst asks, in reply, 'If you felt this, why did you shoot?' to which Forster replies 'I had no choice. The way I'd chosen to live led to that encounter, which was in itself a challenge. Are you so great? Then fire! I fired and the secret flew up leaving only blood on my sleeve. I became human. So I waited.'

The latent unreality of all public action has also in *Marching Song* another kind of echo from some of Whiting's other plays, namely the question of the effects of government on the individual. The descriptions by Dido, Harry, Cadmus and Matthew Sangosse of the city only just emerging from a period of foreign occupation is very reminiscent of the descriptions of the city and its life in *Noman* and even more of that shadowy yet vivid city described in *Not a Foot of Land*. In all three there is discernible Whiting's scorn for a shallow gregariousness and for a society founded solely on the worship of purely material benefits. In *Marching Song* too, he shows considerable impatience with the facile belief that these and all other social ills can be cured by the indiscriminate application of something called 'democracy'. Cadmus, talking about the new form of government which has come into being now that the country is independent again, says: 'This country has been compelled to accept that system of government from the conquerors. It is known as democratic. It means that I have an opposition party. This of course is a great novelty. My opposition party is liberal-minded and they have all the savagery possessed by good men. They say it is love but they bare their teeth when pronouncing the word.' It is safe to assume that in this instance the character is acting also as *raisonneur* for his author. Whiting's concept of human relations is a fastidious one and it automatically precludes any attempt to account in glib, simplistic terms for the complexities of either personal relationships or relationships between the individual and the community at large.

A further word perhaps ought to be said about the naming of characters in this play. Dido Morgen's surname has already been discussed and the inferences in that instance do seem legitimate. There is great temptation to pursue her forename also for erudite symbolic significance, with thoughts of the *Aeneid* and of the Carthagian queen's taking her own life on her funeral pyre when deserted by her lover. This approach seems unrewarding, however, and leads only to confusion, as do similar speculations on the names of Catherine de Troyes and Cadmus. The Trojan reverberations which Catherine's name tends, perhaps, to set ringing, do not really chime with *Marching Song* at any point and to think of Catherine as Andromache awaiting the return of Hector from the war is not helpful. Similarly with Cadmus: in Greek mythology, he was the brother of Europa and the founder of the city of Thebes; he killed a dragon and sowed its teeth in the earth, the crop being a field full of warriors completely armed; these he thinned out by tricking them into fighting amongst each other, only five surviving; the five became the ancestors of the Spartans and of the noble families of Thebes. Cadmus was also the one who introduced writing into Greece and, when he became old, he turned into a serpent. If one wished to pursue the argument to a *reductio ad absurdum* one might also point out that he was married to a lady called

Harmonia. The John Cadmus of *Marching Song* is passionately fond of music and he is both old and cunning, but the comparison seems to produce as much mystification as clarification and, more important, seems to deal in things which, if not irrelevant, are certainly only peripheral. Ultimately it becomes dangerous. Whiting's own explanation was this: [13] 'Well, I like a sort of euphony and before I start a play I run through the names to make certain that the Christian names or the surnames are not all one, two or three syllables. Dido, Catherine, Rupert, John, Harry – so that you get a sort of pattern . . . I don't think there is any greater significance to my use of names than that.' He must have known, after the event at least, this was not true in at least some cases. And in *Marching Song* he would perhaps have been well-advised to avoid gratuitous false echoes, or irrelevant ones, by choosing more 'neutral' names. There was a special problem in this play, however, as he himself explained in the same interview: 'I was faced with a problem in that play, of course, because I didn't want to use names like von Rundstedt, von Manstein, and so on. Therefore I chose a name like Forster, which is found in Germany, applicable in France and is found in England; and the same thing with the Christian names, which are interchangeable in most European countries.' Attractive though his choices were, one still feels that happier ones could have been made, even though the echoes of a vague and general classicism do serve to emphasise the sense of the dilemma's being an everlasting one and part, therefore, of the very blood and bone of all humanity, not a twentieth-century political problem to be settled at a conference. This same sense of eternal warfare is also reflected visually by an ancient helmet, found by Forster on the field of battle, a relic of some other battle, long ago. The helmet, on a plinth, is now part of the decoration of Catherine's room.

Although the play, when it opened in London on 8 April 1954, ran for only forty-three performances, it was accorded a critical reception a good deal more respectful than that which greeted either *Saint's Day* or *A Penny for a Song*. Even so, most critics stopped a good deal short of rapture. The most laudatory of them were T. C. Worsley, of the *New Statesman*, recanting his former antagonism to make public obeisance, and Harold Hobson in the *Sunday Times*. 'With his new play', said Worsley, 'John Whiting confounds those of us who were too dense to recognise his talents in the famous Arts Theatre prize play *Saint's Day*. The talent in *Marching Song* is indubitable and impressive.' Hobson's notice contained one particularly perceptive comment: 'He has a troubled and uneasy poetry whose shadowy tides never wash against the shore of our own land of cricket bats and football pools . . .' Whiting himself seemed to change his mind about the play. When it was published in *The Plays of John Whiting* in 1957, he wrote of it: 'Of the three plays, *Marching Song* is the most important, both in content and structure. It has a single and undeviating line in story and treatment . . . There are no sub-plots . . . My intention was to strip from the play everything unimportant to the theme, both in action and speech.' In 1961, however, in the *Encore* interview (that is to say, after *The Devils* had been both written and produced) he said: '*A Penny for a Song* is rather clumsy in its structure but it's a better play than any of the others, curiously enough. It has a much lighter texture but it *is* the best play of the three. *Marching Song* is not a successful play – it is much too dense . . . I could have done it with far less of both resources and material. There are pieces of music like this. It's got a thickened sense about it. It suffers slightly from a kind of intellectual elephantiasis.'

Now that the play has had time to find its own proper level and enough time has elapsed for an objective judgement to be made, one feels that Whiting was to some degree mistaken in both of his judgements. Though of considerable merit and importance and a major work of high seriousness, *Marching Song* does not, in point of fact, seem to be 'the most important' of his plays. *Saint's Day* is that, whether one judges importance by historical position and influence or by intrinsic artistic merit. On the other hand, one would not subscribe either to the view that *Marching Song* was not a successful play, or that it is heavy and overladen. If anything, it is too spare, too self-consciously austere, especially in the matter of language. Something of the spontaneous luxuriance of *Saint's Day* would have helped rather than hindered. The experience need not have been pared to its centre as much as it was: some bifurcation would not have distracted from the central growth and would have given an added fulness to the whole plant. But even as it is, the existence and the vigour of that central growth cannot be denied, nor its stature and importance set aside. Those critics who, when the play first appeared, found it cold and without charm (both points were made by two or three different critics) were largely guilty of the same error that actuated Johnson's famous misjudgement of *Lycidas*: they were looking for the wrong things – though it is only fair to them to add, while not regarding it as proving anything, that Whiting himself described it as 'glacial on a human level' and as having 'no private parts'. It still reads magnificently and of all his plays – especially in view of its political subject matter – it is the one which ought now to be given the acid test of revival. It has had no major professional stage production in English since its opening in 1954 (unles one counts the rather skimpy and scrambled version at the Greenwich Theatre in 1974) though it has had two different productions on British television.

Raymond Williams, in *Drama from Ibsen to Brecht* (the revised version, published by Chatto and Windus in 1963, of *Drama from Ibsen to Eliot*) has, among the material added to the new version, a brief but interesting passage about *Marching Song*: his comment on its structure is useful, as is – particularly – his description of the play's relationship to the patterns of development of twentieth-century thought and dramatic expression: '*Marching Song* is unusual', he says, 'in a special sense: in its concentration, into a single and restrained form and tone, of the representative themes and gestures of a late liberalism, a settled naturalism. It is not penetrating: not the savagely exposing, disturbed and distorted action of the post-liberal collapse.' There is more to it than this, but the statement is valuable in helping to place *Marching Song* in its context. Williams ends his note on the play by observing 'It is less showy, less crude, than the forms which succeeded it . . . At the same time its anxious restraint shows clearly, if negatively, what would happen to this complex if controls were relaxed: a rush of feeling and a loss of form.' Whiting was acutely aware of this, as his dramatic criticism – as well as his struggles with style in his own work – shows. He was also aware that a major work of art cannot exist without the fusion of these two elements of form and feeling, that the former is not an inhibition of the latter but is its necessary complement in determining the work's posture and transmitting its meaning. *Marching Song* is, among other things, an example of Whiting's constant efforts to establish and maintain the proper balance.

IV   *The Gates of Summer* (1953–1956)

Some critics have tended to assume that because *The Gates of Summer* never reached London (it opened at Oxford in September 1956 for a pre-London provincial tour, was dogged by ill-luck in that Dorothy Tutin, who was playing Caroline, became ill, and it closed in Brighton in late October, without ever coming in to London) it can safely be ignored. Gabrielle Scott Robinson in one of her articles in *Modern Drama* described it as 'a minor play' – not a judgement that it is easy to endorse. It is, in fact, a play of considerable interest and stature, both as a study of Whiting's developing style and as an autonomous work with an identity of its own. It is probably the most playable of all Whiting's plays and, though the dialogue – like that of the other plays – shows again that struggle with the problems of style which has already been discussed and shows it in an acute form, with considerable mixing of conventions, yet the play contains some of the smoothest and most effective of all Whiting's dialogue and two or three descriptive passages of quite startling beauty.

It is a play about love. Where his other plays have treated or considered love among other subjects or related to other things, *The Gates of Summer* makes love its theme solely. True, this theme is seen in the wider Whiting context of the impossibility of virtue, the smirching of innocence (again one thinks of Anouilh) and the search for some absolute value, a search foredoomed to failure; but love is not, in this play, merely incidental to that search, nor is it cited simply as one example of the dilemma: it is the only example and it is examined as if it might have some special right or claim in the matter. Equipped with passions as we are, there is a reasonable temptation to suppose that love between man and woman ought to be or could be the very means by which the longed-for absolute is attained. Has sexual orgasm no meaningful symbolism outside its own physical existence? With a wan little smile, the play shakes it head and tiptoes away at the end, leaving mundane compromise in charge of the field.

The lovers are John Hogarth and Caroline Tremayne and they meet when Hogarth arrives in Greece from England. The play is set in 1913 – a cunning piece of timing that gives interesting and sometimes poignant perspectives, though at plot level it also places something of a strain on the credulity, since the characters, especially the two lovers, are so pervaded by the dark unease of the middle of the century that it is sometimes difficult to associate them with the twilight of the Edwardian era.

John is a libertine who has explored the possibilities of love with the assiduity of a Don Juan. And this is not the only Byronic echo: unfulfilled by love and disgusted with the crass philistinism of England, he has sold all his possessions, given the money (£100,000) to a Greek revolutionary cause and come to Greece now to offer his services as a soldier in the revolution. The revolution is led by Prince Basilios, whom John has originally met in London. The arrangement is that they should meet again just outside Athens at the house of Sophie Faramond, an old mistress of John's who is now married to Selwyn Faramond, an archaeologist. Caroline is Selwyn's daughter by his first marriage. Her husband, Boysie Tremayne, has recently deserted her after a few years of married misery. Caroline is twenty-five and, in her own word, 'finished'; John is thirty-five; Sophie is fifty-four.

Sophie is writing her memoirs or, rather, is dictating them to Cristos, a Greek who has rented the house to Selwyn and Sophie. Like all the other characters in this strange play, Cristos is a frustrated and failed Romantic. He was educated in England, a country he still loves, but because he lost all his money gambling there, he had to return to Greece and live quietly almost as a servant, not being able to afford to go back to England. The memoirs, we gather, have John Hogarth as a central figure, a hero twice over, in that Sophie has remembered him in heroic terms and Cristos is not, in fact, setting down what she dictates but shaping it, with Hogarth as hero, into a work of fiction that satisfies his own artistic standards. Selwyn, Sophie's husband, has for eighteen months been working on archaeological excavations which lead during the course of the play to the discovery of an ancient temple of Aphrodite and this activity has brought to the place Henry Bevis, a special correspondent from *The Times* who is writing a regular column on the progress of the 'dig'. In his timid way, he also has fallen in love with Caroline, though she treats this partly as a joke and partly as a bore. With John, however, she has no such hesitations or reservation: by the end of Act I she has entirely abandoned her despair and her position of objective reserve, has fallen thoroughly in love with him and told him so, to his extreme annoyance – since he also finds her very attractive and since he has just run away from what he swears is his final love affair. The progress and the nuances of their relationship form the central motion of the play.

On the periphery of this is Selwyn's discovery of the temple of love, Sophie's jealousy of Caroline (very faintly sketched) and Henry Bevis's ineffectual regret at losing Caroline. John tells Caroline that, though he loves her, he will not be deflected from his original plan of joining the Greek revolution: love and all personal relationships seem now to him to be evanescent, no matter how marvellous at the time; love degenerates into marriage, into the compromise of everyday living and he longs for something that retains its meaning and its splendour. Caroline tries to persuade him, but fails. She then offers him a glass of wine and they drink together to his going: when they have both drunk, she tells him that the wine is poisoned – she has made a distillation from some berries, locally called 'Man's Friend' to which Cristos had once, on a country walk, drawn her attention and told her of the local legend: 'We'd been talking of the unhappiness of love,' she says, 'the impossibility of absolute oblivion. Then Cristos took a handful of the berries and told me that many people in this tragic country believed they held the secret.' The berries are said to take effect in about eight hours, so they have the length of the night before them, which John refuses to spend with Caroline. When John tells Sophie what has happened, she says: 'Yet it makes a much better ending.' 'For me?' enquires John. 'No. The book, dear boy. Better than the battlefield. Less confusion.' Meanwhile, Henry Bevis has run into what is for him a major problem: the archaeological discovery that Selwyn has made turns out to be a major one, which is what Bevis had hoped for because he is counting on his reporting of it to make his reputation for him. However, he feels now that he has seen it that he cannot describe it in any detail for so august a journal as *The Times* because the discovered temple is decorated entirely with life-size bas-relief figures all engaged in various stages of the acts of courtship, pursuit and love. In Selwyn's words, it represents 'ostensibly man and woman's progress from the cradle to the grave, with overwhelming emphasis on a certain aspect'. 'These golden children' is John's description of them. While John, on the assumption that he has only a few more hours to live, has retired to his room to ponder on life and its events, Cristos comes to tell him that Basilios has arrived to conduct him to the revolutionary forces. John tells Cristos of the poisoned wine and the latter merely laughs. Caroline had mis-understood him about the berries, he explains: they are not poisonous but are by legend reputed to possess aphrodisiac properties. This is what he had meant when he said to her that 'many people in this tragic country believed they [the berries] held the secret.' Basilios also has a shock for John: he cannot lead his revolution after all, because he has squandered all the money John gave to him: at the request of a beauti-ful woman he organised an enormous garden party designed to raise more money, but no one came except the woman herself. The magnific-ent, elaborate affair was presented for just the two of them, as in a dream world; and all the money was lost. So Basilios is in flight and there is no revolution for John to drown his sorrows in and lose himself in. In every respect love seems to have triumphed (Sophie has just been down the hill to attend a peasant wedding) and there seems now no reason at all why John should not surrender and stay with Caroline. She, indeed, now assumes that he will but the matter is kept in doubt until the final moments of the play. In no less than six slightly varying draft endings which are still extant (though unpublished, of course) he *does* stay and the tone, though either muted or troubled, in these versions is 'happy' – at least to the extent of leaving the lovers together. But in the penultimate and final versions (the latter appears in *The Collected Plays*, vol. 2), John leads Caroline to think he is staying but while she is undressing to go to bed with him, he tiptoes out of the room, deliberately handing her over to Henry.[14]

When one recounts the outline of the story in this way, it sounds more like the scenario for a comic operetta than anything else and, given a different treatment, it might well have been. As it is, though the play is a comedy and the touch is light, yet firm, the overall tone and gesture is not merely serious, it is downright sombre. Whiting describes it as the 'harshest' of his plays and in a way it is. Paradoxically, however, it also contains the purest and the most persuasive lyrical passages that he ever wrote, though over all of them hangs an autumnal sadness. Caroline comes almost to believe in the lyrical joy at two points in the play, but John never does and it is his voice to which the play gives the greater authority. The title of the play is the centre of one such group of lyrical images, invoked in all seriousness and sincerity by Caroline, but transmuted to ironic use by the play. It is taken from the following passage:

JOHN: All my life I've treated every opportunity as the last chance. I've looked – oh, sadly – on each encounter as the last. But I was cheated. The sun came up and the sun went down and, damn it, life had to be lived. And opportunity didn't knock once. It beat a positive tattoo at my door.
CAROLINE: Which every time you opened.
JOHN: It was never shut. (*He kisses her on the forehead*) But now the foot

of time is edging it to. Soon there'll only be space in that doorway for the lightest and most frivolous opportunity to get through. The last – the smallest and least consequential – will have to stay, I suppose, to comfort my extreme age for there'll be no getting out.

CAROLINE: My God! Can't you – (JOHN *kisses her on the mouth*) see? Can't you see – that before you – haven't you eyes? – oh, yes! you've eyes – before you is not a quickly closing door. No, John – darling, my new found one: dear – fool! there before you are the wide open gates of summer. You've lived only – nothing but – the early months of your year of life. Stay on. I'll not mind – never mind – if you go on from me to another – fairer, she may be – but be aware – be'ware – not old, not sleeping but now whilst young – of the fairest to hand. Stay. Go on from me – after all – if you want to go on – on. Go on.

This same image is echoed by Basilios when he describes to John the great garden party, with only himself and his mistress there. ('We walked the garden in silence until the sun went down and the Chinese lanterns were lit. The river pageant moved past in splendour for my lady . . . Her face was to the stars as the firework display was set off.') John asks him: 'Was she beautiful and were you truly happy?' Basilios replies: 'She was beautiful, yes, and for the last time I was truly happy. The last time. For with her hands she closed the gates of love behind me.' John then says 'I wanted to be sure the money wasn't wasted, that's all.'

Love and time and the ache for an absolute are linked in the play in a complicated pattern of concentric circles. 'We were speaking of your future happiness, my child', Sophie says to Caroline. 'Were you, darling', is the acid reply, 'What about my present happiness?' 'We thought it problematic (CAROLINE *has taken* JOHN's *arm*) – or merely affected.' In the present, John and Caroline debate their love and their future; Sophie writes about a past that she knew and half-consciously, half-unconsciously, creates a myth for the future as she writes. Behind and around all this, is the distant past, represented by the ancient temple that suddenly moves disturbingly into the present, with its frescoes that seem as full of life still, after two thousand years, as the newly risen sun. 'The lamps were handed through to me', Selwyn says, describing his discovery 'and in their dancing light the still figures on the wall seemed to be animate. For two thousand years they'd remained until I brought them the light which set them performing again their endless love rites. A great moment. To hear a poem of Anacreon[15] spoken by a voice of the time. The young sun-hot bodies joined by the freshly poured wine and playing their games forever to the silent music.' Sophie, particularly, is sensitive to these time relationships. Of her husband she says, when she realises that work on the excavation of the Greek temple is almost finished: 'Soon he'll be at work again digging up a day that was a thousand years ago and I, nearby, less fortunate, at work on a mere decade. Yes, the future definitely seems to lie in the past.' She describes

John Hogarth as 'the first twentieth-century man' and when pressed for an explanation says: 'He was the only man I knew who seemed perfectly unequipped to face the future. I knew he'd survive.' This is an especially significant comment because it succinctly describes one of the basic concerns of the whole play – the ability of twentieth-century man to survive; and to get at the root causes of his spiritual dilemma, the play attempts to trace them back to their origins in the securer times of the last decade of the nineteenth century and the first of the twentieth. Has modern man, the play tacitly enquires, some special excuse for his sense of desolation, or is the condition endemic to the whole human race, at all times? A sense of history and of the balancing forces of tradition and progress, stability and innovation, are factors whose influence is felt in all John Whiting's plays, but they are clearer in *The Gates of Summer* than in any of the others: there is considerable cunning in the choice of 1913 as the time of the action of the play, as there also is in the pivoting of the mechanics of the plot upon the progress of an archaeological exploration. Together, these devices ensure that none of the actions or moments of the play are observed in isolation: all are related in a sophisticated and significant pattern to a host of images both past and future, so that the poetic complexity and sensibility of the play is vastly increased. The corridors of human time are made to reverberate with multiple echoes.

In this pattern of times, the impatience of the immediate present is represented by Caroline. Like Dido Morgen in *Marching Song*, she is an archaeologist's daughter; like Dido, she knows only one reality – that which can be grasped and sensuously apprehended *today*; like Dido, too, she holds archaeology and the reverence for tradition in contempt. Whiting's own instinctive sympathy is with tradition – the observable solidity of past achievement – but he acutely realises also that life must be *now*, that those justly valued achievements of the past were once the disputed and doubtful strivings of the present: of all human activities, art must always be particularly aware of this dichotomy.

These connections and juxtapositions of love and time exist throughout the play, as do the links between love and the desire for an absolute, a complete fulfilment not just of the passionate urge itself but of the whole sense of being. The most extensive and explicit expression of this is spoken by John when he composes for Henry Bevis a mock review for *The Times*. The mockery, though maintained throughout the speech, is subjugated to the lyric intensity of the longing for life to contain one perfect and complete gesture and the speech, therefore, becomes an encapsulation of the beauty and bitterness of the play as a whole:

> 'Athens: Monday. (Have you a pencil?) The expedition led
> by Colonel S. F. Faramond (well, come on, man: take it
> down!) today reached an inner chamber of the excavation

(Shorthand, eh?) The work of eighteen months, as
observed by Your Correspondent (that's you) has been
successful. The find will disappoint many who had hoped
for some revelation of the Periclean age, but will be of
interest to those who have never before had any sympathy
with archaeological science. (Stop sucking the pencil,
Henry. Get it down. Here we go!) This place – (have
you a picture of your ideal reader? I have) – a room stamped
down by time under the earth holds, sir, your youth. This
place, dedicated to the sparrow and the swan, the rose, the
poppy and the lime tree, sacred to Aphrodite, keeps safe
the dark girl, the gay brave one in the language of the
time, who loved you (so she said) most. Your
Correspondent has no wish to use these columns for
confession or reminiscence but yes, she was known to him.
For she was born to many of us among the raspberry bushes
on a hot afternoon in the garden when the younger children
laughed and played, but you and I, sir, older (at least
fourteen) silent, horribly wiser, stayed out of sight: (I speak
personally, Henry. You were probably curled up in a
theatrical basket) born in the fevered heat on that torrid
day with the sun falling out of the sky. She stayed with
you, growing in beauty and experience as your imagination
and longing swept you into manhood (Were you swept into
manhood, Henry? I was. It entailed swimming the length
of an ornamental lake at four o'clock in the morning. You're
right. Another story). She was so nearly met. There was
always the chance of absolute discovery in so many
encounters. And yet. And yet. Where was she? The dark
girl with the wit of the sparrow, the viciousness of the swan,
the arrogance of the rose, the vulgarity of the poppy and
the contentment of the lime tree. Shall we say she was with
you until you lost your ambition? Yes, sir, age is
responsible for too much. That's agreed. It's responsible,
you'll remember, for the loneliness which made you do with
that angel in tweeds across the breakfast table . . . The dark
girl, the ideal born in the garden, has been protected after
all. Here, sir, are your boyish scribblings on the wall, the
formal patterns of desire scratched on the end papers of
your Liddell and Scott, the undergraduate poems and the
solitary drinking of your thirties, all translated to beauty
and truth. How foolish you were, dear reader of *The Times*,
to think she was lost. She was here in every way. Playing
the games, laughing, lying, acting all the scenes and being a
woman. She was in this place. Waiting. Ah! sir, in two

thousand years she has not aged. Her bed is still a jousting
ground: yours is now a place of rest. Her way of adoration
has become a goodnight kiss pecked into the forehead.
There are other differences too painful for this journal to
print...'

Both Ronald Hayman and Simon Trussler construe the discovered
temple as an obscenity and therefore a symbol of disillusion since something noble and 'uplifting' was expected and this expectation has been
disappointed. They both compare the difference between expectation and
realisation with Rupert's discovery, in *Marching Song*, that the goat
songs he had believed in as symbols of love were in fact obscene. Surely
the passion and sincerity of the long speech of John's that has just been
quoted, however, militates against such a reading. All the speech's irony
is directed against the 'angel in tweeds' who is fond of dogs; the dancing
figures in the temple are treated with seriousness but with delight as
uninhibited expressions of, and embodiments of, that spirit which
touches every individual life, but only glancingly, that longed-for
absolute which for most people is unattainable and of which they feel
only the faint, poor, broken echoes. The fullness of the life embodied
in these carvings is the central image of the play, a symbol of the errant,
instinctive, full-spirited life that erupts suddenly from the ground, compared with which the careful, attenuated, calculated life of the twentieth-
century everyday bourgeoisie is thin and tame.

Sexual love, the play seems to say, ought of its very urgency to be
the one human experience in which an absolute state of perfection could
be attained. Yet it proves, in everyday practice, to be otherwise. The
comic interlude of the great garden party is a conscious counterpoint to
this main theme. The garden party *is* perfect, whole, self-contained,
complete; and it is a celebration of all the aspects and all the rites of love
('But for us the fiddles sang – and sang until their voices were faint
to us through the empty corridors of the house which led us dancing
to our further sport'). So Basilios, who is a failure in material, worldly
matters and who as a character is treated wholly comically (though not
unsympathetically) by the play, is shown as attaining the ideal which
permanently eludes John. Clearly, however, Basilios is, by virtue of his
special and minor position in the pattern of the play, the exception
that proves the rule. The whole frame of the play makes the rule itself
plain: and that rule is the pervasiveness of disillusion. Just as the yearn-
ings for an absolute, attained through political idealism in *Not a Foot of
Land* and through a life of action in *Marching Song*, both failed of
achievement and led to the choice of self-destruction rather than the
acceptance of compromise, so John, disillusioned and spiritually exhausted by love's compromise, elects death on the battlefield (as he
hopes). Caroline, on the other hand, with her grand gesture of dying

together, feels that love, in the sense of individual, sexual attachment, can still be made the crown of life, the very epitome of its purpose, greater and more apt to succeed than a devotion either to political solutions or to material progress. 'Let's show them, John', she says 'Let's show this whole damned century with its passion for steam engines and plotting in cellars that there were two people who were unafraid to give themselves to the oldest passion of all. The beauty and the sacrifices are all in the story books now. I want them as you do to be here in life.' John. though he came to Greece with no other purpose in mind but to die, feels that to die for love in the way Caroline has devised is too glib, too sentimental, too unreal; but later, when he has heard from Cristos that the berries are not poisonous, he changes his assessment of her, though not his determination to leave her:

CAROLINE: Nothing lasts for ever, not even bad weather. Some dawn or other it clears and you find yourself a long way out. You're safe. But you're drifting. And you're alone. Reason, the poor soaked fool, is fished out, hauled aboard, restored to its seat and at once starts giving advice. You take it and paddle on. This time I wanted to go down with all hands. And with you.

JOHN: It's not going to happen.

CAROLINE: Oh, yes it is.

JOHN: No, you made a mistake. The berries are harmless.

CAROLINE: But Cristos said . . .

JOHN: You misunderstood. The stuff has a certain effect.

CAROLINE: What effect?

JOHN: Well, shall we say that it strikes at a more private part than the immortal soul.

CAROLINE: I didn't know.

JOHN: Are you sure?

CAROLINE: Of course I'm sure.

JOHN: I'm glad.

CAROLINE: You're glad I thought we'd both be finished?

JOHN: Yes. No one's ever balanced my life so precisely with their own before.

CAROLINE: My God! You love me, don't you?

JOHN: Very much.

CAROLINE: Wait a minute. Have you forgotten? There's going to be a tomorrow after all. Can you say it knowing that?

JOHN: Yes.

CAROLINE: But, John, it's going to be for quite a while. Now say it.

JOHN: A man takes leave of a woman he's loved and an art he's practised in much the same spirit. He loves but he goes. That's what I'm doing now.

All these various utterances from the play have the same import – life is useless and worthless unless one has some recognisable, verifiable objective, greater than oneself, to which that life can be devoted, some belief to which one may give oneself with total confidence that it will not diminish in stature or evaporate at the breath of reality, something which *is*, in fact, itself the ultimate reality. And in the face of this need, neither hedonism nor hypocrisy will serve as substitutes, nor will humility, Christian forbearance or a cheerful acceptance of compromise. There is in the nature of life that which demands some absolute manifestation of purpose. Whiting in one of the interviews he gave, said in relation to *Marching Song* that it was strange that no one in the play mentioned God. Given the texture of the play of course, it is not strange at all; nor was Whiting suggesting that it was a mere oversight on his part that the mention of God had been omitted from the play. The true significance of his comment, surely, is that it pinpoints his awareness of the difficulty of expressing, in a fragmented and secular society, the sense of desire for an absolute which lies at the root of all his own plays.

The focusing of this desire, in *The Gates of Summer*, upon the love relationship produces in the work some curious echoes of other dramatists, not all of which are equally happy or advantageous to the play. One of these – and one that here and there threatens to wrench the play from its true bias – is an odd Strindbergian overtone. Sophie says to Caroline : 'My dear child, it's a fact that men sometimes get sick of us; not individually or personally, but sick of our whole ravening sex. They then take up soldering or achaeology, throw themselves into politics or find other things to do which we don't understand – such as revolution.' In the same act there is the following passage between Caroline and John:

JOHN: Time, Caroline, and time again I was well on my way to being in love with a person.
CAROLINE: That's behaviour. Got no more to do with it than the angle of your hat. You speak of formalities. Didn't you suffer?
JOHN: Horribly. About the fourth week. Oh, to stop playing the dancing ape.
CAROLINE: Poor animal!
JOHN: Yes! You'd blubber over such lack of freedom for your doggies and birdies and dear, sweet gee-gees. But a man? Why you only bite your finger to stop your laughter. Goad the beast and it will give tongue. Do you recognise human speech? What is it you want to hear? Surely not the beaten desperate cry: Will you please go away and leave me alone!
CAROLINE: We always go. There's that to be said for us.
JOHN: Go? Yes, but you leave behind a long, backward look.
CAROLINE: We have to fight with outdated weapons. We hope the dull edge of remorse stays sharp enough to penetrate the heart.

This conversation ends with John's saying 'No, Caroline, love can never stand up to the onslaught of your sex. Never' and at an earlier moment, he has said to Sophie when they were discussing Basilios and his revolution: 'Basilios is a man – the one sex I don't make mistakes about.' All this springs from, and adds to, the play's pervading mood of world-weary cynicism and is effective in this context. It makes for witty dialogue and theatrically powerful situations, too. Its disadvantage, though, is that, at best, it distracts attention from the play's central purpose; at worst, it threatens to disrupt and dissipate that purpose by substituting a different one – the old, familiar War of the Sexes. Fortunately, the threat remains unfulfilled: the digressions are not extensive enough to affect the balance more than momentarily.

A very different echo, and one which is more germane to the central issues, comes from a particular play, namely Fry's *The Lady's not for Burning*, which was written some five years before *The Gates of Summer* (by a man who was a personal friend of Whiting's and who had been largely responsible for the award of the competition prize to *Saint's Day* three years before: so the influence is not surprising – in any case, Fry's verse plays were of considerable, if temporary, influence on almost everyone in British theatre at that time). The general tone of the relationship between John and Caroline has some distinct resemblance to the feeling of the scenes between Thomas Mendip and Jennet Jourdemayne in the Fry play: the sense of love's illogicality in a world of violence, mendacity and decay; and the sense of the comic inconvenience[16] in rejoicing over that which, rationally considered, should produce, at best, an ironic detachment and a quiet exit. In *The Lady's not for Burning*, the lovers say to each other:

THOMAS: *I defend myself against pain and death by pain*
And death, and make the world go round, they tell me,
By one of my less lethal appetites:
Half this grotesque life I spend in a state
Of slow decomposition, using
The name of unconsidered God as a pedestal
On which I stand and bray that I'm best
Of beasts, until under some patient
Moon or other I fall to pieces, like
A cake of dung. Is there a slut would hold
This in her arms and put her lips against it?

JENNET: *Sluts are only human. By a quirk*
Of unastonished nature, your obscene
Decaying figure of vegetable fun
Can drag upon a woman's heart, as though
Heaven were dragging up the roots of hell.
What is to be done? Something compels us into
The terrible fallacy that man is desirable
And there's no escaping into truth. The crimes
And cruelties leave us longing, and campaigning
Love still pitches his tent of light among
The suns and moons.

Notice, in passing, that in the last two lines of this Fry himself has an echo, though *au contraire* (so to speak), of: 'But Love has pitched his mansion in/The place of excrement.'[17] – which is Yeats, from whom Whiting took the titles for two of his plays (and whose name he comically bestowed on a *female* character in a third play).

In *The Gates of Summer*, John says to Caroline, 'It's difficult to believe that you who occupy little space as a person and the trivial act of writing a poem could in time crowd out the many necessary and amusing ways of living.' And at the end of the play, Caroline says to John: 'Damn, oh damn and damn! This is what Cristos warned me about. Falling in love with a legend. You're a man. Just a man. Two a penny. That's what you are', to which John replies 'Seeing me that way is the penalty of winning, Caro. You've never been anything but a woman to me. I've never asked that anyone I've loved should be more.' She replies: 'You mean, however splendid the pursuit and however corrupt the trickery, I'll end up with a man. Just a man.'

The images are even more explicit – and closer still to Fry's – in some of the earlier versions of the scene: 'You. Going bravely on two feet. You. Creedless. Useless . . .'; 'The whole bag of tricks can be tumbled and forgotten in a hole in the ground in a nod'; 'Then what can make you, a mere acknowledged man, God? A religion in my arms, a philosophy between my legs . . .' (see Appendix I)

However, although the two plays take initial views of love which are somewhat similar, their final postures are quite different. Both plays end as a new day is beginning: *The Lady's not for Burning* greets it, if a little wryly, with gaiety and confidence; *The Gates of Summer* with an autumnal melancholy. In the Fry play the lovers set out together, not expecting very much of the world but at least prepared to face it together; in the Whiting play, the man sets out alone, expecting nothing and leaving the woman by a sad little cynical trick. All in all, the love scenes in *The Gates of Summer*, though they do have echoes here and there of other plays and other playwrights, have a style, a beauty and a flavour which is their own. To an extent they are reminiscent of some parts of *A Penny for a Song*, though never so innocently gay: it is rather as if the instinct to joy is being, in the later play, acknowledged, warily examined and finally rejected as either spurious or misleading. Yet here and there it is present in the play, bubbling up through the hard surfaces of frustration, disbelief, cynicism and ennui, only to be frozen in the icy air.

The extent to which the figure of John Hogarth is intended deliberately to invoke the image of Byron and invite comparison with the poet is impossible to determine definitively but provides grounds for some fascinating speculation. There are certainly *some* connections, whether conscious or unconscious. The name of the character – John Hogarth – conjures up at once the phrase 'the rake's progress' (Hogarth himself mentions it at one point) and this accords nicely both with the image of himself that John Hogarth is at pains to create in the play and with one of Lord Byron's reputations – 'mad, bad and dangerous to know', according to Lady Caroline Lamb, who once sent him a curl of her pubic hair, tied with a ribbon. Basilios mentions Byron's death at Missolonghi and directly compares John with Byron: The full passage reads as follows:

BASILIOS: Ah! my wonderful boy, you came to bring freedom to a country and instead you're content to bring happiness to an old man.
JOHN: Shall I be honest with you, Basilios? I wasn't concerned with the freedom of the country. I wanted freedom for myself. I'd have died in your cause, Basilios, whatever it was.
BASILIOS: My dear boy, you come from a country which has always spoken lightly of dying for the cause. Your great predecessor, Noel[18] Byron, said, you remember:

> *'If thou regret'st thy youth, why live?*
> *The land of honourable death*
> *Is here – up to the Field and give*
> *Away thy breath!'*[19]

God took him at his word, though, and fetched him off here.

Caroline, too, compares Hogarth directly with Byron when she says: 'Now why should it embarrass you to have a woman see you as you see yourself? You act the last of the romantics and carry his accessories. Then you must damned well expect to be treated as such. You can't brood over your pistols and your past, your copy of Malory and your death in battle and have me see you as I see Henry. He's trying to make his way in the world. You're trying to make your way out of it.' Caroline – even though her phraseology may not be justified in terms of the history of English poetry – obviously means Byron when she says 'the last of the romantics', though this is obscured by a misprint in the 1969 *Collected Plays*, which has 'You *are* the last of the romantics . . .'. Clearly this is an error, since it does not really make sense of Caroline's speech (why should she say that John is the 'last of the romantics'? With whom, in 1956, is she comparing him?). But to accuse him, mockingly, of acting the part of a known great romantic figure, of *imitating* him, has great ironic force at this moment in the play. All the manuscripts and typescripts confirm this meaning: they all have '*act* the last of the romantics', not '*are* the last of the romantics'.

A further irony of the comparison with Byron is that the poet was fighting on behalf of a popular uprising, a 'people's war': the revolution John Hogarth was to have aided, had it not aborted itself, was a *counter-revolution*, an attempt to restore power to the aristocracy. 'We are', says Basilios to Sophie, 'a few brothers bound by a belief in a former way of life' (which links this piece of conversation with those other examples, already mentioned, of discussions of the relative merits of tradition and progress).

Byron was certainly someone in whom John Whiting was especially interested. Among the books on his shelves after his death were fifty-four volumes relating to the poet, including such rare items as Ralph Milbanke's *Astarte* and a complete set of the original printer's galley sheets, bound in white buckram, of the anonymous *Lady Noel Byron and the Leighs*. The bookseller's letter was still tucked inside the front cover: Whiting had bought the book for twelve guineas from Hall's Bookshop in Tunbridge Wells in 1960. 'STRICTLY PRIVATE', the letter said of the book, 'only 32 copies printed for the descendants of Lord and Lady Byron, 1887.' Alongside the strictly private volume on the shelves were more public ones from both the nineteenth and twentieth centuries: two copies of Thomas Moore's *Byron's Life, Letters and Journals*; Dallas's *Recollections of the Life of Lord Byron*; the 1871 *Vindication of Lady Byron* with its antagonist, Harriet Beecher Stowe's *History of the Byron Controversy*; Ethel Colburn Mayne's *Life of Lady Byron*; the anonymous *Journals of the Conversation of Lord Byron with the Countess of Blessington*; *My Recollections of Lord Byron*, by Teresa, Countess Guiccioli (Byron's last mistress), the notorious *Amours de Lord Byron*, anonymously published in Paris in 1843; critical and biographical studies by Harold Nicolson, G. Wilson Knight, Andrew Rutherford, André Maurois, Leslie A. Marchand, Doris Langley Moore, Paul West, Karl Elze, William Parry, Thomas Medwin and Malcolm Elwin; Lord Broughton's *Separation of Lord and Lady Byron*; the six-volume edition of Byron's *Letters and Journals*, leather-bound; nineteenth-century editions of most of the poems and the twentieth-century variorum edition of *Don Juan*. And he chose a quotation from Byron as the title of that early play, *No More A-Roving*. That he would have a spontaneous sympathy with the Byronic hero is easy to understand: he was something of one himself. The fierce self-disgust and the contempt for the shoddiness of human society, coupled with an instinctive belief in what ought to be the nobility of life and of man, the half-longing, both at the conscious and unconscious levels, for death – consciously, intellectually, as a way of leaving behind a situation that is, of its nature, beyond repair or remedy; unconsciously as the instinctive turning of the spirit towards peace and darkness – are all characteristics which are shared by Byron's early heroes on the one hand and the John Whiting of the plays on the other. Manfred pleads for forgetfulness and 'oblivion, self-oblivion' and says:

> '*I tell thee, man! I have lived many years,*
> *Many long years but they are nothing now*
> *To those which I must number: ages – ages –*
> *Space and eternity – and consciousness,*
> *With the fierce thirst for death – and still unslaked!*'

Though he would never express it in terms of such extravagant rhetoric, this is very close to one side of John Hogarth's personality. He says to Caroline: 'I think you've misunderstood. The pleasures you've talked about had become as bitter to me as any penance. Every one was the harshest reality which I couldn't stomach. For they're only tolerable when they're more than themselves. When the food feeds more than the body, when sleep is more than an escape to a dream and the comfort of women is more than a cushion.' And when Caroline says to him, referring to his proposed revolutionary activities. 'You may come through the whole affair untouched. I hadn't thought of that', he replies: 'I had. It would be just my luck.' He is one of that company, along with Timothy and his fellow-revolutionaries in *Not a Foot of Land*, with Southman, Procathren, Charles Heberden, Rupert Forster, Sister Jeanne and Urbain Grandier, who were 'half in love with easeful death'. Caroline, too, if she cannot have the fullness and immediacy of the love she has imagined for herself, chooses death, or at least thinks she does. Cristos says of her, when he hears of the conclusion to which she jumped about the berries: 'I should have remembered that Caroline is apt to see everything in terms of mortality.[20] She thought it was poison. Oh, dear, I must tell the poor child at once.' The weakness of Caroline's position is that, though she would prefer death to an act of compromise, she does not see, as John does, that an easy domesticity would *be* an act of compromise so far as her impossibly impassioned love is concerned. John on the other hand, prefers to leave the figures and images of love fixed frozen for ever in their dancing postures and accept a real and known emptiness rather than a spurious and pretended fulfilment.

John Hogarth, then, has — whether by conscious intention or not — something of the sombre and overheated quality of the earlier Byronic hero, tempered with the gay cynicism of the Byron of *Don Juan* (though largely without the latter's vitality and energy). Like Childe Harold, 'self-exiled' he 'wanders forth again, / With nought of hope left, but with less of gloom' and with Harold he seems to say 'From mighty wrongs to petty perfidy / Have I not seen what human things can do?' In spite of the connections of plot and incident between Hogarth's libertine life in London and the Don's traditional reputation, it is more the Byron of *The Corsair, Lara, Childe Harold* and, most closely of all, *Manfred* that John Hogarth represents, rather than the much gayer, more vigorous, more rounded personality of Byron's Don. And in spite of the Byronic overtones both of situation and of mood, he remains also, at the same time, a typical Whiting figure, with so many characteristics of his author so overtly worn that one is bound to think of him as being, in some respects at least, a self-portrait — though not necessarily deliberately so, of course. Deliberate or not, his sophistication is Whiting's, as are his wit, his charm and his gentle melancholy. He is also, be it noted, represented as being exactly the same age (it is referred to by Sophie in the first five minutes of the play) as Whiting was when the play was written – thirty-six; and his forename is John – the only character Whiting ever called by his own forename, except John Winter and John Cadmus, neither of whom is normally referred to as 'John', the former being addressed habitually as 'John Winter' and the latter, except on one occasion by Catherine, as 'Cadmus'. Whether Whiting intended to create a deliberately Byronic character or not, there is a very happy coalescence of images and reverberations arising from the combination of archaeological discovery, the placing of the action in that fading peace before the First World War, the name of Hogarth and the inevitable thought of Byron which rises in the mind when one hears of a young Englishman who runs away from love affairs at home to assist in revolutionary politics and war in Greece. Whiting makes rich and skilful use of these elements and allows the chemistry of their mixing to work in a remarkable way. The fact that the girl's name is Caroline and that Hogarth once or twice calls her 'Caro', which was Byron's diminutive and pet name for Lady Caroline Lamb, is probably no mere coincidence either.

In addition to the main theme and its obvious connections with his other plays, a number of other recurring Whiting leitmotivs appear in the play. The imagery of childhood, first noted in *Not a Foot of Land*, is far less dominant in *The Gates of Summer* than in any previous play, but it is present in one or two places. 'All the best games end in destruction', says John: and Caroline replies: 'We never get out of the nursery, where everything finishes broken up.' This is a very similar use of the adult-child metaphor to one that appears in the unfinished *Noman*:

PETER: Walter, when you were a little boy, did you smash up your toys?
WALTER: Can't remember. I expect so.
PETER: I did. Remember very well. I deliberately broke them up.
WALTER: What are you talking about?
PETER: I used to get punishment every time. That made me think of it. I used to get so scared. If I don't do it, I thought, things will go on as they are. I shan't get hurt. But in the end I'd want to finish it. Be done with it. That was a long time ago. You can take toys away from children. But you can't take all this away from grown men.

The dubious efficacy of political revolution and the contrast of this with the passionate earnestness and idealism with which the revolutionaries approach their task is a theme which constantly fascinated Whiting. It appears in *Not a Foot of Land*, *Marching Song* and *Noman*. In *The Gates of Summer* it is incidental, not integral ('Revolution is for the man who can't love,' Caroline says), but it *is* there, nevertheless. And as in the other three cases, it is there in close juxtaposition with sexual activity, as if the two were in some way alternatives, or complements the one of the other. In *The Gates of Summer*, the revolution is set aside, laughed out of court by its rival, but in all four plays the two energies – sexual and revolutionary – are seen as springing from the same root.

Sophie sees the completion and fulfilment of John's life as being the creation of a legend around himself as a revolutionary hero, a legend that future generations will honour and worship, so that, so far as Sophie's book is concerned, John will become a figure rather similar in position to Lang in *Noman* and 'The Master' in *Not a Foot of Land*. So far as the play is concerned, however, this is regarded with a sceptically quizzical glance, as though the whole business of revolutions was now being looked at from another angle and not being found able to command serious attention.

Glancingly, and then more by general implication than by specific and explicit reference, another Whiting theme is stated – the reality of action, action as the only repository of reality. John, a person of feeling and sensibility, abandons these (hence his leaving of Caroline at the end) because he now has come to believe them unreal, an anodyne at best: he must seek the possibility of a permanent reality in *doing*. When he first tells Sophie about his decision to join the revolution, he says: 'Basilios talked to me in a language I've known since childhood. Yet until that night I'd never heard it spoken.' 'Do you mean Greek?', Sophie asks: and he answers: 'I mean the language of action.' This sounds very like Rupert Forster, in *Marching Song* and, indeed, the two characters, though in most respects very different – and treated in different aesthetic conventions by Whiting – do hold this trait in common. Sophie, without knowing it, points out one other characteristic common to these two when she says 'It's an unfortunate fact, Caroline, that the qualities needed for survival as a person are the same unusual qualities which can destroy an individual, a community, or even a nation. So the lack of moral equipment of the genius and the great criminal are much the same. It's what you haven't got that matters.' Hogarth had sensibility and shed it in favour of action; Forster was a man of action purely, until he was suddenly assailed by, interrupted by, sensibility. We see the processes working both ways.

In one of the speeches already quoted, John Hogarth likens the lover's position to that of an artist ('A man takes leave of a woman he's loved and an art he's practised in much the same spirit') and *The Gates of Summer* has a particularly sophisticated version of that image of art as a way of fixing and making permanent the reality of life, which also appears in several other Whiting works. John's search for a real and final posture is reflected in Sophie's account of it in her book and there it acquires a larger, or at any rate more complicated, view of reality because it is modified by Sophie's own search; and presently still further compounded by Cristos in his own quest for a truth and an artefact to contain and perpetuate it. In addition, John's particular suspicion of where the ultimate truth lies is also reflected – down a long corridor, so to speak: in a muted light but a clear mirror – by another work of art, namely the fresco in the newly unearthed temple. This parallel of art with living events, with its implication that meaning is not meaning until it is translated into art, is strongly present in the play ('You're keeping me in suspense as to what the final chapter of my book is going to be,' Sophie says to John, 'But under no circumstances can I allow it to be farce. That's Henry's part') and reminds one forcibly of the puppet play in *Not a Foot of Land*, where the outward action is actually *foretold* by the work of art. The completion of the picture by Charles's painting of the figure of Stella in *Saint's Day* is another example of the same device and though they do not operate in quite the same way, since the immediate actions of the plays in which they appear are not directly reflected by them, the presence of artists is important in *No More A-Roving* (an actor), *The Conditions of Agreement* (a circus clown) and *Marching Song* (a film director); and *Saint's Day*, of course, has two poets, as well as a painter. It is not an accident or a coincidence, of course, that this should be so: Whiting was always vitally concerned about the function of the artist, whom he saw not only as an abstract and brief chronicler of the times but also as the one who, by a strange alchemy, crystallises into permanently living and permanently truthful form, that which was transitory and subject to flux.

This conscious, sometimes self-conscious, concern with artistic form led him once again into the old battle over style and produced, as well as some remarkable passages of a clear beauty, a number of others in which the writing style is an encumbrance to the play and an impediment to actors. Often, it is a single, unspeakable sentence that obtrudes in an otherwise fine speech. Observe, for instance, the one that begins with the words 'That slow and heavy circle . . .' in the following:

> 'There's been a wedding. One of the workmen. Down there
> the men and women are making the bond. That slow and
> heavy circle will tread the pattern into the earth through
> the night. There's a tribute to love if ever there was one:
> Can you hear the music? It'll be a thin pipe. Listen.'

It is not just that that one sentence is not conversational prose. Neither is the one immediately before it: no one would ever say in twentieth-century conversation '. . . the men and women are making the bond.' Yet it is gravely impressive and exactly right while the 'slow and heavy circle' seems stilted, almost pompous. The line is a very thin one and fiendishly difficult to judge. In Act I Caroline has an even more remarkable example, one that almost discusses the problem explicitly, as well as providing an apt example of it. The false sentence is the last one: the rest of the speech is racy, eminently speakable stuff:

> 'It's not a matter of words, Henry. That's the mistake
> you're making. Read poetry, you said. There you were off
> the mark. I went through a poetical marriage. Boysie knew

about every art except one. Life with him was never too
damned beautiful for words. There were so many to be
spoken, sung, whispered, written, rhymed, scratched on
the window pane, carved into wood and stone – words for
everyday use and casually slung at each other, words for
public abuse and shouted from the housetops, words with
simple meaning and words with double meaning, good
words, bad words, holy words and dirty words. And when
the day was over and you'd think the talking would have
to stop – no, there'd always be that dribble of stale words
for explanation of failure, betrayal, misery and horror.
Buried beneath, suffocated, dead, was love.'

Judging from Norman Shrapnel's review in the *Manchester Guardian*,
something of the difficulty did show in the 1956 production of the play
in England. 'As for the talk,' the reviewer said, 'it shifts with too little
control through too many gears: desultory, direct, highfalutin, downright vulgar.' This now seems too harsh. We no longer demand an
absolute homogeneity of style as the early 1950s tended to and Shrapnel's
comment could be applied equally well to *Love's Labours Lost*. Nevertheless, there is *some* substance in it: the mixture is too great always
to be acceptable and, much worse than this, it includes here and there
lines which are outside the range of the medium for which they are intended. They are not theatre words, capable of being spoken easily and
fluently by actors. They belong, if anywhere, to the printed page and this
is, for those moments, a weakness in a work which is intended to be
spoken aloud in public.

In one particular this same criticism – of an incompatible mixture of
styles – can also be made of the characterisations in this play. Henry
Bevis, who, says Caroline, was made 'to be made unhappy' strikes one
as being created in a convention different from that of the other characters. He is not only made 'to be made unhappy' but also to be made fun
of and he comes dangerously near to existing in the play only for that
reason, without having an entity of his own. He is, in fact, a lightly drawn
caricature, a figure of farce, in the middle of a comedy of manners in
which the other characters are seen in terms of psychological complexity and causation. He is a little reminiscent of Epihodov (or
Yepikhodov), 'Two-and-Twenty Misfortunes', in *The Cherry Orchard*,
except that he is not integrated with the rest of the play with nearly
the delicacy and gentle skill that Chekhov brings to the task. Where
Epihodov serves to show the closeness of farce to both comedy and
tragedy and to illustrate the infinitude of shades of which the colours of
life are capable and the way they change and flow into each other, the
presence of Henry Bevis tends to suggest that the colours must not
be mixed, that you have to make up your mind and stick to it. He is

an irregularity in the fabric of the play where Epihodov is a *variation* in the fabric.

But he is the only serious one; and the language blemishes noted above, though present, are not large enough or frequent enough to be really damaging.

5

THE INTERREGNUM (1955-1960)

I   Film Scripts

By the time that *The Gates of Summer* failed to reach London, in 1956, John Whiting was already fairly extensively involved in writing for the cinema. Following the 1951 production in London of two of his plays, his literary agent, A. D. Peters, had begun to arrange for him to work for some of the film studios. His first actual commissions were in 1952 – three 'treatments' for the Group Three company. They were adaptations of other people's work, arrangements of already existing narratives in film-scenario form; their titles were *One Touch of Larceny*, *Love on Paper* and *The Golden Legend of Shults*. By 1956 he had also written three full screenplays, though none of them was original: all were adaptations of novels, prepared specifically at the request of the film companies who had already bought the film rights of the novels in question. Whether, after the failure – commercially speaking – of *The Gates of Summer*, he took a deliberate and conscious resolve to leave the theatre in favour of the cinema or whether, as offers of film work increased, he *drifted* into the position of being a film-script cobbler rather than a dramatist it seems impossible now to determine, but the fact remains that from 1956 until 1961 no new Whiting play appeared. He had bought a big and beautiful old house in Sussex in 1956 and left London to live in it. The financial rewards of writing for films, larger and – once established – more certain than theatre royalties, must have been a considerable temptation since they helped very substantially to sustain for himself and his growing family that pleasant country life. The house was in the tiny village of Nutley, on the edge of Ashdown Forest, in one of the loveliest stretches of countryside in the south of England. That he felt some bitterness at the way the critics and the public had received his theatre work can be judged from some of the press interviews he occasionally gave and also, by implication, from

199

some of the dramatic criticism which he himself later wrote. And this bitterness on his part is scarcely to be wondered at. There were times too, in his darker moments, when his confidence in his own capacities was shaken – as what artist's is not at some times? But the fact remains that his writing for films was an interruption of, not an extension of, his real work and he remained, in spite of the occasional sense of bitterness and of shaken confidence, a dramatist who for extraneous reasons was for those years working at something other than his true trade. As was remarked in Chapter 1, one would like to argue that what he was doing was exploring a new dramatic medium or searching for a way to make theatrical contact, via a modern form, with a larger and more 'popular' audience – to whom the film could speak more unselfconsciously than the theatre – but there is no evidence at all for such a belief. Whiting talked in great detail on various occasions about his theories of and his attitude to theatre: never once (so far as I know) did he discuss the cinema in this way. For the theatre he wrote profoundly original, disturbing, moving and important works; for the cinema – with one or two exceptions – he wrote well-carpentered trivialities. Even the exceptions are more important for the light they cast on other aspects of his work and on him as an artist than for any great intrinsic significance. On the other hand it would be false to argue that since his film scripts are not literary[1] productions in any real sense of the word and since they cannot be regarded as part of his serious artistic work (again, with one or two exceptions), they should not be considered at all. This might be true of an activity that had no connection at all with a writer's craft: if a writer stopped writing and took up farming or accountancy the details of his farm jobs or accountancy jobs would in all probability have no bearing on one's assessment of his standing as a writer. But writing for films, though its *purpose* might be different from that of writing for the theatre, employs techniques and processes of thought which are quite similar. The use to which these crafts are being put and the ways in which these techniques are being applied have, therefore, a distinct bearing on the overall consideration of the writer's work and should be taken into account. In Whiting's case the study is a particularly interesting one in that even in the most conventional and machine-made of the scripts, obviously designed by the original story to do nothing but titillate the taste for what is conventionally regarded as 'excitement', one can discover an odd line of dialogue or a moment of description that has recognisable links with Whiting's more serious work (reference is made to a few of these moments elsewhere in this book). Even when he is subjugated by someone else's narrative and characters, his own sense of the world makes itself felt here and there, usually with the result that the shallowness of the surrounding material is emphasised. This film work is important, too, for the obvious influence it had technically on his writing for the stage when he returned to it. The most obvious example of such influence is, of course, *The Devils*, but the fragmentary *The Nomads* (and the notes for this) shows it, too, as does also the one completed act of *Noman*.

One must bear in mind, of course, in any attempt to assess the value of a film script, that it is not meant to be purely and solely a literary work, nor should it be judged as such. This does not mean that the literary parts of it are negligible or that they can be of inferior quality without affecting the quality of the whole, but it does mean that, even more than in the theatre, the visual elements are the dominant ones and are meant to be: the writer calculates his work with this in mind. And when one considers the final product – the film itself – it must be remembered that once the writing of the script is complete the writer has little or no influence on its destiny. Unlike the script of a play, the script of a film is sold outright, the writer retaining no rights in it or control of it: it is – in the jargon of the trade – a 'property'. The author does not attend rehearsals of it, as he does in the case of a play. His opinion on performance and setting and music is not invited. We are, therefore, in the present instance considering the scripts Whiting wrote and their *potential* as finished films, rather than some of the films as they actually turned out. This, in any case, is all we *can* do with some of them, since in several instances the script was completed and paid for but never 'made'. Of his three most interesting, one (*Hedda Gabler*) never reached the film company, though it was completed; one (*The Reason Why*) was commissioned and paid for by Michael Powell, but was never made into a film; the third (*Young Cassidy*) did become a film, though not a very good one.

Whiting had a hand, to a greater or lesser extent, in twenty films altogether. He wrote no *original* script for a film; all his scripts are adaptations of other people's work: nor did he ever write a film version of one of his own plays. He wanted to do the film script of *The Devils* himself, but died before he was able to: it was done later by Ken Russell, with disastrous results. Except in the case of one or two of the later films, the choice of subject cannot be taken as any indication of Whiting's own preferences: he accepted such commissions as were offered to him and did the best he could with them. Thus, the triteness and sentimentality of *Thanks for a Lovely Day* (1952) belongs much more to Godfrey Winn, who wrote the original story, than to John Whiting. Indeed, several of the scripts seem now to read like epitomes (caricatures, almost, in some cases) of all the run-of-the-mill films one ever saw in the 1950s. It is interesting to observe – though it does nothing to illuminate Whiting for us – the extent to which the style of popular entertainment has changed in the intervening twenty years: the accepted and expected norms of these scripts, both visually and so far as plot and characterisation are concerned, seem very distant and stilted now. Which goes to show, I think, not that films have improved since then or that popular taste has become either more sophisticated or more discriminating, but merely that popular entertainment is as subject to the whims of fashion as women's hats used to be and young people's clothes are now. Whiting largely followed the fashion.

This shows amusingly in some of the descriptions of particular camera shots and visual effects. In *The Golden Fool*, written for Associated British in 1956 (an earlier version was called *Gold!*) one of the characters is described as being 'fifty, clean-shaven, with a face that might be carved from wood', which sounds as if it came straight out of a woman's magazine; and when there is a pause in the argument as to whether to go after the gold or to continue with the quiet, healthy life of the farm, the 'stage direction' says *He is silent: there is the sound of night insects* – as in every warm-climate movie ever made. In *Thanks for a Lovely Day* there is a bumper crop of film clichés: a montage representing the end of a working day (machines slowing down, workmen turning switches off and pulling levers, workers pouring out of the factory, whistles blowing, conveyor belts stopping, etc.); *suddenly the screen is filled with a mass of beating wings*, says one description of a shot, about a flock of pigeons; as Edna walks along the pier at Blackpool, she *thrusts her hands deeply in her coat pockets* to indicate independence, self-reliance, determination and so on – which is a cliché in its use of words as well as in the action described; and there is a scene in which the main characters all gravitate to a fairground and there behave in 'characteristic' ways, which must be the biggest film cliché of them all. Yet even in the middle of this morass of sentimentality and stock response, there is one image that is a faint flicker of the real Whiting and reminds one of several of his plays: *The crowd is standing around the Laughing Clown – a mechanical, larger-than-life automaton that roars with laughter all day long to cheer up the visitors to the Pleasure Beach. They all start to laugh at the Clown as they join the crowd – all, that is, except one little girl, who takes one terrified look and promptly bursts into tears, burying her face in her father's jacket. And the scene goes back to a final close-up of the Clown rocking with laughter.* Clowns and children and the ambivalence of mirth . . . Given a different context, this is the kind of situation of which Whiting could have made something significant.

Castle Minerva deals in another standard set of film clichés in a style very typical of the 1950s – the Spy story: it has a Grim, Forbidding Castle in it, several Narrow Escapes (including walking on a high, narrow ledge in a rising wind), a fire in a circus (with Escaping Animals), a gun duel in a disused church. Faces tend to be *steely* or *drawn with fatigue* and, after all the sinister happenings, the hero, at the end, walks back into 'ordinary life' (he is a school-teacher), watched by us from the vantage point of a London window, high up, from which we see him mingling with, and gradually being lost in, the busy morning crowd. It has such a healthy, old-fashioned, totally unreal feel about it! How much more interesting it would have been if it had shown David's real life as a school-teacher (omitting all the usual clichés about *that* life, also) and contrasted it with the childish *Boys'-Own-Paper* stuff of the spy incidents. One knows, of course, that this sort of nonsense does, in fact, actually happen in the real world: the extraordinary thing is *why*? Why do apparently adult people allow themselves to be inveigled by mere governments and officials into such adolescent posturings? This could have been explored, contrasting the solid, real world of human relationships in the classroom with the paper-thin, melodramatic make-believe of the espionage world. A school-teacher might be quite intelligent and imaginative: some of them are. Why, supposing he is, would he get mixed up in this sort of nonsense? But the film does not enquire into this. Instead, it goes off into a predictable rigmarole of novel predicaments, standard sentiments and synthetic tensions.

And so with most of the other scripts: *The Gypsum Flowe*r, though it has a little more character than some of the others, describes a girl, a French resistance worker, waiting in her room at night for news: *She is awake, staring at the ceiling. A cheap alarm clock ticks noisily at her head*. One pauses in reading it to wonder whether Whiting copied this from all the other films in which this tension-producing device was used, or whether they all copied it from him. By now, it's hard to tell. Or take the following, from *Nya*: *The single lonely figure of Nya is seen going along the great stretch of sand in the curve of the bay. She skims flat pebbles out over the surface of the water and then goes into the distance.* Pensive young people, especially pensive young people in love, have been doing this ever since movie-making began. *Nya*, though, does have some points of genuine interest in it, probably because it is about a young girl growing up and this immediately, I suspect, caught Whiting's imagination because of his perennial interest in the relationship of childhood experience to adult experience. There is one very good moment when Nya, who is fourteen, arrives at her new boarding school in England before term has begun. It is done entirely in visual terms; no dialogue. Left alone, the girl – who has recently come from South Africa, following her mother's death – wanders round the empty building: *A long, stone corridor: Nya appears at the far end. She wanders along. She stops for a moment looking up at a big ornamental board holding the names of past prize winners. She walks on. She hesitates at a door. Opens it. A classroom, echoing with emptiness: desks ranged, black-board clean. Nya shuts the door and goes on. A line of tennis courts: unnetted. Nya passes them, dragging her fingers listlessly across the wires. The swimming pool: empty. Nya walks alongside the pool, her footsteps echoing beneath the vaulted glass roof. Near the school chapel: beneath the stained glass windows and running beside* *the chapel is a cloister. Cool, monastic, of white stone. Nya appears beneath the furthest arch. She stops. At the far end of the cloister is a girl. She is at an easel, painting.*

The story of the film is rather improbable and the dialogue in some cases is stiffly over-explicit, especially in those passages where characters have to talk not because it is really natural for them to do so but because they have to explain their motivations to the audience. Most of the characters are cardboard figures, straight from stock: the exception is Nya herself. In her case the character is fresh, original and well-drawn and her dialogue rings true throughout.

Among the film scripts, *The Reason Why* (1958), is altogether more interesting than anything that precedes it. It is based on Cecil Woodham Smith's book of the same name and is concerned with the infamous Charge of the Light Brigade in the Crimean War. Whiting's script is very faithful to the book and translates it well into visual and dramatic terms, providing a much cooler, more objective and more subtle comment on that fatuous event than the Tony Richardson film on the subject that *did* reach the screen. The two central imbeciles, Lord Lucan and Lord Cardigan, are both vividly drawn and the plotting keeps their individual lives prior to the start of the war equally and skilfully before us. Indeed, the structure of the whole script is very skilful: some of the juxtaposition of scenes is extremely telling and the actual cutting from scene to scene, especially when moving from one preposterous noble lord to the other, is done with considerable wit and a keen eye for detail. Most of all, the film keeps in mind throughout its central purpose, which is not to pave the way to a visual and 'dramatic' climax in the cavalry charge but to account for the existence of that extraordinary occurrence – the reason why. The script makes good use of William Howard Russell, the famous *Times* reporter who, for the first time, exposed the nonsensical goings-on of a military high command in a series of newspaper articles. Though he occupies relatively little space as a character in the film, he serves as a lens to bring the whole thing into focus and at the same time to give a suitable distance and objectivity to the view of it. It is a great pity that this very good script was never made into a film: it could have been a fine one.

Young Cassidy is adapted from the autobiography of Sean O'Casey, chiefly from vols 2, 3 and 4 (*Pictures in the Hallway, Drums under the Window* and *Inishfallen, Fare Thee Well*). It was commissioned in 1961 by Robert Graff and Robert Ginna, of Sextant Films, New York and the finished film appeared in 1965 after the deaths of both Whiting and O'Casey (the latter having died in the autumn of 1964, at the age of 84). From the start, the correspondence about it indicates that it was intended to be a film of major importance. Carol Reed and Lindsay Anderson were both invited to direct it, though both turned it down. On 19 November 1962 Robert Graff, writing to Whiting, said:

> Now about stars and directors. Dick Burton says no, that he
> doesn't think he's Irish enough. I think the real reason
> quite other and has to do with a complicated problem with
> Miss Taylor. I hear from Mary Keane that Peter O'Toole
> wants desperately to do it but his manager, Jules Buck,
> says no, presumably because he smells big money somewhere
> else. I've written Peter about this to see if there's a way
> through. Meanwhile Richard Harris has read the script and
> loves it. I think I'm in favour of offering him the part but
> I want to see *Mutiny on the Bounty* next week before I do.

Whiting flew to New York for consultations about the script and on
other occasions the producers flew to England to discuss it with O'Casey
himself, who made various suggestions about details and actually rewrote a few lines of dialogue here and there. O'Casey wrote to Graff,
when sending him the last of these amendments, saying:

> I've read the script-plan for the photography and it seems
> very fine to me. The way in which the sequences are evolved
> from the 3 books is very clever, though some of them are,
> necessarily, wide of the facts. For instance, the real 'Nora'
> never came near me through the stress and strain. Apart
> from the towering Titan, Yeats, I stood alone. I never saw
> the real 'Nora', neither did she get into touch with me,
> or even write a line. She stayed hidden. I never saw her
> from 1922 and left Ireland without a glimpse of her. She
> had no courage; unlike my Eileen who stood by me in the
> matter of *The Silver Tassie* and all through, representing
> me in your country and facing the Irish when *The Bishop's
> Bonfire* went on there; a brave and undaunted lass.

This particular departure from the original was not altogether
Whiting's fault. Ten months before O'Casey made his comment,
Whiting had received a letter from Robert Graff, making some suggestions. Graff and Ginna had received and studied the 'treatment'
Whiting had sent to them in January of 1962 (A 'treatment', in the
jargon of the trade, is a kind of expanded, extended scenario, giving
the story and plot in detail and sketching in a good deal of the dialogue.
It is prepared by the writer for the approval of the film company before
he embarks on the writing of the full screenplay.) On the whole, Graff
and Ginna liked the 'treatment' ('We are elated by the possibilities it
presents') but the first of their suggestions read thus:

> To our eyes the basic problem of the film you present is the
> lack of a dramatic romance between the hero and a girl.
> Daisy is fun but frivolous, Nora cold, distant and
> unsympathetic. We feel that the entire story could be

> improved dramatically by fusing the characters of the two
> women into one and making her – Nora – an Irish shop
> girl who is warm, gay yet parochial and for whom the ideals
> of Ireland are those of Sean's cronies rather than Sean's.
> Such a character would permit an enormous wrench when
> Sean decides he must leave not only Ireland but also a girl
> who represents much that is fine in Ireland behind. A rousing
> and continuing relationship between Sean and a girl would
> subsume all the girls he's known before and whatever girls
> he may know afterwards.

Whiting managed to fend off some of the force of this single-minded and instinctive drive for vulgarity. The script does not fuse the characters of Nora and Daisy and both appear in the finished film, played by Maggie Smith and Julie Christie, but Nora's part is extended to include some good, juicy love scenes and she is duly incorporated in the film's climax, as the producers had suggested she should be, by bringing her to the Abbey Theatre for the riots which occurred during performances of *The Plough and the Stars* and by having her make her decision to leave Sean actually in the theatre. We see them come back into the empty auditorium after the angry audience has left and on the stage, in the middle of the set for *The Plough and the Stars*, Johnny (Sean) suddenly asks Nora to marry him. She refuses, saying 'No, Johnny. You love me, it's true, but love can hold a man back. You'd be stopped from doing things. Nora won't understand that, Nora won't like that. And you'd not do it and so you'd diminish yourself. I'm a small, simple girl and I need a small, simple life. Not your terrible dreams and your anger, Johnny. I'm just an Irish girl; and your talent makes you more than just an Irishman.' The scene finishes with Nora backing slowly away up the aisle of the theatre, while Johnny remains on the stage. As she reaches the exit, Johnny says 'I love you, Nora.' 'I love you, Johnny', she replies and slips through the swing doors, leaving him alone.

This kind of oversimplification of the many-coloured, finely shaded, highly ambivalent original autobiography characterises the whole of the script of *Young Cassidy*. 'Johnny is a powerfully-built young man of twenty-six' says Whiting's script, introducing a scene in which Cassidy (O'Casey) is seen on his first day as a pick-and-shovel navvy, a job that the real O'Casey, who was a little man who suffered a good deal of ill-health and who was not strong, had taken in desperation because no other was available to him. So what in the original book was a description of a terrible physical fight to keep going becomes in the script and the film an amusing and good-humoured escapade. Johnny, in the film, happens to be rather inept with a pick and shovel because he has not used them before: but for a *powerfully-built young man of twenty-*

six this will obviously not be a difficulty for very long. He will soon pick up the knack: it is easy for him. And Rod Taylor, who was eventually cast for the part, in the film plays it this way. With a cheerful, personable, rather simple-minded grin and that smug self-confidence and sense of superiority of the stock American folk hero (clumsy exterior hiding a heart of gold and all sorts of other potential besides) he makes it apparent that digging trenches and writing plays and fighting, both metaphorically and literally, with all and sundry, would all come easy to him. There is no more possibility of his being defeated than there is of John Wayne's being defeated, or of Batman's being defeated. A simple, fictional figure has replaced the struggling, courageous, doubting yet resolute man whom one senses in every page of O'Casey's autobiography. O'Casey describes, for example, the constant battle with pain from his weak and afflicted eyes (he suffered acutely with them all his life) when he was struggling to write *The Plough and the Stars*: 'Coming close to the first night, Sean's eyes filled with inflammation and ingrowing eyelashes made the inflammation worse. Dr J. D. Cummins, now an intimate friend, did all he could to lessen the searching pain; but on the night of the first performance, Sean found it hard and painful to keep his eyes fixed on the bright zone of the stage.'[2] Early in the negotiations for the writing of the film the decision was taken that 'the affliction of Sean's eyes is absolutely unnecessary' (Graffe, in a letter to Whiting, 12 February 1962).

And so on: there is no need to give further examples of the constant diminution of the rich subtleties of the original. One only wonders at the kind of timorous banality that makes even intelligent men instinctively strive to make every piece of poular entertainment as much like every other as possible. The popular cinema is riddled with this: in its tepid insipidity it hates originality, but loves novelty. Reading the correspondence about the script of *Young Cassidy*, it is impossible to suspect even the producers of down-right cynicism. In their own way and up to a certain point (a point which is determined automatically and spontaneously in a producer's mind by a series of commercial reflexes) they genuinely believed in the artistic validity of the venture. It is ironic that the two dramatists involved should be O'Casey and Whiting, for no twentieth-century playwright has been more uncompromising in his own standards than these two and none so outspoken or so scornful about the crass surrender of art to commerce in the theatre and elsewhere. 'Why is the English theatre so low in mind, so scanty in fancy and imagination?' demanded O'Casey, in that same autobiography and Whiting's dramatic criticism is full of inveighings against sentimentality and mindlessness in the theatre. Eileen O'Casey, in her book about her late husband (*Sean*, edited by J. C. Trewin and published by Macmillan in 1971) points up the sad little moral. Writing of the last few years of O'Casey's life she says (pp. 283–4):

Soon, too, we received from Bob Graff an offer to buy for
the cinema Sean's six autobiographies, published together
under the collective title of *Mirror in My House*. Though I
was against any film, especially during Sean's life, Sean
himself was determined to accept. In a state of health far
worse than I knew, he wanted to leave me as comfortable
as possible; at heart he did not believe that he had all that
time to live. The film contract provided that the money was
to be paid over three years. Once Sean had consented, Bob
Graff and Bob Ginna had a script prepared by John Whiting,
an able writer, but far in style from Sean, with nothing of
the same tragi-comic sense or the gift for Irish
characterisation. When the script of *Young Cassidy* arrived,
I read it myself as I was now going through all scripts and
theses, trying to ease the strain upon Sean's sight. Bob
Graff told me it was suitable; but, without knowing the
technique of a film script, I was conscious that the warmth
and beauty of Sean's work had not come through. Sean,
very tired and suffering from his bad nights, was weary of
it, and Dr Doran was anxious for him to be free of any care;
he did rewrite a few scenes but naturally they were not in
key with the rest of the script. It was an unhappy period,
though the deal did not alter Sean's regard for the two
Bobs, who were striving hard; we hoped the film might be
better than we imagined. Personally, I consider that because
Sean had devised his autobiographies much as a dramatist
might, the entire film could have been worked up from the
dialogue as in Joyce's *Ulysses*. [Other films can be made
from the books; perhaps they will be one day, especially
the tragic life and death of Sean's sister, a poignant story
in waiting.] *Young Cassidy* was not released until after
Sean died; again one has little courage in saying what one
believes when friends have toiled so sincerely. There was
bad luck here in both the casting of the main characters and
in the production, but I do think of Donal Donnelly's
magnificent performance as an undertaker's man and of
Maggie Smith – an actress I have never ceased to applaud
– as Sean's first love. The cast included such names as
Flora Robson (Sean's mother), Michael Redgrave (Yeats),
Edith Evans (Lady Gregory), Jack MacGowran (Sean's
brother) and Sian Phillips (his sister). Rod Taylor played
Sean. It was a relief, at any rate, that our finances had
improved so sharply. Sean had been accustomed to complain
that the only big things he could leave me were his
manuscripts, and he hoped somebody would buy them.

In a letter to Whiting dated 24 October 1961, Robert Graff says 'The theme of the film should be the making of a man, the struggle for wholeness against overwhelming odds of poverty and scorn.' Whiting, in a preface to the script (and the presence of such a preface, an unusual thing in a film script, can be taken as an indication of the importance attached to the script by all concerned):

> I am in complete agreement with this. It is essential that
> the figure of the man, Sean Casside,[3] should be set against
> his time. But the story must not become the story of a
> period of history. In short, the character must dominate.
> Social and historical considerations must give way to the
> highly personal struggle of a man against his time and the
> conditions of his life. By these means we shall hope to
> widen the appeal of the film. For throughout Europe and
> the world today the struggle of young people for recognition
> as individuals, their need to free themselves from past
> tradition, from the rigidity of class distinction, and their
> necessity to gain the liberty to do the job they love, is
> unaltered from the time of Sean Casside in Dublin.

Perhaps Whiting's agreement with his producer's rather glib thesis was all too thorough for his artistic good. One can only guess at possible motives for such a capitulation. And the utterance 'we shall hope to widen the appeal of the film' does not sound very typical of John Whiting, either. Perhaps the search for a too-easy relevance, in the sense of a 'theme' that would be easily and instantly accessible to the most casual of viewers, foredoomed to failure any real attempt to capture the delicate and austere lyricism of the O'Casey original. Nor can it be claimed that, though untrue to the original, the film has a subtlety and significance of its own; is, in fact, a new work of art. It is not. It is a very ordinary, run-of-the-mill melodrama, devoid of real sensitivity, but decked in expensive trappings.

The film version of *Hedda Gabler*, on the other hand, is a very different matter. Here, the artistic integrity is complete and there is no question of softening or watering-down the original to make it more palatable to an audience that does not care to have its stereotypes disturbed (which perhaps accounts for the fact that this script was never made into a film). Whiting follows very closely the development of the characters as drawn by Ibsen. He uses the same main plot incidents as are represented in the original play, sometimes with extremely interesting touches added. Hedda, for example, in the conversation with Brack in Act 2 of the play, tries to explain her motives for marrying Tesman and in doing so to find such excuse and consolation as she can for a situation which she instinctively despises. In the Ibsen play she says 'And Jörgen Tesman . . . you must allow that he's a most worthy person in every way.'[4] Brack sardonically agrees with her and she goes on to say 'And I can't see that there's anything specifically ridiculous about him . . . Or what do you say?' In both the first and second drafts of the film script, Whiting follows this exactly, but then in the second version, though not the first, he makes Hedda add 'Of course, he has a disgusting way of walking when you see him from behind.' This comment does not appear either in the final version of Ibsen's play or in an earlier draft which is still extant, but in one of Ibsen's notebooks which relates to *Hedda Gabler* there are some scattered notes which were obviously written when the play's development was at a very early stage (Hedda is not yet named and is referred to simply as 'the married lady') Ibsen jotted the following: 'He has such a nasty way of walking when you see him from the back. She hates him because he has a goal, a life-task.'[5] Ibsen eventually decided not to use the line in the play's dialogue, but Whiting found it, liked it and used it to good effect in the film. Towards the end of the film there is an addition to Hedda's spoken thoughts which is very typical of Whiting: she is describing to Brack – and being incited by him to do so – the manner of Lövborg's death as she imagines it to have been, a glorious demonstration of the freedom of the soul, with no mean or diminishing circumstances attached.

HEDDA: He would have found some lonely place . . .
BRACK: Go on.
HEDDA: Yes, it would have been a lonely place. He would have gone out of the town – to the moors – the little road where . . . (*Suddenly*) Was it in the head?
    (*She lightly fingers her temple.* BRACK *shakes his head*)
HEDDA: Well, the chest then. It doesn't matter. He would have looked up just before . . . before . . . and he would have seen the morning sky . . . the hills . . . the house where I was a child . . .

That last phrase – 'the house where I was a child' – is not there in Whiting's first draft of the film: it appears only in the second, though the rest of the speech is there in both. And, of course, it is not there in Ibsen. It is quintessentially Whiting and it reminds one vividly of his short story, 'A Valediction' and of Timothy's memories, in *Not a Foot of Land*, of the house where he spent his childhood and to which he was never able to return. Childhood as the source of the overpowering longing for a life that is clean, pure, innocent, uncompromised, uncompromising and possessed of a magnificent dignity. Ibsen never *says* all this, but it is implicit in all that is said, both by herself and others, of Hedda's relationship with her father (and it is there in several other Ibsen plays, too). And, as has already been pointed out elsewhere in this present study, it is one of the basic elements of Whiting's vision.

'You are like all men, haunted by the past', Whiting makes Hedda say to Brack, but the line could equally well have been written by Ibsen.

Rosmer is haunted by the past in *Rosmersholm*; so is Solness in *The Master Builder*. The powerful grip of tradition is something to which Ibsen over and over again returns; and Whiting, too, is always aware of the conflict between the eager present and the heavy past. It is easy to see how the character of Hedda would fascinate Whiting and, reading the two versions of this film script, one could almost imagine that she is a wholly and solely Whiting character. In her contempt for compromise; in her instinctive belief that human life was meant to be noble and glorious and, so to say, more than life-size; most of all in her dark embracing of death (both her own and Lövborg's) as a cleanser and as infinitely preferable to the farce and the grubbiness of a safe and unspectacular bourgeois existence, she has a direct kinship with Paul Southman and Grandier and John Hogarth and those who destroyed the shrine in *Not a Foot of Land*. For her, as for them, the dark journey to the dark home is sweeter than the summer's day. It is easy to see why, though still not an original work, this film script strikes one as the best of those that Whiting wrote. Hedda's romantic and selfish search for an impossible perfection would make an instant appeal to him. 'It's a liberation to know that an act of spontaneous courage is yet possible in this world. An act that has something of unconditional beauty' Ibsen makes her say:[6] it might well be Caroline, in *The Gates of Summer*, speaking. Or even, if it were translated into Synge's rich Anglo-Gaelic, Pegeen Mike. Like Pegeen, Hedda is too big to live in the circumscribed circumstances of domestic daily life, but unlike Pegeen, Hedda escapes. Pegeen, because of a momentary failure of her courage, is left in the trap, with the bitterness of realisation in her heart; this is what produces that final lamenting cry, 'Oh my grief, I've lost him surely. I've lost the only playboy of the western world.'

Like Synge, Whiting would understand the wild, uncontrollable figure of Hedda and the sharp ambivalence of her final act. Was her suicide merely a confirmation of her self-confessed cowardice? Or was it rather a final, triumphant rejection of that cowardice? While the ethical issue cannot be resolved, the reality of her response and her dilemma would be something that a man of Whiting's particular bent would instantly recognise, as he would also instantly understand Ibsen's comment in his notes written in preparation for the writing of the play – 'Subterranean forces and powers is what it is about.'

The contrast between aspiration and actuality Whiting expresses slightly more explicitly than does Ibsen in the original. Hedda's dialogue with Brack, quoted above, continues from the point at which she mentions the house where she was as a child, as follows:

BRACK: Hedda . . .
HEDDA: He would have . . . Yes?
BRACK: Life just won't work as you think it should.

HEDDA: You can make it.
BRACK: No.
HEDDA: My father did.
BRACK: Soldiers in war are privileged. Nothing like that happened to Tom.[7]
HEDDA: But he left me here . . .
BRACK: I know he did. With one of your pistols in his pocket. And he
    walked down to the town. He must have been very frightened, poor man,
    because he got hold of some drink. And he walked round and round.
(HEDDA *is staring across the room at* BRACK. *Quietly, insistently, he continues*):
BRACK: It wasn't in a lonely place, Hedda. It was in a street in the town.
    Tom was drunk. People were on their way to work. The first buses
    had just started. Tom fell under one. He was run down. That's all. Just
    a silly little accident.
            (HEDDA *has her hands to her face. She cries out*):
HEDDA: Oh, Christ, Christ! Everything I touch becomes sordid and
    ridiculous.
BRACK: You must learn. The business of living is sordid and ridiculous.
HEDDA: No, no!
BRACK: And you must learn something else, too. You walk out of one trap
    into another.
HEDDA (*Staring at him*):   You mean you.
BRACK: Yes.
HEDDA: I don't want anymore to do with you.
BRACK: You may have to.

As will be inferred from the mention of buses, Whiting has moved the
plot forward into the twentieth century, with some gains in clarity, I
think. The small university town is, in his version, in the industrial
north of England. Tesman's honeymoon trip, which he also uses as an
opportunity for visiting libraries in pursuit of his academic research,
is made in the United States, the subject of the book he is writing
being 'The Condition of Man in Mid-Twentieth Century Industrial
Societies' (instead of an account of domestic crafts in medieval Brabrant).
Brack, in the first draft, is an American businessman whom they meet
in New York and who happens now to be in England on business. This
device is abandoned in the second draft, which has Brack as another
member of the university faculty, a colleague of Tesman's. Eilert
Lövborg's name is changed to Tom Kelsey and Thea Elvsted becomes
Thea Fraser. The social structures of the grimy, depressing town are
skilfully employed to serve the play's purpose, Hedda's dislike of the
belittling effects of ordinary, everyday living being related to her contempt for the lives of the working-class people in their blocks of slum-
clearance flats. Thea, who lives in one of these herself and who is well
aware of Hedda's scorn, remarks with irony 'Yes, Mrs Tesman, you
may well look. That's how things go on at our end of the town. Drunken
fathers go out with women all the time and then come home and nearly
kill their kids. It's terrible how the working classes live.' In two of the

main conversations between Eilert-Tom and Hedda, the 'flashback' device is used to *show* their previous relationship – covert meetings on the moor and by the disused canal and in cheap hotel bedrooms. The Ibsen purist may wince a little at the idea, but it seems to me perfectly justified in the cinema and, while it helps to clarify the delineation of the two characters, it neither distorts nor overexplains them.

There is one last sad little postscript to John Whiting's interest in *Hedda Gabler*. It is this: when he died, he was just beginning work on a film treatment of another Ibsen play – *The Lady from the Sea*. The play has distinct connections with *Hedda Gabler*: it is the work which immediately precedes *Hedda Gabler* in the chronology of Ibsen's works, being written in 1888 while the date of *Hedda Gabler* is 1890; and Ellida, the heroine of *The Lady from the Sea*, has in a way the same choice to make as has Hedda, the choice between the wild, romantic, noble and free life on the one hand and the steady, gentle, responsible, domestic life on the other. The existence of the choice represents the existence of contrary impulses in the spirit of life itself, the dichotomy between the deeply instinctive responses and the rational, intellectual ones, the division between the urge towards self-fulfilment, self-realisation and the recognition of duty and interdependence; and in Ibsen's hands, as in Whiting's, this becomes also the choice between self-destruction and self-preservation, the choice between life and death. Given this choice, Hedda chooses one way and Ellida the other, but their kinship is obvious.

Whiting's work on *The Lady from the Sea* never got past the stage of his preliminary notes and from them it is impossible to judge how successful the venture might have proved. One interesting little detail emerges: there is in the original play a character to whom Ibsen refers simply as 'The Stranger', though he is a very important part of the story: the character himself calls himself by different names at various times, one of these names being 'Friman'. He represents the daemon in Ellida, the instinctive impulses, and he comes to persuade her to leave her husband and family and return to the wild, free, uncontrollable life that is all the way through the play represented by the sea and the influence of the sea. Whiting's notes indicate that he was proposing to give this character a permanent name. He was to be called Freeman – and one is reminded of the strange, compelling atmosphere of that little, unfinished radio play, *The Quarry and the Prey*, nearly twenty years before, which also had a character in it called Freeman.

II   A television play

John Whiting's only play for television was written in 1959 and was called *A Walk in the Desert*. He himself said that it derived from *The Conditions of Agreement*, though one needs to look carefully in order to recognise the connections between the two. Spiritually such connections do exist, but this does not mean that *A Walk in the Desert* is a rendering for television of the plot of the earlier play: the narratives are entirely different from each other. Stylistically, the television play is more closely related to the film scripts than to any of Whiting's plays, the dialogue being nearer to a flatly naturalistic representation of the conversational phraseology of everyday speech than Whiting ever employed on the stage. This results in an oversimplified quality in the piece and, especially from Peter (the central character) too great a need to explain (and thus *tell* us what the play is about). Paradoxically, this produces at some moments a rather artificial and stagey feeling. It is the old, familiar trap of the naturalistic play, risked here, perhaps, because Whiting felt that a play designed for a mass television audience ought to be 'simpler'. Nevertheless, the play has a powerful and savage central sense, some very good theatrical moments and an ironic edge that is very telling.

The plot concerns Peter Sharpe, a young man of twenty-four who is lame: he lost a leg during his compulsory military service, not in any fighting or military action but in an automobile accident – he was standing about, day-dreaming and not paying attention, when a recruit who was learning to drive a truck backed the vehicle into him and crushed his legs. He can now walk again, with some difficulty, but spends most of his time lying on the sofa rather than endure the difficulty of walking and the embarrassment of showing his lameness. His parents are wealthy enough to be able to support him so he has not attempted, since his accident, to find work that would be within his capacity. He spends his days in idleness and bitterness, feeling the pettiness and aimlessness of the vacuously comfortable bourgeois life of his parents and of the small town in which they live and feeling that he himself has been cheated by life. In particular, he resents – quite irrationally but nevertheless deeply – the easy success of Brian, who lives next door. Brian is the same age as Peter; they went to school together. And Brian was always the lucky one. While Peter's National Service has left him a cripple, Brian's has given him the idea for a popular, comic book about army life, a book which has now been made into a film. So Brian is rich and famous, while Peter is a cripple. Peter is far too intelligent not to know that Brian's book is worthless, that success of this kind is cheap and most of all that the differences between his own fortune and Brian's are simply matters of luck and chance. Though he knows this intellectually, he still responds to it at the emotional level with resentment and it becomes for him a symbol of the general shoddiness and contemptible quality of an aimless small-town existence.

The play shows him on a Sunday evening, lying on the sofa, reading the Sunday papers and sneering at his parents who are just going off to a rehearsal by the local amateur dramatic society, to which they belong.

Tony, a friend of Peter's, arrives as they leave. He is older than Peter, lazily good-natured, with enough money to be able to use as an anodyne such trivial amusements as a small town has to offer. He has come, as he frequently does, to keep Peter company. While they are struggling with the ennui of a Sunday evening, trying to decide what to do – Tony being flippantly bright and Peter being savagely morose – the doorbell rings. It is a girl of twenty who has got to the wrong house: her intention was to call at the next-door house, where Brian lives, to apply for a job as secretary to the now-famous author. She produces from her handbag a crumpled copy of the advertisement she came across in the local paper. When he answers the door to her Peter, on an impulse, decides not to tell her of her mistake. In response to her question he pretends to be Brian and proceeds to 'interview' the girl. Tony at one point tries to halt this cruel practical joke, but Peter brushes aside his objections and continues, subjecting Shirley, the girl, to a ruthless cross-examination which reveals that she, too, like Peter, has been damaged by circumstance and repudiated by her fellows. She is, in a sense, a cripple. Her particular disability is that she has had an illegitimate child and has found herself rejected by her own circle in consequence. Peter who, even before he hears her story, instinctively recognises a fellow-victim, forces Shirley to confess that the brave face she puts on and her optimism about being able to pull out of the mess are both assumed, illusory. 'It's the young chaps' forgiveness you want and they'll never let you have it', he says to her. 'I'll find somebody', she replies: to which he savagely says 'Never'. And he goes on:

> 'Look at me. And then say it. We are eruptions on the
> smooth face of society . . . The welfare schemes and help
> in the home try to soothe us out of existence. More is being
> done every day . . . Kindness is now an official state. It
> wears a uniform and badges. But where is ordinary human
> kindness? The thing that passes between men without
> thought. The kindness of love. For you know perfectly well
> that no-one has given you that sort of kindness. Your
> father. You say he was good to you, but you only say that
> because you wish he had been. Really, he's ashamed of
> you . . . Now you pretend you're going to start all over
> again. You can't. The job, the money, won't alter a thing.
> You're done for. Like me . . . Both of us insults to the present
> perfect way of life.'

Eventually Tony does intervene to tell Shirley that there is no job, that she came to the wrong house and after she has left, disappointed and numbed by the experience, Tony asks Peter why he did it. Peter's reply is this 'She was standing out there on the steps and I saw her – go on, laugh – I saw her as if she was undressed . . . I saw her body shrinking

from the cold, shrinking from disappointment, withdrawing from love –
Don't look at me like that! – and I wanted to hurt her.' Tony asks
him why:

PETER: If you live as I do it all goes into your head. All the devils. And
it's all thought, no feeling (*He has groped for this word*) Saints. Nomads.
Me. What other people experience – all that just goes to the head and
becomes a possibility. It sometimes gets pretty crowded up there with the
maybes. I'm trying to explain. That's what you want, isn't it?

TONY: Yes.

PETER: She was standing there on the step. And I didn't feel anything.
Some common tart come to the wrong house. Then I saw her . . . saw
her . . . as I said. And I remembered a song. From years ago. I was
once in love, believe it or not. Keep me to the point, for God's sake.
So there she was. Enquiring. Unknown. And I wanted her to feel something about me. Recognise me, I suppose.

TONY: You wanted to make an enemy.

PETER: Yes. (*Pause*) Yes! Something positive. It's not often now that
people approach me. Either by chance or wish. There she was. I wanted
to be remembered by someone. With hatred? Why not? How can I
ask for love? And it was meant to be a joke. At first. This'll make Tony
laugh. I remember thinking that. But when she told me about the child
it wasn't any good. I found I was talking to one of my own kind. I was
talking to myself. And it hasn't made you laugh.

TONY: No.

This is the core of the play and though a bit prosey and overexplanatory
it has a certain acrid sense of reality. And the lines of connection can
be clearly seen flowing out from it to Whiting's other plays and to his
general sense of the world. It is worth noting that speech of Peter's
which opens the passage quoted above: several very familiar Whiting
images are contained in it, so much so that the actual *titles* of three of his
other plays make their appearance cheek-by-jowl in its brief span –
The Devils, *The Nomads* and *Saint's Day*. Peter here announces himself
in terms almost too obvious as another example of the archetypal
Whiting person, an absolutist with a passionate longing for nobility and
perfection, an alienated cynic wandering in a desert and vainly searching
for home. Peter himself uses this metaphor: he says 'At one time I
believed that this waste ground must have boundaries. And I thought
that if I made my way towards that limit I'd at last meet with people . . .
In his next speech he adds, 'I've heard of people who live in places where
talent and opportunity for a kind of joy in life can flourish. And I really
believe they exist. I don't want to make the mistake of thinking that
all people in all places are like me. But there are far too many of us.
You shouldn't crowd a wilderness. It contradicts its purpose.' Recalling
Whiting's adaptation of *Hedda Gabler* and the affinities between his
vision and Ibsen's, one might well take very special note of the phrase
'opportunity for a kind of joy in life', for it is an extraordinarily close

echo of the attitudes and the exact words of two other of Ibsen's wild young women – Rebecca in *Rosmersholm* and Hilde in *The Master Builder*: even the qualification 'a *kind of* joy' is used by both of them, as if it were impossible to define this aspiration and this climactic experience precisely. In this central scene between Peter and Shirley can be found, too, the real kinship with *The Conditions of Agreement*: the sense of a futile, pointless, cruel and – above all – farcically humiliating world, the mirror-image of which is, for both plays, the smug complacency of small-town life; the paranoiac inferiority complex of the self-aware social misfit, his alienation from society being in both cases dramatically symbolised by physical lameness and disability; the curious love-hate of this character for another instinctively recognised as a 'victim-type' – Nicholas for A.G., Peter for Shirley; the seeking for an accomplice to assist in the perpetration of a practical joke which will in itself typify the world's casual, heartless cruelty – Nicholas recruits Bembo against A.G., Peter seeks to recruit Tony against Shirley (Tony, however, is much more passive than Bembo and finally changes sides, which Bembo does not do). *A Walk in the Desert* is less elaborately figured and less highly stylised, however, than *The Conditions of Agreement* and is the poorer on that account.

Shirley, too, is a less willing and a less pathetic victim than A.G. Whereas the latter is made to accept defeat completely and to retreat abjectly and without protest at the end of the play, Shirley in fact returns, undefeated. After Peter's cruel trick, she leaves the house in humiliation; she goes next door and is seen by Tony to be turned away without even being invited in, so we know that Peter's trick has robbed her of even the chance of the job she hoped for; then from Peter's mother and father, returning from their dramatic society, we hear of some accident they have seen by the canal – the police wading in the water and dragging something or someone out of it; Peter and Tony are terribly afraid, until Shirley suddenly comes back to collect her handbag, which she had accidentally left behind. Her final words are a sturdy assertion of the value of sensible compromise: 'Why can't people take things as they are? Look at you now. Inventing a sad story for me. She ended up in the river. It'd never be like that. Never. Still, it was nice of you to be worried. Matter of fact, it was a cat.' She describes how the police had carefully rescued the cat from the canal and, because it was a stray, had then taken it to be destroyed. 'Someone had complained', she says, 'Its screams were upsetting the neighbourhood. (*She looks at* PETER) He's right. No doubt about it. The place must be kept quiet so that you and all the other people in this street can die in peace. Goodnight.'

Whiting does not leave the play finally in Shirley's hands, however. He returns it to Peter. His final speech is a description of life's desolation. 'They say you walk in circles in a desert . . .' While he speaks, we see not him but the town, which Whiting describes as follows:

> *Shirley is seen walking through the town. The lights from*
> *shops fall on her. She looks ahead. Her movements are*
> *definite and hurried. The rain has made her hair ugly to look*
> *at ... Shirley has gone from sight down the street ... The*
> *town square: swept with rain ... The station: a train is*
> *leaving ... A by-pass road, lit by sodium lamps and*
> *deserted, goes straight into the distance.*

Over these visual images of desolation Peter's voice is heard: his last speech begins 'The moment I set eyes on her I knew she was an enemy. She believes in the good land. I don't any more ...'

To an extent, then, *A Walk in the Desert* is, as Whiting claimed, a rewriting of *The Conditions of Agreement* (which was, of course, in 1959 when the television play was written an unpublished, unperformed, entirely unknown play of which no one but Whiting himself was aware: indeed, as recently as 1957 *he* had claimed, in the Introduction of *The Plays of John Whiting*, that it was lost): but only to an extent. To be more exact, it employs one theme from *The Conditions of Agreement* but omits entirely the exploration of the peripheral reverberations of that theme. It is, in other words, essentially a one-act play, as compared with the fully developed full-length play of *The Conditions of Agreement*, a cameo as compared with a canvas. It is, within these limits, a good piece of work, well-observed and tautly constructed, with some excellent use of the visual element that television provides: the combination of voice and picture at the end of the play is especially skilful and moving.

III   Translations

Between 1953 and 1957, Whiting translated five modern French plays into English. These were *Une Fille pour du vent* (André Obey), *Les Invités du Bon Dieu* (Salacrou), *Pour Lucrèce* (Giraudoux, *Madame de ——* (Anouilh) and *Le Voyageur sans bagage* (Anouilh).

Three of the five were produced and published in Whiting's lifetime: the other two – the Salacrou and the Giraudoux – have never been either produced or published. These two unpublished ones are the most substantial plays of the five and in many ways are the best examples of Whiting's work as a translator. The publishing of Whiting's *Lucrèce* was, no doubt, inhibited by the publishing of Christopher Fry's *Duel of Angels*, which was an English version of the same Giraudoux play and which had, in 1953, a distinguished stage production with Vivien Leigh and Claire Bloom in the leading roles. There seems to be no adequate reason for the lack of publication and stage production in the case of the Salacrou play, unless it was that Whiting was, in this regard as in

218

others, before his time for the British theatre. His typescript of the translation of *Les Invités du Bon Dieu* is dated 1955 and one needs to remember that it was not until 3 August of that year that *Waiting for Godot* was seen in London: the first British production of Ionesco, by Peter Hall, had taken place in the previous year, having been suggested to Hall by Whiting. The Salacrou play, though not absurdist *tout court*, has a strong streak of that influence in it. Its sense of the world is too coherent and its ending too lyrical and trusting for it to be considered as a true absurdist piece, but some of its individual *effects* are absurdist in nature (for example, the Young Woman who is both herself and her twin sister, the mistress of the father in one of her personalities and of the son-in-law in the other: but Salacrou abandons the true absurdist implication of this situation by having the Young Woman give a purely naturalistic explanation – she is merely *impersonating* a twin whom she has deliberately invented for the purpose of being able to carry on a 'double life'). The play's structure, too, has something of the zany inconsequence of that of an absurdist play, though here again it is not developed into a fully absurdist image and metaphor.

Whiting's translation of the play is sprightly and firm and eminently playable. Both the texture of the dialogue and the use of startling images reminds one sometimes of *A Penny for a Song* (in the happy and comic moments) and of *The Conditions of Agreement* (in the sombre moments). The scene, too, in which Leonie, the wife, accepts the Young Woman (whose name has also now become Leonie) as a surrogate in her husband's mind for her own lost youth, might almost be original Whiting, though it is entirely true to Salacrou's play. It produces in Whiting's hands an English version of the scene which has great charm:

YOUNG WOMAN: Have you ever been to the opera, Madame? I'm his Carmen, his Manon Lescaut, his Lakmé . . .

LEONIE: So you're a singer!

YOUNG WOMAN: No, I'm his mistress.

LEONIE: What a charming idea! Why, Leon?

LEON: Your conduct is inexcusable!

LEONIE: Mine, Leon?

LEON: No, not yours, darling. I love you: always have loved you. I'll explain . . .

LEONIE: But love doesn't need to be explained, Leon.

LEON: I've always loved you, Leonie, and only you.

LEONIE: I've never doubted it, Leon.

LEON: Don't you think that girl has a resemblance to you when we were married?

LEONIE: Perhaps. But one never sees oneself as very beautiful.

AURILLON: He wasn't put off by the difficulty of the name, Leonie.

FRANCOIS: She represented the youth of his wife. How could he call her anything but Leonie?

AURILLON: But that's not her name.

LEONIE: Neither is it mine, Monsieur Aurillon.

LEON (*To* LEONIE):   I looked for the charm and the grace of your youth in that girl. I've loved you so much, Leonie, but so clumsily. With her I made good our youth, I sweetened and mended my ways. Through her I asked your forgiveness. Do you understand?

LEONIE: Yes, Leon.

AURILLON: Aren't you jealous?

LEONIE: Why should I be jealous of myself?

AURILLON (*To* LEONIE):   But you can't have understood, or you'd be blind with anger.

LEONIE: Why should I be angry at having been loved so well all my life? (*To* YOUNG WOMAN) Tell me, did you go to the opera? And to Saint Michel? Ah, those little restaurants at Saint Michel! And . . . I hardly dare ask you this . . . did you go to Andelys?

YOUNG WOMAN: Yes, we went to Andelys.

LEONIE: I'm glad. You never spoke of it again, Leon, and I was afraid that you'd forgotten Andelys. (*To* YOUNG WOMAN) We were very happy there, you see.

YOUNG WOMAN: Madame, I'm ashamed of myself. Try to forgive me, Leon. I'm sorry I said anything.

LEON (*Angrily, to the* YOUNG WOMAN):   What does it matter? You're no longer Leonie!

LEONIE: Forgive us, Leon. Have you forgotten that I, too, was not very bright at twenty and that I also made many mistakes? She must make them good and mend her ways. (*To the* YOUNG WOMAN) I'll help you.

Whiting's translation of the Salacrou play was, in fact, never completed. It had been commissioned by Hugh ('Binkie') Beaumont, of H. M. Tennant Ltd, who was so shocked by its contents when he read Acts 1 and 2 that he withdrew the commission and Whiting, in disgust, did not finish Act 3.

The instinctive sympathy between John Whiting's work and that of the leading French dramatists of the day is not surprising: both were greatly in advance of the contemporary average British dramatic fare. Kenneth Tynan remarked on it at the time in an article in *The Observer*[8]:

> The bare fact is that, apart from revivals and imports, there
> is nothing in the London theatre that one dare discuss
> with an intelligent man for more than five minutes. Since
> the great Ibsen challenge of the nineties, the English
> intellectuals have been drifting away from drama. Synge,
> Pirandello and O'Casey briefly recaptured them and they
> will still perk up at the mention of Giraudoux. But –
> cowards – they know Eliot and Fry only in the study: and
> of the native prose playwright who might set the boards
> smouldering they see no sign at all. Last week I welcomed

> a young Frenchwoman engaged in writing a thesis on
> contemporary English drama. We talked hopefully of John
> Whiting; but before long embarrassment moved me to ask
> why she had not chosen her own theatre as a subject for
> study. She smiled wryly. 'Paris is in decline' she said. 'Apart
> from Sartre, Anouilh, Camus, Cocteau, Aymé, Claudel,
> Beckett and Salacrou we have almost nobody.'

It is interesting that in 1954 the one British name that came to Tynan's mind, as a contrast to the general and pervading dreariness, was Whiting's and that his young French friend – if, indeed, she existed at all and was not simply a dramatic device introduced by Tynan to make his point more vividly – had eight French names to add to that of Giraudoux (who died ten years before, in 1944), which Tynan had already mentioned.

The Giraudoux play which Whiting chose to translate, *Pour Lucrèce*, has one figure and image in it that might have come straight from the realm of Whiting's own private mythology – the young woman who is the symbol of purity and who rushes with a kind of ecstasy into the arms of death in order that her purity might be preserved. The Obey play, too, has a similar figure – though in all other respects the two plays are utterly different. 'I laughed just now when you said I was defeated', says Lucile at the end of *Pour Lucrèce*, 'Because I already held the remedy in my hand. A remedy I had from a small girl, with my name, who swore when she was ten years old never to tolerate wicked people. She swore to prove, by death if necessary, that the world was a good place and mankind pure. Now the world has become empty and filthy to her, life is a disgrace. But it doesn't matter, it's not really true, because she took a vow!' And with that she swallows the poison which she has until that moment concealed in her hand. Iphigenia, in *Une Fille pour du vent*, expresses similar sentiments: 'I'm going to escape from them. They disgust me so much. They're loathsome to me. They've filled every part of me with such an angry, sick hatred that even if they went on their knees and asked my forgiveness I should run away. I'd tear myself from their company, from their earth and from their air!' It is Calchas, the politician–priest and Agamemnon, the commander-in-chief and her own father, of whom Iphigenia is speaking. She is supported and seconded by the young Dead Soldier, the first man to be killed in the campaign against Troy. She alone can hear him (for she herself is already, in effect, of the company of the dead) when he says to her:

SOLDIER: On our way, lass, on our way. We others are not afraid any more.
IPHIGENIA (*Quietly*):   Just a little.
SOLDIER: Not at all.
IPHIGENIA: Yes, yes; I am afraid. To die.

SOLDIER: Not die! To escape! Die laughing, dearest. Die to avoid being
a woman of the empire of Calchas! Die to keep from being the mother
of subjects of Calchas! Die so as not to grow old in the world of
Calchas! Die to stay young and free forever! Die to stay alive!

It is easy, in the light of what one knows of his own plays and other
works, to see why these two French plays, with central figures of this
kind, would attract Whiting. Of all the five translations that he did –
all of them extremely competent and workmanlike – perhaps the most
successful is the Giraudoux play. Its French text, though passionate, is
elegantly formal in language and this formality is one of its strengths.
Whiting's own style, a kind of highly charged poetic prose, is peculiarly
suitable for the rendering in English of the internal sense and spirit of
the Giraudoux original because it can preserve through its formality
something of the original's outward literary shape. This is truer of
Whiting's figured prose than it is of Christopher Fry's version in *Duel
of Angels*. Fry, when he is not writing that scintillating, dancing, decor-
ative verse, writes rather flatly: his natural style was not so close to
Giraudoux's as was Whiting's. It had to be suppressed, with predictably
less happy results. Whiting's on the other hand, could be allowed its
head in a play whose vision was close in kind to his own. His text is
fuller, too – at any rate as compared with the published version of
Duel of Angels, though one cannot predict, of course, what might have
happened, in way of cutting the original text, to Whiting's version if
it had gone to production or publication. What one can say, however,
is that the passages preserved by Whiting and cut by Fry are to the
play's advantage, whatever might have been the exigencies of tailoring
the play to conventional theatre length.

Le Voyageur sans bagage, a play in which the dialogue is much
more conversational than in the Giraudoux play, illustrates the stylistic
problem from the opposite angle. A perusal of one of the early typescripts of Whiting's translation of Anouilh revealed some very interesting emendations of diction. 'I shall not allow harm to come to the
weasels on any land I may own', says the amnesiac Gaston as he con-
templates the row of stuffed animals left by the murderous small boy
who was, perhaps, his own former self. In the typescript Whiting has
crossed out 'not allow harm to come to' and has pencilled in 'defend'.
The speech continues 'But how can I comfort these for their long night
of pain and fear, held in relentless jaws, and not understanding why?'
The phrase 'held in relentless jaws' has been amended – after one or two
attempts – simply to 'trapped'. In an earlier scene, Gaston says 'In that
case, why didn't I go to see him every day and keep him company in
his room? Why didn't I give up my games in the sun so that he didn't
feel the injustice too much?' Whiting has crossed out 'games in the
sun' and in its place written 'all my half-holidays'. One sees him at

work here 'cutting the plush'. And, at the end of the play, when Gaston decides to slip away and evade the past which he now knows for certain is his, but which he finds repulsive and overwhelming, he says in the typescript 'Tell Georges Renaud that the fickle ghost of his brother surely sleeps safely in some common grave in Germany.' Whiting has excised the words 'the fickle ghost of' and 'surely'. One need not multiply the examples: those given above are sufficient to show that Whiting realised the play's need for a fairly quiet, conversational style with which the more highly coloured and obtrusive literary metaphor was out of place and would have the effect of falsifying rather than heightening the sense of reflected experience. Of course, this would not be true of all Anouilh's plays, some of which are themselves much more mannered than is *Le Voyageur sans bagage*. Whiting, indeed, in translating the one-act *Madame de* —— has neatly caught in English the sardonic, brittle artifice of the dialogue of the original.

As in the dialogue of his own original plays so in these translations can be seen Whiting's perennial interest in and battle with the stylistic problem of diction in the twentieth-century play. How realistic, how conversational, how 'ordinary' should talk in a play be? When should one and when should one not, to use Whiting's own phrase, 'cut the plush'? Though in a general way he never solved the problem completely (since there *is* no complete solution now) his adaptation of his own style, in the translations, to suit the spirits and senses of other men's visions is as remarkable as the style itself and the translations, as a result, are eminently stage-worthy and evocative renderings of their distinguished originals. After these modern plays Whiting undertook, at Peter Hall's request, a translation of Molière's *Don Juan* but as far as I can trace this was never completed. It was certainly never played or published.

IV   *No Why*

No Why is a one-act play which was originally intended to be played as a curtain-raiser to Whiting's translation of *Le Voyageur sans bagage*. Peter Hall, however, who was directing the Anouilh play, felt that *No Why* would be too austere and forbidding for the audience and persuaded Whiting to translate *Madame de* —— to fill up the bill. *No Why* was then published in *London Magazine* without being produced. Later, it was produced as a radio play by Martin Esslin and finally received a stage production in 1964, when it was presented by the Royal Shakespeare Company in a programme of one-act plays. As has already been mentioned in Chapter 2, the central figure of the play is a small, silent boy who is being punished by being locked in the attic while his family enjoy themselves at a party downstairs; but one somehow feels that it works more in the mode of a short story than in that of a one-act play. The two forms are, of course, utterly dissimilar and *No Why*'s disadvantage as a play is its fragility, a quality which would be an advantage to it as a short story. For the theatre, it is too delicate and also almost too single-minded: to give it theatrical strength and variety the texture has had to be rather dangerously coarsened here and there. Though it may sound paradoxical to say so, it needs – fully to realise itself – to be even more tenuous and, in certain senses of the words, enigmatic and gnomic; but there is a strict limit, in the theatre, to the extent to which a play can be tenuous, enigmatic and gnomic without also being either impenetrable and dull or sententious and vulgar. *No Why*, though it does not fall into these errors, hesitates on the brink of them and loses force accordingly. It is not that Whiting failed to solve the problem, but that the material is, for the theatre, intractable and the problem insoluble.

Jacob, the small boy, becomes even in the brief space of this very short play the image both of the unjustly oppressed and of that dogged purity which refuses to surrender to the shady, compromising world. From being at the beginning of the play just a small boy being harassed by grown-ups, he becomes in the middle scenes an archetypal figure and is spoken of at one point almost as if he were Mankind itself: 'Remember how we planned him', says his father to his mother, 'What should he be like, our son? Should he walk on two legs or on four? We decided two, remember? So his head should be nearer the clouds. *You* wanted that with your love of pansy poetry. The more feet on the ground, the more realistic his outlook, I thought. But you kissed me and I gave in. And he turned out just as our conception of him.'

Henry, the father, does not believe this: all the way through the play he talks like a public relations officer or advertising man, a liar down to the very roots, and this glibly sentimental account of Jacob's origins is thrown in by him as the merest propaganda. The irony is that it turns out to be true. Jacob *has* become the two-footed creature, standing erect, head nearer heaven, rejecting those who crawl. His silence is the silence of Jesus before Pilate, or Cordelia before Lear; it is a condemnation of the cackling political world, the world of bargains, deals and the doctrine of expediency.

The nature of the alleged offence which they say he has committed is deliberately not specified, though the hint is dropped that it is something terrible and shocking and quite outside the pale. By not tying it to the naturalistic structure of the play – what there is of it – Whiting makes it possible for the 'offence' to acquire much more metaphorical and poetic resonance. In turn it becomes, in the minds of his accusers, a dereliction of personal ties – an offence, that is to say, against love; a legal dereliction – an offence against justice; a moral dereliction – a sin and an offence against God. Or so the accusers would have us believe. But Jacob's silence, combined with their own shifty posturings and over-protestings assure us that though the offences they speak of are real enough, the offenders are themselves – and us. Jacob's real offence is in being different and insisting on the difference. All he needs do is apologise. All they ask of him is 'Say you're sorry, Jake', then he will be accepted back into society; then he can come to the party. 'Come back to the family party before it is too late', his father says to him. But he will not say he is sorry; he will not barter with them; he will not give them the submission they want. And so he is left in a locked, dark, empty room to die alone.

The rest of the figures – 'characters' would be the wrong word – in the play are broadly drawn, deliberately two-dimensional, expressionistic. Only Eleanor, the mother, wavers occasionally into humanity. This expressionism and caricature produces some very good moments. Gregory, the grandfather, for example, becomes a judge-like figure who is called in as a last resort to settle the matter. 'Please try and make him say he's sorry', Eleanor pleads with Gregory. Whiting's stage direction says, GREGORY *and* JACOB *stare at each other*, then Gregory says 'Why should I? It doesn't matter now. Not when you get to my age. It's not important, I tell you. All that matters is something called – (*He hesitates*) justice.'

He hesitates. Why? Because he cannot even remember the name of the concept? Or because he is ashamed? Or because he fears the very word may blister his tongue? All those ideas and possibilities are there.

The austerity and the uncompromising severity of this little play are entirely typical of Whiting and it is perhaps significant that in 1957, when he wrote this piece, he was even less inclined than usual to make concessions to the entertainment aspects of theatre. The theatre, after all, had rejected him. He, in turn, was treating its flippancy with scorn. He was not even sure at that time that he was going to return to it and if he did it would be on his terms, not those of the lighter-minded audiences. And yet, in spite of the estrangement and in spite of his own austerity, of which *No Why* is a good example, there must clearly have been in him a great urge to return to writing for the stage. He knew perfectly well – as we now know – that he was first and foremost, and most significantly, a dramatist.

6

RETURN TO THE THEATRE
(1958-1963)

I Noman (1958–1960?)

In 1958, while still busy with his writing for films, Whiting began the composition of yet another version of a play he had made several false starts on the year before. This time, he returned to the central theme and image of his very first work, the novel called *Not a Foot of Land*. Clearly there was something about this image that was integral to his view of things and it is much more likely that, in 1958, it was this image that disturbingly returned to him, compelling him to begin the new play, rather than that he decided *in vacuo* to write another play and then looked round for a subject. The image is that of the attack by a group of fervent revolutionaries on a museum–shrine dedicated to an assassinated leader who had himself been a revolutionary in his day. This plot situation is taken bodily from the centre of *Not a Foot of Land* and is made the central incident of the new play. Whiting obviously felt that he had not yet said all there was to say about it. It is significant that it was his first major artistic image to which he now returned and it is also significant that, having written one act of the new play, he laid it aside, feeling that he did not know how to complete it. 'Never worked . . . ,' he said in the 1961 *Encore* interview, 'boring beyond words so I put that away.' But although he put it away, he returned to it again, several times. He never completed *Noman* and never managed to give full expression to that complex of images that had dominated almost all of his writing, but one can see now, in retrospect, how that one dramatic confrontation of popularised, emasculated idealism with frustrated, passionate, personal belief represented for Whiting the very crux of twentieth-century experience. It is an image of astonishing sophistication and richness, containing within its small compass much that would relate contemporary man's sense of personal isolation and

226

alienation to the political history of the century. Whiting never managed to bring this relationship into completely clear dramatic focus but he acutely realised its presence and its importance. According to his own account, this difficulty of establishing a meaningful relationship between personal commitment and communal, public life applied to his own private life and thoughts as well as to dramatic expression and artistic problems. 'It's only in recent years that I've been prepared to commit myself on any very definite opinion about things', he said in the 1961 interview: 'I suffer very much from being able to see both sides of the question. I suppose it's because of my age, and coming out of the late thirties, and then the war and . . . I don't know.' He mistrusted the glib solution, the too-readily-acquired opinion, the large public pronouncement; he knew that the purely socio-political solutions constantly propounded made for shallowness and a diminishing of the spirit. But he also instinctively recognised that the frame of modern society had been cracked and must be replaced if the growth of the individual spirit were to be protected and encouraged.

His revolutionaries in *Noman* are all young, except one: Walter, the theorist of the group, is forty-six; Meyer, Jacob, Peter and Leonie are in their early twenties. Though Walter is not as old as Old Tim in *Not a Foot of Land*, the general structure of the conspiratorial group is the same in both works – three young men, a girl and an older man. The personal relationships within the two groups are different, however, and Walter is a less dominant – and less interesting – figure than Old Tim, at least as far as one can judge from the one act of the play that Whiting completed. At the beginning of that act, the conspirators assemble at the museum just before closing time, go in and hide themselves and wait for the caretaker to lock up the building after the public has left. When he has done so, they come out and confront him. The intention and possibility of violence is painfully and vividly present in the scene, but no overt violence actually occurs: the confrontation is rather one of ideas and ideals than of physical onslaught. The real leader of the revolutionary group is Meyer (he is never given a first name) and his intention it to destroy the museum and all its contents. His primary motive for this is immediately clear – the museum building is in fact the house in which Lang died; Lang had been the great leader of the people and had (presumably by revolution, though this is not stated in so many words) established a new state and a new government in the 1920s; he had been assassinated by his own brother on the steps of the house and his memory is now venerated by the whole country, the museum–house having become almost literally a shrine, a place of pilgrimage; and for Meyer all this is anathema; he hates Lang and all his works. The ritual destruction of this house is the symbol of all that hatred: the hatred is the reason for the destruction. The equation, in one sense, is as simple as that, but beyond the primary motive are secondary ones and these are much less clearly defined. As they make their appearance during the course of Act 1, it becomes clear that Meyer is a character of great complexity and with contradictions built into his personality. He is a strange mixture of idealism and nihilism. When Walter, deriding Lang's materialistic approach says to the girl, Leonie, 'You can have your unconstrained span of years of pleasure and goodness and love and then you can rot in the earth for ever and ever and ever and ever . . .' Meyer passionately shouts 'Shut up! Shut up!' and turning to Brendel, the caretaker, who is his antagonist in the argument, he says 'That's how we were taught. That's what we were taught. And the children today. Who was this man?' Brendel says Lang was persecuted for his ideas and Meyer snaps 'Persecuted! He should have been crucified. Who was he?' At this point, then, Meyer is what we might by now almost regard as the standard Whiting hero-idealist, insisting that life is tawdry and worthless unless there is something outside oneself and greater than oneself which automatically commands one's devotion. Scornfully he says, looking at a photograph of Lang, 'Was it *this* that destroyed God?' and at another point he speaks of 'Lang's hateful ideas'. Yet he rejects with a sneer Walter's image of him (Meyer) as 'lonely, solitary, friendless, impossibly dedicated to some nonsense', saying that it was 'one of Walter's poorer efforts, shamelessly borrowed from nineteenth-century fiction'. And at the end of Act 1, when the climax is at its height and one feels that the promised act of violence is imminent, Meyer praises that act because of its senselessness. When Brendel says 'It seems such a senseless thing to do', Meyer replies 'That's it! It's pure. All, beautiful . . .' and adds a little later 'But this . . . it's a senseless thing . . . there's no feeling . . . even a motiveless, gratuitous act gives you something. But this. Nothing. Nothing. So that's why we're here. That's why we're here. That's what it's all about.' Of course, Meyer's idealism and nihilism, though contradictory on the surface and though they give rise to contradictory manifestations in practice, are linked beneath the surface. In effect, he is pursuing an argument that goes something like this – life must have some absolute sense, some meaning which transcends the immediate and material world; this *must* be so because all instinct, all reason, all life itself tells us it must be so; but direct personal experience in the passing moment, the mundane, day-to-day, ordinary experience seems to show it is not so, that there is no such absolute; so day-to-day experience contradicts the 'inner' experience, and what we conceived to be the spirit of life is mocked; that being so, there is nothing left, nothing of any significance and the only satisfactory act left is to ally ourselves senselessly – that is, beyond the reach and realm of the senses – with that Nothing.

Meyer expresses all this mistrust of life and the consequent disgust, including self-disgust, in his hatred for Lang. From the moment when he faces Brendel, the caretaker of the museum, for the first time – and

Whiting sets up this opposition at the beginning of the act by having Meyer alone invade Brendel's private room in the museum and fetch him out to confront the others – it becomes obvious that Brendel will act as Lang's defender, attempting to defend both his reputation and the collection of memorabilia in the museum. At first, this seems perfectly ordinary and to be expected: he is after all the caretaker of the museum and one would expect him to take care of it, to protect it. Gradually, however, one gets the feeling that Brendel's defence of Lang is something more than his duty as a physical custodian. He rarely answers Meyer's arguments and never at any length, yet the sense develops during the act that his defence of Lang is both broad and deep and he somehow seems to become closely identified with the dead leader. The group of invaders notice and comment on this:

WALTER: Then why are you so concerned?
BRENDEL: Leave it. Let it alone. You can destroy this place. You can. I know. All right. But you won't touch the man. Lang. He doesn't exist here. So leave this place as it is . . .
WALTER: Why are you so concerned?
MEYER: Because it will be his place we break up. He lives here. He looks after it. He's responsible. Like a priest in a church. He's responsible.
WALTER: He doesn't care about Lang. Do you mean that?
MEYER: Why should he? (*To* BRENDEL) Why should you?
BRENDEL: I do care. I care very much.

This exchange occurs almost at the end of the act, which finishes without letting us know *why* Brendel cares so much for Lang's reputation and memory. This was to have been revealed in Act 2, which Whiting never managed to write. His notes for it are still extant, however, and they give the reason for the degree of Brendel's concern. The reason is that Brendel *is* Lang, literally. The assassination of Lang, though thought by everyone to have been successful, was not so. Lang was gravely injured but not killed. By what means he was rescued and nursed back to health the notes do not reveal, but now, twenty years after, he is here, in disguise and under a false name, employed as caretaker of a museum in his own memory. There is in this situation, as Ronald Hayman remarks, a richly ironic vein which Whiting presumably intended to exploit in Act 2, for now – unlike the situation in *Not a Foot of Land* – there is an authoritative spokesman for the earlier regime, the one against which the present revolutionary gesture is aimed. Now the earlier Master can speak for himself and tell us whether the arid materialism of the society to which Meyer objects (and to which Timothy similarly objected in *Not a Foot of Land*) is what he had intended. Did something go wrong with the earlier revolution? Was Lang intending further developments that were cut off by his death? Did he fail because he somehow lost power to other, more reactionary or more doctrinaire forces? What has he learned since, in his twenty years of silent watching? Would he change the form of society and the country now, if he could? The potential is enormous and the possibility of the spectacle of revolution and counter-revolution in headlong collision is fascinating. It could have embraced the whole history of twentieth-century political upheaval, all the questions of popular revolutions that go awry and lead not to a fuller life for the individual but to a regressive totalitarianism or a dreary bureaucracy, or both. And what is a 'fuller life' for the individual, especially when one tries to interpret this question in political terms – two cars instead of one, a summer cottage by the lake, more spare time (that he doesn't know how to use)? To have, in effect, the figure of the Master simultaneously both dead and alive is obviously a much more complex and sophisticated concept than the single lyric gesture of defiance that is the centre of *Not a Foot of Land* and illustrates the advance in Whiting's contemplation and probing of his subject. Apparently he felt, however, that this complexity could not be brought into theatrical focus, or at any rate he did not succeed, in the years between 1958 and 1963, in discovering how this could be done.

One sign of the increased richness of texture, as compared with the novel of 1946, is the treatment of the group of insurgents. In the former work they had been, with the exception of Tim and Sara, very shadowy figures, hardly present as people at all. In *Noman*, they have much more individual definition, even including a long and rather uncharacteristic stage direction at the beginning of the act, in which detailed physical descriptions are given, almost as if Whiting were reminding *himself* that more definition was needed, both to give the work a firmer grip generally and, in particular, to make it stageworthy. This stage direction begins as follows: *The five figures in the darkness have come forward into the first room. They are:* MEYER, WALTER, JACOB, PETER *and the girl,* LEONIE. *Let us look at these people.* Then follow the descriptions, with details like '*His pale eyes – perhaps he needs glasses – sometimes become hooded as if with tiredness. This is not likely to be affectation. His teeth are bad. His clothes show that he looks after himself, and his body is well exercised.*

The five conspirators are as sharply differentiated in character as they are in outward physical appearance and Whiting obviously intended, in Act 2, to develop and examine these differences. 'The breakup of the group', note no. 14 laconically says. 'What makes a revolutionary?' is the question he is asking. What burning common purpose binds these five different people together? As far as one can tell from Act 1 as it exists, by far the most interesting of these intra-group relationships was going to be that between Meyer and Walter. Walter is the older man and, one would have thought, would be the leader of the group, especially as Meyer introduces him to Brendel as 'Our theorist'. This turns out not to be so, and later in the act, Walter himself gives at least part of the explanation, though much is left to be resolved between these two:

WALTER: You and I could have done this job alone.
MEYER: Yes.
WALTER: Yet you had to bring the others. Why?
MEYER: You seem to know. Tell me.
WALTER: Because you can't see yourself as a leader unless you've got someone to lead. I'm no good to you because I gave you the ideas. You decided to put them into action, certainly. Something that was beyond me. But you can't lead me because I'm a step ahead. I knew what should be done. You know how to do it.

What Whiting seems to have had in mind, judging from the existing first act and his notes for the second, was some kind of examination of the nature of revolution and the revolutionary mind. As has already been noted in other chapters of this book, he had a profound and continuing interest in the relationship between socio-political structures and the aspirations and responses of the individual. This shows in many of his plays and what he is now doing in *Noman* is examining the nature of this relationship and of the instinct to rebellion by concentrating on each in turn of a heterogeneous group of revolutionaries, bound only by their instinct toward revolution. One of the things that comes most powerfully out of this examination is the sense of the non-intellectual, ritual, atavistic element which is a constituent part of the revolutionary mind and process, even in people of forceful intellectual grasp.

The whole of the first act of *Noman*, then, is a single confrontation between five revolutionaries with nothing in common but their revolution and the single, unknown, disguised ex-leader. Nothing actually 'happens', in the sense of plot incident, except that Meyer, in a kind of ecstasy, at one point suddenly smashes the glass top of a museum showcase and takes out the plaster cast of Lang's hands which the case contains. At the end of the act, he picks them up again. *He holds them before him for a moment and they make by their structure an expressive gesture. Then Meyer smashes them together and they fall in pieces.* Despite this lack of 'action', the play has both tension and forward movement.

Noman takes place in an unnamed, imaginary country. It seems to have some of the characteristics of an Eastern European Communist country in its official 'abolition' of religion and its insistence that everyone must revere the dead Leader. On the other hand, its reported devotion to comfort, consumer goods and materialistic targets is very much an echo of the more affluent West. The truth is that the play is concerned not with a particular country or a particular political system but with the texture of twentieth-century society generally – the rise of the arid, technocratic, bureaucratic community with its glibly proclaimed 'ideals' of material advancement. The fact that Brezhnev's Russia and Nixon's America *both* seem to be echoed in the play (and seem, when one thinks of it, to be dangerously, frighteningly, depressingly alike) is only a mark of the play's astonishing prescience. The target of its irony is neither communism nor capitalism, but the easy acceptance of a tawdry, cocooned existence, the willingness to see life squeezed of its vital juices for the sake of mere safety and freedom from trouble. This utter desolation of a society is savagely satirised in one scene, in which – to illustrate the warped teachings to which they have been subjected – the revolutionaries play a charade for Brendel's benefit. Walter takes the part of a school teacher and the others pretend to be the pupils. Meyer arrives late to class and is asked why. His reply is: 'It was such a fine morning, sir. I stopped in the park. The band of the Tramway Workers' Guild was practising. The flowers were bursting like bombs. A breeze swept off the boating lake and carried the idiotic language of children. Birds were shitting on the public statues. Four park-keepers were hanging by their necks from the historic oaks. I stopped, sir, just for a moment, to be happy. I'm ready for my punishment.' What sticks in Meyer's craw and makes him furious about this mock-idyllic scene is the stupid, mindless, unthinking acceptance that it implies. This is the basis of his hatred of Lang who, in Meyer's submission, induced this moronic response by setting up a society that, for reasons of political safety and survival, demanded a sedated and silent people, a people who would not ask awkward questions or demand to be consulted. Meyer rejects the society which results from such views for the same reason that he rejects Walter's image of the lonely idealist 'impossibly dedicated to some nonsense' because it is empty, affected, unreal. His rejection of both is a rejection of the stock response to the stock image: the thing for which the human heart is impelled to search must spring from direct personal perceptions and experience of life's spirit; it must be *real* and be known to be so. It must in this sense be a new experience and a new response every time, never a repeat or an imitation. Walter, when he had first recruited Meyer for the revolutionary cause, had painted for him pictures of all life's possible satisfactions, trying to find out the basic cause of Meyer's discontent. Asking him what he *does* want, Walter has said 'There must be some known pattern of life which could apply' and Meyer has answered 'None'. And in describing to Brendel their disillusionment with the form and frame of society, Meyer says – about the Sunday when he and Walter sat and watched the 'happiness, leisure, desolation' of the populace – 'We sat at a safe table. Everything was laid on to impress us with the urgent need to accept ourselves as we are.' It is the unquestioning acceptance – especially of oneself – that strikes Meyer as iniquitous.

Yet two or three times during the act, Meyer is compared with Lang. Indeed, he makes the comparison in one instance himself. Brendel also makes it. Meyer has just said to Walter that the time for absolute leaders of the autocratic sort has passed and that he, Meyer, could not have initiated the present revolutionary action if the rest of the conspirators had not supported him and had an active part in the making of the decision. Brendel says that Lang was just the same and that it was this trait in him that led to his being murdered. This is never explained but perhaps implies that Lang (rather like poor Alexander Dubček) had realised the greyness of his revolution, was trying to do something to give it a more 'human face' and was murdered by a doctrinaire 'hard-liner' who wanted no truck with softness.

Walter, during this discussion of the responsibilities and limitations of leadership, mockingly compares Meyer to 'A chairman, a committee member', a description from which Meyer does not dissent. The whole question of the proper relationship between individual and society, with which the revolution itself is concerned, is mirrored in smaller scale within the revolutionary group and becomes at several levels one of the interwoven themes of the play. Leonie, the girl revolutionary, states one extreme of the argument: she diagnoses Meyer's impulse as purely destructive and of frustrated sexual origin. 'He's simple. He could find what he's looking for in a bed. It's all there, all; yes, Jacob, all there! The destruction and the shame.' And she contemptuously dismisses the Romantic ideal: to her a Holy Grail is nonsense. 'Look, we live now,' she says, 'Yes? All right? All this waiting till you're dead. What's all that about? It's now or never.' A moment later she adds, to Jacob 'I don't want the taste of blood and dust in my mouth, I want the taste of your sex. Let Meyer get rid of his energy this way, but you come to me.'

One is constrained to ask, in that case, what she is doing there at all. Perhaps she came reluctantly, dragged along by Jacob? It is not explained in the play as it stands but would perhaps have come out in Act 2 under 'breakup of the group' (note no. 14). Another note does say 'Girl: Why bring her? Woman's place. Balls!' So Whiting was aware of the problem raised by her presence. The truth is that she is some-thing of a weakness in the play's structure. She is useful to Whiting because she can state, as is shown above, the *opposite* of all the revolu-tionary ideals, which is useful by way of contrast (she is, in fact, a fair example of the society they are trying to get rid of). But this does not provide within the plot a logical reason for her presence, which is going to have to be ingeniously explained away, rather than genuinely ex-plained. She is, one suspects, there for dramaturgical rather than truly dramatic reasons. She is also there, in a sense, as the result of an accident – the accident of being left over from *Not a Foot of Land*, from which work she is an echo of Sara, though temperamentally quite different from that ethereal, half-real creature.

Some of the weaknesses resulting from Leonie's presence would no doubt have disappeared if Whiting had reworked the play again and had written the second half of it. There are other slacknesses, too, that would certainly have been tightened. As Ronald Hayman says, it is unfair –

and, indeed, misleading – to judge *Noman* alongside Whiting's finished work. Nevertheless, it is a powerful piece, even as it stands; and it illustrates very vividly the clear line of continuity in Whiting's essential vision, while showing also the deepening complexity and profundity of that central Whiting figure, the self-immolating Romantic still in search of an absolute.

II *The Devils*

As has already been pointed out in Chapter 1, *The Devils* was written in 1960 and was based on a book by Aldous Huxley, called *The Devils of Loudun*, which was first published in 1952. Huxley subtitled his book 'A Biography' and based it directly upon original documents and historical commentary relating to certain historical events which occurred in seventeenth-century France. Whiting has taken only one part of Huxley's book, has intensified it considerably for his own purpose and has omitted entirely the long historical perspectives which Huxley gives to the events.

The central figure of Whiting's play is Urbain Grandier, the vicar of the town of Loudun who was, in point of historical fact, burned to death as a witch and sorcerer in August 1634. The play relates the events leading up to this judicial murder. Grandier is shown at the start as a man who loves the things of the temporal world but who yet is troubled with a self-disgust and a deep unease. He is proud and sophisticated and handsome and well-educated, all of which makes him a desirable and eligible friend in the homes of the wealthier and more powerful people in the town, the 'top people'; but in the minds of those a little lower down the scale, whose noses have been put too badly out of joint by his coming to Loudun, these same qualities excite only envy and enmity, especially since Grandier takes no pains to conceal his contempt for their small-town, cloddish stupidity. With the women of the town, of whatever social station, he is universally popular. Attractive, urbane and not hindered by any puritanical scruples, he has already made several of them his mistresses. His reputation as a lover spreads, making more enemies for him; in spreading, it reaches the ears of Sister Jeanne des Anges, the Mother Superior (though she is only twenty-five) of a small Ursuline convent. Sister Jeanne is a nun who has entered the convent for reasons of family convenience, rather than upon the urgings of faith. She has no real vocation. She is, moreover, a hunchback and is both bitter and filled with a sense of inferiority and disgust about this deformity. She has never met Grandier but on the strength of his reputation alone she conceives for him an intense sexual passion which she cannot acknowledge, of course and which she finds it impossible to dismiss. Conveniently for her, the old priest who has been the convent's spiritual director dies and Sister Jeanne takes this opportunity to invite Grandier to take over these duties. When he refuses, her passion for him becomes a passion of hatred and she claims that, through super-natural powers, he visits her at night in the shape of an evil spirit and debauches her. Not to be outdone, other nuns of the convent begin to make the same kinds of claims and very soon it is common knowledge in the town that the whole convent is possessed by devils and that it is Grandier, the sorcerer, who has, in the name of Satan his master, conjured these devils and commanded them to torment, violate and take possession of the nuns. Grandier's enemies, smarting under the lash of his pride, confidence and cleverness, recognise this new rumour as the chance for which they have been waiting. They seize it and bring charges of witchcraft against him. Even then the forces of charity and reason prevail for a time and d'Armagnac, the governor of the town, with the help of de Cerisay, the chief magistrate, succeeds in protecting Grandier and showing up the charges against him for what they are – a mixture of ignorance, superstition and malice. But at that point a greater force enters the lists against Grandier: Cardinal Riche-lieu is busy subduing local authority and making himself the political master of all France, as he is already the political master of the King. Grandier has supported d'Armagnac in his resistance to Richelieu's domination and has spoken out against the Cardinal's schemes for demolishing local fortifications. This makes him Richelieu's enemy. Richelieu, in the name of the King, sends Baron de Laubardemont as special commissioner to Loudun, his commission being to prosecute the case of withcraft against Grandier. The vested interests of Church, State and various disaffected private individuals unite forces; suitable witnesses are bribed; the nuns are only too ready to oblige with spectac-ular public demonstrations of demonic possession, stage-managed by Canon Barré, an exorcist who sees devils in everybody and everything and derives enormous pleasure and satisfaction from his continuous – and very public – battle with Satan. The end is, of course, a foregone conclusion: after a mockery of a trial and the solemn mumbo-jumbo of sentencing, Grandier is put to the Question, both ordinary and extraordinary (that is to say, subjected to the most hideous and brutal torture in an effort to get him to confess) and then burned alive.

Given the facts of the historical story, there are obviously several levels at which they can be handled and several different tones or essences that can be derived from them. This was aptly demonstrated, in a negative way, by the lamentably silly film on the subject by Ken Russell, who chose to make it a vehicle for a cheap and modish sensa-tionalism, an exercise in *Grand Guignol*, trivial and childish, lacking both the coolly ironic and objective tone of Huxley's book and the darkly serious, metaphysical exploration of Whiting's play. And this, in broad general terms, describes the difference between Huxley's approach and Whiting's. Whiting also has irony – as, indeed, he almost always has – and within the prescription of the play's aesthetic his vision is clear and objective, but there is nevertheless a dark intensity in his treatment, a desperation almost, which is wholly absent from Huxley's. Contemplating the history and the events, Huxley centred his work more on Sister Jeanne than on Grandier. Whiting's contemplation led him in the opposite direction. Huxley at one point[1] describes his book as a comedy and Sister Jeanne as an essentially comic figure. (This is not the place for a long digression into the vast and complicated and semantically confused subject of the nature of comedy or the definition of the term, but it should just be remarked that 'comic' does not simply mean laughable or amusing and, indeed, need not mean either of these at all.) Huxley's description of his own book is an accurate one and his comments on the comedic elements in Sister Jeanne's character as it existed in historical fact are interesting and illuminating. Whiting's treatment is not a tragic one – though it embraces some of the elements of tragedy – but it certainly is not comic. Reading Huxley's book – and his predilection in Huxley's favour has already been commented upon – John Whiting saw in Grandier another of those Byronic–Whitingesque figures who so exactly reflected his own sense of the world, one who had, through his wit and his culture and his sensibility tasted all the joys of sense and intellect and yet found within himself a black and bridgeless void, one who longed for and searched for what Huxley, in relation to both Grandier and Sister Jeanne, calls 'self-transcendence'. It is from this angle that Whiting instinctively approaches the story. This is not a perversion either of Huxley's book or of the historical fact, but an attempt to account for that fact. Though Grandier has nothing of this metaphysical yearning in Huxley's narrative, there are points at which, one can see, Whiting might well have taken such a hint. On pages 170–1 of the 1961 edition, for example, Huxley has the following:

> Laubardemont lost no time. By 6th December he was back
> again at Loudun. From a house in the suburbs he sent
> secretly for the Public Prosecutor and the Chief of Police,
> Guillaume Aubin. They came, Laubardemont showed them
> his commission and a royal warrant for Grandier's arrest.
> Aubin had always liked the parson. That night he sent
> Grandier a message, informing him of Laubardemont's
> return and urging immediate flight. Grandier thanked him;
> but, fondly imagining that innocence had nothing to fear,
> ignored his friend's advice. Next morning, on his way to
> church, he was arrested.

Then later, on pages 232–3, Huxley allows himself some speculation. In the description of Grandier in prison, alone, at night, knowing now

that the trial was a rigged one and that there was no hope, there is this
passage:

> The parson lay down again – but not to sleep. He had the
> will to heroism; but his body was in a panic. The heart
> throbbed uncontrollably. Shuddering with the mindless
> fears of the nervous system, his muscles were made yet
> tenser by his conscious effort to overcome that purely
> physical terror . . . It was all completely unthinkable; and
> yet it was a fact, it was actually happening. If only he had
> taken the Archbishop's advice and left the parish eighteen
> months ago! And why had he refused to listen to Guillaume
> Aubin? What madness had made him stay and let himself
> be arrested?

Whiting's interest is much more in questions like these than in the fact
of Grandier's arrest and imprisonment. He starts from the facts: the
fact of the arrest, the fact of Grandier's conniving at it himself and
taking no steps to avoid it. And from there he makes his play pursue
those questions. Why? Why *allow* this to happen to oneself? What kind
of man would do that? And, later, why suffer the extremes of torture
go through the fire itself when a little discretion and circumspection –
just for the sake of not making the required confession? Why, finally,
especially for a man as clever and articulate as Grandier – could have
avoided the whole thing? Why? Speculating – as a poet must and
should – much more widely, boldly and thoroughly than the historian–
biographer, Whiting finds the questions leading him once more to an old
concept, seen now in ever more complex form and in darker colours than
ever before.

The contrast between Huxley's Grandier and Whiting's is evident
from the very beginning. Here is Huxley's description, on p. 27 of his
book, of Grandier before the trouble began:

> The pattern of Grandier's life at Loudun was now set. He
> fulfilled his clerical duties and in the intervals discreetly
> frequented the prettier widows, spent convivial evenings
> in the houses of his intellectual friends and quarrelled with
> an ever-widening circle of enemies. It was a thoroughly
> agreeable existence, satisfying alike to head and heart, to
> the gonads and the adrenals, to the social *persona* and his
> private self. There had as yet been no gross or manifest
> misfortune in his life. He could still imagine that his
> amusements were gratuitous, that he could desire with
> impunity and abhor without effect. In fact, of course,
> destiny had already begun to render its account, but
> unobtrusively. He had suffered no hurt that he could feel,

only an imperceptible coarsening and hardening, only a
progressive darkening of the inner light, a gradual narrowing
of the soul's window on the side of eternity. To a man of
Grandier's temperament – the sanguine–choleric, according
to the Constitutional Medicine of his day – it still seemed
obvious that all was right with the world. And if all was
right with the world, then God must be in His Heaven.
The parson was happy. Or, to put it a little more precisely,
in the alternation of his moods it was the manic that still
predominated.

Whiting's Grandier, even in the early stages, is much more self-aware
than this, and much more troubled. On the ninth page of the play he
enters the church alone, kneels at the altar and prays:

'O my dear Father, it is the wish of Your humble child
to come to your Grace. I speak in the weariness of thirty-five
years. Years heavy with pride and ambition, love of
women and love of self. Years scandalously marred by
adornment and luxury, time taken up with being that
nothing, a man. I prostrate myself before You now in
ravaged humility of spirit. I ask You to look upon me with
love. I beg that You will answer my prayer. Show me a
way. Or let a way be made. (*Silence*) O God, O God, my
God! Release me. Free me. These needs! Have mercy.
Free me. Four o'clock of a Tuesday afternoon. Free me.
(*He rises: cries out*) Rex tremendae majestatis, qui salvandos
salvas gratis, salva me, salva me, fons pietatis!'

But though Whiting, looking at the history of these events at Loudun,
sees Grandier in his own particular way and sees him, moreover, as in
some sense archetypal, not merely a seventeenth-century figure but an
eternal and recurrent one, he does not entirely succeed in making the
play maintain this focus and this sense of direction. Deflected partly by
the sheer weight and richness of the material, partly by the recalcitrance
of history and historical event, partly by a certain unsteadiness in the
author's own approach, the play remains more rewarding in its parts
than its whole: separate scenes, some of them immensely powerful and
most moving, develop more promise of the final total gesture of the play
than in fact materialises. The ultimate test of the play's stature and
worth is not how well or badly it dramatises Huxley, or how faithful
it is to historical incident, but how true it is to itself, to what extent
it fulfils its own declared intentions and to what extent these intentions
seem, by the acid tests of the onlooker's sensibility and experience, to be
valid and of some real consequence. Viewed in this way, as an artistic
entity in its own right, the play displays some weaknesses.

The trouble, one suspects, centres on the character of Sister Jeanne. Though she has some good moments – and one or two very fine speeches which are most germane to the play's central purpose – her presence in the play is in fact disruptive, in two ways. First, because in Acts 2 and 3 so much time and space is spent on her 'possession' and the antics it leads to that our attention is distracted from Grandier's spiritual problem to the much more superficial and much less interesting matter of the hysteria, the play-acting and the devils. In the play's true pattern, these things are incidentals, mere instruments by which Grandier is enabled to consummate his longing for death. It is this longing and its realisation that should form the central pillar of the play, but the architectural pattern is obscured and the edifice itself dangerously weakened by too much weight's being allowed to fall on the incidental structure of Sister Jeanne's exploits. (This suggests, by the way, that the play should never have been called *The Devils* at all, but by some title that urged the centrality of Grandier). Quite apart from the diffuseness and dividing of interest that results from the overemphasis on Sister Jeanne – an overemphasis which comes partly from a ruthless insistence on incident and happening – the instrument of Jeanne's 'possession', whether produced by God, the Devil or human hysteria, is too crude a one, too simplistic, to use against so subtle and sophisticated a person as Grandier. It has theatrical excitement, but no real power; it is, in the context of Grandier's maimed sense of life, an irrelevance. As such, it tends to dissipate the play's real energies. It is for that matter – and especially in its theatrical manifestations – also too crude to be compatible with the deepest and best levels of Sister Jeanne's own character, for there are signs that Whiting saw her, too, as a lonely soul on a tortured pilgrimage. 'I wish to be pure', she says when she is alone and the devil within her replies 'There's no such thing.' She should have been a twin study, another equal and parallel example, of the same search for an Absolute that Grandier is, but somehow the two stories divide the play instead of uniting it, vitiate each other's power instead of reinforcing each other. And Jeanne's story develops the crudity and false theatricality which makes it superficial, even at times a bit silly. Part of the difficulty may have been that, somewhere deep in his unconscious mind, Whiting saw – or, rather, felt – women as being peripheral to the idealistic search which dominated his soul's horizon. Ultimately, perhaps, he thought of it, quite instinctively and without stopping to consider it, as a *male* search. His women characters are often startlingly well observed and sensitively, sympathetically, portrayed: Patience, Stella, Dorcas, Dido, Catherine de Troyes and Caroline Traherne. But they are not central to the spiritual action and conflict of the plays in which they appear: the Promethean protagonist in these plays is always a man. This need not be thought of as a flaw or a disadvantage. It should, however, critically speaking, be borne in mind as a possibility: it may account for some of the posture and balance (or imbalance, as the case may be) of some of the plays. It is worth recalling, in this context, the strangely and even intrusively Strindbergian note that one was rather surprised to find in some moments of *The Gates of Summer*. Applied to *The Devils*, it may mean that Sister Jeanne cannot ultimately be allowed to rank as Grandier's fellow-sufferer but must occupy, principally, the position of his torturer, a stumbling-block in his path and one over which he deliberately chooses to fall. From this would stem the weaknesses that have already been noted. Here and there, though, she shows in better and in deeper colours. At one point one of the other young nuns asks her, concerning the displays of daemonic possession 'Have we sinned? Have we mocked God?' Sister Jeanne's reply is this:

> 'It was not the intention. But to make a mockery of Man.
> That's a different matter! For what a splendid creature
> he makes to be fooled. He might have been created for no
> other purpose. With his head in the air, besotted with his
> own achievement, he asks to be tripped. Deep in the
> invention of mumbo-jumbo to justify his existence, he is
> deaf to laughter. With no eyes for anything but himself,
> he's blind to the gesture of ridicule made in front of his
> face. So, drunk, deaf and blind, he goes on. The perfect
> subject for the practical joke. And that, my sisters, is where
> the children of misfortune – like me – play a part. We do
> not mock our beloved Father in Heaven. Our laughter is
> kept for His wretched and sinful children who get above
> their station and come to believe they have some other
> purpose in this world than to die. After the delusions of
> power come the delusions of love. When men cannot
> destroy, they start to believe they can be saved by creeping
> into a fellow human being. And so perpetuating themselves.
> Love me, they say over and over again, love me. Cherish
> me. Defend me. Save me. They say it to their wives, their
> whores, their children, and some to the whole human race.
> Never to God. These are probably the most ridiculous of
> all and most worthy of derision. For they do not understand
> the glory of mortality, the purpose of man: loneliness and
> death.'

It might almost be Grandier himself speaking. Jeanne is thinking of Grandier as she speaks and speaking of him in a tone such as he himself might use. But she is thinking of herself also: she, also, is one of those who 'get above their stations' and she, too, has to cope with the 'delusions of love' and knows she has. She is for a moment Grandier's equal in suffering and in self-knowledge; but the moment does not last and much of her time in the play is spent on overlong and over-detailed scenes of demon antics and exorcism, in which she is a woman seen from outside by a man, one of the instruments acting upon him, for good or ill.

There is a tendency also for the political detail in the play to become top-heavy and exert a similarly divisive effect. For the play to function at its highest level, Grandier must not appear simply – or even mainly – as an innocent and heroic victim of a corrupt political system, sacrificed in the cause of freedom. And there is some danger of this. Especially in the second half of the play the issues of Richelieu's rapacious ambition and contempt for justice and of de Laubardemont's insolence of office loom large, too large. The whole question of local autonomy and the fortifications is really quite incidental to the play's main purpose. Grandier *uses* this issue, as he does that of the daemonic possession, to work his own end, which is his own destruction: he does not get caught unwittingly in its toils. Unless the initiative, morally, mentally and spiritually speaking, remains firmly with Grandier, the play loses impetus and focus. The true dramatic dichotomy is not between him and the forces of ignorance, superstition, jealousy and chicanery: it is between his disgust with humankind, including himself, on the one hand and his indefinable but passionate longing for a purity of meaning and a nobility of purpose on the other. This is the play's true ambience; this is the area of experience at its heart which it should reflect. And this is the focus which sometimes blurs, to the play's detriment. If this could be kept firm and clear, then the multiplicity of detail and incident could be a constant enrichment instead of an occasional distraction. Whiting's original version of the play,[2] before production cuts were made, was superior in this regard to the version that finally got into print. It was rather more formally structured in one regard and this helped considerably, not only to keep the focus on Grandier but also to emphasise his position as a churchman and Christian, someone, in other words, whose day-by-day profession is belief. This directs our attention to the right areas of interest, as well as producing some useful ironies. The device that Whiting used to produce this effect was to punctuate the dialogue several times with parts of sermons: Grandier in full canonicals in the pulpit of his church, preaching to the audience-as-congregation. The cutting of these scenes seems mistaken. Though the restoration of them to the text would not entirely correct the tendency the play has to break its own back, it would have helped, even if only by giving a greater degree of structural cohesiveness to the piece.

Simon Trussler, in *The Plays of John Whiting*, also comments on this imbalance. 'Greeted as little short of a masterpiece', he says, '*The Devils* strikes one, in retrospect, as a tired, almost dispirited piece of writing, manipulating stage effects and emotional dead-certainties to achieve a deceptive forcefulness on stage. In most of Whiting's work the core is so dense that gravity plays funny tricks at the crust: but here the inner world of the play is too flimsy to support the intensity of action on its surface. And the result is melodrama.' This, though unnecessarily harsh and denying by implication those merits which the play *does* possess, is a piece of very acute observation indeed.

The nature of Whiting's vision being what it is, there was a special logic in his taking a specifically Christian figure as the centre of a new play. Not that the vision is itself ultimately compatible with Christian theology, nor that Whiting sets up as an apologist – far from it – but the thrust of the artist's vision in Whiting's case had, all the way through his work, been towards the contemplation and reflection of that life which sees itself in terms of an absolute belief, a life ennobled and given meaning by some Absolute Meaning outside itself, a life which can devise and hold an ideal of such purity and power that it will transcend the gross and disgusting elements of human living, or, if it cannot, will prefer self-annihilation and oblivion to compromise. In this context, the possibility of Christianity's being the basis for such a life, the question of the reality (or otherwise) of so-called religious belief and the relationship of that belief to human life in general, present themselves quite obviously as possible expressions of Whiting's central sense of experience, so his gravitation towards a figure tortured first by religious doubts and then, in a literal sense, by allegedly devout men, was a very natural one. It will be recalled that Whiting himself said, about *Marching Song*, that it 'is a play in which one might think somebody somewhere would mention God, but nobody ever does'. He was right: *one* of the possible ways of expressing that Absolute, for which his central characters all yearn, is to describe it as a search for God and in *The Devils* this is the convention and symbol that Whiting adopts and explores. His search, like that of any artist in any medium, was for some all-encompassing meaning and this search is echoed by Grandier himself. Towards the end of the play, when he thinks that he has begun to divine something of the true nature of God, he tells the Sewerman (who has been his confidant throughout) about the experience. There follows this exchange:

SEWERMAN: You've found peace.
GRANDIER: More. I've found meaning.
SEWERMAN: That makes me happy.
GRANDIER: And, my son, I have found reason.
SEWERMAN: And that is sanity.

The original version of the play made a point of establishing this search, in terms of Christian belief and Christian practice, at the very start. Instead of beginning quietly, conversationally, sardonically, with short snatches of conversation from various of the contending groups (which is what happens in the final published version), it began with a formal set statement by Grandier himself. This was one of the speeches – miniature sermons – delivered from the pulpit, to the cutting of which reference has already been made. Either it was considered too 'untheatrical' a way of beginning a play, or else the play was considered too long *in toto* and had to be cut for that reason. For whatever reason it was made, however, the cut seems unfortunate: the speech would surely have strengthened the play both structurally and poetically. Here is the speech which was cut:

> 'A man finds it hard to understand the ways that can bring
> him peace. It seems that his sins are so heavy, so
> irredeemable, that the torture of hell could bring nothing
> but solace. His self-disgust is so great that the most
> calculated cruelty could only ease his wretchedness. Listen to
> me. There can be no respite. You are alive and so you
> must conflict. The battle is lifelong. It will go this way and
> that. It will be fought horribly under the sun, bitterly in
> the night. The enemy will be met in the meadows and at
> the river crossing, in lonely rooms with those who would
> destroy you. The wars of nations are like the squabbles of
> children when put beside Man's struggle to free himself
> from the love and gentle care of God. And this battle will
> be won and lost again and again. Triumph and despair. O
> my friends, the heart's cry! But between victory and defeat
> lies the still, unassailable point of sanctity. My dear
> children, we must come to that point if we are to live. We
> must come to it if we are to live, not in the squalid span
> of earthly life, but eternally in the light of grace. And we
> must seek it, each man in his own way. A way we find so
> hard to understand.'

The speech not only puts the play unequivocally within the right frame of reference and gives it a spine and a shape, it also allows us to see Grandier at the outset as a 'serious' man. The lechery and the cleverness which comes later are incidental to his seriousness of soul and purpose, not the other way round.

Setting the search for the Absolute in Christian terms is, however, ultimately unsatisfactory for the expression of Whiting's vision. While the metaphors of religion will serve for some part of the way, the equation eventually breaks down and it is one of the weaknesses of this oddly unequal play that it illustrates that breakdown itself but then evades the issue and passes on as if nothing had happened. Grandier, like Timothy, Southman, Heberden, Procathren, Forster, Hogarth and Caroline before him, makes several references to the desirability of self-destruction in preference to a meek acceptance of the disgusting humiliations of an 'ordinary' life. This is entirely in keeping with the high

Roman fashion of Whiting's Gothic–Romantic vision, but it creates insoluble doctrinal problems in a Christian context. The question is raised in specific form by d'Armagnac in the conversation, already quoted in Chapter 2, in which Grandier says: 'Politics, power, the senses, riches, pride and authority. I choose them with the same care that you, sir, select a weapon. But my intention is different. I need to turn them against myself.' D'Armagnac, later in the conversation, says 'I'm not one for sophisticated argument, but tell me something. I can see that the obvious short-cut, self-destruction, is not possible. But isn't creating the circumstances of your death, which is what you seem to be doing, equally sinful?' Grandier does not answer the question but says 'Leave me some hope.' D'Armagnac, in effect, rephrases his question: 'The hope that God will smile upon your efforts to create an enemy so malignant as to bring you down, and so send you – up?' To which Grandier says only 'Yes'.

Grandier's evasion of the question of suicide is dangerous to the play's integrity. If the search for the Absolute, the imperishable Ideal, is to be worked out wholly in Christian terms, d'Armagnac's question must be answered. Suicide is a sin, in the Christian system, because it denies God and thinks only of self. It indulges despair, which is itself sinful. Though Grandier does not literally take his own life, he not only allows it to be taken when he could easily have escaped, but he also actively encourages the emergence of a set of circumstances in which his death is – as he well knows – inevitable. Is that not equally sinful? When this question is first raised by d'Armagnac and Grandier avoids it, one feels that this may be only because he is going to return to it at a later time. But he does not and neither does the play. It is not from the theological or philosophical point of view that this evasion is so damaging, but aesthetically, because it means that to be true to the spirit of Whiting's vision, the central figure could not properly be Christian. Conversely, if the given figure were Christian, then it could not be made to reflect truly Whiting's sense of the inner nature of things: one or the other would be either blurred or distorted. Whiting, albeit unconsciously, chose to blur the outlines and by dramaturgic sleight-of-hand to try to contain both visions within the compass of the one character, but there is an uneasy feeling of hollowness about the operation. 'Why didn't he reply to d'Armagnac's question?', we keep asking ourselves.

In the original version there was another, similar near-collision but this was avoided by cutting the passage for the play's first production and the passage did not appear in any of the published versions. Its presence would, in fact, add to the difficulties, but cutting it does not really help, either: one is simply left with a hole – a hole which can, in fact, be observed by looking at p. 172 of vol. 2 of *The Collected Plays*. In this scene, in which the Sewerman describes how he uses a caged bird to test for toxic gases in the sewers, there is a speech which says 'So I always approach it with this creature on a pole before me. His many predecessors have died in the miasma. When this happens I know it's no place for me.' In the published version, the Sewerman continues his speech, following straight on to the above, to say 'So I let the drains run foul for a day or two and I spend my time catching another victim to shut up here. You'll understand what I mean.' A silence follows. Neither Grandier, to whom the Sewerman is speaking, nor the audience, could really be expected to understand what he means, since the symbol has become hopelessly obscure by reason of the cut. In the original version, after the Sewerman has said 'When this happens I know it's no place for me', the scene then goes as follows (bearing in mind that the Sewerman, speaking of the bird, has earlier said to the priest: 'He's my saviour. Who's yours?'):

GRANDIER: Your intended analogy appals me. Are you suggesting that because of the death of God, *this* is no place for me?
SEWERMAN: Is it? From what I know of the scriptures, and from what I see of the images you put up in your churches, he died in despair.
GRANDIER: But later, my son. What happened later?
SEWERMAN: That happened in the minds of men, not in the pattern of God. Men who were not brave enough to despair.
GRANDIER: Are you saying that the philosophy of the Catholic Church is a philosophy of optimism? And false at that.
SEWERMAN: You'll find out.
GRANDIER: How?

(Silence)

Now the silence is significant, for it indicates that the Sewerman declines to explain to Grandier what the latter is wilfully refusing to acknowledge in his own mind. The total *geste* within the play of the character of Grandier as Whiting represents him leads logically and indeed inevitably to the conclusions which the Sewerman correctly draws. Grandier, according to all the rules, *ought* to agree with him, but from the set and given position of the Christian, he cannot. Trapped thus, the play is impaled; it cannot move to its own true and natural position. And it is not just this particular scene, or the one which contains d'Armagnac's question about suicide. These two are symptomatic of the crack that goes right down through the whole structure, overlaid and more than half-hidden though it be. Whiting saw Grandier as echoing a sense of the world which was native to Whiting's own vision; but he saw him, in the ultimate analysis, wrongly, if the figure of Grandier-as-Christian is to be maintained, which the play says it is.

However, though this basic flaw is there and must prevent the play's ever fully uniting the strength of its separate parts into the tremendous and powerful overall drive that one somehow feels ought to be in it, there is so much about Grandier that *is* right (and incidentally about

245

some of the other characters, too) that an authentic, even though partial, vision of truth does emanate from the work. One of the elements that most conveys this sense of absolute veracity is the concern which the play has for the connections between sex and love and between both of them and that hopeless, holy quest on which Whiting sees humanity embarked. How, in a word, to reconcile – if reconciliation be ever possible – soul and body? 'The act of passion is an act of revelation', says Jeanne in the original version (though not, unfortunately, in the published version). 'It's entire purpose is abasement of self. I think you will agree that this gives it a sort of holiness which makes it acceptable.' This is very reminiscent of several of the earlier plays and especially of *The Gates of Summer*. Does the great weltering that love makes in the individual heart really mean, as we feel it ought to mean, that the thing has more than momentary and individual importance? Or is it, when all is said, merely an *ignis fatuus* that leads the victim into fatal swamps. Constantly, Whiting sees sexual and spiritual energies linked, yet also sees the sex act itself with constant disgust. 'Every man is his own drain. He carries his main sewer with him', says the Sewerman, adding 'What makes a man happy? To eat, and set the drains awash. To sit in the sun and ferment the rubbish. To go home and find comfort in his wife's conduit.' And Grandier does not contradict him: indeed, the Sewerman functions in the play almost as Grandier's *alter ego*. Yet, Grandier, in defiance of his sacerdotal vow of celibacy, conducts a secret 'marriage' ceremony with Phillipe Trincant, himself both priest and bridegroom, and afterwards says to the Sewerman who is questioning him sardonically about so rash a step: 'Come now, even at this hopeless hour you must admit more passes between human beings than the actions which provide you and the laundry with a job. There is a way of salvation through each other.' D'Armagnac describes a morning when, unobserved, he watched Grandier in his garden, glorying in the world of the senses, and again the image is connected with sex: 'He fondled a rose as if it were the secret part of a woman.'

The whole play is concerned throughout to seek a viable equation between the force of sex and the power of love, between love of man and love of God and between love and reality. Is not love the greatest evidence of reality? is the question the play asks. Is it not the reallest of all real things? And yet, has it any objective existence? Or has 'reality' itself any objective existence, for that matter? As well as Phillipe and Grandier, Jeanne too – in her best moments – is an expression of these same concerns. There is one strange, evocative scene in which Jeanne, alone in her cell at night with a book of devotions, having just learned of Grandier's refusal to accept her invitation to become the convent's spiritual director, speaks a kind of litany of love that links her and Phillipe and Grandier together. It springs from frustration and jealousy, but it moves out into gentleness and understanding and while she speaks we see, in another part of the stage *Phillipe, naked, making love with Grandier. They will continue to be seen in the touching formal attitudes of passion throughout Jeanne's words.* The speech epitomises the agonising dilemma which is at the true centre of the play's experience and is worth quoting in full:

JEANNE: You wake up. Dawn has broken over others before you. Look at the little grey window. Then turn. She lies beside you. The attitude is of prayer or the womb. Her mouth tastes of wine and the sea. Her skin is smooth and silky, rank with sweat. The native odours of her body have exhausted in the night the scents of day. Look at her. What do you feel? Sadness? It must be sadness. You are a man. Ah, now she stretches her arms above her head. Are you not moved? This is not the sophistry of a whore, whatever you may pretend. She shifts her legs, entwines them, lays a finger on your lips and her mouth upon her finger. She whispers. Those words were taught. She only repeats the lesson. Such filth is love to her and the speaking of it is an act of faith. What was that you did? Stretching out to clutch the falling bed-clothes. Was it to cover your nakedness? Is there modesty here? (*Silence: in wonder*) How strange. Can you laugh, too? That's something I didn't know. Pain, oblivion, unreason, mania. These I thought would be in your bed. But laughter . . . How young you both look. Quiet again. The girl is heavy in your arms. She yawned and you have taken up the shudder of her body. You tremble, in spite of yourself. Look, the sun is breaking up the mists in the fields. You're going to be engulfed by day. Take what you can. Let both take what they can. Now. (*She weeps*) This frenzy, this ripping apart, this meat on a butcher's slab. Where are you? Love? Love? What are you? Now. Now. Now. (*She falls on her knees, convulsed.* GRANDIER *and* PHILLIPE *can no longer be seen*) O my God, is that it? Is that it?

Again, as was noted in an earlier case, Jeanne speaks almost with Grandier's own voice. Certainly the general posture of the speech is more male than female. The two characters have coalesced into a joint expression of the play's central sense. This speech brings the play very close to *The Gates of Summer*. This search for reason and meaning and an absolute belief and commitment – surely human love and passion is the truest expression of this? This, and its counterbalancing doubt, is the question which is the heart of *The Gates of Summer* and is close to the centre of *The Devils*. The involvement of Jeanne with this question, rather than with her wounded pride and her plans for a frivolous and terrible revenge, is clearer in the original version than in the final one and is an advantage.

Sometimes the detailed imagery, as well as the general tone and sense of direction, echoes *The Gates of Summer* very closely. In the original version Grandier has a speech (which was cut in the final version) that said:

'To walk on with as much dignity as the pathetic two-legged
animal I am allows me, and to tumble into the pit. To crawl
forward on my belly, a humble Christian, and to tumble
into the pit. That is my choice. It is any man's choice. Here
I stand. Look at me. Something has been achieved. I am
upright. On two legs. But between them hangs a bag of
tricks supposedly quietened in the Name of God. Praising
him by its very inaction. O holy thing! I have come again
from the widow. I am on my way to church. From one
temple of adoration to another.'

The images of Man, upright on his two legs and of him tumbling into
the pit were used by Whiting in some of the alternative endings of *The
Gates of Summer*, as is shown in Appendix 1 (see, particularly, variants
nos 2 and 4, where the expression of these images are retained, but
changed from one character to another). In passing, it may also be noted
that this speech of Grandier's is another of those – hence, perhaps, the
cut – that makes it difficult for him to die as a Christian in a Christian
cause. His sense of the world and of his own potential nobility is true,
his Christian humility is false. He is at loggerheads with dogma again
and the play, instead of making use of this as part of the dramatic
dichotomy and conflict, evades the issue – which, given the historical
facts, it was almost bound to do.

In any event, dogma and drama are hard to combine. Dogma is, by
definition, fixed, static, unassailable – that is its function; drama, of its
very nature, is a mutable flux, a matter of change, reversal and vicissi-
tude.

Though attention has been drawn to several instances in which
speeches which seem valuable were cut, for production purposes, from
the original script and though, in fact, that original version is, in total,
superior to the published 'official' version, there is at least one case in
which the cutting of the original version was wise. It is a speech of
Grandier's which, though critically very interesting, is a bit ponderous,
a bit literal and a bit sentimental. Its interest for us is the way that it
suddenly echoes, once again after a lapse of time, Whiting's abiding
sense of childhood as a mirror of manhood. Here, again, is the Whiting
child victim. It occurs in that final scene with the Sewerman when
Grandier, returning from a deathbed and a walk home through the
countryside, relates his finding of a sort of meaning and a sort of peace.
He likens the old man's death and his own spiritual torment to a childhood experience of his own:

GRANDIER: I have been out of the town. I sat with an old man through the
    night. He died at first light of day, and then I too turned homeward.
SEWERMAN: It's a comfort. Always a comfort. Sit by me. You're drunk
    with mystery.

GRANDIER: When I was a little boy I once wandered far off. It was summer. Long days.
SEWERMAN: They always were in childhood. Fine, too.
GRANDIER: But the day ended at last. You must have known it. When the earth loses its warmth and the sweat of night is rank and chilling. I was afraid, alone and lost. I'd believed on setting out that however far I went into unknown country someone would come to gather me up. My father, my mother, perhaps a stranger. But no-one came. Christ, how still it was! The world lay quiet and watched me. Twelve years old. I tried all the tricks, of course. There were tears and there was whistling in the dark. There was anger. First at those I thought to be neglecting their duty. I may die, I said to myself, and then they'll be sorry. And I was satisfied. Only to be angry with myself. Silly boy, silly boy. I cried out. And still no-one came. I must have slept. The rain woke me. I stared round. Desperate sadness. I knew that if I was to find my way back it had to be alone. And so I began a journey which has lasted until this morning.

This, stylistically, is a very interesting speech. In general concept it is like those formal, set, individual speeches – poems or arias, almost (and neither analogy is intended as a derogation) – in *Not a Foot of Land* and *Saint's Day*. But its texture is coarser, its imagery more commonplace and its energy flagging by comparison. It is a good example of Whiting's tempering the extravagance of his literary style at the cost of vigour and liveliness. It actually *needs*, if it is to work (and there is no intrinsic reason why it should not work: it is a perfectly acceptable theatrical convention), some of that wildness of imagination and luxuriance of language that the earlier examples in his work have. Its central picture, incidentally, of straying wilfully on a beautiful summer's day and then being overtaken by the cold, dark night calls irresistibly to mind an old, sentimental, Victorian, children's hymn:

> *A little lamb went straying*
> *Among the hills one day,*
> *Leaving the gentle shepherd*
> *Because it loved to stray.*
>
> *And while the sun shone brightly*
> *It knew no cause of fear . . .*

The Good Shepherd, however, comes to rescue the Victorian child. Whiting's child must find his own way home.

There are many examples in *The Devils* of these formal, set, 'literary' speeches, some of them very fine, theatrically viable and entirely germane to the play's purpose. They mingle notably well with Whiting's increasingly terse, laconic conversational passages, no sense of strain being felt. Perhaps the nature of the subject matter lends itself particularly well to a 'mixed' style of this kind – the contrasts between public face and private heart; between personal conviction and public commitment; between private meeting and public encounter. The number of occasions in the play calling for formal public declarations – by both sides – makes the use of these set speeches particularly apt and gives good occasion for their carefully considered literary shape (often quite exquisite). The 'religious' usages, both as to formality of occasion and as to sonorous expressiveness of language, tend also to militate in the same direction as, to some extent, does the fact that the period represented is an historical, not a modern, one. There is, it must be confessed, little logic in this last consideration, but it is a fact of theatrical life, nevertheless.

The reception accorded *The Devils* when it was first produced was more favourable than that for any other Whiting play. T. C. Worsley, who had berated *Saint's Day* and *A Penny for a Song* in such scornful terms, and who had conducted with Whiting a rather acidulated debate in print in the *New Statesman* in January–February of 1957, not only praised *The Devils* extravagantly in his review in the *Financial Times*; he also sent Whiting a personal telegram saying 'Congratulations on a masterpiece'. He used the same word in his written review: 'I don't remember in twenty years of reviewing plays ever before having been tempted to use the word masterpiece about a new English play . . . I shall not resist the temptation.' H. A. L. Craig, in the *New Statesman*, compared the power of the play with Webster, and Kenneth Tynan said 'language like this has too long been absent from our stage. Those aphorisms steeped in vinegar, those phrases with tails like scorpions, could have come from only one pen; and there are speeches of the most limpid tenderness to soften the prevalent mood of Swiftian distaste.' 'A play rich in ironic implications', said *The Times*. Suddenly, for a brief moment, everyone who took any interest at all in the theatre (the kind of interest that reads theatre reviews but wouldn't dream of reading plays) had heard of John Whiting. *The Devils* is the only play of Whiting's, up to now, to be presented in New York and the only one to be made into a film. These are the tests of popularity in the theatre, not of excellence: there is no correlation between the two. *Some* excellent plays do become popular; many do not. Many popular plays are the merest, sheerest rubbish; a few are not. Fame is not only capricious, in the theatre as elsewhere: she is also quite devoid of judgement or good sense.

To sum up, one would say that *The Devils*, though fatally flawed by the intrinsic nature of the material on which it is based, has about it, nevertheless, the indefinable sense of being a major work, a 'big' play. It has many incidental glories and felicities, is often most moving and powerful and if it finally fails to integrate all its strengths and senses into a totally satisfactory work, nevertheless it hints (and truly) at the complexity of the experience of searching for reality in a world

mostly given over to chicanery, pretence, wilful ignorance, vanity, ambition, comfort, power-seeking and material possessions. But the play
does not develop this complexity aesthetically, nor explore it. It evades
it, and progressively more so as the play proceeds. The historical
characters are, ultimately considered, too mundane for Whiting's purpose. He *almost* makes them mean more than they really did: but not
quite. Except Grandier, nearly all the time, and Sister Jeanne in some
moments: they are authentic exemplars of that corrosive Whiting vision
of things and stand in the true line of succession in his work. Grandier,
moreover, is himself more conscious than any previous Whiting protagonist of the nature of the search in which he is engaged and the impossibility of success in such a quest. He, of all of them, is most sensitive to
the evil of the world's slow stain. In him the exquisite dilemma of
humanity trembles most noticeably and closest to the surface; and if the
play that contains him fails fully to develop, this serves only to make us
long for the Whiting play that should have followed this one, the play
we never received.

III   Revision of *A Penny for a Song* (1962)

So far as the effect upon the play is concerned, little need be added concerning the revising of *A Penny for a Song* to what has already been
said in Chapter 4. Two things, however, do make it worthwhile to consider it again in its chronological sequence. One is the immediate,
practical, professional reason for its being undertaken and the other is
the indication it gives of Whiting's changing attitudes.

The popularity of *The Devils*, in its 1961 production by the Royal
Shakespeare Company at the Aldwych Theatre in London, encouraged
them to take it that year to the Edinburgh International Festival and,
further, to retain it in their repertory for the 1962 London season. At
the same time, they decided to include in the 1962 season a revival of
A Penny for a Song. Whiting, who had not had a new play presented in
London for nearly seven years, was suddenly the house dramatist for
the best theatrical company in the country. Since he started to write for
the theatre, the 'New Wave' of British dramatists had arisen and by
1962 Osborne, Pinter, Arden, Wesker, Simpson and several others were
recognised as exciting and important playwrights, but Whiting, in effect,
was being put in the position of doyen of the new 'serious' dramatists.
It is in this context that he set about revising *A Penny for a Song* for its
new production. The idea of revising the play, rather than having it
revived just as it stood, was, Peter Hall told me, Whiting's own. Clearly,
he viewed it almost as a new play and wanted to bring it into line with
his other work of that time, as well as making it into a new play worthy
of its elevated place in the Royal Shakespeare Company's programme.

The revision was undertaken immediately after the period of very intensive work on *The Devils* and alongside attempts either to complete the unfinished *Noman* or to turn it into *The Nomads*. When one considers the general tone of all these three, it is hardly surprising that the alterations to *A Penny for a Song* tended to move in the direction of sombreness and harshness. However, even given the play's position as a talisman of Whiting's return to the theatre as the leader of the leaders, the attempt to bring it 'up to date', to make it more 'serious' or 'significant', either in terms of current political views or of his own changes of heart since 1951, was mistaken on Whiting's part.

The changes, though they produce a less satisfactory play, do here and there have the incidental merit of confirming in explicit form some of the personal attitudes of Whiting himself which we have recognised in his other plays. 'Mr Matthews is the kind of man who laughs to stop himself from crying', says the reconstructed Edward; and we think of Whiting himself. Dorcas, in this second version, says 'All right, go, then. But don't become one of those men for whom the idea of people gets to be more important than people themselves', a statement with far too great a polemical content for the first Dorcas to have uttered but one that reminds us sharply of Whiting's own distrust of 'movements', causes and parties. The two unfinished plays which lay on his desk at the time he was revising *A Penny for a Song* were both concerned with this; the notes for the unwritten Act 2 of *Noman* are especially explicit about it: 'Group action – revolutionary action – opposed to that of the individual', one note says. Whereas, however, the structure of *Noman* and *The Nomads* could perhaps have been made strong enough and suitable enough to carry the weight of such direct explication, the delicate tracery of *A Penny for a Song* is overburdened by it. It is not that either Whiting or the play altogether approve of or give their support and authority to the new Edward Sterne's glum self-righteousness, but Whiting, finding the atmosphere of 1962 drenched with 'protest', somehow felt that it should be represented in the play. This seems mistaken, now. There is one exchange in particular, in the new version of the play, that illustrates neatly both Sterne's moral earnestness and Whiting's own instinctive reaction to it:

HALLAM: You're quite wrong. My money doesn't come from the sweat of the poor. I got it by gambling and loans from friends. It's all perfectly respectable.

   (*There is silence.* DORCAS *looks from one to the other*)

DORCAS: Do go on.

HALLAM (*To* EDWARD): Your turn.

EDWARD: For the last four years I've been walking about Europe. I've seen such horrible things that it broke my heart. Poverty and disease, love and friendship ruined by war, men and women living like animals in a desperate attempt to stay alive. I was one who sold himself for war so that he could eat, and I've had women sell themselves to me so that their children could eat. Now I may be simple, Matthews, but there's cause for all this. And the cause is laziness and indifference. There are only a handful of tyrants at any one time, but there are millions who don't care. I saw all this, I smelt it, I lay down with it at night, and at last I decided to fight. I carried in my pocket a book which is a weapon. It has a title which will mean nothing to you. It's called *The Rights of Man.*

(Silence)

HALLAM: That was most unfair. You were serious.
EDWARD: I'm afraid I was. I'm sorry.
HALLAM: May I bring the discussion back to a more acceptable level?
EDWARD: Please do.
HALLAM: Very well. Don't address me as if I were a society, Mr Sterne. I am a private individual. One of the few remaining in England.

Hallam is here practically quoting his author verbatim: Whiting had said about himself, to an interviewer: 'I am one of that disappearing species, the private individual.' It provides Hallam with a good repartee – almost Wildean – even if it does set up a faint echo of Queen Victoria and it does nothing, in this instance, to damage the play; but the fact remains that it demonstrates the way that Whiting was, in this revision, writing from the outside, so to speak, superimposing upon his characters.

Not that all the emendations are for the worse: in matters of *detail* there are some distinct improvements – tauter phraseology, pithier and more telling *bons mots*. The mischief is in the overall concept and effect, but some of these incidental improvements are worth noting in passing. Hallam, in the revised version, describes himself, on his arrival at the Bellboys' house, as 'pursued by the agony of love, the danger of war and the misery of democracy', which gives him a stronger speech than in the original and helps to establish his character more quickly and more firmly than the corresponding speech in the first version. The changing of the silent child, Jonathan, into a French boy is also, as E. R. Wood observes in his Introduction to the 1964 edition, an improvement, since it avoids the slightly fey and sentimental flavour of the first Jonathan, who is described as being on a journey to Bethlehem because he has heard of a baby's being born there. Even in the greater fantasy of the original script this particular detail seemed a little coy. To make the child French and a refugee, rescued by an Englishman from a battlefield in Bavaria where the victorious army was French, produces its own ironies without a word of explanation. And this Jonathan, like the previous one, never speaks. His silent figure on stage is as appealing and looks as vulnerable as that of the first Jonathan, but he manages to convey this essence of childhood without the faint suggestion, which hung over his predecessor, of being an illustration from an early twentieth-century child's picture book. Edward Sterne, too,

253

has one excellent speech in the revised version which, though the first Edward could not possibly have spoken it, one feels it would be a pity to lose. Both E. R. Wood and Ronald Hayman quote it, with approval, in their commentaries on the play. Dorcas, at the more imminent approach of the alarms of war, says to Edward: 'You know about this sort of thing. What does one do?' His reply is this:

> 'Don't stand under a flag, stay far away from anybody in
> a fine bright uniform, take a look at the sun so that you'll
> always know which way you're running, if there's a loaf of
> bread about put it in your pocket, and if there's a hole in
> the ground, sit in it. Ignore all cries for help, stay deaf to
> all exhortations, keep your trousers tied tight about your
> waist. In any difficulty, look stupid, and at the first
> opportunity go to sleep.'

A speech like this is an actor's delight, of course, and it is a good illustration of the increased verbal felicity – theatrically speaking – of some parts of the revised script (though this must not be taken to mean that the original version was dull of speech or unstageworthy – far from it). The improvement, however, is intermittent and, in the final analysis, minor. The weakening it brings with it is major because it is a weakening of the fable, the mythic quality, the true action of the play. And that weakness centres on the change in Edward Sterne, from whom it flows out to affect many other things in the play. It would be untrue to say that the play is ruined by this influence: much of its charm and gaiety and poetry survive. But one is aware of the presence of a foreign body, a distraction, a divisive influence. And one is aware, too, of a surfeit of explanation, such as this: 'Men are cursed with ideas and ideas aren't much use unless they're put into practice. This means travelling far, going to war, parting from people you love. But there'll come a day, if I have my way, when women will be able to go with men, equally.' The sentiment is irreproachable. How could one disagree and who would possibly want to? But it is out of the place. *A Penny for a Song* is not that kind of play, as a glance at the Yeats poem from which its title comes will confirm.

IV   *The Nomads* (1961–1963)

When the Royal Shakespeare Company commissioned *The Devils*, Peter Hall specified that one of his requirements was that the first modern play to be done by the company must be a costume piece, so that the wrench of Shakespeare to modern play would not appear too great. With the success and acclaim earned by *The Devils* as a springboard, the Royal Shakespeare Company then commissioned another play from John Whiting, this one to be on a contemporary, twentieth-century theme. *The Nomads* was to have been that play.

All that we have of it is a set of fairly detailed notes and fragments of four scenes. The longest of these fragments is three pages; the others, less than a page each. The notes and the fragments are all included by Ronald Hayman in vol. 2 of *The Collected Plays*. It is impossible to form any very definite impression of what the play would have been like had it been finished. One infers from the 1961 *Encore* interview, to which reference has already been made several times, that it was of *The Nomads* that Whiting was speaking when he said:

> I did begin two plays. I wrote half of one. It was hopeless,
> it wouldn't work at all. I put it away and I started another
> one, of which again I wrote half.[3] A very fascinating subject.
> Couldn't ever work, never worked, boring beyond words,
> so I put that away. It was only recently that I realised that
> the first play I started is perfectly all right. I've just
> changed the place[4] and I've changed the basic idea. It was
> simply that I was writing the wrong play, that's all.

There is nothing actually to prove that *Noman* and its earlier version, called *Nomad*, were the half-plays he took and tried to rewrite in some other form, but the inference does seem a reasonable one to draw: though there is no correspondence either of plot or of characters between either of them and *The Nomads*, there are strong connections of idea. All three concern the spiritual brankruptcy of continental Europe after the Second World War; all examine the disintegration both of personal relationships and of persons as being paradigmatic of more widespread and wholesale disintegrations; and all, it may be remarked, have their roots in that first work fifteen years before, *Not a Foot of Land*. This novel and *Noman* both adopt the device of setting the story in an imaginary country, one to which no name is ever given. *The Nomads* follows precisely the opposite technique. An opening stage direction says *The action of the play takes place in the city of Munich. The time is the present day*; and one of Whiting's preliminary notes says 'The idea of the city. Munich. A known and identifiable place. Use it.' Clearly he had begun to feel that in order to make general points and to give the play wide and general reference, he had to begin from a scene that was absolutely specific and, by realising that scene sufficiently vividly, allow the more general implications to emanate of themselves from the particular.

He includes in his notes a list headed 'Places' and among these are steps leading up from a river, the entrance to a theatre, an unrestored bombed building, a museum or art gallery and a library. All of these figure somewhere in *Noman* or *Not a Foot of Land* or both, though not in *Nomad*. Whether named or unnamed, whether referred to by specific particulars or in general and symbolic terms, the damaged cities of the European continent after the Second World War obviously held for Whiting a dark fascination.

The notes for *The Nomads* are a good deal more interesting than the fragmentary scenes. From the latter there is really very little to be gathered, so embryonic are they, but in the notes can be seen the drawing together of many familiar Whiting threads, both technical and ideological. Much the most important is note 2 of those written on 4 June 1961. It says: 'The play is basically about the destruction of our ideal. Or at least, Western Europe's inability to come up to the ideal.' So here, almost at the end, it still is, now stated plainly in documentary terms, that 'leitmotiv' which we have observed running all the way through his work. It was, however, going to be given a new shape and even darker colours, if Whiting had been able to finish the play. He had worked out a pattern by which three decades of the century would be typified by small groups of characters. Those of the first decade (the 1930s, roughly) are characterised thus – 'Have lived violent lives'; the second decade – 'Have partly engaged'; the third decade, represented by one young man – 'Refused to engage. Totally withdrawn'.

One of the main characters of the play was to have been Robert Anderson and in the notes are a number of background biographical details of him – born 1917, father a professional soldier, mother a countrywoman; spent his childhood in the country, not the town; went to a preparatory school in the country and was happy there; went to a public school and was miserable; married in 1940; child born in 1946. There are a lot of other details about him, too, which do not concern the present point. What strikes one about those which I have picked out and listed above is that every one of them applies not only to Robert Anderson but also to John Whiting. There is no indication in the rest of the notes or in the few written scenes or parts of scenes that he intended to make the play in any overt or specific sense autobiographical – none of the other details of Anderson's life correspond in the least with the details of Whiting's own life; what Whiting apparently did intend to do, however, was to anchor the play's experience securely upon a generation whose mood and feeling he intimately knew – his own; the generation that grew up under the shadow of one huge war in preparation for its ghastly part in another. This sense of the declension of the spirit from one generation to the next and the basing of this play (and consider its title!) upon this movement of the generations seems one of the most significant and remarkable insights of this remarkable writer.

There are signs in the notes of that life-long struggle with style. Whiting once remarked, in one of his less guarded moments towards the end of his life, that he was no longer interested in or concerned with technique, the implication being that his interest by then was on content alone. This simply was not true and when he was working, as opposed merely to *talking* about work, he knew that this division was, in any case, false, that there is no division in real art between form and content. His first notes, preparatory to writing *The Nomads*, read:

> 1. An absolute scheme *must* be made before beginning
> the play. Remember writing *The Devils*.
> 2. Total narrative. The necessity of 'the happening'.
> 3. Define the *poised* position of each person early. *What
> will they do?*

A little further on is the note, already quoted once or twice, in which he emphasises to himself the necessity for a harsh, direct, idiomatic style – in the dialogue, that is. His first three notes are concerned with the overall shape of the play, the later one with language. Here he was, the author of three or four of the most distinguished plays in the language in the present century, worrying about the attainment of a style sufficiently pure and sufficiently strong to contain and communicate the essence of a twentieth-century sense of life to a twentieth-century audience. 'The play can be a remarkably pure form', he wrote once in his note-book: 'I find it strange that so many playwrights now introduce song and dance. Or is it the directors? Historical precedent[5] is often invoked. Am I the only person who reaches for his hat when the actors begin to chant and hop?' As we have seen, he never entirely solved the stylistic problem in his own works, though he came closer than all of his contemporaries, except perhaps John Arden and Harold Pinter. Perhaps *The Nomads* would have been the play in which he found the way to combine veracity, power, size and shapeliness in a major work of recognisable stature – the masterpiece which he said was his avowed artistic aim.

7

DRAMATIC CRITICISM
AND ESSAYS

After his death, in an understandable but not always altogether wise desire to preserve *everything* he ever wrote, two collections of John Whiting's casual and occasional pieces, along with some scraps and remnants of creative work, were published. These were *John Whiting on Theatre* (*London Magazine* Editions, 1966) and *The Art of the Dramatist* (*London Magazine* Editions, 1970). The creative work – short stories, outlines for projected plays and films, and so on, much of which has been referred to elsewhere in this present book – is much the most important of these posthumous publications, illustrating again for us the nature of his basic imagery and demonstrating, also, the obsessive quality of that imagery. One or two of the short stories – especially 'A Valediction' – are in any case extremely well-formed and important works in their own right: the others are useful and interesting (indeed fascinating) for the light they shed on the major works and on Whiting as an artist generally. These creative pieces are all contained in *The Art of the Dramatist*. The other book, *John Whiting on Theatre*, is a collection of thirteen pieces written for the *London Magazine* between April 1961 and August 1962. Most of them are reviews of productions; one or two are book reviews; one is a rather general and not especially illuminating comment on actors and acting. The striking thing about this little collection is the demonstration it gives of Whiting's capacity for seizing on the essential heart of a play and of brilliantly summarising this for the reader. It is in the third category of these posthumous pieces that one begins sometimes to wonder about the advisability of giving them permanent form. They occupy about two-thirds of *The Art of the Dramatist* and consist of one complete lecture, notes for two other lectures, seventeen pieces of more-or-less casual writing about the theatre, culled mostly from the pages of various

258

magazines, five book reviews and three short excerpts from Whiting's private note-books, one of these excerpts consisting entirely of aphoristic quotations from Henry James during *his* traumatic experience in the theatre. (The derivative nature of these is not made clear by the editor of *The Art of the Dramatist* and an uninformed reader may be forgiven for thinking that they are original Whiting, which they are not.) One would like to suggest that together they set forth a consistent and recognisable view of theatre, but that is not altogether true: they do, in fact, tend here and there to contradict each other and even to have contradictions within a single lecture or article. They all suffer stylistically from the fact that they are obviously ephemera and the lectures suffer further from a kind of conversational smartness, designed at the time, no doubt, to make points simply and strikingly enough, especially at the ends of paragraphs or sections or arguments, for the audience to grasp and appreciate and be borne along on the tide. The magazine articles have, in some cases at least, a distinct air of special pleading, even of a slightly peevish self-pity sometimes. In view of the way his work was misunderstood and abused, this is both understandable and forgivable, but this aspect of his journalistic writing should perhaps have been left to be buried decently with the time that bred it, not paraded for posterity.

In spite of these strictures, however, these pieces, especially when considered alongside the dramatic criticism, do have two virtues. First, they contain dozens of examples of ringing phrases that hit off particular aspects (sometimes contradictory, but none the less impressive for that) of both life and the theatre with accuracy and brilliance. These two little books together read like a collection of theatrical aphorisms, in both senses of that phrase. Second, and ultimately more importantly, though no closely reasoned critical view of the theatre emerges from the collections as a whole, what does emerge is a general sense of Whiting's instinctive reactions to certain aspects of theatre and drama, deeply felt rather than cogently argued. These are very revealing and are valuable adjuncts in the task of understanding and interpreting his work as a dramatist. They are worth detailing and defining here, since they are so clearly discernible and recognisable.

The first is his intense sense of seriousness about his work and about the position and potential of theatre as an art form. Over and over again, sometimes glancingly, sometimes in direct terms, he returns to the debasing influence of the commodity theatre on the art theatre, to the old arguments about the duty to entertain, and so on. 'Is it possible to make a play in performance a work of art?' he asks, in an article written for *London Magazine* in 1956:

> That is, performances in a playhouse under the stringent
> conditions of time and place which have been dictated by

> the caprice and fashion of the audience. It is this condition,
> more than any other, which gives to play-writing an air of
> servility. Also the fact that actors have a strange love for
> humiliation. It was, I believe, David Garrick who first
> used the phrase 'servants of the public' in reference to
> actors. It was a mistake. From that moment the mob were
> at the throat and have never let go. Now it is shaking the
> life from the theatre, and still the words are, 'We exist by
> your favour.'

And in his lecture called 'The Art of the Dramatist', given at the Old Vic in 1957, he said:

> A work of art is the statement of one man. It is one of the
> noblest, because it is one of the most selfless, activities of
> human existence. It has nothing to do with an audience or
> a wish to please. It does not necessarily entertain, instruct
> or enlighten. It can do any one or all of those things, but
> that it should is not the artist's concern. That is the work
> of art in its perfect state. The thing is there: an audience
> taking from it what it can. It is not the artist's job to
> simplify the means of communication.

This sense of the seriousness and high calling of the artist had been a basic tenet of Whiting's faith from the very beginning and was not merely something connected with his profession: it was a part of his whole approach to life and purpose at its deepest levels. In his war-time diary there is a note written in 1940, long before he was a dramatist and even before most of his experience as an actor. In it, he talks of the other soldiers in his unit:

> I find myself shocked by these men. Not by what they are
> but by what they do. Not by their drinking, swearing and
> talk of women: indeed, I like such men as these to be noisy:
> but by their unrestrained carnality, which seems to control
> their lives. There is a difference between this animality
> and the lusting for the good things which is inherent in all
> men. There is no fastidiousness in this: no choice. Nothing
> to divide these men from the veriest beast. Indeed, no man
> has but one thing which raises him from animal and that is
> a distinctive and exacting use of his mind. This trait is
> found at a higher standard in artists, for it is an artist's job
> to discard all material unworthy of attention for fear that
> his mind and his sensibility become clogged with waste
> matter.

This sense of the duty and responsibility of the artist is seen again in another of its aspects years later when, in a review of the Henry

Livings play, *Stop It, Whoever You Are*, he likened the theatre to a lunatic asylum, not so much for the overt craziness of its happenings but for its current tendency to isolate itself from life and reality.

> Alienists say that the mad have no sense of the past and the future is nothing but a vague foreboding to them. This seems to apply, frighteningly, to many young dramatists. Contemptuous of history, terrified of the future, trapped within the limitations of birth and death dictated by humanism,[1] they are transfixed in the time they like to call the present. And on this fine edge, which does not exist, they attempt to create works of art. These men are even shy of using normal terms concerning their job. If, when they come before the public, which is often, such a phrase as a 'work of art' should slip out, it has to be apologised for, laughed away. The desire for the commonplace has become so great an obsession that it is now an affectation in its own right.

This is a brilliant piece of observation, strikingly expressed, devastatingly accurate and years ahead of its time. Indeed, in relation to the twentieth-century theatre, the truth of what Whiting says is beginning to be recognised generally only now, twenty years later. It is the artist's responsibility to keep in touch, not with the simple, obvious and immediate surface of life, but with the underlying reality of it, making sure that his view of reality is itself clear and strong, that the very word itself is not just the latest in the never-ending series of artistic shibboleths. 'These people', he goes on, still castigating the younger generation of playwrights, actors and directors, 'believe themselves to be stridently engaged in life. Reality – these words! – is the new myth-making substance. Fix it with absolute accuracy and it will transcend itself to the point of revelation. That is what many people in the theatre believe. So do madmen.' Though these two books show that he changed his mind as to the details and though, in struggling for definition, he contradicted himself fairly frequently, what does emerge is his unshakable conviction, throughout his whole life, of the supreme importance of the artistic vision and the necessity for the absolute dedication of the individual to its service. Provided, that is, that the individual in question really *is* an artist and not either a pretender or a pathetically mistaken aspirant. On these he invariably lavished his scorn. One of his notebook entries reads:

> There is something very mysterious about the amateur theatre in this country. Why do they do it? And in such numbers. This behaviour, this public performing, does not square with the accepted view of our national

characteristics. We are a nation of secret actors, there's no
getting away from it. In university cities professional
theatres wither and die, yet every college has a group of
young men dressed in sheets declaiming hours of Fletcher
or Dekker or Ford, which must have taken them weeks to
memorise. It's all very strange.

And in the original, though not the final, version of *The Devils*, he has
put in a bit of conversation with just such an amateur:

TRINCANT: So good of you to call, Father Grandier.
GRANDIER: Not at all. I've brought back your poetry.
TRINCANT: So I see.
GRANDIER: Tell me, why do you write it?
TRINCANT: Well…
GRANDIER: Go on. I'm very interested. It concerns me, what's more. Be-
              cause if a man looks for immortality through the recording of his thoughts
              in some form such as this, I'd say he's going to be disappointed. It
              rarely occurs to him in these days to ask that his body should be pickled
              or stuffed. Why should he expect it for his mind?
TRINCANT: I wanted to make a small contribution to civilisation, I suppose.
GRANDIER: I see. Art – which I'm very fond of, by the way, in moments of
              relaxation – has always seemed to me one of the greater human vanities.
              It is, after all, the supreme expression of self. Or should be. It is allow-
              able, I think, when it is done to the greater glory of God, but I can find
              no mention of Him in these pages.
TRINCANT: I'm afraid I've never thought of it in this way.

Closely connected with this concern for the seriousness of purpose of
art, and cropping up at least as frequently and in many guises, is the
question of the right attitude to the audience. Whiting comes back
to it again and again and his statements do not always tally with each
other. In spite of this, there is a consistency of general attitude, of
stance: he feels very strongly that a play is not a play until it exists in
performance and is received by an audience (though, it should be
noted, 'received' does not necessarily mean 'approved of'); a play is
not primarily a literary work; he regards the serious theatre as naturally
and properly a thing that can ever appeal only to a minority, but he
feels that this minority *is* there, should be found and, having been
found, should be educated in its tastes. He argues, in other words,
for an élite theatre, a theatre for the initiated. He debated this hotly in
the *New Statesman* with T. C. Worsley in 1957. On 26 January of that
year, Worsley, who was the drama critic for the *New Statesman*, published an article under the heading 'Minority Culture', in which he
quoted from an earlier article by Whiting in *London Magazine*.
Whiting in this earlier article had said 'A playwright must not think
that he will extend his audience beyond that of the novel or poetry. It

is a mistake to see the theatre as a popular art.' Worsley took Whiting to task for this and said that the playwright's business is 'to articulate on behalf of the inarticulate, to express for those unable to express themselves what they want to hear expressed'. Predictably, this ham-fisted (and, indeed, quite wrong-headed) attempt at definition brought a sharply acid reply from Whiting. His letter on the subject was published the following week and is reprinted in *The Art of the Dramatist* (though there it is headed by the editor 'A letter to *The Times*', it appeared, in fact, in the *New Statesman* of 2 February 1957). In it, Whiting says:

> The writer's job is to make the statement. Therefore, he
> must dictate the premise. If he does not do so then his
> audience will lead and the writer will be forced to follow.
> Together, they will go from bad to worse, ending up in
> the hell of accepted opinions which is reserved for those
> who sell out politically, socially or intellectually. My
> argument was developed from the dangers of applying the
> methods of present-day public entertainment to that silly
> old nineteenth-century thing, art. Numbers should not
> come into it.

Another of his perennial themes connects with and leads on from this, namely his deep ambivalence about the other sort of theatre, the 'popular' theatre. In his 1957 lecture at the Old Vic, he said: 'I would like to approach the theatre in future with a great austerity. I am a little sad about this because I have a strong inclination towards the baroque theatre. And on a pure level of entertainment I love the theatre at its silliest: Lehar, and that sort of thing. But all that is part of the museum now.' And the dichotomy appears again, this time in a piece of self-mockery, in his *London Magazine* review of one of Noel Coward's less felicitous endeavours, a 'musical' called *Sail Away*. 'A dramatist selects his material, his method and his audience, in that order', Whiting wrote. 'Mr Coward's mistake is that he is doing this, but backward. It cannot but lead to the gravest errors of taste. And these Mr Coward commits in abundance.' He goes on to say that Coward ought to return to the style and subject matter of his early plays and then adds:

> Could we not have next a court play? Hush, I don't mean
> a Royal Court[2] play. I mean a play designed to be performed
> before the very best people, such as myself and my friends,
> not more than two hundred of us in all. It should be given
> one performance and published in a limited edition of
> fifteen copies. The loudest sound in any of its three acts
> should be the shutting of a door ... Must we wait for the
> day when the aristocracy rises before we get this play? I

hope not. Mr Coward adores excitement, that's obvious.
Well, nothing would give him a greater kick than an
outright bid for unpopularity. God knows, he might succeed.
Many of us do.

In one of those brilliant aphorisms of his, Whiting hit off exactly the difference between 'popular' theatre and 'serious' theatre: 'The purpose of art is to raise doubt: the purpose of entertainment is to reassure.' This was jotted in one of his notebooks.

Another of the leitmotivs which run through all these essays, articles and critical pieces, expressed in various forms, is the sense of the absolute integrity and inviolability of the play as a work. For Whiting a play was not a negotiable document that could be adjusted to meet the needs or suit the expediency of a particular circumstance; it was not a starting point for the actors' and directors' experiments (though on the question of the relationship of writer to actors he appeared to change his mind several times and this will be discussed in a moment). In a piece called 'Some Notes on Acting' in *London Magazine* (January 1962) he said 'There is a general belief nowadays that a play is created, rather as a social act, at rehearsal. This is not true.' In spite of the occasional self-contradictory comments, one gets the very firm impression that he regarded the written-down play as an actual artefact, an entity – a personality, almost – a discrete, finite, objective reality incapable of being dismembered without being either maimed or killed. He wrote several times of the desirability of devising some precise system of notation in the scripts of plays that would make the job of translating script into performance less subject to chance, accident and caprice, some way of ensuring that actors *could* not misinterpret it: and he said often that it was part of the dramatist's duty so to shape and design his dialogue as to lead actors *inevitably* to the correct interpretation of the words and to the essential action that should accompany the words. This matter of the absolute integrity of the play was connected, in Whiting's mind, with the more general idea of the sanctity of all artistic purpose. He quoted Thomas Mann: 'A work of art is something which is worth doing for its own sake' and, when challenged on this, quoted Charles Morgan in reply: 'Charles Morgan once wrote about this in one of his plays. "Does the thing exist once it is written down or does it only exist with an audience?" I should say that it exists anyway.' And he went on to elaborate the point: 'But this seems to me to be the very essence of the personal level of our art. I mean there are many things in life on the personal level which are worth doing for their own sake. Making love, for example. They don't need to have repercussions outside themselves.'[3] He admits that this view carries with it the danger of a retreat into a Pater-like aestheticism, but insists that, in spite of the danger (which, in any case, is not unavoidable), 'the thing *is* worth doing for its own sake. It doesn't have to have another purpose.'

There are, throughout these occasional pieces of writing, several discussions of and a large number of passing references to the vexed and difficult question of the artistic relationship – that is to say, the relationship of artistic functions, not the mere personal relationship – between playwright and actor. As has been suggested already, Whiting appears to have changed his mind about this from time to time during his career and this change was undoubtedly the result, in part, of the change in his own status, from his being an actor who was beginning to write plays to his being a full-time dramatist whose plays were being interpreted – or, in some cases, misinterpreted – by other actors. This purely personal response, however, does not fully account for the change of view, which must have been actuated, or at least influenced, by two other factors – the deeply divided opinions on the issue held by many theatre people; and the very difficult nature of the problem itself. Briefly, Whiting moved from the position of seeing the actor, director and playwright as collaborators, artistic co-equals in the creative process (though never, even then, did he see them *writing* the play together at rehearsals, trying bits out to see how they would go and then making a selection) to the position of regarding the actor as an *interpretive* artist, wholly dependent upon the writer for the original impulse and the vision. The matter crops up in many different places in these two books, but its progress can particularly be traced in three magazine articles which are all included in *The Art of the Dramatist*: 'Writing for Actors' (first published in *The Adelphi*, 1952), 'To the Playguehouse to See the Smirching of Venus' (in *Act*, 1956) and 'The Writer's Theatre' (in *London Magazine*, 1956). In the first of these, he says, talking about actor, director and dramatist: 'More important, surely, is that they are interdependent. It is an author's vanity to claim creation because he is the mere starting-point. His play would be no play if it remained words on paper.' By the time he comes to the second of these essays, the sentiment has changed: 'The danger lies', he says, 'in the play becoming a mere vehicle, in the subordination of language to action,' (though in 'Writing for Actors' he had said 'The action must never become subordinated to the dialogue'). By the third essay, the danger has become a dominant reality for Whiting: 'A sad parting of the ways has occurred between the playwright and his interpreters. To the writer, drama is a basic form: the theatre is a toy, an ingenious piece of machinery. It exists for the interpretation of plays. To many actors and directors it has become a thing in itself, tiresomely dependent on some form of content.'

Quite apart from the change of mind – and there is nothing reprehensible about a man's changing his mind – there is also some overstatement and oversimplification in that last quotation. It is scarcely true that to many actors and directors the theatre '*has become* a thing in itself': to many actors and directors it always was. The tendency to substitute theatricality, the virtuosity of performance, for the true dramatic values of the play, is no new problem. Shakespeare knew about it and so did Aristophanes. And to say that the dramatist regards the theatre only as a toy is not only untrue but a little silly. The point Whiting is trying to make is clear enough and is indisputably sound: namely that the mechanics of the physical stage should be subordinated to the sense and spirit of the play; but this does not mean that the writer treats the stage as a toy. Rather, he treats it as a sensible working tool which is essential to his craft and which he must employ in the achieving of his own purpose. It follows from this that he must *understand* that tool, intimately. Whiting himself *did* understand it and there are countless instances in his own plays of the brilliant application of this understanding to the task of making the play, when it reached the stage, reflect that inner sense from the perception of which the play itself had been born. To introduce into the argument emotive and in-exact language, like 'toy' and 'ingenious piece of machinery', serves no other turn, apart from a momentary smartness, than to bedevil the issue. But by the time that was written, in 1956, Whiting had suffered a good deal at the hands of actors and directors. He voiced his views even more firmly in a lecture at Vaughan College, Leicester, in 1958, when he said 'Too many people think it is always the text should be changed. There is a lack of flexibility in the modern theatre.' It is a pity that his later personal experience should have led to this sense of disillusionment because his earlier ideas of co-operate creativity in the theatre were basically sound in theory and were founded solidly on his own experience as an actor. Whiting was right, later on, to say that they often did not work – more often than not – but he was wrong to assume they never could or would. The present phase through which Western theatre is passing, a phase in which the emphasis falls far too heavily on the immediate, the thoughtless, the spectacular and the sensational and in which the tendency is almost always to sacrifice the play to the actor and the director, is unfortunate; but it is not necessarily permanent. It has happened before and has passed; it will pass again. One under-stands Whiting's impatience and despair but one need not take them as the final word. In some ways, his early thoughts on this question are both more valuable and more interesting. When he was an actor with the York Repertory Theatre in 1947–8, he frequently complained about the poor quality of the plays in which he had to appear ('My God, the junk they do as new plays in this place!', he said in a letter to a friend and, in another letter 'There is a limit to the amount of tripe I can play and I believe I am approaching the limit'), but when he was playing in a good play, he was immediately exhilarated and felt the lift which the play gave to the actor. In a letter to Caroline Hooper, an actress friend,

written in September 1947, he records a particularly exciting experience as an actor and one which vividly illuminates for us both his
theories about the actor–writer relationship and his own practice as a
dramatist. He was playing the part of the Inquisitor in Shaw's *St Joan*,
which was, apparently, one of his best performances at York. He describes the experience thus:

> On Wednesday, I experienced one of those sublime moments
> of sympathy with the part when you feel so exalted that
> all the miseries not only of the profession but of life generally
> seem nothing at all . . . I have spoken of this before – the
> moment when the words are spoken with a new and absolute
> meaning, the moment when the movement runs pure and
> true and there is something within you that is inspired –
> but it is not mental, physical or intellectual – and is as
> terrifying and as exquisite, well, psychically I suppose, as
> an orgasm is physically. A moment of supreme achievement.
> To me it came, strangely, in a moment of complete stillness
> and silence. The moment when I have spoken the sentence
> of perpetual imprisonment. I am high on a rostrum and
> Joan is far below me. There is a tremendous pause whilst
> the appalling significance of what I have said communicates
> itself to her. She rises, staring at me, and then says 'Perpetual
> imprisonment. Am I not then to be set free?' It was during
> this pause when we stare at each other that I knew
> everything. What is it that happens? I think I know. I think
> it is the moment when one manages to get the images of
> impersonation and truth absolutely coincident so that they
> become truth. Do you know what I mean? In the army I
> used to work an instrument which, when you looked into a
> lens, you saw two of the same object. By means of a little
> knob it was possible to bring those two images together :
> this was easy if the object was stationary but very much
> more difficult if it was moving, as then constant adjustment
> was necessary. Now in every part in every play – no matter
> how good or bad – there is, as with everything that exists or
> happens, a basic truth (I call it that for want of a better
> term) : perhaps essential rightness would be better. That
> basic truth is the actual image and our impersonation of it as
> actors is the false image. I believe it is when we make these
> images coincident and so achieve truth that we experience
> these moments . . . This is obviously very much more
> easily attained in a play like *St Joan* because it is a great
> play and one is helped by the genius of the author. That
> is why, as you know, these moments occur more frequently

in the great plays than in, say, topical comedies and farces.
Dear Christ! It is all most exciting, this job of ours! I
think I'd give up anything in the world for it and so would
you, wouldn't you? ... Lots of things don't matter but
that does and I thank God that I can say that when I am
nearly thirty. I pray God I shall be able to say it to the end
of my life.

This is not only more whole-hearted and enthusiastic than *any* of his later pronouncements about actors and acting, it is also more profound, more cogently argued, nearer the heart of the matter. The reason is not far to seek – this was written directly from personal experience, a day or two after the actual occurrence and written at white heat; the magazine articles were written from a rather vague, generalised position, not relating very closely to any specific situation or example, and with some 'political' and public relations factors half in mind. The letter, moreover, was written for no other reason than that the writer himself desperately wanted to write it; the magazine articles were written because somebody else asked for them.

There is one other subject that has not yet been mentioned, to which he returns many times, both explicitly and by implication, in these pieces of dramatic theory and dramatic criticism. Again, his remarks are often fragmentary, often so elliptic as to be obscure, sometimes seemingly contradictory; but his general stance on the question is, nevertheless, fairly clearly adumbrated. This is the question of the essential function and essential nature of drama. In 'Writing for Actors', he says 'The basic, the unalterable factor of drama is the moment "when"; the moment of happening which is contained in the action. The dramatist must concern himself with this moment of action and not leave it, as so often happens, to be imposed by the director or the players. In other words the dramatist must create what is done and *when* and not only the words to be spoken.' He goes on to explain that he is not here pleading for fuller stage directions but for the writing of dialogue that implies and impels the essential action unavoidably in its structure. Needless to say, 'action' in this context does not merely mean stage movement and 'business' but is used in a sense rather close to the Aristotelian sense of the *inner* action of the plot, the mainspring of the forward movement of the drama itself. On the question of what language can best provide this implicit action in a twentieth-century play, Whiting shifted ground several times. His *theories* tended to move more and more toward the austere and the naturalistic, but his practice in his own plays did not always (or, for that matter, often) follow his theories – for which we should be very thankful. At one point in the lecture 'The Art of the Dramatist' he said, 'Now I believe that all language for the theatre should be taken from life. It is no longer permissible to invent. This means the concern will not only be for the highly articulate man using words with care and for effect, but also with the idiot mumblings of the half-wit who lives down the lane.' This sounds very like a description of out-and-out naturalistic speech, yet earlier in the same evening he had said, 'When I say austere I don't mean bare stages with actors chanting hieratical drama. I mean rather a greater sense of truth. Not naturalism. The sense of truth which makes plays of apparent fantasy such as *Fin de Partie* and *The Chairs* more moving and more truthful than the examples of neo-realism and social significance we get offered in the English theatre.' In allowing these two statements to appear side by side in the same lecture, Whiting seems to overlook two things: first, that the most 'naturalistic' of speech 'taken from life' is, if the dramatist is a good one, 'invented' (his own taut, spare, laconic dialogue is an excellent example of this: even when representing the mumblings of idiots it is shaped and fashioned to the highest degree); second, that if one takes the first-quoted statement as it stands, without qualification or explanation, it surely leads inevitably in the mind of any ordinary, intelligent listener to the 'examples of neo-realism and social significance' which Whiting (rightly) deplores. His ultimate artistic position is sound and can be gathered from a slow and careful reading of all his pronouncements, but his critical, intellectual, debating position is distinctly shaky. One could add further to this confusion by noting that in regard to the first point raised above – the 'invented' quality of so-called 'naturalistic' speech – he himself elsewhere actually comments on this and makes precisely the same point that is made here, namely that when you get down to it, there is no such thing as purely naturalistic speech in any play and that if there were the thing would cease to be a play.

The 'invention' of the artist was, in fact, a thing which with John Whiting held a place of absolute primacy. From the start of his work to the finish he knew it, identified it, spoke of it and practised it. He realised instinctively, moreover, what it implied in the question of shaping a play and of selecting for the play just the right parts of the essential experience and just the right point of entry. His statement that 'the basic, the unalterable factor of drama is the moment "when"' is at once one of the most succinct and one of the most exact definitions in modern criticism of the exact nature of an art form. It immediately distinguishes the nature of drama from the nature of the novel and the nature of poetry, of neither of which is it true that 'the moment "when"' is the basic factor. It is not true, nor did Whiting assert, that this makes drama in some way superior to its sister arts; but it does make it *different* from them and different in the precise way that Whiting noted – drama deals with that facet of human experience which reflects the exact moment of change, the exact moment when the dichotomous nature of experience itself is suddenly borne in upon us. This sense of life, more-

over, will come *obliquely* from the work in question, not by direct statement or argumentation – hence the paramount importance of artistic
'invention'. Whiting was neither logician nor aesthetician and was incapable of building this knowledge into a philosophical system, but
his instinctive command of it is clear enough, nevertheless, and its effect
is observable in all his own dramatic works.

Apart from these recurrent main themes, there are, scattered through
these random writings, no end of good isolated moments. In a review
of Jean-Paul Sartre's *Les Séquestrés d'Altona* he says 'However, this
play may be of more than academic interest to this country in the near
future because one of the things it deals with is the ruthless methods
needed in this century for the survival of the individual'; one is instantly reminded of all Whiting's other pronouncements upon the
sanctity of individual life and mind, about which he obviously cared
passionately. Particularly in the case of that ultimate development of
individuality, the artist. In a review of Wesker's *The Kitchen* (which
Whiting much admired, though he disliked most of Wesker's work) he
said:

> Most of us, if history has left us any fragment of humanity,
> feel that we would be better occupied in the refugee camp,
> the hospital or (Mr Wesker's favourite activity) sitting on
> the pavement outside the Ministry of Defence than putting
> words on paper or paint on canvas. But in Mr Wesker's case
> it is a temptation which should be resisted. He should put
> aside his scruples, take his courage in both hands, be cold
> and calculating, and commit for our benefit another crime
> like *The Kitchen*. And while he is engaged on it let him
> remember that it is as difficult for a writer to be a *reasonable*
> human being as it is for him to be a gentleman.

Talking of current trends in stage production of Shakespeare he acidly
remarks 'There is a school of thought which seems to believe that by
coarsening the very formal language, a humanising effect is reached.'
Of actors he at one point says 'Give an actor an inch and he will take
a column – and probably want a photograph, too.' And in one of the
excerpts called 'From a Notebook' in *The Art of the Dramatist* he has
this piece of advice to give (it has been quoted often before, but is worth
repeating): 'A way of salvation: make enemies.'

8

CONCLUSIONS

John Whiting was always highly conscious of his responsibility and his position as an artist; acutely aware, too, of the relationship of the arts to other human activities. The particular nature of his vision and the particular bent of his talent tended jointly to promote an especially sensitive realisation of the sort of function an artist ought to fulfil and the fact that his particular art was that of theatre made conscious definition a necessity both as a way of renewing his own resolution and as a means of self-defence.

He always saw life raised to the order of art. Art was the higher form, a transmutation of the quintessential substance of life: it would not have occurred to him to think of the arts as extrinsic decoration, or as a means of communication, or as a kind of comment on life. The art *was* the life.

On things of that remark from his notebook, quoted on p. 264: 'The purpose of art is to raise doubt; the purpose of entertainment is to reassure.' And Ronald Hayman quotes him as writing elsewhere:

> The most dangerous tendency of modern criticism towards
> the work of young writers, especially in the theatre, is that
> it sets out to destroy by ridicule or abuse the writer's private
> mythology. Yet it is this private world which prevents the
> play becoming mere bombast, or journalism. If we are
> normal human beings we live surrounded by terrors, clowns,
> dead loves and old fears, represented by, say, a painting on
> a wall, some reels of photographic negative, a rose garden
> and a call from another room. The artist, admitting their
> significance, naturally reaches out for them in the desperate
> emergency of creation. They are nothing in themselves,
> these material things, but what they evoke for us as writers
> matters very much.

271

These two statements between them succinctly adumbrate Whiting's conception of the origins, the methods and the purposes of all art. The artist's endeavour, as Whiting saw it (and surely he was right), would always be to translate those terrors, clowns and dead loves, by means of his own particular private mythology, into a new entity – a formal, balanced, self-declaring and self-contained entity called a work of art. The reason for this endeavour would always be solely that the terrors, clowns and loves *existed* and, existing, carried with them the smell and taste of reality: no other reason, no explanation or excuse extrinsic to the artistic act and artefact itself, was needed or could suffice. Part of the design of the work, of the new entity, must be that it should sufficiently declare the nature of the 'private mythology' in such a way as to give both a structure and a frame of reference to the work. By 'private mythology', it is clear from the statement quoted above, Whiting meant that those things and memories drawn from personal experience would, in the hands of a real artist, develop into a system of symbols carrying meanings far beyond their own importance – ultimate meanings, in fact. These private symbols, if they can develop sufficient power, will become substitutes for, and will function in the same way as, those great 'public' symbols which are drawn partly from literature and partly from folk cultures. Thus the private symbol will acquire the energy and the significance of a mythology and will operate in the same way (though rarely on the same *scale*) as, for instance, a character or story drawn from a Greek legend or from the Christian myth, the only difference being that the private mythology will be restricted in its ambience to the work in question and will not carry the huge reverberations which are set up by the great public mythologies.

Though the belief in art as its own justification is everywhere apparent in Whiting, there does also seem to be – ambivalently and parodoxically – a perceptible movement, throughout the plays which have been discussed in this present book, away from the private world and toward the 'ordinary' world, at least so far as the *means* of expression are concerned. Though he knew he must not take it into account in the making of artistic decisions relating to the work itself, he longed, nevertheless, to find that the plays really did speak and speak powerfully to audiences and that audiences really did receive and were moved by them. This movement from private vision to public world shows, in the succession of his plays, both in the way his characters talk and in the plot situations he invents for them. *Not a Foot of Land* and *Saint's Day* are his most private works and yet in many ways his most complete and most fully realised. Later he seems more inhibited, or more anxious to talk to the 'ordinary' world. In this pattern a legitimate exception can be made of *No More A-Roving* (which does seem to contradict the theory by being a work belonging largely to the 'ordinary', public world yet occurring early in his career) because it is so patently an attempto explore the

medium, to apprehend its possibilities and its capacities: it was a range-
finder. The pattern can clearly be seen if one examines the dialogue of
Saint's Day, Marching Song, The Gates of Summer and *The Nomads*,
a progress from luxuriance into inhibition. As to the nature of that
private mythology and the sense of life which it reflects, it is described
very aptly indeed by Ussleigh, the character in *Paul Southman: An
Appreciation for Broadcasting*, when he says about Southman's work
as a poet, 'From the very first pamphlet the writing contained that
quality of savage pity which is the essence of tragedy.' This is the basis
of Whiting's own work, too: his private mythology is essentially tragic
in quality. His vision is one of violence and bleakness, is never sentimental and is highly romantic – that is to say, idealistic, passionate,
irrational, desiring to believe in a heaven of some sort, embracing death.
It is worth pausing to think back over the number of plays in which there
is the conjuration of some violent act, either enacted or described: from
the little radio plays at the very start – an untitled fragment of a play intended for radio has as its chief character a middle-aged woman who
plans to procure the murder of a nineteen-year-old girl because she is
jealous of the girl's influence upon her daughter and her husband – to
the torturing of Grandier in *The Devils*, Whiting is obviously obsessively
moved by the vulnerability of humankind, but his instinct is not to
translate this susceptibility to violence into either spectacle or mere
savagery but into a touchstone by which to test the texture and worth
of life itself and the relationship between men and gods.

The way in which he lived constantly with his private obsessions
has been referred to many times in this book. It is strikingly illustrated
at a very early stage in his career in a letter which he wrote on 21 July
1948 to his actress friend, Caroline Hooper:

> I must admit that I know a fresh start must be made. It is
> a question of returning or of throwing off the accumulated
> sophistications of the past years. Neither can be a solution
> because one will remain haunted by the evil, treacherous
> things one has done, by the tears of the others. Perhaps
> neither of these ways but to take a new road (the direction
> of which is so clear – so clear) as one is, as one has been
> formed by the years. This is the confession of failure.
> Something I have known for months past but about which I
> have never spoken before this night. It is, I believe, a
> common enough dilemma – perhaps I have reached it at a
> rather earlier age than usual. This is the monstrous terror
> of being unable to cancel out completely. The horror of
> living for ever in the ripples caused by a past action. It is
> inescapable. I have lost belief in myself and until it returns
> I suppose there is the family and yourself – all big enough

> people to remain with me and yet remain untouched by me
> as I am at present. No, not quite alone.

This piece of very private writing, though it comes from the beginning of his career as a writer (none of his work had appeared in any form before the public when this letter was written) serves as a very useful and accurate summary of that career in one of its aspects – his dependence upon his private resources. Though it often plunged him into black despair and often made his life a misery to him, it also provided the motive power that kept him going as a writer. He himself recognized this when he wrote in his notebook:

> I suppose nothing is going to make me angry or sad
> enough to write a new play. Sitting in the weak sunshine it
> seems as unimportant to me as it would seem to anyone
> else. Perhaps it really is the climate. In a little over a year
> I shall be forty. All the people who urged me to write for
> the theatre ten years ago have husbands and children now,
> and are not concerned with anger and sadness. I am
> becoming petulant, but it has no irritant value, except to
> others.

This was in 1956 (Ronald Hayman dates it 1960, but this must be an error, since Whiting says he is thirty-nine at the time of writing it), eight years later than the letter to Caroline Hooper (who was, incidentally, one of those who had urged him 'ten years ago' to write for the theatre). In between the letter and the notebook entry he had published in *Plays and Players* in 1954 a sardonic letter to himself from an imaginary correspondent. When published, the article bore the title 'What the theatre means to me', but Whiting's hand-written draft, which begins in letter style 'Dear John Whiting', is headed 'Letter to an Unsuccessful Playwright'. The private resources had, at least temporarily, run out.

A word of caution is needed here, perhaps: when one says that this haunting frustration and near-despair provided the motive power for his writing this must not be construed as meaning that it provided the subject matter for the plays. Considering the obsessively introverted nature of his personality, his plays are astonishingly free from any kind of self-pity or self-parading. But his work fed on his personality, all the same. He applied his personal sense of suffering to the evidence presented by the world around him and from the chemistry of this mixture he produced the dark glories of his dramatic writing. He was a Romantic, his imagination having even something of a Gothic cast about it – empty houses, children's nightmares, mediaeval tortures and burnings: yet throughout his work, from *Not a Foot of Land* to *The Nomads*, the romantic vision is tempered by a coolness and objectivity, a powerful but dispassionate observing of realities. It is as if he saw the world's terrors but refused to be intimidated by them, refused even to get *involved* with them, in spite of his own passionate response to them. He was anything but casual and uncaring, but his primary care was for the absolute integrity of his work.

The talisman by which he tested that integrity – and the integrity of others' work – was the raw experience of life itself. He constantly mocked the theatre of his day for its complacency, smugness and remoteness from reality. There is a nice example of this in the already-mentioned 'Letter to an Unsuccessful Playwright', in which he excoriates the contemporary British theatre as having been 'built as a great museum'. He mocks its unthinking, traditional approach: 'It shelters for us every one of the outmoded ideas and customs, forms of behaviour and morality, which can bring comfort in an age of threats and violence. When we pay our money and enter a theatre we know that we shall find those well-loved, well-remembered themes and situations which, although gone from everyday life, remain enshrined in the English drama.' Yet he was no radical. He was seeking neither to abandon tradition nor to deride it. He sought to *renew* it. He saw the arts of the present as a logical extension of those of the past, connected to the past by the indissoluble bonds of a living tradition, but constantly revitalised by a constant reference of them to the final court of appeal – reality. He does not reject tradition, but he derides dead traditions, sentimentally and unthinkingly maintained. His own plays, though startlingly new in some technical respects, to say nothing of the uniqueness of their vision, stand nevertheless in the main tradition and line of descent of English dramatic writing. It is interesting to note one particular aspect of this and to contrast it with the plays of Harold Pinter, with whom Whiting is often compared. This is the almost invariable use which Whiting makes of characters who are cultivated, articulate, well-educated people. There is no element of snobbery in his plays, but he nevertheless almost never uses working-class characters or uneducated characters and, when he does, they are never the protagonists. It is noteworthy that in the most important exception to this general practice – the three soldiers in *Saint's Day* – he equates them not only with violence but also with *mindless* violence, with pure destructiveness, with the disintegration of society. Although in his lecture at the Old Vic in 1957 he said that room must be made in modern plays for 'the idiot mumblings of the half-wit that lives down the lane', there is no example anywhere in Whiting's work, either before that statement was made or after, of such a character or of the photographic naturalism of speech which his statement implies. The Sewerman in *The Devils* speaks, for instance, with a sustained, laconic elegance.

In this sense, his innate romanticism of vision is modified by an austerely classical longing for pure form. This form is, in Whiting's submission, based on language and stems from a long and continuous tradition. It follows that only those who are acquainted with and sensitive to this tradition and its artefacts can possibly appreciate fully any new manifestation of the artistic spirit and though Whiting never explicitly stated this, it is implicit in all his work and in all his views on art and artists. Now, fifteen years after his death, when we have approached dangerously and depressingly close to the point of dismissing as bad any poem or play or picture whose 'meaning' is not instantaneously obvious to the most careless and casual observer, it is refreshing to find Whiting diagnosing the disease and recognizing its dangers over twenty years ago. With more than a touch of asperity he makes Tony, in *A Walk in the Desert*, say 'I went to the Grammar School when it was a grammar school and not the local louts' reformatory.' The watering-down of a classical education in the names of democracy and vocational training was not a movement that appealed to Whiting. He described himself, as has already been remarked, as a member of that dying species, the private individual: he was a representative also of another species that is in grave danger – the educated gentleman.

Much has been said in these pages of Whiting's struggle for perfect form and little need be added by way of conclusion except to note that, in a way, his original romantic vision, expressed in its own straightforwardly romantic terms in his first works, was the truest and most profound of his career, even though its expression was sometimes crude and sometimes obscure. The story of his short career is the story of his attempts, first, to express that vision and then, later, under the pressures from profession, need for recognition and so on, to tame the vision and tailor it to public requirements (or, at least, to what he saw as the modern theatre's requirements). His desire was not so much the crass desire to be popular or 'successful' but the desire to ensure that neither he nor the theatre be confined to an ivory tower, of no matter how delectable a design. The problem he tried to solve between *No More A-Roving* and *Saint's Day*, the problem of the right artistic relationship between the description of life's surface and the exploration of the inexplicable and reason-less reverberations beneath it, never was solved completely. Having begun, once he had realised the presence of the reverberations, by regarding them as the all-important thing in art, its very *raison d'être*, he then retreated under ever-increasing pressure (pressure exerted by *himself*, that is, as a result of his observation of the responses to his work) towards explicit description again: though not towards an acceptance of superficiality. His hope seemed to be that by a dry, hard description of the surface, the depth below could somehow be reached and plumbed and charted. He was looking, in other words, for plots that could be made to behave as fable or legend and a language that could bear the weight of such legend and fable without sounding precious and pretentious on the one hand or remote from experience and reality on the other. I think he never entirely found what he was looking for, though he often came close; and all the indications are that, with Whiting restored to the theatre in 1961 after a period of disillusion, the play which would have followed *The Devils*, had death not supervened, might well have demonstrated the solution fully and have led on to much greater works. Let us remind ourselves, had Shaw died at the same age as Whiting, the plays we should have lost would include *Man and Superman, Major Barbara, Heartbreak House, Back to Methuselah, St Joan* and *The Apple Cart*.

In the matter of language, Whiting's inclination in the early days was toward the verse drama of Eliot and Fry – the latter, particularly, was an influence upon him personally. But Whiting never, in fact, wrote a verse play. Instead he developed that highly figured, heightened, evocative prose which is unique and is instantly recognizable as his and his only. It is as full of potent imagery as is poetry, yet stays close enough to everyday speech to avoid the remoteness and esoteric quality which seem to be regarded in the twentieth century as the inevitable concomitants of verse in the theatre. It has another, specifically theatrical, virtue too. Several leading actors have commented, both when playing in Whiting plays and in seeing and hearing Whiting plays, on the astonishing way in which his language leaves, so to say, room for actors to act in. It allows for physical characterisation; it automatically anticipates the actor's contribution to the play's total gesture.

In the wide space of spirit which separates the ivory tower from the common street, Whiting stood with Janus-face, looking both ways. 'People should appreciate the pleasure of writing in obscurity', he once said. 'Don't they know the first public notice of the first public performance finishes you? From then on the game is politics.' Yet he returned to the theatre and obviously regarded it as his one true home. Kenneth Tynan described him as presenting the aspect of a born playwright who was determined not to write plays. It was true, in a way; except that the determination broke down in the face of the overriding fact of his very nature: he had to write plays.

He was a meticulous and methodical reviser of his work (almost always, new revisions are dated and carefully filed) and there is a general tendency discernible in nearly all his revisions and which has some significance in the context of Whiting's view of the purpose of art. It is this: his revisions nearly always show a move away from specific description and literal narrative toward a more general 'sense' embedded in the work. It was as if he were trying to capture the *essence* of the event rather than its mere outward appearance and as if he were trying, once that essence had been realised, to link it with all like essences in the generality of human experience, the more clearly to pinpoint and define this particular experience. In the composition of the work, it seemed to be necessary for him first to fix the surface of the experience, to relate it to other parts of life in a way that would make it definable and recognisable, yet not so closely as to trap it at the surface and confine it to a mere documentary statement. Then, this frame of reference having been established, the exploration could proceed into the inner senses of that segment of human reality to which the artist's first impulse led him and as the exploration became better-defined it would build up its own structures and its own patterns. These would gradually become clear in the structure of the work itself and, as they did so, the necessity for the reliance on the surface of events and their descriptions would steadily decline, so that all but the barest outlines of surface things could be pared away, leaving the heart free to absorb the inner, and truer, reality. There is a close parallel to this desire and to this method of revision in the presenting of five different versions of the central incident in *Not a Foot of Land*. The effect, in both the structure of that novel and the method of revision adopted by Whiting, is to *generalise* the experience in such a way as to explore all its possible aspects and senses. And to generalise, in this sense of the term, does not mean to make it vague or less precise, but to imply its relationships with the sum of human perceptions and truth. Whiting's careful and constant revising, making the task of writing itself an act of exploration of the true and ultimate values, is reminiscent of the similar struggles of Rainer Maria Rilke, the Austrian poet, to define for himself the relationship between art and life. He, too, passionately believed that the definition would come through 'the work' (he talked constantly of his poetry as 'the work') and when he was living in Paris with the sculptor, Rodin, whom he greatly admired, he received from him advice which was an endorsement of his own inclinations and convictions: 'Il faut toujours travailler.' It might have been said to Whiting, or about him – or by him.

Finally, when one considers the general posture and the sum total of Whiting's whole *oeuvre*, what stands out is that 'search for the absolute', about which so much has been said in this book's analysis of the individual plays. But a word of caution is necessary: it is dangerous to try to build this idealism – all-pervading though it be in his works – into an intellectual or philosophical system. It was instinctive, not rational. Equally, it is dangerous too firmly to rationalise the sense of nihilism (Meyer, in *Noman*, for instance) into 'death rather than compromise', which would in fact translate it into another form of idealism; it would cease to be nihilism. This would make Whiting into a sort of latter-day Victor Hugo, which he certainly was not. The nihilist impulse was real, and purely nihilist: it said 'Death anyway; destruction in any case, for its own sake. Life was made to be destroyed. Darkness is best.' But the nihilist impulse co-existed in his vision of life with the idealist impulse, both equally vital and both equally a true part of his sense of the world. And together they make that strange amalgam that provides all of Whiting's work with its compelling authority and force. They appeared side by side in that very first work, the novel called *Not a Foot of Land* and there is in it a poem which contains and summarises and celebrates both of them. The poem provides the words for a song sung by Old Tim to cheer himself up as he walks the journey back to 'the city' (and it incidentally makes one wish that more of Whiting's verse had been preserved)[1]:

> *We will walk*
> *To our delight by the ruined road:*
> *Come to me, quietly, for*
> *There is no ending to this time.*
>
> *A child has laughed, a man has died*
> *And it is apposite to sing.*
> *All infinite themes of love*
> *Are yours when our memories are dead.*
> *Come to me, quietly, for*
> *There is no ending to this time.*
>
> *I am old, abhorred, decrepit,*
> *Tired, unsociable, unfriended.*
> *'Better die', the sea has said,*
> *'Far, far better dead are you'.*
> *So come to me, quietly*
> *All time has ended.*

Just as it is mistaken to try to reduce to a formula the general thrust of Whiting's work (or anyone else's, for that matter), so is it wrong to try to simplify the individual plays into some brief factual statement, as though their lives could be dehydrated, frozen for preservation, pre-packaged and handed out like so many fish fingers. They are complex entities, ambivalent (in some cases, ambiguous), unique, in the ultimate analysis inexplicable: they tell us nothing, but they celebrate a mystery. They are not 'about' (as the saying is) the search for the absolute: it happens to be one of the things which is revealed and illuminated when the play is allowed to play upon you. Ultimately, the only explanation of any work of art is the work itself.

John Whiting's first plays were exactly contemporaneous with those of Samuel Beckett and Eugene Ionesco and were of the same order of importance. He was the first major British dramatist to catch, epitomise and reflect the profound unease of the mid-twentieth-century world and this he did in ways unique to himself. It is true that at some points in some of his plays one is reminded strongly of Pinter but Whiting is more than just a precursor of Pinter and Pinter is more than a mere echo of Whiting. Both are major artists and they are more important for their differences than for their similarities. Pinter is the cooler and more objective of the two, Whiting the more feeling and passionate.

Whiting's world is darker than Pinter's, but Pinter's is the bleaker. Pinter apart, no other dramatist since Shaw can compare with Whiting in stature except John Arden, and, at the time of writing at any rate, just possibly Tom Stoppard, David Storey and the temporarily forgotten James Bridie. But comparisons, though sometimes illuminating, are odious and these league tables of achievement after a while become invidious. Let us leave it by saying that John Whiting was a major dramatist whose vision was an austere and splendid one and whose work has been insufficiently recognised.

Notes

Chapter 1

1. These notebooks were not published during Whiting's life. They were discovered after his death and excerpts from them, edited by Ronald Hayman, were published in *London Magazine*, vol. II, no. 3 (August/September, 1971).
2. For more on this, the reader is referred to that excellent essay in biography, *The Quest for Corvo*, by A. J. A. Symons, first published in 1934 (see especially pp. 191–2 in the Penguin edition of 1940).
3. This was not, in fact, a formal newspaper interview but a response to a request from a graduate student of the University of California who was writing a thesis on John Whiting's plays. He had written to Whiting, in 1962, asking him to make a tape-recording giving autobiographical details. Judging from the correspondence, Whiting went out of his way to be helpful: the tape he provided was quite long and detailed.
4. That is, the paragraph in which Whiting requests that news of his illness be treated as confidential.

Chapter 2

1. This was said in the tape-recorded autobiographical note made at the request of the graduate student at the University of California, who required it in connection with the MA thesis he was writing on Whiting's plays. The statement that he made 'no attempt' to get the novel published is not strictly true: he offered it to one publisher (Hogarth Press) who rejected it. It was not offered elsewhere.
2. *Purgatorio*, Canto XXI

'*Brother,*
Do not do that. You are a ghost and you look on a ghost.'

And the other, rising: 'You know the extent
To which my love of you warms me,
When I forget our nothingness,
Treating a shadow like a solid thing'.

(author's translation)

This comes at the moment when, climbing the mountain, Virgil and Dante meet the shade of Statius, the Latin poet, who tells them of his own debt to Virgil's poetry. On learning that he is in the presence of Virgil he kneels to him, but Virgil bids him rise.

3. It should, perhaps, be re-emphasised that this was a *novel* that Whiting was writing, that he had no intention of turning it into a play and that at this point he had written no plays nor, so far as is known, had he even contemplated doing so. It shows, of course, that as a writer he instinctively thought – from the first – not only in dramatic terms but in specifically theatrical ones.

4. The typescript has *proceeded* here, but this does not make sense: *preceded*, for which one would suppose *proceeded* the more likely error, makes even less sense, since the day he left England for good (16 November, 1938) could not *precede* the events of 'his last days in England', of which the models remind him. The context seems to require *succeeded* and I have, therefore, amended the text accordingly. Perhaps *proceeded* carries the sense of the events connected with the models *proceeding into* the day of his final departure, which indeed at the end of the novel they do, but this is really not defensible syntactically.

5. I suggested to Mrs Whiting, who owns the copyright, and to the late A. D. Peters, her literary adviser and formerly John Whiting's agent, that *Not a Foot of Land* should be published. They were friendly about it, reread the manuscript and considered my suggestion seriously; but they both thought Whiting's own view should be respected in the matter. I sympathise with this and understand it, but in view of the importance of the work, I disagree.

6. Air Raid Precautions.

7. For *Encore*, the British theatre magazine which has since ceased publication. This interview was published in January/February 1961.

8. Though Hayman treats this as a direct quotation, I can find no place in the novel where the 'Master' is described as 'holy'. The phrase 'Holy Master' tends to evoke the image of Christ and if this can be maintained and the revolt shown to be against Christ or a Christ-like figure, then the argument of nihilism is much strengthened. On the evidence of the novel, however, I do not believe this can be sustained, since 'Holy Master' is not the novel's phraseology.

9. Here again there are connections with other of Whiting's works. The central character of *Saint's Day* is Paul Southman, an old poet and former political satirist, exiled from society on account of his excoriating denouncements of its weaknesses and failings. Whiting also wrote in 1946, on the same theme, a short radio play called *Paul Southman: An Appreciation for Broadcasting*. It was not, in fact, broadcast: the BBC, when it was submitted to them, rejected it. (For this information I am indebted to Martin Esslin, former Head of BBC Radio Drama, now Professor of Drama, Stanford University.)

10. The leader of the revolution in *Noman*.

11. He has been smirching the walls with paint and writing slogans in paint on them.

12. Like an actor, we may note in passing, not a playwright. The playwright is Timothy.

13. 'It was the sinister, princely death which the chamberlain had carried with him and had himself nourished during his whole life' (Rilke – *Notebooks of Malte Laurids Brigge*, Part I, translated by John Linton).

14. This is unexplained in the novel. 'N' does not appear anywhere else in the work.

15. Included by Ronald Hayman (editor) in *The Art of the Dramatist* (*London Magazine* Editions, 1970), a collection of Whiting fragments.

16. The other occupants of the railway carriage. Note the presence of the child, who weeps silently throughout the journey. He and his mother appear in the story for this moment only, then disappear for good. Sara asks the mother 'Why does he cry?' the reply is 'For no reason. One of his fits.' 'Can't you comfort him?' asks Sara, but the woman does not answer.

17. *The Art of the Dramatist*, ed. Ronald Hayman.

18. This plot-situation, of an invading army halted by an army of children, is almost identical with the central situation of a BBC radio play of 1933. This play was called *The Fantastic Battle* and was written by Leslie Baily, but in it the invaders are successfully halted; no one is killed; the invading armour surrenders to the moral superiority of the innocent children. Moreover, in *The Fantastic Battle*, the device of opposing the defenceless children to the tanks is a deliberate political move invented and organised by adults, not a spontaneous childhood expression. And it is carried out without the passion of Whiting's child-army: in *The Fantastic Battle* the children do not rush out or wave toy swords; they stand, still and silent, in the path of the on-coming armoured vehicles, which halt and eventually turn back. I have

no idea whether Whiting knew this earlier play and consciously drew on it for *Marching Song*.

19.   So in the typescript. I have noticed that elsewhere in the novel, and occasionally in the plays also, Whiting is shaky about the differentiation between nominative and accusative. Perhaps this politely affected form of speech (always 'you and I': never 'you and me' even when the sense demands the accusative) is an indication of the source of Whiting's conversational speech patterns – the polite middle-class English of the professional classes in the 1930s.

20.   That passion for minute detail again.

21.   It is also, be it noted, more or less exactly the period of human gestation, which may be a design or just a strange coincidence. I like to think it is the latter.

Chapter 3

1.   Note the definite article in the play's title. It appears so in Whiting's typescript of the play in 1946 and again when Whiting mentions the play, in 1957, in the Introduction to *The Plays of John Whiting*; but it was dropped when the play was included in *The Collected Plays of John Whiting* (Heinemann, 1969), after Whiting's death. I propose to retain it, partly out of a (perhaps pedantic) desire for academic accuracy and partly because the increased specificity of it provides a more aptly ironic reference to certain incidents in the plot of the play.

2.   Signifying the end of the dance. The National Anthem was always played at the end of all public functions in those days.

3.   The fragment is published in *The Art of the Dramatist*, edited by Ronald Hayman (*London Magazine* Editions, 1970)

4.   I intend the word in a critically precise sense, not in its popular connotation of merely 'exciting' or filled with surprising, violent or alarming incidents.

5.   The image of the artist as both clown and cripple and also as an outcast from normal society can also be found in Wedekind's play *The Marquis of Keith* (1900). The use Wedekind makes of it is wilder and more surrealist than Whiting's, but the similarity of imagery is striking, nonetheless, especially when one remembers that Whiting returned to this same system of symbols several times in different plays and stories. Wedekind in the opening stage directions describes his central character as having 'an exemplary figure were it not for the limp in his left leg' and says of him: 'He is dressed in a suit well chosen for its social elegance, but by no means foppishly. He has the rough red hands of a clown' (trans-

lation by Carl Richard Mueller). Not a peasant or a workman –
which one might have expected – but a clown. There is no way of
knowing whether Whiting knew the Wedekind play: the German
dramatist is never mentioned in Whiting's essays, lectures or reviews of drama. In any case, there is no suggestion of plagiarism;
only of a remarkable correspondence of vision.

Chapter 4

1. *Poor Judas* was included in a volume called *Two Plays* by Enid
   Bagnold (Heinemann, 1951); *Right Side Up* has never been
   published. *Poor Judas*, before its appearance in the Arts Theatre
   competition, had been produced by Esmé Church at the Bradford
   Civic Theatre, a distinguished amateur company, in 1946. The
   other two plays in the Arts Theatre competition, *Right Side Up*
   and *Saint's Day*, were being played for the first time.

2. To this smug criticism, which one hears so often, one feels like
   returning the answer that Turner made about his criticised sun-
   sets: 'Don't you wish they did?'

3. There is a pile of 'human and animal bones' on the floor, according
   to the stage directions at the beginning of the act.

4. In *Modern Drama*, May 1971.

5. The term 'goat songs' is used, in that exact form, several times:
   never 'goat-herd's songs' or 'the song of the goat-herds', but always
   'goat songs'. It is difficult to avoid the conclusion that the term,
   consciously or unconsciously, had for Whiting echoes of the
   Latin–Greek origins of the word 'tragedy'. The Greek word is
   τραγωδία (*tragōidia*), the Latin form being *tragoedia* and the
   usual etymological explanation is that the word derives from the
   Greek *tragos* (goat) and *ōidē* (song). In loose terminology, therefore, the word 'tragedy' means 'goat song' and it is, indeed, often
   so expressed in English. It is virtually impossible to use the term
   'goat song' without awakening in the mind the idea of tragedy
   and Whiting would surely be aware of this. Had he wanted to
   avoid this implication, he would have chosen some other term.
   He did not and we must, therefore, assume that the mixture of
   ironic and tragic overtones at the moment are intentional: they
   certainly deepen the whole mood of the play. In a review of Fry's
   Curtmantle, which Whiting wrote for *London Magazine* in 1961,
   he said 'Mr Fry's play, I suppose, is a tragedy. The origin of the
   word – goat-song – is, I believe, obscure...'

6. 'The crown o' the earth doth melt, My lord!
   O: wither'd is the garland of the war.

> The soldier's pole is fall'n; young boys and girls
> Are level now with men...'
> (Antony and Cleopatra, IV, xiii)

The invoking of a memory of this particular play in connection with his own is not without significance. Though Forster and Catherine are obviously not intended to be *like* Antony and Cleopatra as characters, the image of the man whose reality is achieved in action and the woman whose reality is achieved in love is a valuable overtone to *Marching Song*. I do not know why he changed the title and forfeited that echo, unless that the phrase 'marching song' (which is from Yeats) had some special appeal for him: he uses it occasionally elsewhere, as well as in the title of this play. Caroline, for instance, at the end of the first act of *The Gates of Summer*, says 'Ah! My revolutionary. I'll be your marching song...'

7. Reprinted in *The Art of the Dramatist*.

8. These are the things each of them remembers from other nights, in the past, before they met; they have been talking about them earlier.

9. There is some similarity between the function of Father Anselm in *Marching Song* and of Father Ambrose in *The Devils*. They are both old and fumbling but Anselm affords spiritual comfort and a renewal of strength to Catherine as Ambrose does to Grandier. Catherine says 'It was Father Anselm who in his own muddled way gave me back the words'; and Ambrose says to Grandier 'Even young girls come to me nowadays and confess things I don't know about. So it's hardly likely that I'll understand the sins of a young man of the world such as you. But let me try.'

10. In his Introduction to *The Plays of John Whiting* (Heinemann, 1957).

11. In *The Collected Plays of John Whiting*, ed. Ronald Hayman (Heinemann, 1969), Vol. 2, p. 261.

12. In the 1961 interview with *Encore*.

13. In the *Encore* interview.

14. These eight different versions of the ending of the play are, for comparison's sake, given in full in Appendix 1.

15. Anacreon is noted for his light, gay poems about women and wine and pleasure. He is mentioned by Byron in the first canto of *Don Juan*:

> *Ovid's a rake, as half his verses show him,*
> *Anacreon's morals are a still worse sample,*
> *Catullus scarcely has a decent poem,*
> *I don't think Sappho's ode a good example.*

Whiting's choice of Anacreon's name to illustrate his point may be a mere coincidence or it may be due to his having read or reread the great Byron poem at about the time he was writing *The Gates of Summer* which, as I point out in this chapter, has many other Byron echoes as well.

16. The same quality as is contained in Fry's title for another of his plays – *A Phoenix too Frequent*.

17. These two lines are to be found in 'Crazy Jane talks with the Bishop' which is one of the poems in *The Winding Stair and Other Poems* (1933).

18. Lord Byron's name, of course, was George Gordon, but when he married Annabella Milbanke, one of the terms of the marriage settlement, under which he benefited from his bride's family's estate, was that he should add their family name to his title. Annabella Milbanke's mother had been Judith Noel before her marriage to Sir Ralph Milbanke. This inheritance came from Miss Milbanke's uncle, Lord Wentworth, and there is a statement in writing about it, made on 10 May 1841, by Lady Byron to Bianca Milesi Mojon. It says (in part) 'Lord Wentworth died in 1815, a few months after my marriage. He left a large property to my mother for her life, and afterwards to me for my life; then to a collateral branch of the Noel family, the Curzons, and only if that branch becomes extinct will the property revert to my daughter. The condition of the inheritance was – to take the name and arms of Noel. My mother, who was about 55 when Lord W died, was from that time called Lady Noel instead of Lady Milbanke, and my father Sir Ralph Noel, but neither Lord B nor I assumed the name of Noel till after her death.' In a letter to Tom Moore, written from Pisa on 19 February 1822, Byron tells of Lady Noel's (i.e. Annabella's mother) death and says 'My agents and trustees have written to me to desire that I would take the name directly, so I am yours very truly and affectionately, NOEL BYRON'. He was known by that name, therefore, for only two years, since he died in 1824.

19. This is the penultimate stanza of 'On This Day I Complete My Thirty-Sixth Year', which was written by Byron at Missolonghi: on 22 January 1824. He died there of a fever on 19 April, while fighting for the revolutionary cause.

20. The 1969 *The Collected Plays* has an unfortunate misprint here, giving 'morality' instead of 'mortality'. The typescripts, however, have 'mortality', which obviously makes much more sense. Caroline has no tendency at all to see anything in terms of morality.

Chapter 5

1. It should be noted that while, in the theatre and cinema of the present moment, the word 'literary' is usually regarded as one of disapprobation, it is used here with the reverse intention.
2. *Innishfallen, Fare Thee Well* (London: Pan Books, 1972), p. 174. O'Casey writes of himself in the third person.
3. This, the Irish form of the name, is used by O'Casey in his autobiographies and is adopted in correspondence (though not in the film script itself) by Whiting.
4. The translation is that of Jens Arup, included in vol. 7 of the Oxford Ibsen (edited by James Walter McFarlane and published by OUP in 1964).
5. Again, I am indebted to the magnificent editorial work of James McFarlane (see p. 480 of vol. 7 of the Oxford Ibsen).
6. Jens Arup's translation again.
7. Tom is Whiting's name for Eilert Lövborg.
8. The article was written in 1954 and is reproduced in *Curtains*, the collection of Tynan's dramatic criticism (London: Longmans, 1961).

Chapter 6

1. See the collected works edition of *The Devils of Loudun* (London: Chatto & Windus, 1961), p. 324. The book had originally been published in 1952, also by Chatto & Windus.
2. The 1960 typescript, incidentally, follows Huxley in the matter of the title: the play at that time had the same title as Huxley's book, *The Devils of Loudun*. It was only for the first production, in February 1961, that the title was shortened to *The Devils*.
3. The first half-play to which he here refers was called *Nomad*, written in 1957. Two manuscript versions of Act 1 and a typescript of the same act still exist (in the Enthoven Collection, British Theatre Museum). The play, in this version, is set in Morocco and centres on Robert Anderson, a free-lance photographer, a tortured, savage and riven man. The second half-play is *Noman* (1958). Elements from both find their way into *The Nomads* (1961) and all three share the sense of nihilistic despair that Whiting obviously felt over what he regarded as a crumbling idealism and a ruined civilisation. In many ways *Nomad*, the 1957 version of the play, is the most brutal and terrifying. Though it is as complete (one completed Act) as the 1958 *Noman*, the latter was included in *The Collected Plays of John Whiting* in 1969, while the former was not.

4. From Morocco to Munich: but some of the characters' names were retained, e.g. Robert Anderson, Jessica (who in the 1957 version is Jessica *Lang* – her surname is picked up for the 1958 version, *Noman*).
5. According to Ronald Hayman (*The Art of the Dramatist*, p. 161), what Whiting actually wrote was 'precedence', but in modern English this does not make sense: obviously 'precedent' was intended. I have not seen the notebooks myself.

Chapter 7

1. This idea is an interesting one and had already been used by Whiting in another place. In the completed act of *Noman*, which was written before the review in question, one of the young revolutionaries says 'In the years of pre-history men thought there might be a time before the womb and a time after the grave. Lang's great achievement is that he snapped off these useless tag ends and revealed by its practical length life's true purpose.' (*The Collected Plays of John Whiting*, vol. 2, pp. 241–2).
2. The Royal Court Theatre, in Sloane Square, Chelsea, was (and still is) the theatre occupied by the English Stage Company, directed in those days by its founder, George Devine. It was noted for its productions of plays of social and political commitment by dramatists such as Osborne, Wesker, Arden, etc. Whiting disliked most of these plays (though he made an exception of Arden's work in this) because he felt that they were gauche and didactic.
3. The *Encore* interview, 1961.

Chapter 8

1. Though he once said in an interview that he had, from his early days, written some poetry, none of it was ever published. So far as I know, none of it is now extant. Apart from the two songs in *Not a Foot of Land* I have never seen any of it, except for a short poem, scribbled with a red ball-point pen on a piece of scrap paper among some miscellaneous notes for *The Gates of Summer*. At the top of the page are three lines of dialogue for that play, written in pencil (they never got as far as any of the final typewritten drafts of the play). On the back of the paper are some rough pencil notes about characterisation in *The Gates of Summer*. And under the three pencilled lines of dialogue on the face of the page the poem appears. It reads as follows:

Yesterday it seemed to me (without doubt I was drunk)
That I saw on the arch of a bridge an encounter of horsemen
All armoured in iron, all over-lapped with steel
And decorated with strange harness.

Some dragons cowered muttering on their helmets,
Some Medusas of brass opened their wild eyes
In their great shields with fantastic ornaments,
And some knots of snakes covered like scales their armlets.

At intervals, at the edge of the giant arch,
A wounded rider losing his point of support,
A frightened horse fell into the open water,
Mouth of a crocodile closed on them.

That was you, my desires, that was you, my thoughts
Who try to force a way over the bridge,
And your twisted bruised body clad in false colours
Sleeps swallowed up in the bottomless chasm.

This piece of rough paper I found among notes, papers and complete drafts of *The Gates of Summer* in the manuscript room of the Lilly Library, Indiana University. The Library has a small but extremely valuable holding of Whiting MSS.

There is in Act 2 of *The Gates of Summer* a reference to 'a group of silent horsemen on the hill'. The metaphor is used by both John and Caroline to signify Nemesis – the coming on of inevitable fate.

Appendix 1

Variant Endings of *The Gates of Summer*

Among Whiting's papers at his home in Sussex, I found, apart from the published text, five different versions of the ending of the play; in the Manuscripts Department of the Lilly Library at Indiana University I found two more, as well as some rough notes that indicated that Whiting frequently changed his mind about how the play ought to end. Some of these changes are quite radical: in particular he was obviously very undecided whether John Hogarth and Caroline Treherne, the two principal characters, should remain together at the end or not. In some of his drafts they do; in some they do not.

The play's central concern is that one which shows as an obsessive leit-motiv in many Whiting plays – the hopeless search for an absolute, for an unassailable splendour which will give meaning to all the rest of life, a spirit which will transcend the pettiness of the everyday and of the individual. In *The Devils* this absolute is represented as God; in *Marching Song* it is represented as military achievement; in *The Gates of Summer* it is love. In none of these plays is the absolute attained: in all of them, indeed, it is shown as being for ever unattainable and Grandier, Rupert Forster and John Hogarth, the three protagonists concerned, share in fact that curiously Whitingesque ambivalence, of yearning passionately for the assurance of such an absolute beyond the bounds of self and of simultaneously comprehending intellectually (and how superbly intelligent these Whiting characters are!) that such a yearning is by the very nature of life foredoomed to frustration.

I wanted to find out, if I could, what the exact incidence of the variant endings was and what was the relationship between them and the practical business of preparing and staging the first production of the play, so I consulted with Peter Hall, who had directed the original production and Dorothy Tutin, who played Caroline. Both of them were extremely kind and helpful and offered many valuable suggestions, but no definitive version of the play's end emerged from our talks. Both Miss Tutin and Sir Peter recalled frequent alterations and rewritings during rehearsals, but it is evident from some of the notes and manuscripts that several rewritings of the last three or four pages had already taken place before rehearsals began and while the play was still in its formative stages. The most that can be said with any certainty is that right from the completion of the first draft in 1953 until the end of rehearsals in October 1956 (and, indeed, beyond: Peter Hall told me that he remembers at least two changes of ending after the tour of the play began) Whiting had been uncertain about the proper way of finishing the play. Peter Hall, as director, shared that uncertainty: 'We could never get the ending to *work*', he said.

In a sense the whole bent of Whiting's vision is involved in, and is illustrated by, the dilemma of the play's ending. His austere sense of the truth of things was driving him one way; his desire to achieve a particular theatrical entity was dragging him another. For he had resolved, Peter Hall told me, to write a comedy: not that he was in the least attracted by the thought of a quick and easy 'success' – Whiting openly scorned such cheapness and shallowness – but because he was afraid that the austerity of his own vision, of the forbidding nature of which he was himself acutely aware, would end by cutting him off from communication with his audience altogether. It was not easy laughter and a glib approbation he was seeking, but a more vivid and more broadly based way of reflecting his own perception of the nature of the world. There is a sense in which the tragic and comedic visions of the world are the obverse of each other and Whiting, more consciously than most dramatists, knew this. He was deliberately seeking, in *The Gates of Summer*, to turn from one face of truth to another and the agonised wrestling with the end of the play demonstrates in a fascinating way the difficulties both of style and vision in which this involved him. He was always a consummate and fastidious stylist, searching for the perfect shape both of speech and of plot and one can well see that a sense of falsity at the end of this wry and harsh comedy would worry him profoundly. Mere cleverness would not serve; and sentimentality (which could have been a danger) was anathema; on the other hand, the kind of stark statement which ends *Saint's Day*, *Marching Song* and *The Devils* would be quite unsuitable here.

Two principal elements seem to be involved: first, whether the right bitter-sweet taste can best be obtained by leaving Caroline and John together at the end (presumably on the argument that they deserved each other) or by having John stick to his resolve to treat her as a passing fancy and continue on his way to wars and battlefields; second, to maintain the tone of language and imagery at the right level – not too colloquially casual on the one hand and not too apocalyptically poetic on the other. Among the Indiana papers are a few rough working notes that bear on the first of these considerations. One of these says:

CAROLINE – JOHN (ACT III)

John is in love with Caroline,
He does not know whether she has tried to kill him or not.
He hopes she has – to show her love.
He hopes she has not – for her character.

Another of these isolated notes reads as follows: 'So John has failed as well as Caro. Being forced to stay. What can he do? (Return to England? Go on from here? Where can he go? And why should he?)' But another page of notes contains this comment: 'Caroline has gone. John alone (?)' And in yet a third note Whiting envisaged another possibility: 'End – Caroline & John renew lease of Cristos's house which lapses at end of Selwyn's excavation.' In early versions of the play the idea of having the final duologue between John and Caroline interrupted by Henry Bevis had not yet come into Whiting's mind (Henry Bevis – called Henry Wriothsley in the very early drafts – is the newspaper reporter whose ineffectual love for Caroline is made fun of by both Caroline and the play) but in one of his revision notes one can see the beginnings of this idea: 'John–Caroline: to bed – curtains of bed drawn. Henry enters: "I can't read my own writing. Did you say . . . ?" Henry goes. END'. This scrap of dialogue never got into the play, but Henry's interruption of John and Caroline did, and provided Whiting with as final a solution of his problem as he ever managed to reach.

The second consideration – the question of the tone of language and imagery – is best judged by examining and comparing the variant texts themselves. They are set out below, but the order in which they are set out is not intended to indicate – except in very broad outline – the order in which they were written. This is quite impossible to determine, except to say that nos 1–7 all seem to antedate no. 8 (no. 8 is the 1955 typescript which Ronald Hayman, in editing *The Collected Plays* in 1969, took, correctly, I think, as being the final version) and that all those in which Henry Bevis appears were written later than those in which he does not. Neither Miss Tutin nor Sir Peter Hall could remember – and it is scarcely surprising, considering the number of variants, the degree of uncertainty and the length of time which has elapsed since – in what order the various endings were tried in rehearsal, though both of them vividly recalled certain details and images. The swinging lamp, for example – though it did not find its way into the 'final' version – had fixed itself in the imagination of both of them.

The variant endings, as given below, are drawn from three types of source: full drafts of the play in manuscript; full drafts of the play in typescript; revision notes and revised passages of dialogue, in manuscript, for various parts of the play. Some of these papers are in Mrs

Whiting's possession at her home in Sussex; some of them are in the possession of the Lilly Library, Indiana University. To both I am deeply indebted for their help and for permission to quote from the papers:

Variant 1

(Single sheet, undated, handwritten, found among miscellaneous, non-sequential notes: the sheet is numbered '7', but the rest of the sequence is missing.)

SOPHIE: I sent a cable to the Editor of the London *Times*. It said reports from the mountains spoke of you falling gallantly at the head of your native troops led in a lost cause. Naturally, I signed myself Henry Bevis.

(SOPHIE *goes out of the room*)

JOHN: That's a solution. Will they believe it?

CAROLINE: Why not? They must if you don't show yourself.

JOHN: It has great possibilities. I'll have a freedom I haven't dared think about. I can be young again. I shall be twenty-eight. A new name. That can be decided later. Freedom of activity. Freedom of acquaintance. I need recognize no one from tomorrow morning when the cable gets to London. I'll have known not a single person until that time anyway. I can start again from the beginning.

CAROLINE: Why wait until tomorrow morning?

JOHN: I've been staggering under the past. I'd not understood it until now. Is everyone borne down by it? The hopeless lost blundering [*an illegible word here*] of a turning taken before their eyes were open.

CAROLINE: So now everything's going to be all right. This time. Not like last time. This time. All right.

JOHN: What! No.

CAROLINE: Then why are you happy?

JOHN: I suppose, because there's a chance of making all the mistakes again.

CAROLINE: Was making love to me a mistake?

JOHN: I don't think so, no.

CAROLINE: Then I'll go to my own room.

JOHN: What!

CAROLINE: Why? It's only the mistakes you're going to make again.

JOHN: That's too simple. I've no wish to go back to Ada. She was a mistake on my part.

CAROLINE: Then I'll stay. For it's going to be the first time, not the last chance. How d'you do. Why not take advantage of me?

JOHN: What do you mean?

CAROLINE: You're not the man you were. You may go far. You're a few years ahead. But young again? No. Twenty-eight? Never.

JOHN: You don't think I'll manage it.

CAROLINE: No. But I know you and I'm here. And I love you. You talk about the past and the future. There's a present time. You're not to look so miserable. You've always an escape. Just turn up in London again as yourself. You can do that when you're tired of me and it doesn't look as if there'll ever be anyone else.

JOHN: You're giving me a weapon of blackmail. I shall use it.

CAROLINE: I'll want you to use it.

(She jumps on the bed)
[The rest of the scene is missing]

<h2 style="text-align:center">Variant 2</h2>

(Two pages, undated, manuscript.)

ACT III Revised (2) sheets page 24 [This is Whiting's own note at the head of the first page]

(SOPHIE goes out of the room)

CAROLINE: How sad! How terribly sad!

JOHN: Is it? I wonder.

CAROLINE: I mean because no one will believe me when I say we were here together.

JOHN: No, not a soul will believe you.

CAROLINE: Unless, of course, you turn up in London as yourself. With me.

JOHN: I'll not do that.

CAROLINE: I feel as if I've never seen you before. Damn, oh damn and damn! This is what Cristos warned me about. Falling in love with a legend. You're a man. Just a man. Two a penny. That's what you are.

JOHN: Seeing me that way is the penalty of winning, Caro. You've never been anything but a woman to me. I've never asked that anyone I've loved should be more.

CAROLINE: You mean, however splendid the pursuit and however corrupt the trickery, I'll end up with a man. Just a man.

JOHN: That's all.

CAROLINE: You. Going bravely on two feet. You. Creedless, useless until you are threatened, made to remember that you'll have an eternity for things of the spirit. (JOHN is watching a lamp which hangs on a long chain beside the bed and is behind CAROLINE. Almost imperceptibly it has begun to sway to and fro) You. Tonight. Safe. What is left which might recall you to your duty? Nothing. Basilios has gone: no danger there. The berries in the wine: you'll live. You're threatened by nothing but love. You're safe.

JOHN (He smiles, watching the lamp):   No, Caro. You forget. In this country the very land you walk on may . . . (He kisses her: the window curtains are suddenly disturbed. CAROLINE released)

CAROLINE: Was that you?

JOHN: Yes.

CAROLINE (Looking down):   I felt the ground move. (She looks up at the lamp, which is shifting the shadows: laughs) That's it. There, beneath our feet. Your necessary reminder that time may be short, very short.

There, in that tender movement. (JOHN *reaches up and steadies the lamp, turning it low. With consideration they begin to make love*) My God, they say the land rolls up like the waves of the sea. Does it so?

JOHN: A small tremor. It will pass. Everything does.

CAROLINE: Quickly. There may not be time for regret. All men are threatened! (JOHN *cries out*) There, now. Well, well. Nothing can make it better. So, so. One question, Johnnie. One.

JOHN.   One.

CAROLINE: Do we all get what we deserve?

JOHN: Yes.

CAROLINE: Every time?

JOHN: Yes.

CAROLINE: Hm. Let's take care of ourselves.

(*Silence: they have become lost in the darkness of the bed: there is a whisper of sound through the open window*)

CURTAIN

Variant 3

(Two pages, undated, manuscript.)

REVISED ACT III page 24 line 21 [Whiting's own note]

CAROLINE: How sad! How terribly sad!

JOHN: Is it? I wonder.

CAROLINE: I mean because no one will believe me now when I say we were here together.

JOHN: No, not a soul will believe you.

CAROLINE: Unless, of course, you turn up in London as yourself, with me.

JOHN: I'll not do that.

CAROLINE: I feel as if I'd never seen you. Damn, oh damn and damn! This is what Cristos warned me about. Falling in love with a legend. You're a man. Just a man. Two a penny. That's what you are.

JOHN: Seeing me that way is the penalty of winning, Caro. You've never been anything but a woman to me. I've never asked that anyone I've loved should be more.

CAROLINE: You mean, however splendid the pursuit and however corrupt the trickery, I'll end up with a man. Just a man.

JOHN: That's all.

CAROLINE: Then what can make you, a mere acknowledged man, God? A religion in my arms, a philosophy between my legs. What makes up [*illegible word here*] time with you?

JOHN: Speaking from the lowest level of dignity, this. The sight and sound of a mob, a day ending in exhaustion, a sweet voice, a threat, violence. In short, whenever I remember that I shall have an eternity for things of the spirit. (*He is watching a lamp which hangs on a long chain beside the bed and is behind* CAROLINE. *Almost imperceptibly it has begun to sway to and fro*)

296

CAROLINE: And tonight. What is left which might recall you to your sense of duty? Nothing. You're safe.

JOHN (*He is smiling*): You forget, Caro, in this country you walk on land which may . . . (*He kisses her: the window curtains are suddenly disturbed:* CAROLINE *released*)

CAROLINE: Was that you?

JOHN: Yes.

CAROLINE (*Looking down*): I felt the ground move. (*She looks up at the lamp: laughs*) Time's short. There's the threat. Violence. Your necessary reminder. There in that tender movement. Personal as an obscene word. (JOHN *reaches up and steadies the lamp, turning it low. With consideration they begin to make love*) My God, they say the land rolls up like the waves of the sea. You're looking down one minute and up the next to a little hole in the sky. Nothing left but that, no light but that. Nothing, in the long tussle to bring to light nothing. Nothing but the animal smells and tastes which even the most [Whiting has left a gap here for the later insertion of a suitable adjective] habits crushed from s . . . [the word is illegible] distilled chemistry – cannot make polite. One question, Johnny. One.

JOHN: One.

CAROLINE: Another time.

(*They are lost in the obscurity of the bed: there is a whisper of sound through the open window*)

CURTAIN

Variant 4

(A separate sheet, undated, manuscript.)

Revised Act III page 24, line 21 Second draft

NOTES: Cut lines (telegram) Page 21 Line from Cristos about house

(SOPHIE *goes out of the room*)

CAROLINE: How sad! How terribly sad!

JOHN: Is it? I wonder.

CAROLINE: I mean because no one will believe me now when I say we were here together.

JOHN: No, not a soul will believe you.

CAROLINE: Unless, of course, you turn up in London as yourself. With me.

JOHN: I'll not do that.

CAROLINE: I feel as if I'd never seen you before. Damn, oh damn and damn! This is what Cristos warned me about. Falling in love with a legend. You're a man. Just a man. Two a penny. That's what you are.

JOHN: Seeing me that way is the penalty of winning, Caro. You've never been anything but a woman to me. I've never asked that anyone I've loved should be more.

CAROLINE: You mean, however splendid the pursuit and however corrupt the trickery, I'll end up with a man. Just a man.

JOHN: That's all.

CAROLINE: But you were – can be – I know, I know – to me you can be, my God, God! What puts you up there? What is it changes you, a mere acknowledged man, into a religion, faith, into a bloody philosophy?

JOHN: Going on two feet. The whole bag of tricks can be tumbled and forgotten in a hole in the ground in a nod. Find it hard to believe? So do I. So strange waiting for the threat, the violent act, which will prove it. In short, whenever I remember that I shall have an eternity for things of the spirit (*He is watching a lamp which hangs on a long chain beside the bed and is behind* CAROLINE. *Almost imperceptibly it has begun to sway to and fro*)

CAROLINE: And tonight. What is left which might recall you to your duty? Nothing. You're safe.

JOHN (*He smiles*):   You forget, Caro. In this country the very land you walk on may . . . (*He kisses her: the window curtains are suddenly disturbed:* CAROLINE *released*)

CAROLINE: Was that you?

JOHN: Yes.

CAROLINE (*Looking down*):   I felt the ground move. (*She looks up at the lamp, which is shifting the shadows: laughs*) There's your threat. Violence. Your necessary reminder that time is short. There in that tender movement. (JOHN *reaches up and steadies the lamp, turning it low. With consideration, they begin to make love*) My God, they say the land rolls up like the waves of the sea – does it so? – leaves no one free – not even men of God – gods of men – no one, least of all you – are threatened! (JOHN *cries out*) There, now. Well, well. Nothing can make it better. So. One question. Johnnie. One.

JOHN: One.

CAROLINE: Another time.

(*They have become lost in the darkness of the bed: there is a whisper of sound through the open window*)

CURTAIN

Variant 5

(Typescript, undated.)

This one is almost, but not quite, the same as no. 4, of which it is obviously intended to be a fair copy. It is headed 'Revised sheets, page 24' and differs only in three speeches from the manuscript text shown above in Variant 4. The three changed speeches read in Variant 5 as follows:

CAROLINE: But you – were – can be, I know – to me, my God, God! What puts you up there? You a mere acknowledged man, become a religion, faith, a bloody philosophy! How?

JOHN: By going on two feet. The whole bag of tricks can be tumbled and forgotten in a hole in the ground in a nod. Find it hard to believe? So do

I. But there's always the threat, the violent act, which will prove it. Divinity? No. Just let me remember that I shall have an eternity for things of the spirit.

CAROLINE: My God – they say the land rolls up like the waves of the sea – does it so? – all – men of God – gods of men are – threatened! (*John cries out*) There, now . . . [etc.]

Variant 6

(End of both the manuscript drafts of the complete play, dated 1953.)

(SOPHIE *goes out of the room*)

CAROLINE: How sad! How terribly sad!

JOHN: Is it? I wonder.

[In the first draft John says 'Yes, isn't it' but this is crossed out and the new line added]

CAROLINE: I mean because no one will believe me now when I say we were here together.

JOHN: No, not a soul will believe you.

CAROLINE: Unless, of course, you turn up in London as yourself. With me.

JOHN: I'll not do that.

CAROLINE: I feel as if I've never seen you before. Damn, oh damn, damn! This is what Cristos warned me about. Falling in love with a legend. You're a man. Just a man. Two a penny. That's what you are.

JOHN: I'm more fortunate. You've never been anything but a woman to me. I've never asked that anyone I've loved should be more (*He lifts* CAROLINE *in his arms and puts her on the bed. Then by pulling on the heavy silken cord he draws the curtains which quite surround the bed. There is a knock at the door*) Yes?

(HENRY *comes into the room*)

HENRY: I want to apologise. I'm afraid the worry about my article made me lose my sense of humour and then my temper.

JOHN: It's all right. Sorry I couldn't be more helpful. I hope you'll get it straightened out.

HENRY: I think I have. I took another long walk and I had an idea.

JOHN: Why don't you sleep with it?

HENRY: No, I must get it down on paper. I think I've found the right approach. After the usual introductory paragraph about the date of the excavation I shall continue something like this: 'It is encouraging to see from the statuary in the excavation that the Greeks of this period very much resembled in their habits the Englishman of today. Your Correspondent found the same emphasis on the sanctity of marriage which is to be found in British social life. Also, it is clear they had much the same sense of fun. This can be seen in the frieze representing an old man chasing a group of laughing girls who are in turn chasing a bull which is chasing a young man who is running after another girl. The resemblance to many English pastoral games will be understood.' And so on.

JOHN: And so on.

HENRY: I shall sit up until morning getting it down on paper. Then I can think about going home.

JOHN: Wait a minute. (*He looks in his pockets. Whilst he is doing so* CAROLINE'S *bare forearm comes through the curtains of the bed. She is holding out the telegram to* HENRY. *He takes it and, at once staring towards the bed and taking the telegram from the envelope, moves to the door.* CAROLINE *speaks from the bed*)

CAROLINE: May I ask one question? Just one.

JOHN: What is it?

CAROLINE: If you're not the legend I can believe in, what is? Love?

(HENRY'S *cry comes from beyond the closed door for he has gone from the room*)

HENRY: No!

JOHN: Yes.

CURTAIN

Variant 7

(pp. 26–8 of the complete typescript of 1953.)

(SOPHIE *goes out of the room*)

CAROLINE: How sad! How terribly sad!

JOHN: Is it? I wonder.

CAROLINE: I mean because no one will believe me now when I say we were here together.

JOHN: No, not a soul will believe you.

CAROLINE: Unless, of course, you turn up in London as yourself. With me.

JOHN: I'll not do that.

CAROLINE: I feel as if I've never seen you before. Damn, oh damn, damn! This is what Cristos warned me about. Falling in love with a legend. You're a man. Just a man. Two a penny. That's what you are.

JOHN: I'm more fortunate. You've never been anything but a woman to me. I've never asked that anyone I've loved should be more.

(*He lifts* CAROLINE *in his arms and puts her on the bed. Then by pulling on the heavy silken cord he draws the curtains which quite surround the bed. There is a knock at the door*)

Yes?

HENRY: I want to apologise. I'm afraid the worry about my article made me lose my sense of humour and then my temper.

JOHN: It's all right. Sorry I couldn't be more helpful. I hope you'll get it straightened out.

HENRY: I think I have. I took another long walk and I had an idea.

JOHN: Why don't you sleep with it?

HENRY: No, I must get it down on paper. I think I've found the right approach. After the usual introductory paragraph about the date of the excavation I shall go on something like this: 'It is encouraging to see from the statuary in the excavation that the Greeks of this period very much resembled in their habits the Englishman of today. Your

300

Correspondent found the same emphasis on the sanctity of marriage which is to be found in British social life. Also it is clear they had much the same sense of fun. This can be seen in the frieze representing an old man chasing a group of young girls who are, in turn, chasing a bull which is chasing a young man who is running after another girl. The resemblance to many English pastoral games will be understood.' **And so on.**

JOHN: And so on.

HENRY: I shall sit up until morning getting it down on paper. Then I can think about getting home.

JOHN: Give my regards to your mother. Home! Wait a minute!

(*He looks in his pockets. Whilst he is doing so* CAROLINE'S *bare forearm comes through the curtains of the bed. She is holding out the cablegram to* HENRY. *He takes it and, at once staring towards the bed and taking the cablegram from the envelope, moves to the door.* CAROLINE *speaks from the obscurity of the bed*)

CAROLINE: May I ask one question? Just one.

JOHN: What is it?

CAROLINE: I want to know. Do we all get what we deserve?

(HENRY'S *cry comes from beyond the closed door for he has gone from the room*)

HENRY: No!

JOHN: Yes.

CAROLINE: Every time?

HENRY (*Distantly*): No!

JOHN: Yes.

CURTAIN

<h2 style="text-align:center">Variant 8</h2>

(The 1955 typescript and *The Collected Plays*.)

(SOPHIE goes out of the room)

CAROLINE: How sad! How terribly sad!

JOHN: Is it? I wonder.

CAROLINE: I mean because no one will believe me now when I say we were here together.

JOHN: No, not a soul will believe you.

CAROLINE: Unless, of course, you turn up in London as yourself. With me.

JOHN: I'll not do that.

CAROLINE: I feel as if I've never seen you before. Damn, oh damn and damn! This is what Cristos warned me about. Falling in love with a legend. You're a man. Just a man. Two a penny. That's what you are.

JOHN: Seeing me that way is the penalty of winning, Caro. You've never been anything but a woman to me. I've never asked that anyone I've loved should be more. (*He lifts* CAROLINE *in his arms and puts her on the bed*)

CAROLINE: You mean, however splendid the pursuit, and however corrupt the trickery, I'll end up with a man. Just a man.

301

JOHN: That's all. (*He gently pulls on the heavy silken cord and draws the curtains which quite surround the bed. There is a knock on the door*) Yes?

(HENRY *comes into the room*)

HENRY: I want to apologise. I'm afraid the worry about the article made me lose my sense of humour and then my temper.

JOHN: All forgotten.

HENRY: I took another long walk and came to a decision. (*He is a little wild-eyed*) I'm going to tell the truth about Selwyn's discovery.

JOHN: That's brave of you.

HENRY: Then I shall be called home in disgrace.

JOHN: Yes. Home! Wait a minute. (*He looks in his pockets. Whilst he is doing so,* CAROLINE'S *bare arm comes through the curtains of the bed. She is holding the cablegram out to* HENRY. *He takes it, staring at the bed. He pulls the cablegram from the envelope. He reads it. Slowly, his face crumples.* JOHN *has moved to* HENRY *and now puts an arm round his shoulders. Together, in silence, the two men stand staring down at the cablegram. Then, quietly,* JOHN *speaks*) Do you have a little badge, or something? (HENRY *shakes his head*) Go home. To mother, incognito. Keep your mouth shut. Your articles will go on arriving. I shall also sign every one Henry Bevis. (JOHN *gently takes the cablegram from* HENRY *and begins to move to the door.* CAROLINE *speaks from the obscurity of the bed*)

CAROLINE: May I ask one question? Just one.

JOHN: Yes.

CAROLINE: I want to know. Do we all get what we deserve?

JOHN: Yes. (*He is at the door*)

CAROLINE: Every time?

JOHN: Yes. (JOHN *gives a sad smile to* HENRY *and quietly goes from the room.* CAROLINE'S *arm is still extended between the curtains of the bed. Suddenly, imperiously, she snaps her fingers. Slowly,* HENRY *moves to the bed and takes her hand in his*)

(*There is a pause*)

CURTAIN

Though we do not know the exact order in which these variants were written, we do know that nos 1–5 *must* pre-date nos 7 and 8, since the page references on the former do not correspond with the pagination of either of the typescripts and must, therefore, refer to earlier, handwritten, versions (though not to the two MSS referred to in no. 6). We know, moreover, because both are dated, that no. 7 pre-dates no. 8. This means that Whiting, as usual with his revising, was moving from the specific, the descriptive, the explicit to the more general, the wider implication, the oblique; and, also as usual, was strengthening the poetic statement in the process. It also means that he gradually changed his mind about the actual plot details. In nos 1–5 he either says or implies that John will now stay with Caroline permanently, as she wishes; in no. 6 he hits on the idea of tempering the passionate, gloomy romanticism with irony by bringing Henry in, though still leaving John with Caroline at the end. Then in no. 8, having got Henry in, he suddenly sees that the true logic of the situation is for Henry to remain and John to leave, as he always intended to; and, by introducing John's neat trick of exchanging places with Henry, several problems are solved simultaneously: John can now, by impersonating Henry, lose himself in a much bigger war than the little Greek revolution he had planned to join – the telegram is to tell Henry to 'proceed incognito to expected trouble centre Bosnia' (this is 1913, just before the assassination of the Archduke Ferdinand at Sarajevo in Bosnia, the event which was made the excuse for the beginning of the First World War); Henry can be given ironically to Caroline, who will teach him a good deal very quickly about men, women and reality; and Caroline, who has herself prophesied that her predatory instincts will leave her with 'just a man', will live to regret the truth of her prediction. It is a far stronger ending than any of the others and carries the real ring of truth. Its irony is more consonant with the general spirit of the play than the 'softer' earlier endings and, paradoxically, it makes a more heroic figure of John, which somehow seems right. The only problem that in Variant no. 8 remained unsolved was the one of clothing the idea in suitable dialogue. The verbal device of Caroline's 'May I ask one question?' does not spring naturally from what goes before it: in fact, it does not 'spring' at all. It is left over from the more overtly philosophical questioning of some of the earlier versions (see nos 2, 3, 4 and 5, above) and, though that questioning should be implicit in the ironic-comic ending, it needs some hint to start it off. As it is, the business of 'getting what we deserve', while it carries clearly enough the comic and ironic implication that Caroline will get Henry and that is what she deserves, quite fails to carry also the darker and more serious implications which come from the earlier dialogue about men and gods, which Caroline really has in mind when she says 'May I ask one question?' If her question, when she asks it, could somehow be made to serve both the serious *and* the comic purposes, the irony and the pattern would be complete. One feels that the best solution, perhaps, would have been to keep the moment of seriousness between John and Caroline, before moving to the ironic ending with Henry's entrance. The business of the swaying lamp is impressive as a visible symbol of the hidden power of God in the earthquake and something of that image and metaphor could, with advantage, be retained. The sombre colour of such a moment would serve to remind us that both John and Caroline 'see everything in terms of mortality' (as Cristos says of Caroline earlier in the play); and it would also effectively set off the irony of the coda.

Simon Trussler, in *The Plays of John Whiting* (Gollancz, 1972), sums up the ending of the play by saying 'and the best John Hogarth can do is to accept his death as a public man (effected by Sophie's dispatch of a premature obituary notice to *The Times*), and seemingly prepare to make the best of life alone with Caroline.' This, apparently, was true in the early drafts of the play but not in the last two or three. Certainly the only published version does not support this view. Trussler quotes the final six lines of this version down to John's final 'Yes' and then adds 'There the action ends.' But of course it does not end there: Trussler omits, without explanation, the final (and surely crucially important) stage direction, which was written by Whiting, not added by the director, and which flatly contradicts Trussler's assertion. John *quietly goes from the room* and it is Henry's hand that takes Caroline's, though she is obviously expecting it to be John's. This, surely, is the force of John's question to Henry: 'Do you have a little badge or something?' – so that John can impersonate Henry the more readily as a newspaper man in Bosnia, having some sort of credentials. The implication of this final version is that up to the moment of Henry's entrance, John has uneasily concluded that he must remain with Caroline, at least for the time being, though there is nothing to indicate that he has abandoned his original stance or that he means to stay permanently. His love for her is genuine, but so is his conviction that love, like all ideals, degenerates rapidly in keeping and most rapidly when kept domestically. Henry's entrance and the telegram, between them, give John the idea of using Bosnia instead of Greece as the scene of his Byronic self-immolation. London already thinks he is dead (because of Sophie's telegram to *The Times*): even if he does not actually die in Bosnia, he will have ceased to exist as himself: he will write reports to *The Times* signed with another man's name. Meanwhile Caroline, who with half her nature yearns for domesticity, can – the one brief moment of glory over – be shipped back to London with the anonymous Henry. It is an ending that has a curious blend of idealism and cynicism that fits and summarises the play exactly and beautifully.

As has already been remarked, two or three different endings were tried during the actual tour of the play, without any finally satisfactory solution's being reached. As far as Peter Hall could remember, when I talked to him, the version given in Variant 8 (above) was the one which was regarded as coming closest and the one that was being played when the production was finally abandoned in Brighton. It was certainly the difficulty of finding a satisfactory ending for the play that, at least in part, led to the decision not to take the production into London. Sir Peter's one very clear recollection was that it was John Whiting's feeling that John and Caroline could not be left together at the end, that this would falsify the whole structure. Dorothy Tutin, on the other hand, recalled playing Caroline in the play's week in Glasgow and at that time John and Caroline *were* left together, lying on the bed in each other's arms. Miss Tutin left the cast, because of illness, after the week in

Glasgow and so was not aware of changes made after that. She herself felt that there was something vaguely unsatisfactory or incomplete about the ending as it stood when she played it, but she did also feel that a point could be made by *leaving* John and Caroline together, uninterrupted by Henry, if the playing were sufficiently 'dry' and ironic, Caroline suddenly realising right at the end that she *still* hasn't got what she wanted, though she *has* got what she deserves – a failed romantic and a failed revolutionary who will quickly become a very dull domestic dog. For my own taste and sense of the play, this deflates John too much and in the wrong way, though I agree that the focus and emphasis of such an ending would be right so far as the character of Caroline is concerned. John should fail, but with a certain aura of sombre glory: he should not be debunked.

Perhaps the various endings could have been combined in something of the following manner (and I should here say that while the words are Whiting's, the responsibility for shuffling and juggling with them is entirely mine; and I should add that I am much indebted to Miss Tutin and Sir Peter Hall for giving me very sensitive impressions of what the production over twenty years ago was trying to do and for helping me to identify the spirit of this elusive play):

CAROLINE: How sad! How terribly sad!

JOHN: Is it? I wonder.

CAROLINE: I mean because no one will believe me now when I say we were here together.

JOHN: No, not a soul will believe you.

CAROLINE: Unless, of course, you turn up in London as yourself. With me.

JOHN: I'll not do that.

CAROLINE: I feel as if I'd never seen you before. Damn, oh damn and damn! This is what Cristos warned me about. Falling in love with a legend. You're a man; just a man. Two a penny. That's what you are.

JOHN: Seeing me as anything more is the penalty of winning, Caro. You've never been anything but a woman to me. I've never asked that anyone I loved should be more.

CAROLINE: You mean, however splendid the pursuit and however corrupt the trickery, I'll end up with a man. Just a man.

JOHN: That's all.

CAROLINE: Then what can make you, a mere acknowledged man, God? A religion in my arms, a philosophy between my legs. (*She gazes at him*) You. Going bravely on two feet. You. Creedless, useless, until you are threatened, made to remember that you'll have an eternity for things of the spirit. (JOHN *is watching a lamp which hangs on a long chain beside the bed and is behind* CAROLINE. *Almost imperceptibly it has begun to sway to and fro*) You. Tonight. Safe. God or man, what is left which might recall you here to your duty? Nothing. Basilios has gone: no danger there. The berries in the wine: you'll live. You're threatened by nothing but love.

JOHN (*Smiles, watching the lamp*):   No, Caro. You forget. In this country the very land you walk on may . . . (*Kisses her: the window curtains are suddenly disturbed*)

CAROLINE (*Pulling away from him suddenly*):   Was that you?

JOHN: In a manner of speaking.

CAROLINE (*Looking down*):   I felt the ground move. (*She looks up at the lamp, which is shifting the shadows. She laughs*) That's it. There, beneath our feet. Your necessary reminder. Personal as an obscene word. There, in that tender movement. (*With one hand she follows and imitates the movement of the lamp. There is a low mutter of thunder.* JOHN *kisses her. She reaches up and steadies the lamp, turning it low; then returns to the kiss.* JOHN *picks her up in his arms and carries her to the bed, putting her down gently on it. The thunder mutters again. They begin to make love*) My God, they say the land rolls up like the waves of the sea. Does it so? Leaves no one free – not even men of God – least of all, you. All – men of God, gods of men – all threatened! (*Another distant rumbling*)

JOHN: A small tremor. It will pass. Everything does.

CAROLINE: Quickly. There may not even be time for regret. All men are threatened! (JOHN *cries out*) There, now. Well, well. Nothing can make it better. So, so. (*Their love-making quietens. They are still.* JOHN *half-rises and very gently pulls on the heavy silken cord, closing the curtains on the bed so that they are out of sight*) One question, Johnnie. Just one.

JOHN: One.

CAROLINE: Do we all . . .

(*There is a knock at the door.* JOHN *calls in answer to it and comes through the curtains from the bed, leaving the curtains closed and* CAROLINE *out of sight*)

JOHN: Yes?

(HENRY *comes in*)

HENRY: I want to apologise. I'm afraid the worry about the article made me lose my sense of humour as well as my temper.

JOHN: All forgotten.

HENRY: I took another long walk and came to a decision. (*He is a little wild-eyed*) I'm going to tell the truth about Selwyn's discovery.

JOHN: That's brave of you.

HENRY: Then I shall be called home in disgrace.

JOHN: Yes. Home! Wait a minute. (*He looks in his pockets. Whilst he is doing so,* CAROLINE'S *bare arm comes through the curtains of the bed. She is holding out the telegram to* HENRY. *He takes it, staring at the bed. He pulls the telegram from its envelope.* JOHN *has moved to* HENRY *and now puts an arm round his shoulders. Together, in silence, the two men stand staring down at the telegram. Then, quietly,* JOHN *speaks*) Do you have a little badge or something? (HENRY *shakes his head*) Go home. To mother. Incognito. Keep your mouth shut. Your articles will go on arriving. I, also, shall sign every one of them Henry Bevis. (JOHN *gently takes the telegram from* HENRY *and begins to move to the door*)

CAROLINE (*From the obscurity of the bed*): You didn't answer my question. Johnnie.

JOHN (*Gently*):   You didn't ask it.
CAROLINE: It's this. I want to know. Do we all get what we deserve?
JOHN: Yes. (*He is at the door*)
CAROLINE: Gods and men?
JOHN: Yes.
CAROLINE: Every time?
JOHN: Yes.
(JOHN *gives a sad smile to* HENRY *and quietly goes from the room.* CAROLINE'S *arm is still extended between the curtains of the bed. Suddenly, imperiously, she snaps her fingers. Slowly,* HENRY *moves to the bed and takes her hand in his. There is a pause*)
CURTAIN

Appendix 2

Letter from John Whiting to Peter Brook

On Tuesday, 5 December 1950, Whiting met with Hugh Beaumont and
John Perry, of H. M. Tennent Ltd, and Peter Brook to discuss the
forthcoming production of *A Penny for a Song*, which Tennent's had
recently accepted for production and which Peter Brook was to direct.
Some time during the following week (his letter is undated), he wrote
to Peter Brook about the play, as follows:

Dear Mr Brook,

I have been thinking over the details of our conversation
last Tuesday at the Globe Theatre about 'A Penny for a
Song.'

Concerning the character of Hallam Matthews which
appears to be obscure: may I indicate the idea more fully?

At the opening of our conversation you referred to the
spirit of English eccentricity with which the play is invested.
I want Hallam Matthews to be a Dandy *of the period*
(Dandyism – one of the most genuine products of our native
eccentricity – has remained, in spite of the French influence
which brought about a decadence of the philosophy, an
essentially English quality). Together with this I want
Hallam to have an appreciation of humour and a delight in
the absurd which is certainly alien to the philosophy of the
true Dandy – because the Dandy's behaviour as we know it
was undoubtedly conditioned by the fact that he was
constantly observed by his fellow clubmen. In other words,
Hallam in the play is the *man* beneath the Dandy. That is
why I have positioned him a little way outside the
happenings of the day, yet at times participating – indeed
entering into the lunatic action with whole-hearted
enjoyment – but able at a moment to extricate himself should
he so wish. You mentioned the fact that he holds the power
to determine the course of action of the other characters.

But he does not avail himself of this power to bring them to practical reality and this is, to me, an indication of his personal philosophy. Hallam is, intentionally, a more artificial person than any of the clowns; he is truly sophisticated. All the other people have illusions – delusions, perhaps – in their hearts but Hallam has none and so he attempts to create a sense of danger, of fear, of humour by dramatising every situation.

All this, however, from what you tell me, is not immediately apparent from the character within the play. May I suggest as to how I think I can clarify it?

It seems to me, in view of your suggestions, that Hallam must state this personal philosophy determining his behaviour on that day. First, it could be spoken of by Lamprett and Dorcas in Act I – this being an objective statement. Secondly, Hallam could discuss his attitude with his servant, Breeze, later in the same Act – this being a subjective statement. Thirdly, I could re-write Hallam's opening speech in Act III to the child Jonathan – this, coming late in the play, could be a restatement with variations. (I must admit that I had considered I had established Hallam well enough to play, in his scenes with Ned, Dorcas and the child, on the paradox of his belief in the innocent things – belied as it is by his way of life outside the Bellboys' household). Perhaps the element of diabolism of which you spoke and which is, of course, inherent in dandyism could also be introduced in these scenes. I don't, however, want Hallam entirely to lose the air of enigma personifying, say, the showman with his human puppets – nor do I want him to lose his quite obvious love for them.

I feel that having invested him with the enigmatic it is this which has made him tenuous and clouded in human personality. He is a man from town set down among country folk and this determines his deviation from the excessively formal behaviour of the classic dandy. As you will understand, his behaviour in town would be very different but he is, shall we say, taking a holiday of the heart

Now, as to the point of Timothy's second descent of the well in Act III when you suggested he might be observed by the Volunteers which would initiate A Chase. I quite understand you making this point to bring the action on stage instead of being, as at present, a little way off.

Part of the action, at least, could be brought into the scene by something like this:

Selincourt (the leader of the Volunteers) knows that
Timothy is in the tunnel – he gives a short exposition on
elementary ballistics – he then expresses his intention of
using the tunnel as a kind of gigantic gun – packing one end
with explosives and blowing Timothy out of the other end,
possibly as far as France – 'returning the damned fellow
to his native heath' – maybe blowing him literally to Hell.
Selincourt and his men can lower kegs of explosives in the
bucket of the well – the fuses will be burning brightly –
there will, of course, be a certain amount of confusion.
Selincourt will station himself in the gateway ready to
observe the 'muzzle' end of the tunnel – it has already been
stated that it is in view from the gateway and Humpage, on
the wall, can watch through his telescope. The explosion
within the well occurs. There is a pause. And then, I think,
Timothy's ariel [*sic*] progress might be conveyed, not by
words, but by nothing more than the movement of
Selincourt's and Humpage's heads. That is until he comes
to earth – when, of course, it is apparent to Selincourt that
something is quite dreadfully wrong – and the chase can
begin. (Do you think this scene can be played almost
entirely in pantomime?) This occurrence can reduce
Timothy to a state of physical decrepitude making him
unrecognisable to the Volunteers – a point made by Mr
Beaumont. This will entail a considerable revision of part
of the last Act. Hallam's oration on Timothy would go –
no great matter this – I felt it slowed the action to the
pace required for the scene between Ned and Dorcas which
I would like to retain in its original form, leading to Hester's
entrance in armour. Part of the chase for Timothy could
pass through the garden at a point where it is now merely
indicated – that is, at the few lines between Brotherhood
and Hester. It could then continue – deleting the present
scene between Hallam and Selincourt which would be
redundant giving, as it does, the details of Timothy's
ejection from the tunnel – to Timothy's entrance and
continuing to the end of the play as written.

You criticised the scene in Act I where Hallam meets
Selincourt and is told of the mock invasion relating to the
later scenes in which Hallam pretends he has dreamt the
occurrence. If my explanation of Hallam's character in the
re-writing still does not make this pretence feasible may
I suggest that it would be better to delete all reference to a
dream, leaving it that Hallam merely retains a silence for
the sake of his anticipation of the comic consequences? I

don't really want to do this because I would like so much
to retain the fact that Hallam is 'acting' just as much for the
benefit of the other characters in the play as he is for any
audience.

We talked about the belief of the characters in their
actions. To me they all have a passionate faith in what they
do but, of course, it is a faith for the wrong purpose.
Lamprett's love for his fire-fighting obliterates any concern
with so trivial an occurrence as war. Timothy's belief in his
power of impersonation, the assertion of himself, completely
nullifies in him any sense of personal danger – even
responsibility. Ned and Dorcas, being so very young, are
too concerned with the sudden awareness of Life, through
falling in love, to have any serious comprehension of
Death. Selincourt – now, this is by no means unusual from
personal experience of military men – has so great a pride in
his unit of volunteers that he is completely oblivious as to
the practical use for which they were formed.

This preoccupation with an object for the pure purpose
of itself and not for its use is surely the essence of all
eccentricity – the great 'follys' of the 18th and early 19th
centuries, for example.

To me, Ned, Dorcas and the child Jonathan should
contrast with the other characters by their sheer, startling
physical beauty. (Jonathan should look like a della Robbia
angel). The quality of personality in Ned, the tumbler, is
certainly rather difficult. He must contain the passion which
is exalté – he can be, in fact, unEnglish to contrast with
Dorcas.

I will get to work immediately on a draft revision of the
points I have mentioned so that should you consider them
to be any contribution they will be at least in a state of
preparedness. Should I think of any further details for the
clarification of these points I will write to you again.

Yours sincerely,
JOHN WHITING

To Whiting's copy of this letter was attached a pencil note in Whiting's
own hand-writing. It related to the character of Hallam and said: 'I see
him physically as a very big man who is quite obviously able to take
excellent care of himself in any emergency. I believed much of the
humour would come from the fact that in spite of this he behaves at
times like a big baby. He should be shepherded around and his childish
tantrums generally soothed by his servant, Samuel Breeze.'

311

Appendix 3

First productions of the plays

A Penny for a Song

First produced at the Haymarket Theatre, London, on 1 March 1951

William Humpage	George Rose
Sir Timothy Bellboys	Alan Webb
Samuel Breeze	Dennis Cannan
Lamprett Bellboys	Denys Blakelock
Hester Bellboys	Marie Lohr
Dorcas Bellboys	Virginia McKenna
Pippin	Joy Rodgers
Hallam Matthews	Ronald Squire
Edward Sterne	Ronald Howard
Jonathan Watkins, a small boy	Derek Rowe
George Selincourt	Basil Radford
Joseph Brotherhood	Kenneth Edwards
James Giddy	Peter Martyn
Rufus Piggott	Alan Gordon

Directed by Peter Brook and designed by Rowland Emett

Saint's Day

First produced at the Arts Theatre Club, London, on 5 September 1951

Paul Southman	Michael Hordern
Stella Heberden	Valerie White
Charles Heberden	Robert Urquhart
John Winter	Scott Harrold
Robert Procathren	John Byron
Giles Aldus	Donald Pleasence
Christian Melrose	Ralph Michael
Walter Killeen	Robert Mooney
Henry Chater	William Morum
A Child	Peggy Palmer
Judith Worden	Anne Padwick
Thomas Cowper	Bertram Shuttleworth
Women of the Village	Judith Nelmes
	Maureen Moore
	Sabina Ward

Directed by Stephen Murray and designed by Fanny Taylor

Marching Song

First produced at the St Martin's Theatre, London, on 8 April 1954

Harry Lancaster	Hartley Power
Dido Morgen	Penelope Munday
Matthew Sangosse	Robert Sansom
Father Anselm	Philip Burton
Catherine de Troyes	Diana Wynyard
Rupert Forster	Robert Flemyng
John Cadmus	Ernest Thesiger
Bruno Hurst	Michael David

Directed by Frith Banbury and designed by Reece Pemberton

The Gates of Summer

First produced at the New Theatre, Oxford, on 11 September 1956

Sophie Faramond	Isabel Jeans
Cristos Papadiamantis	Martin Miller
John Hogarth	James Donald
Henry Bevis	Lionel Jeffries
Caroline Traherne	Dorothy Tutin
Selwyn Faramond	Harold Scott
Prince Basilios	David Kossoff

Directed by Peter Hall

The Devils

First produced at the Aldwych Theatre, London, on 20 February 1961

Mannoury	Ian Holm
Adam	James Bree
Louis Trincant	P. G. Stephens
Phillipe Trincant	Diana Rigg
D'Armagnac	Patrick Allen
De Cerisay	Peter Jeffrey
Sewerman	Clive Swift
Grandier	Richard Johnson
Ninon	Yvonne Bonnamy
De la Rochepozay	Derek Godfrey
Father Rangier	David Sumner
Father Barré	Max Adrian
Sister Jeanne	Dorothy Tutin
Sister Claire	Stephanie Bidmead
Sister Louise	Mavis Edwards
De Laubardemont	Patrick Wymark
Father Mignon	Donald Layne-Smith
Sister Gabrielle	Patsy Byrne
Prince Henri de Condé	Derek Godfrey
Richelieu	John Cater
Louis XIII	Philip Voss
Bontemps	Stephen Thorne
Father Ambrose	Roy Dotrice
A Clerk	John Cater

Directed by Peter Wood and designed by Sean Kenny

A Penny for a Song
(revised version)

First production of the revised version was at the Aldwych Theatre, London, on 1 August 1962

William Humpage	Newton Blick
Sir Timothy Bellboys	Marius Goring
Samuel Breeze	Colin Jeavons
Lamprett Bellboys	James Bree
Hester Bellboys	Gwen Ffrangcon-Davies
Hallam Matthews	Michael Gwynn
Dorcas Bellboys	Judi Dench
Pippin	Margo Andrew
Edward Sterne	Mark Eden
A Small Boy	Robert Cook
George Selincourt	Clive Morton
Joseph Brotherhood	Robert Webber
James Giddy	Roger Swaine
Rufus Piggott	Henry Woolf

Directed by Colin Graham and designed by Alix Stone

No Why

First produced at the Aldwych Theatre, London, on 2 July 1964 as part of a programme called *Expeditions One*

Jacob	Garry Van de Peer
Henry	Tony Church
Eleanor	Juno Jago
Max	John Steiner
Aunt Sarah	Elizabeth Spriggs
Aunt Amy	Caroline Maud
Grandfather	Ken Wynne
1st Servant	Mary Allen
2nd Servant	Wyn Jones

Directed by John Schlesinger and designed by Barry Kay

The Conditions of Agreement

First produced at the Little Theatre, Bristol, on 12 October 1965

Emily Doon	Eithne Dunn
Peter Bembo	Terence Hardiman
A.G.	Frank Middlemass
Nicholas Doon	David Burke
Patience Doon	Jane Lapotaire

Directed by Christopher Denys

Appendix 4

The John Whiting Award

John Whiting was, from 1955 until his death in 1963, a member of the Drama Panel of the Arts Council of Great Britain. Two years after his death the Council instituted an annual award designed to give recognition and some modest financial assistance to younger British playwrights whose work is just beginning to be known. The following list shows the announced winners of the Award from its inception to the date of going to press (Autumn 1978):

1965: Award inaugurated.

1966: Awarded jointly to Wole Soyinka for *The Lion and the Jewel* and *Trials of Brother Jero*, and Tom Stoppard for *Rosencrantz and Guildenstern are Dead*.

1967: Awarded jointly to Peter Nichols for *A Day in the Death of Joe Egg* and Peter Terson for *The Ballad of the Artificial Mash* and *Zigger Zagger*.

1968: Awarded jointly to Peter Barnes for *The Ruling Class* and Edward Bond for *Narrow Road to the Deep North*.

1969: Awarded jointly to Howard Brenton for *Revenge, Christie in Love, etc.* and *The Freehold Company*, director Nancy Meckler, for *Antigone*.

1970: Awarded to Heathcote Williams for *AC/DC*.

1971: Awarded to Mustapha Matura for *As Time Goes By*.

1972: Awarded to John Arden and Margaretta D'Arcy.

1973: Awarded to David Rudkin for *Ashes*.

1974: Awarded to John McGrath, but not accepted on a technicality.

1975: Awarded to David Edgar for *Destiny*.

1976: Awarded to David Len for *The Winter Dancers*.

(For the information in this Appendix I am indebted to John Faulkner, Drama Director, Arts Council of Great Britain.)

Bibliography

1. John Whiting's Published Works

Collections

The Plays of John Whiting (London: Heinemann, 1957), (contains *Saint's Day, A Penny for a Song* and *Marching Song*, with Introduction by John Whiting).

The Collected Plays of John Whiting, ed. Ronald Hayman (London: Heinemann Educational Books, 1969), (New York: Theatre Arts Books, 1969), (vol. 1 contains [*The*] *Conditions of Agreement, Saint's Day, A Penny for a Song, Marching Song*; vol. 2 contains *The Gates of Summer, No Why, A Walk in the Desert, The Devils, Noman* (incomplete), *The Nomads* (incomplete). Introduction and Notes for both volumes by Ronald Hayman).

John Whiting on Theatre (London: Alan Ross and *London Magazine* Editions, 1966), (contains all the dramatic criticism written by Whiting for *London Magazine*).

The Art of the Dramatist, ed. Ronald Hayman (London: *London Magazine* Editions, 1970), (contains short stories, critical comment on theatre, the texts of lectures, etc.).

Single Works

Saint's Day (London: Heinemann Educational Books, 1963), (with Introduction by E. R. Wood).

Saint's Day in *Plays of the Year*, vol. 6, ed. J. C. Trewin (London: Elek, 1952).

A Penny for a Song, revised edition, (London: Heinemann Educational Books, 1964), (with Introduction by E. R. Wood).

Wo wir fröhlich gewesen sind (Frankfurt-am-Maim: S. Fischer Verlag, 1960), (the German version of *A Penny for a Song*).

Marching Song (London: French's Acting Editions, 1954).

Marching Song in *Ring Up The Curtain* (London: Heinemann, 1955).

Marching Song in *New English Dramatists*, vol. 5 (Harmondsworth: Penguin, 1962).

Marching Song (London: Heinemann Educational Books, 1962), (with Introduction by E. R. Wood).

No Why (London: French's Acting Editions, 1961).

No Why in *London Magazine*, May 1961.

The Devils (London: Heinemann, 1961), (New York; Hill & Wang, 1961).

The Devils (London: French's Acting Editions, 1962).

The Devils in *New English Dramatists*, vol. 6 (Harmondsworth: Penguin, 1963).

Sacrifice to the Wind, translation from the French of André Obey, in *Plays for Radio and Television*, ed. Nigel Samuel (London: Longmans, 1959).

Sacrifice to the Wind in *Three Dramatic Legends*, ed. Elizabeth Haddon, (London. Heinemann Educational Books, 1964).

Madame de——, translation from the French of Jean Anouilh, (London: French's Acting Editions, 1959).

Traveller without Luggage, translation from the French of Jean Anouilh, (London: French's Acting Editions, 1959).

No More A-Roving (London: Heinemann Educational Books, 1975), (with Introduction by Eric Salmon).

2. John Whiting's Unpublished Works
(typescripts and manuscripts lodged in The Enthoven Collection, British Theatre Museum)

Not a Foot of Land, a novel.

Nomad, unfinished play (one completed act).

Paul Southman: An Appreciation for Broadcasting, a play for radio.

Eye Witness, a play for radio.

The Stairway, a play for radio.

Love's Old Sweet Song, a play for radio.

The Quarry and the Prey, unfinished radio play.

Lucrece, a full-length play translated from the French of Jean Giraudoux.

The Image of Majesty: A Narrative for Good Friday, a television programme.

An incomplete translation of Armand Salacrou's *Les Invités du Bon Dieu*.

An incomplete translation of Molière's *Don Juan*.

24 filmscripts on various subjects.

3.   Critical Works by other Authors about Whiting

Books

Ronald Hayman: *John Whiting* (London: Heinemann Educational Books, 1969).
Simon Trussler: *The Plays of John Whiting* (London: Gollancz, 1972).

Articles in Journals and Magazines (a selection)

Ronald Bryden: 'Whiting's Way', *The New Statesman*, 14 May 1965.
Adrian Cairns: 'The Significance of John Whiting's Plays', *International Theatre Annual*, no. 1, ed. Harold Hobson, 1956.
James Ferman: 'The Theatre of John Whiting', *Granta*, 24 April 1954.
James Ferman and Peter Hall: 'John Whiting, un nouvel auteur dramatique anglais', *La Revue des Lettres Modernes*, août–septembre 1954.
Christopher Fry: 'John Whiting's World', *The Listener*, LXXII, 1964.
Christopher Fry: 'The Plays of John Whiting', *Essays by Divers Hands*, XXXIV, 1966.
Ronald Hayman: '*Marching Song* and John Whiting', *Nimbus*, autumn 1954.
Ronald Hayman: 'Tragedy in the Holiday Camp: the Plays of John Whiting', *London Magazine*, September 1969.
Jacqueline Hoefer: 'Pinter and Whiting: Two Attitudes towards the Alienated Artist', *Modern Drama*, December 1962.
Charles R. Lyons: 'The Futile Encounters in the Plays of John Whiting', *Modern Drama*, May 1968.
Tom Milne and Clive Goodwin: 'John Whiting: An Interview', *Encore*, January/February 1961. (Reprinted in *Theatre at Work*, ed. Charles Marowitz and Simon Trussler, London: Methuen, 1967).
Garry O'Connor: 'The Obsessions of John Whiting', *Encore*, July/August 1964.
Gabrielle Scott Robinson: 'A Private Mythology: The Manuscripts and Plays of John Whiting', *Modern Drama*, May 1971.
Gabrielle Scott Robinson: 'Beyond the Waste Land: An Interpretation of John Whiting's *Saint's Day*', *Modern Drama*, February 1972.
Eric Salmon: 'John Whiting's Unpublished Novel', *London Magazine*, February/March 1973.
Eric Salmon: 'John Whiting's New-Found Play', *The Spectator*, 31 March 1973.
Eric Salmon: 'John Whiting, the Neglected British Dramatist', *Nagyvilág* (Hungary), June 1974.
Simon Trussler: 'The Plays of John Whiting', *Tulane Drama Review*, winter 1966.
Kenneth Tynan: 'Out of Touch', *Observer*, 6 October 1957, reprinted as 'The Purist View' in *Curtains*, (London: Longmans, 1961).

Index

Note: Some of Whiting's works are referred to so many times throughout the book that to list these in the Index would serve no purpose and would be confusing rather than helpful. The following have, therefore, been omitted from the Index: *The Devils, The Gates of Summer, Marching Song, Not a Foot of Land, A Penny for a Song, Saint's Day*. All other Whiting works except the film scripts are listed alphabetically by title.